INTERNATIONAL ORGANIZATIONS
UNDER PRESSURE

International Organizations under Pressure

Legitimating Global Governance in Challenging Times

KLAUS DINGWERTH, ANTONIA WITT,
INA LEHMANN, ELLEN REICHEL,
AND TOBIAS WEISE

OXFORD

UNIVERSITY PRESS

OXFORD
UNIVERSITY PRESS

Great Clarendon Street, Oxford, OX2 6DP,
United Kingdom

Oxford University Press is a department of the University of Oxford.
It furthers the University's objective of excellence in research, scholarship,
and education by publishing worldwide. Oxford is a registered trade mark of
Oxford University Press in the UK and in certain other countries

First Edition published in 2019

Impression: 1

Published in the United States of America by Oxford University Press
198 Madison Avenue, New York, NY 10016, United States of America

British Library Cataloguing in Publication Data
Data available

Library of Congress Control Number: 2018957735

ISBN 978–0–19–883789–3

Printed and bound in Great Britain by
Clays Ltd, Elcograf S.p.A.

Acknowledgements

In this book, we document how the list of normative expectations that international organizations confront has become longer and more heterogeneous over time. Today, international organizations are not only expected to serve their member states, but also advance the interests of the individuals and communities in these states. In addition, international organizations are not only evaluated based on what they accomplish, but also based on the ways in which they organize their work and manage themselves. Taken together, the combined rise of 'people-based' and of 'procedural' legitimacy standards, we argue, makes the legitimation of international organizations more challenging, notably because traditional norms remain in place while new norms are added to the menu.

While we have contributed in various constellations to the chapters that follow, our study is best seen as a monograph. The research we present is based on a truly collaborative effort from the very beginning, and all of us have contributed concepts, ideas, and arguments that go well beyond the individual authorship of single chapters. In the years we have worked on this book, moreover, numerous people have contributed in the background. It is therefore time for us to say a few words of thanks. In terms of institutions, we thank the Deutsche Forschungsgemeinschaft for taking our project under the wings of its Emmy Noether Programme. We are particularly grateful to Katja Fleischer, Heide Horstmann, Dr Eckardt Kämper, and Petra Tierling for their generous advice and for the patience they showed in dealing with the complexities of what eventually became a transboundary research project. Next, we owe much to the truly wonderful Institute for Intercultural and International Studies (InIIS) and its host institution, the University of Bremen. They provided an intellectual home for our research during the first years. At InIIS, we are particularly grateful to Peter Mayer, Patrizia Nanz, Lothar Probst, and Bernhard Zangl who helped with the initial grant proposal, provided advice and friendship throughout the years, and convinced us that the InIIS was the right place for us. Moreover, we owe special thanks to Tina Menge, Vicky May, and Peter Arnhold who helped with the project administration, as did Britta Wulf and her team for the University of Bremen. Finally, we can no longer thank the late Stephan Leibfried in person but he, too, helped bring our project to Bremen.

Since 2014, the University of St Gallen's Department for Political Science has provided a new and no less supportive home base for our research. We thank our colleagues there, in particular Daniele Caramani and James Davis who supported our project in their functions as head of the department from day one. In addition, the transition to St Gallen would have been impossible without the administrative know-how and assistance Martina Flockerzi, Cornelia Kappeler, and Thomas Rempfler provided. Finally, the Global Public Policy Institute in Berlin served as an academic basis for Klaus' work in summer 2014, and the Goethe University Frankfurt and Peace Research Institute Frankfurt have become new homes for Antonia Witt since 2014. Since 2016, Ina Lehmann's work on this book has greatly benefited from the supportive working conditions at the University of East Anglia's School of International Development and the University of Bremen's artec Sustainability Research Center.

Beyond institutional support, our work benefited from the excellent work of several generations of student assistants. They include Felix Anderl, Marret Bischewski, Benjamin Brast, Carolin Carella, Igor Fayler, Sebastian Gomez, Nicole Gonyea, Nele Kortendiek, Malte Lellmann, Elias Lingnau, Jishuo Ma, Anne Reiff, Helge Staff, and Jonas Wodarz—thank you all!

Moreover, we are highly grateful to the staff members and stakeholders of the organizations we examine in this book. Whether they shared information or their views and experiences in interviews, or pointed us to specific issues and sources that we may otherwise have missed, their help was central in preparing the case studies we present in this book. Without the insights thus provided, this book would not have been possible.

Over the years, we were able to discuss first drafts of our work at workshops organized at the Global Public Policy Institute in Berlin and the Environmental Policy Department at the Vrije Universeit Amsterdam, and to present preliminary findings at invited lectures at the European University Institute, the University of Freiburg, and the University of Portsmouth—we remain indebted to all five institutions. On these as well as on numerous other occasions, colleagues have generously and critically commented on the work that has gone into this book. Their scrutiny has helped us improve our research in important ways. We particularly thank Thorsten Benner, Steven Bernstein, Magdalena Bexell, Dominika Biegoń, Frank Biermann, Andrea Binder, Martin Binder, Malte Brosig, Mlada Bukovansky, Tony Chafer, Eugénia da Conceição-Heldt, Christopher Daase, James Davis, Matthew Eagleton-Pierce, Sophie Eisentraut, Orfeo Fioretos, Ulrich Franke, Katharina Glaab, Catia Gregoratti, Alex Grigorescu, Jennifer Gronau, Tine Hanrieder, Monika Heupel, Gisela Hirschmann, Anna Holzscheiter, Tobias Lenz, Andrea Liese, Peter Mayer, Aysem Mert, Darrel Moellendorf, Aletta Mondré, Patrizia Nanz, Martin Nonhoff, Frank Nullmeier, Henk Overbeek, Diana Panke, Philipp Pattberg, Jürgen Rüland, Frank Schimmelfennig, Klaus Schlichte, Henning Schmidtke, Steffen Schneider, Andrea Schneiker, Jan Aart Scholte, Dieter Senghaas, Thomas Sommerer, Fred Söderbaum, Jens Steffek, Michael Strange,

Jonas Tallberg, Anders Uhlin, Lora-Anne Viola, Clara Weinhardt, Oscar Widerberg, Bernhard Zangl, Dominik Zaum, Fariborz Zelli, and Michael Zürn.

At Oxford University Press, moreover, Dominic Byatt deserves special thanks for his efforts to bring our book to the publication stage. Moreover, we are indebted to Margaret Karns as well as three anonymous reviewers for the tremendous effort and intellectual rigor they showed in reviewing our initial manuscript. Their commitment and generosity in engaging with the details of a long text were truly exceptional, and we have tried our best to do justice to their efforts in our own revisions of the manuscript. At the final stage, Daniel Iszak helped with language editing, for which he, too, deserves our thorough gratitude. Klaus Dingwerth also thanks Routledge for the permission to reuse parts of his book chapter 'Democracy' (published in *The Language of World Trade Politics: Unpacking the Terms of Trade*, edited by Klaus Dingwerth and Clara Weinhardt, Routledge, 2019, pp. 80–96; © 2019 selection and editorial matter, Klaus Dingwerth and Clara Weinhardt; individual chapters, the contributors, and reproduced with permission of the Licensor through PLSClear) in the section 'The Doha Deadlock and the Long Legacy of Seattle' of Chapter 3.

And then, of course, we all remain indebted to the individuals who mattered in very different ways. On the one hand, there are those colleagues who—early on in our careers as well as later, in one way or another, and very often unconsciously—inspired us and gave meaning to the broader project we call 'the social sciences and humanities'. On the other hand, we could not have written this book without the steady and reliable support our families and close friends provided in this endeavour as in so many others. Thank you!

Contents

List of Figures

List of Tables

List of Acronyms

ASEAN	Association of Southeast Asian Nations
AU	African Union
BBP	Business and Biodiversity Programme
CBD	Convention on Biological Diversity
CIDO	African Citizens' Directorate
CSO	Civil society organization
CTE	Committee on Trade and Environment
DDA	Doha Development Agenda
ECOSOC	United Nations Economic and Social Council
ECOSOCC	African Union Economic, Social and Cultural Council
EU	European Union
ExCom	Executive committee
GATT	General Agreement on Tariffs and Trade
GEF	Global Environment Facility
HCR	(League of Nations') High Commissioner for Refugees
IAEA	International Atomic Energy Agency
ICC	International Criminal Court
ICFTU	International Confederation of Free Trade Unions
IDP	Internally displaced person
ILO	International Labour Organization
IMF	International Monetary Fund
IOM	International Organization for Migration
IPBES	Intergovernmental Science-Policy Platform for Biodiversity and Ecosystem Services
IPEP	International Panel of Eminent Personalities
IR	International Relations
ITO	International Trade Organization
IUCN	International Union for Conservation of Nature
IUPN	International Union for Protection of Nature
MFN	Most-favoured nation
MSRP	Management Systems Renewal Project
NGO	Non-governmental organization
NIEO	New International Economic Order

NPT	Treaty on the Non-Proliferation of Nuclear Weapons
OAU	Organisation of African Unity
OCHA	United Nations Office for the Coordination of Humanitarian Affairs
OPEC	Organization of the Petroleum Exporting Countries
OSCE	Organization for Security and Co-operation in Europe
PAP	Pan-African Parliament
PoWPA	Programme of Work on Protected Areas
PSC	African Union Peace and Security Council
SCO	Shanghai Cooperation Organization
TEEB	The Economics of Ecosystems and Biodiversity
TILCEPA	Theme on Indigenous and Local Communities, Equity and Protected Areas
TMI	Three Mile Island
UK	United Kingdom
UN	United Nations
UNCTAD	United Nations Conference on Trade and Development
UNDP	United Nations Development Programme
UNDRIP	United Nations Declaration on the Rights of Indigenous Peoples
UNEP	United Nations Environment Programme
UNFCCC	United Nations Framework Convention on Climate Change
UNHCR	(Office of the) United Nations High Commissioner for Refugees
US	United States
USD	United States dollar
WCC	World Conservation Congress
WCED	World Commission on Environment and Development
WCS	World Conservation Strategy
WHO	World Health Organization
WTO	World Trade Organization
WWF	World Wide Fund for Nature

1

International Organizations under Pressure

Introduction

Klaus Dingwerth, Antonia Witt, Ina Lehmann,
Ellen Reichel, and Tobias Weise

One problem of the World Bank is that it is called a bank.

Robert B. Zoellick

INTERNATIONAL ORGANIZATIONS
UNDER PRESSURE

The March/April 2012 issue of the *Foreign Affairs* magazine marks a sobering point in the history of international organizations. In a contribution to the issue, outgoing World Bank president Robert Zoellick (2012) elaborates 'Why we still need the World Bank'. The title suggests a deep-seated crisis. *That* we still need a core institution of the post-war international order, he seems to acknowledge, is no longer taken for granted. *Why* we need it requires an explanation, a convincing argument, a foundation in the norms, values, and beliefs on whose support the Bank depends. Yet, while the proposals for how to turn the Bank into an organization more deserving of our support are manifold, they often point into different directions. So, which path should the Bank take?

For scholars of global governance, the episode is central in at least two ways. First, our introductory quote hints that the paths the World Bank may choose are in fact limited. Like any organization, the Bank cannot simply press the reset button and reinvent itself. Instead, it is constrained by the identity it has acquired up until today. That identity is neither under the full control of the organization itself, nor can it be changed quickly. When Zoellick seeks to defend 'why we still need the World Bank', he thus notes the problem of 'being called a Bank'; but at the same time, he speaks of member states as 'clients' and is quick to draw further corporate analogies himself (see Moretti and Pestre 2015).

Second, the World Bank is not the only international organization that has come under pressure. Others, too, are challenged for what they do and how they operate, or feel a need to explain 'why we still need them'—in brief, to legitimate themselves. Take the United Nations (UN). In the early 1990s, many had hoped that the collective security system which the UN had envisaged could finally be put to work given that the 'veto paralysis' resulting from block confrontation was finally over. Yet history followed a different path. Already in 1994, John Bolton, who would later become a United States (US) ambassador to the UN, suggested that 'there is no such thing as the United Nations' and that, if the UN Secretariat building in New York lost ten of its 38 stories, 'it wouldn't make a bit of difference'.[1] In the following year, the inability of the world organization to halt the genocide in Rwanda contributed to a deep sense of failure that was only exacerbated when UN protection forces could not defend the 'safe area' the UN had declared in Srebrenica against Serbian troops, leaving over 8,000 Bosnian men and women massacred in yet another genocide (Barnett 2002). If that was not enough to question 'why we still need the UN', the 2000s gave birth to a further legitimacy crisis. This time, it resulted from the inability of the UN 'to constrain the unilaterally inclined hegemonic US in its efforts to bring about regime change in Iraq (Morris and Wheeler 2007: 214). And finally, the question of UN Security Council reform loomed large since the end of the Cold War, as many UN members believed the Council was no longer representative of a membership that had changed dramatically since 1945 (Fassbender 1998; Grigorescu 2015: 47–88).

Beyond the UN, the European Union (EU) comes to mind. That the EU is under pressure is hardly a novel insight. In 2010, polls revealed that, for the first time in the history of the *Eurobarometer*, the number of respondents saying they do *not* trust the EU had exceeded the number of respondents that do trust the EU (Eurobarometer 2011: 43). Studies of media discourse echo that feeling. They reveal that, in comparison to the national political systems of Germany, Switzerland, the United Kingdom (UK), and the US, as well as to other international institutions like the G8 and the UN, the quality press evaluates the EU most negatively on a broad range of legitimacy standards (Nullmeier et al. 2010). Finally, if anyone still needed further proof of crisis, the 'Leave' vote of the British electorate in June 2016, combined with a rise of nationalist parties in many other member states, has unsettled the organization's very foundation. The efforts of political actors to mobilize generalized

---

[1] Both quotes were subject to debate in the Senate hearing of Bolton's nomination as US ambassador to the UN; see *U.S. Congressional Record—Senate*, Vol. 151, Pt. 8 (May 26, 2005), p. 11520.

support for the European integration project and give reasons for such support has not kept pace with the changes that have occurred in the organization and its environment. In a veritable crisis like this one, to regain legitimacy with citizens becomes a matter of survival. But while the EU's legitimation narratives have changed significantly in the past—from peace to welfare to democracy (Biegoń 2016; Sternberg 2013)—just where a renewal of the EU's legitimacy may come from this time remains open.

We can continue the list further. Facing a more persistent standstill in multilateral trade negotiations than ever before in its history, those commenting on the state of the World Trade Organization (WTO) frequently resort to metaphors of life and death (see Chapter 3). Elsewhere, protesters in Greece and Ireland shout that they want the 'IMF out!' (International Monetary Fund), while a stand-off among Russia and Western member states of the Organization for Security and Co-operation in Europe (OSCE) makes others wonder why that particular organization still deserves our support (Peters 2013). In a similar vein, Burundi, Gambia, and South Africa either threatened or decided to leave the International Criminal Court (ICC). As all three states charged the ICC with suffering from a political bias against African governments, the *New York Times* was quick to call the defections of the three members an 'unprecedented blow to [the Court's] legitimacy' (Cuvellier 2016; see also Vilmer 2016). The same diagnosis would be apt if contemporary public debates in Switzerland and the UK were to lead both countries to put an end to the rule of 'foreign judges' and decide, as campaigns in both countries demand, to turn their back on the European human rights regime. Finally, few observers doubt that the United Nations Industrial Development Organization needs to reinvent itself: while the US, Canada, and Australia had already left the organization in the 1990s, eight European members and New Zealand have terminated their membership since 2012.

This book is about the crisis of international organizations, understood as a situation in which key constituencies no longer take the need for international organizations for granted. To be sure, organizational crises are not a new phenomenon. But the history of the League of Nations also illustrates how serious they may get; and it seems fair to say that the pressure on international organizations has become exceptionally high in recent years. When we ask where these pressures might come from, several drivers come to mind. In general terms, however, we could say that the mounting pressures result from a widening gap between adaptive needs and adaptive capacities. On the one hand, international organizations are thus asked to adapt to changes in their environments more frequently, more fundamentally, and more quickly than in previous times. The challenges are multiple: international organizations are required to adapt to global power shifts, with China, India, or Brazil asking for a stronger role and traditional powers seeking to maintain their privileges (Zangl et al. 2016). They need to cope with a growing density of international institutions that allows dissatisfied states to shift their agenda to a different forum (Morse and Keohane 2014). They have to respond to the rise of a transnational civil society that demands access (Tallberg et al. 2013) and shows a growing capacity to make and monitor transnational rules itself (Abbott et al. 2016). And, like most other organizations, they need to adapt to a process of social acceleration that has become a defining feature of modern societies (Rosa 2013).

On the other hand, international organizations are not particularly well equipped to meet these adaptive needs. While it might be exaggerating to claim that their adaptive capacities have diminished, the claim that they have not kept pace with rising adaptive needs appears much less controversial. So how might the gap have widened? First, membership in international organizations has grown. It has expanded from twenty-three states in the original General Agreement on Tariffs and Trade (GATT) to currently 162 states that make up the WTO, from fifty-one UN members in 1946 to 196 UN members in 2016, and from the six states launching the European Coal and Steel Community in 1951 to the twenty-eight-member union from which the UK now seeks divorce. However, a growing membership usually means that more heterogeneous interests need to be taken into account in making decisions, thus making any adaptation to new circumstances a more tedious affair (Hale et al. 2013).

Second, many intergovernmental organizations have expanded their areas of activity over time. On the one hand, organizations search and adopt new mandates for themselves. On the other hand, international bureaucracies actively help to create new organizations: a process Tana Johnson (2014) has termed 'organizational progeny'. In many cases, the expansion of mandates and the proliferation of international organizations implies a greater need to coordinate with other actors, a greater likelihood of failure in some areas, and a greater challenge when it comes to integrating the various activities into a coherent legitimation narrative.

Third, international organizations are known for their legal-rational culture. Yet, as they become more institutionalized, international organizations are also likely to lose flexibility and thus adaptive capacity. One reason is that the rules that govern the organization have been formally stabilized (Goldstein and Martin 2000); another that the bureaucracies that administer the day-to-day activities of the organization develop formal or informal routines that reduce the scope for deviating practices (Barnett and Finnemore 2004; Steffek 2003). Moreover, we can also expect processes of 'layering' to make international organizations more cumbersome over time, as institutional reforms create 'disjointed' patterns as well as high levels of 'institutional incoherence' (Streeck and Thelen 2005). For the World Health Organization (WHO), for instance, Tine Hanrieder (2015) has shown that reform efforts that sought to centralize the organization were usually blocked by regional veto players and, when reforms eventually materialized, they commonly increased rather than decreased the power of the regions within the WHO. In addition, headquarter efforts to secure centralized competences for particular issues led to the creation of additional centres of decision making. As more, not fewer veto players were thus generated, this made governance of the organization more difficult and ultimately 'fragmented' the WHO.

In short, existing accounts can help us to understand the mounting pressures international organizations confront. This argument suggests that the crisis of international organizations has, at least in part, structural origins that lead to a widening gap between adaptive needs and adaptive capacities. Our study sheds further light on this argument, and hence on the crisis of international organizations. Yet, it examines the idea that international organizations have come under pressure from a different angle, namely from the perspective of their legitimation. This legitimation matters because it is 'foundational': how an organization ends up justifying its existence will reverberate in its work, including its institutional design, its policies, and the ways in which these policies are implemented.

Broadly speaking, we conceive of legitimation as the social process in which political actors seek to generate and promote, among relevant audiences, generalized support for political institutions. More precisely, we are interested in the reasons actors give when they defend or challenge international organizations—or, stated differently, in the *terms of legitimation* that provide the normative yardsticks to which international organizations are held.[2] The normative yardsticks relevant audiences apply mark the paths that lead to *legitimacy*, understood as the belief in the rightfulness of a political order or its constituent parts. Consequently, the normative yardsticks we trace in our study also set the boundaries that international organizations leave only at the risk of losing some of their legitimacy.

The primary question we ask is *how and why the normative yardsticks that underpin evaluations of international organizations have changed since the end of the Cold War.* In asking this question, we refer to the 'end of the Cold War' as a period rather than an event. Hence, the phrase denotes not merely a change in the confrontation between East and West. Instead, we use it as a shorthand for a series of transformative changes that unfolded around the same time. These changes include a further wave of democratization at the domestic level, the birth of a new world order at the international level, a new phase in the globalization of economic relations, a revolution in communications technologies, and the proliferation of 'new wars' (see Chapter 2). Our

---

[2] We use the terms international organization and intergovernmental organization interchangeably in this study to refer to formal organizations that are established by treaty or by the decision of another international organization and that have states, governments, or government agencies as an important or exclusive category of their membership.

inroad for understanding how the legitimacy standards to which international organizations are subjected have changed are what we call *legitimation contests*. In these, a diverse set of actors more or less constantly (re)negotiate the terms of legitimation for an international organization (see Chapter 2). We examine these negotiations through in-depth case studies of normative change in five international organizations. Our cases include the GATT and its successor, the WTO; the Organisation of African Unity (OAU) and its successor, the African Union (AU); the International Atomic Energy Agency (IAEA); the International Union for Conservation of Nature (IUCN), and the Office of the UN High Commissioner of Refugees (UNHCR).

Taken together, the five case studies allow us to trace how the normative foundations of global governance have been renegotiated after 1989/90, a date that is commonly seen as a major turning point in world political history. Because legitimacy standards give expression to how we think about our common institutions and about the values that should guide them, knowledge of such shifts is relevant not only within, but also beyond academia. In brief, which ways of doing politics a community finds acceptable is one of the most fundamental political questions, and those who wield the capacity to define the conceptual terrain on which legitimation takes place wield power (Boltanski 2011; Forst 2015). When we study the terms of legitimation, we therefore also study a particular form of power in global governance.

We understand the *terms* of legitimation in a literal as well as in a figurative sense. In a literal sense, our interest in the terms of legitimation leads us to examine how the values that underpin efforts to legitimate or delegitimate international organizations have changed over time. What were international organizations said to be good for back then? What are they being criticized for now? In a figurative sense, however, the terms of legitimation also stand for the rules of the 'legitimacy game' (van Rooy 2004). How and why do new standards of 'good global governance' arise, while others disappear or change their meaning? How does change in the broader world political context affect the ways in which international organizations need to gain and maintain their 'social licence to operate'? Finally, how do specific actors come to acquire the power to control the normative terrain on which international organizations can claim legitimacy?

What we find in our research boils down to a central message. The legitimation narratives of the national constellation of the post-1945 era remain in place; but they are increasingly complemented by the legitimacy standards of the 'post-national constellation' that is characteristic of the post-1989 world. The result is that today's international organizations need to live up to a *longer list of legitimacy principles* than in previous times. Two changes are particularly noteworthy. First, international organizations need to demonstrate not only what they do *for their member states*, but also *for the individuals in member states*. Second, while international organizations continue to be evaluated in terms of *what they achieve*, they are increasingly also measured by *how they operate*.[3]

As our case studies show, the more pluralist patchwork of legitimacy principles that results from the shifts we observe has multiple origins, but similar consequences. Notably, it renders the legitimation of international organizations more complex, and it requires international organizations to reconcile a diversity of normative expectations. Strikingly, then, at a time when many feel international cooperation is needed more than ever (Hale et al. 2013), legitimating the forms in which such cooperation takes place has become most difficult. International organizations have come *under pressure*.

THE STATE OF THE ART

International Relations (IR) scholars have not overlooked the phenomena we describe. To the contrary, special issues, conference panels, and edited volumes abound in which the authors take issue with the allegedly swindling legitimacy of international organizations (Bexell 2015; Brassett and Tsingou 2011; Hurrelmann et al. 2007; Reus-Smit 2007; Scholte 2011; Zaum 2013a). Yet, while this 'legitimacy turn' allows us to build on existing IR literatures, we also move beyond the latter. In particular, we seek to overcome three limitations: a tendency to examine legitimacy primarily in terms of citizen attitudes and media debates; an inclination to neglect the historical dimension of legitimation processes; and a proclivity to build general claims about international organizations on evidence gathered from only a small number of relatively large, powerful, and visible international organizations.

Moving beyond Attitudes and Media Debates

The IR literature on legitimacy commonly distinguishes between 'normative' and 'sociological' perspectives. In the former, authors develop arguments about the normative principles international institutions *should comply with*

---

[3] We link both shifts to Jürgen Habermas' notion of a 'post-national constellation' because they respond, at least in part, to the 'post-national challenge' societies face under conditions of economic globalization, namely the challenge to maintain their capacity for democratic self-control and self-realization. Where political boundaries have become permeable and states have come to share sovereignty with international agencies, the rise of people-based and procedural legitimacy standards in relation to the latter thus resonates with the need to identify 'the appropriate forms for the democratic process to take *beyond* the nation-state' (Habermas 2001, 60–1, emphasis in the original).

to deserve legitimacy (Buchanan and Keohane 2006). In the latter, authors are interested not so much in moral principles that should guide evaluations but rather *in actual legitimacy beliefs*, held by individuals or social groups, and in the explanatory factors that shape such beliefs.

Our study contributes to the sociological literature on the legitimacy of international institutions. That literature commonly takes the distinction between a normative and a sociological perspective as its starting point. Distinguishing itself from the normative debate, it argues that, whichever views political philosophers might hold, what matters *politically* is how those on whose allegiance political institutions rely, relate to these institutions. Consequently, an important part of the empirical literature conceptualizes legitimacy as 'trust' or 'confidence' citizens or elites express in an institution. Its primary interest is to measure systemically the level of trust or confidence various constituencies display at different points in time, and to identify what determines variation in these levels.

Summarizing the state of the art in survey-based research of this kind, Lisa Dellmuth and Jonas Tallberg (2016: 6) identify three major explanations for varying levels of confidence in international organizations. The first assumes that the individual attitudes towards international organizations build on 'rational evaluations of the processes and outcomes of international cooperation'. In contrast, the second explanation ties these attitudes to the trust individuals have in their domestic political institutions. Finally, the third explanation argues that individual attitudes depend on identity constructions, with 'cosmopolitans' evaluating international organizations more favourably than those who identify more strongly with their compatriots. In line with these explanations, Benno Torgler finds that trust in the UN depends on the capacity of respondents' countries to act in global policy making, on respondents' perceived level of corruption in their own country, and on how strongly respondents identify 'with the world as a whole' (Torgler 2008; see also Ecker-Ehrhardt 2016).

The literature on public attitudes towards international organizations ties into research on the contestation of international institutions in important ways. Notably, it shows *that* support levels vary among groups as well as over time and it helps to identify *who* holds particularly negative views of international organizations. At the same time, its contribution has been limited when it comes to the grounds on which relevant audiences assess international organizations as either 'good' or 'bad', or to the question whose views matter.

More recently, survey experiments have addressed these challenges by randomly assigning cues that contain information about how well political elites believe an organization meets certain values. Dellmuth and Tallberg, for instance, show that respondents pay equal attention to elite information based on the performance and the procedures of international organizations. Moreover, the views respondents hold of international organizations are susceptible to cues from their governments as well as from non-governmental organizations (NGOs), but not from the international organizations themselves (Dellmuth and Tallberg 2016; see also Anderson et al. 2017; Hyde et al. 2017). While this approach takes *legitimacy* research one step further in the direction of *legitimation* research, the fact that respondents are confronted with isolated statements remains an important limitation. What 'level of confidence' respondents would express if they were confronted with the legitimation discourse in its entirety is thus a question survey-based research cannot answer.

Likewise, content analyses of media debates about the value of international organizations (Nullmeier et al. 2010), of debates within international organizations (Binder and Heupel 2015), or of the ways in which international organizations present themselves to various audiences (Dingwerth et al. 2018) have considerably advanced our knowledge. They have helped us to sort out which legitimacy principles matter. They have shed light on which legitimacy standards a particular organization meets relatively well. And they have also advanced our knowledge of the normative yardsticks specific types of actors— for instance governments, international bureaucrats, NGOs, or journalists— uphold most strongly. From Henning Schmidtke's study on media evaluations of the UN, for example, we can learn that media discourses in Western democracies evaluate the principles on which the UN is founded in very positive ways, while they judge specific UN bodies—the General Assembly, the Security Council, and the Secretary General—negatively (Schmidtke 2010).

Overall, survey research and media analyses shed light on various aspects of the 'legitimacy game'. Yet, both are limited when we seek to explore the dynamics of 'justificatory orders' (*Rechtfertigungsordnungen*; Forst 2015) to which international organizations are subjected. To reconstruct the latter, we will need a complementary approach that looks at *discursive interaction* and seeks to understand not only which standards matter, but also how the struggle between different standards of legitimacy plays out in global governance. We therefore ask: who are the protagonists of legitimation contests involving international organizations? How do they interact? And how do the sets of legitimacy standards, which actors refer to—the justificatory orders—shift as a result of change in the organizational environment and of the manifold discursive interactions among the protagonists themselves?

Taking History Seriously

A second strand of writing on which we can build deals with the history of international organizations and their role in constructing a world of global governance (Frey et al. 2014: 3; Cottrell 2016; Iriye 2002; MacKenzie 2010; Reinalda 2009). This literature seems particularly relevant since the claim that contemporary international institutions experience a legitimacy crisis seems to imply that international organizations did not face similar kinds of pressures in the past. We know this view is incorrect. Legitimacy contests have, for example, shaped the major international economic institutions from their very beginning, and knowledge of past conflicts is often key to making sense of today's crises (Buzdugan and Payne 2016; see also Biegoń 2016; Cottrell 2016; Grigorescu 2015; Hanrieder 2015; Sternberg 2013; van Walraven 1996; Wilkinson 2006). Nevertheless, many of the case studies that inform our thinking about the legitimacy crisis of international institutions remain rooted in the present. To our knowledge, our study is the first systematic effort to study the legitimation contests around international organizations *across organizations as well as over time*. At the same time, we can build on the rich literature on the history of international organizations in general. From that literature, we draw four main conclusions.

First, a historical perspective clarifies that *innovation* in the dominant system of governance has always required legitimation in the international realm. In fact, Mark Mazower (2012: 15) shows that in the early days, it was international organizations as such which needed to be legitimated. When the major powers of the day established the Concert of Europe in 1815, the 'collective interests of the continent' still justified a hierarchy among states in which international organizations did not play a major role. Only later did major principles underlying the Concert of Europe come to be seen as 'a symbol of the very problems—autocratic leadership, bellicosity, and incomprehension of the value of freedom and the power of social change—that a true internationalism was needed to solve' (Mazower 2012: 7 and 12). This internationalism prevailed from the 1860s to the 1930s but waned again in the post-war era, when the idea and practice of 'governing the world the American way' gained ground and shifted the foundations on which the legitimacy of international organizations rested.

Second, not only major powers but also individual leaders played key roles as crafters and promoters for new legitimacy standards. In today's world, and in our case studies, such crafters are often bureaucrats working for international organizations or activists from NGOs (Barnett and Finnemore 2004; Johnson 2014; Jolly et al. 2009; Keck and Sikkink 1998; Sending 2014). In the eighteenth and nineteenth centuries, the legal profession and the sciences were similarly relevant for the rise of internationalist norms. The former mainly did so by promoting international law as a 'path to peace', the latter by providing the information required to steer (international) society—a task in which the statistical services offered by international organizations would later come to play a key role (Mazower 2012: 23 and 65–115; Ward 2004). Yet, new ideas did not fall from the sky. Historically, they often originated in societies that occupy a dominant role in the world political system, and diffused by gaining relevance in one field that reached out to neighbouring fields. The idea that 'associations' constitute a 'motor of modernity' provides a good example. Initially referring to societies, its transfer to the interaction among societies turned this idea into an early foundation for the legitimation of international organizations (Mazower 2012: 23).

Third, a historical perspective on the politics of international legitimation underlines how legitimacy standards not only require crafters and promoters but also a 'fit' with political and economic contexts. In his *International Organization and Industrial Change*, for example, Craig Murphy shows how the rise of different types of intergovernmental organization was inherently linked to the economic order in which they were established. International organizations, he argues, were created to serve the interests of the dominant forces within an economic order, allowing them to expand the markets for their products. The public international unions of the nineteenth century, for instance, provided infrastructures and established international standards for industrial expansion; moreover, they helped states to manage tensions with other states as well as the social conflicts that resulted from the expansion of markets. Similarly, the League of Nations and the UN system helped to rebuild Europe, foster growth beyond its borders, and manage interdependence (Murphy 1994).

Finally, international organizations of the past were usually legitimated not as isolated institutions but rather as constitutive elements of the broader political orders. Contests over the legitimacy of international institutions should thus be viewed as negotiations about the acceptable reach and specific form of governance, about its protagonists, and about the inequalities that are accepted, (re)produced or deepened by it. For many international organizations, this became particularly visible when the number of their Southern members rose and the North–South divide became a defining cleavage (Buzdugan and Payne 2016; Helleiner 2014a). This cleavage made it difficult to represent an 'international community' that was increasingly disparate, forcing them to gloss over inequalities among its formally equal members (Viola et al. 2015). In a similar vein, today's international organizations are treated as emblems of particular governance regimes—like the 'nuclear non-proliferation regime' for the IAEA and 'global trade' for the WTO—that not all states and societies perceive as theirs. International organizations serve to maintain and legitimate these governance regimes. But the contestation of the latter's rightfulness also challenges the legitimacy of the international organizations. Ideally, then, tracing the changing terms of legitimation for international organizations is more than a venture into the norms that structure the international realm. Rather, it could help us understand the making of that very realm as a political realm—marked by power and power disparities—and to appraise the specific role and place international organizations take therein.

Beyond the Big Five

Finally, while numerous empirical studies have advanced our knowledge about the legitimacy of international organizations, many insights come from only a handful of organizations: the EU, the IMF, the UN, the World Bank, and the WTO (see for instance Grigorescu 2015; Morris and Wheeler 2007; O'Brien et al. 2000; Seabrooke 2007). Since they face particularly intense contestation, these five organizations lend themselves particularly well to studying the dynamics of contestation—they leave more traces of justificatory discourse than most other organizations. For the same reason, however, these organizations are also unlikely to be representative of international organizations as such. In contrast, their visibility in public debates, the strong authority they exercise, and the comprehensive activities in which they engage are more likely to make them international organizations of a special kind, at least when it comes to their legitimation. As a result, the focus on the 'big five' might have led the contemporary literature to describe the legitimation challenges that a broader set of international organizations confront in narrow or even misleading terms.

The case studies in Dominik Zaum's (2013a) *Legitimating International Organizations* help to illustrate the argument that contestations of the legitimacy of international organizations are more diverse than we commonly assume. While the legitimation of the EU or the UN Security Council is strongly conditioned by the public contestation of the authority these organizations wield, the same is not true for organizations like the Association of Southeast Asian Nations (ASEAN) or for the Shanghai Cooperation Organization (SCO). ASEAN, for example, builds its legitimacy on regional norms and has only recently sought to address Western states as an additional legitimation constituency. The legitimation contest it experiences has since then become marked by the tension between regional norms on the one hand and global standards of legitimacy on the other (Ba 2013). In contrast, the SCO internally legitimates itself as 'an alternative type model to Western-type international organizations' while it draws its external legitimacy from its recognition 'as an important regional organization' by the UN and other international organizations (Prantl 2013: 177–8). To broaden our theoretical understanding of how international organizations are legitimated, we should thus neither ignore the 'big five', nor limit our sights to the contestation of the latter.

RESEARCH DESIGN

In many ways, our study builds on the 'legitimacy turn' in the IR literature. At the same time, we seek to go beyond conventional accounts of legitimacy crises by investigating the normative foundations of legitimacy and the dynamics of their contestation, by adding historical depth, and by broadening the range of empirical cases on which we base our analysis.

Case Selection

To accomplish the latter goal, we reconstruct the legitimation contests in relation to five international organizations that differ in the authority they wield, in the issue areas in which they operate, and in their membership:

- the *World Trade Organization* (WTO), including its predecessor, the *General Agreement on Tariffs and Trade* (GATT);
- the *African Union (AU)*, including its predecessor, the *Organisation of African Unity* (OAU);
- the *International Atomic Energy Agency* (IAEA);
- the *International Union for Conservation of Nature* (IUCN); and
- the *Office of the UN High Commissioner for Refugees* (UNHCR).

The first three organizations, in descending order, have gained considerable *political authority*—defined in terms of pooled or delegated decision-making competences (Hooghe et al. 2017)—during our period of investigation. In contrast, the UNHCR has increased the scope, but not necessarily the depth of its mandate, while IUCN has largely maintained its status quo. As Michael Zürn has argued, if international organizations gain political authority they will also face greater public contestation—or 'politicization'—and therefore confront broader normative demands (Zürn 2018; see also O'Brien et al. 2000). Selecting these five organizations gives us the opportunity to test this argument as well as to examine more closely *how* the transfer of political authority comes to affect the legitimation game (see also Chapter 2). Within-case comparisons among different areas of organizational activity and different instances of norm change facilitate this task. For example, the IAEA has gained competences in the field of nuclear security, but not in the field of nuclear safety. This allows us to draw comparisons in the ways in which legitimation dynamics play out in these two areas of organizational activity.

Moreover, all five organizations are active in different issue areas, ranging from security to economics, human rights and humanitarian assistance, the environment and regional integration. At the same time, they all serve as focal organizations in their respective issue area. This provides us with a means to examine whether issue areas develop their own, field-specific legitimation cultures or whether, in contrast, there is convergence among policy fields. In short, while scholars of 'world culture' or 'world polity' would expect isomorphic pressures to generate a homogenizing trend across issue areas (Drori et al. 2006), proponents of systems theory would expect functional differentiation to increase heterogeneity over time (Albert et al. 2013).

Finally, the five organizations also vary in terms of their membership. While the IAEA, the UNHCR, and the WTO reach or aim at universal state membership, membership of OAU/AU is confined to states on the African continent. Finally, while all four have only states as their members, IUCN counts governmental as well as NGOs among its members. In terms of the legitimation process, this allows us to examine the specific dynamics that unfold between members and non-member audiences in legitimating or delegitimating an organization, and the inclusion of IUCN can also provide information on how far the normative changes we observe travel. Do they hold only for *intergovernmental* organizations? Or do they also apply to *global governance institutions* (Koppell 2010) more broadly? Again, within-case comparisons facilitate our work since all five organizations have experienced considerable growth in their membership since 1970, though again at different rates.

Taken together, our case selection comprises a set of international organizations that is diverse in political authority, issue area, and membership— hence in relation to three major explanations for variation in normative foundations.[4] It includes large organizations like the WTO, but also goes beyond a narrow focus on the 'big five'. Overall, the advantages of our selection thus has some resemblance with a most different systems design, notably the ability to uncover some of the general structures and mechanisms that shape the legitimation and delegitimation of contemporary international organizations. If we find common normative changes across such a diverse range of international organizations, we can thus assume that they will exist in other international organizations, as well. In addition, the process-tracing approach we employ in our case studies allows us to pay attention to the specific factors that made normative change possible in the diverse cases we examine.

The Period of Investigation

To do justice to the history of organizational legitimation is virtually impossible in case studies limited by the length of one chapter. As a result, we seek to strike a balance between the desire to take the historical dimension seriously and the benefits of a cross-sectional research design. Our primary

---

[4] As one reviewer of our original manuscript rightly noted, this does not rule out the possibility that other organizations could have served the same purpose. For example, we could have replaced the OAU/AU with another regional organization that gained political authority over time, or environmental governance with a different issue area like development. Our claim is thus that we have identified a useful selection for our purposes, but not that that selection is the only one that would have fulfilled the criteria discussed above.

focus lies on the four decades from 1970 to 2010. In addition, each case study chapter also considers developments that are more recent. This allows us to assess whether developments that have taken place since 2010 tend to confirm or disconfirm the arguments we develop in this book.

At first glance, the decision to observe legitimation contests over a period of forty years might seem at odds with our claim that we are interested in how legitimacy standards have changed *after the Cold War*. Our justification is that a longer period of investigation allows us to trace incremental change as well as organization-specific continuities that we might otherwise miss. At the same time, the decision to focus on the specific period from 1970 to 2010 reflects our interest in the early 1990s as a watershed in world politics. In pursuing this interest, we do not presuppose a Westphalian world before and an entirely different, post-Westphalian one after 1989/90. Rather, we seek to empirically examine whether—and if so, to what extent—1989/90 was indeed a turning point for the legitimation of global governance institutions, as the Commission on Global Governance (1995) and many other observers at the time would have it.

Including the last two decades of the Cold War, we thus follow Andrew Hurrell's (2002: 142) advice that investigations into world political change should not fall into the trap of 'a stark and highly implausible choice: between a grossly simplified image of Westphalian past and an invariably complex, but usually underspecified, post-Westphalian present and future'. In brief, if we are interested in how legitimacy standards evolved *after 1989/90*, we also need to examine their development *before 1989/90*—first, to obtain a baseline for comparison and second, to make sense of what we see. Studying two decades on each side of the presumed turning point provides the common baseline across the five cases we study. At the same time, our cut-off points are indicative rather than carved in stone. On the one hand, all case studies thus also discuss whether the dynamics we observe have continued or interrupted after 2010, in a world political context that has seen considerable turbulence. On the other hand, where events prior to 1970 appear of particular relevance for a given case, individual case studies discuss their implication for the post-1970 legitimation discourses as our main object of study.

Beyond the Founding Documents: The Empirical Material

How do we find out how the selected five international organizations have been legitimated since around 1970? Intuitively, we could assume that a simple look at an organization's charter or constitutive act provides the answer. Do they not clearly spell out what an organization is supposed to do, hence what makes it a 'good' organization?

It is true that charters and foundational documents contain important information about the norms and values on which the social acceptance of international organizations rests. The UN, for example, can expect public support to the extent that it succeeds in promoting peace, human rights, justice, and 'the economic and social advancement of all peoples' (United Nations 1945: preamble). Similarly, if the WTO truly contributed to 'raising standards of living, ensuring full employment, and a large and steadily growing volume of real income and effective demand' (WTO 1994: 1144), while pursuing all these goals in accordance with the principle of sustainable development and the specific needs of developing countries, who would dare to question its legitimacy? And if the World Bank actually managed 'to assist in the reconstruction and development of territories of members by facilitating the investment of capital for productive purposes' (IBRD 1944: article I), some of the legitimation challenges it faces might equally never have arisen. In short, we might be inclined to wonder: are not the terms of legitimation a direct reflection of the functions for which an organization was created, just as those functions define the agendas of those who seek to openly challenge an international organization? To delegitimate the UN, its critics can—and do— argue that the organization *fails to provide peace* where it matters most. Similarly, those opposed to the WTO or the World Bank claim that the two organizations *neither promote prosperity nor help making poverty history.*

Yet this is only part of the story. First, we know that normative systems are 'inherently dynamic' (Sandholtz and Stiles 2008: 6). The norms they embody give rise to disputes over the meaning and proper application of those very norms. And thus, the outcomes of such disputes also imply normative change: they broaden or narrow the scope of application of a norm, or—slightly or radically—redefine what a particular norm means. If that is true for social norms in general, it should also apply to the norms that define which forms of governance are appropriate. Just like other norms, we should expect legitimacy principles to be subject to disputes, arguments, and change (Deitelhoff and Zimmermann 2013).

On a grand scale, events like the French and American revolutions remind us that this is indeed the case: the two revolutions have transformed standards of rightful government from a conception of divine authority to one based on popular sovereignty (Bukovansky 2002; Roth 1999). On a smaller scale, and more closely linked to the theme of this book, major international organizations have recently come to feel the normative pressures associated with principled ideas about 'democracy', a standard to which they were only rarely held in the past (Grigorescu 2015). Democratic norms like transparency, accountability, participation, inclusiveness, and representation thus transform our ideas of a good international organization, even though they do not commonly form part of the founding treaties of these organizations. If founding treaties were all that mattered, how do we account for such changes?

In addition, the international political environment in which the UN and other organizations operate has changed dramatically over the past decades.

The Cold War has ended. Many states around the world have become democracies. Economic globalization has transformed the way societies relate to each other. Rising powers like Brazil, China, and India have gained influence, both economically and politically. The revolution of communications technology has altered the way people interact with each other. In view of the history of international organizations we have discussed above, it would be a major surprise if the tectonic shifts that have affected our societies so deeply had left untouched how we believe our societies—as well as their interactions in an increasingly interdependent world—ought to be governed.

Finally, communication geared to (de)legitimate international organizations includes more than simply references to the foundational values of an organization. For example, the Organization of the Petroleum Exporting Countries (OPEC), in its 1982 Annual Report, takes pride in the fact that its news agency has disseminated 372,000 words 'in 2500 stories for a daily average of 1471 words', representing a '20 per cent increase in comparison with 1981' (OPEC 1983: 60). While it shows that the OPEC bureaucracy is anything but lazy, the achievement reported here is linked in only indirect ways to 'the coordination and unification of the petroleum policies of Member Countries and the determination of the best means for safeguarding their interests, individually and collectively', as the two central purposes of OPEC (OPEC 2012 [1961]: article 2A). Similarly, anti-WTO protesters at the 1999 ministerial conference in Seattle prominently claimed that the WTO undermined democracy, even though democracy was not a particularly central norm in the way the WTO had traditionally understood itself. In a nutshell, these examples illustrate a simple point: the discursive processes, in which the legitimacy of international organizations is gained, maintained, and repaired, include but are not limited to debates about the proper meaning and application of the norms and values that are explicitly written down in founding treaties. To understand how international organizations are legitimated, and how the norms that underpin such legitimations change over time, we need to look beyond these documents and reconstruct how conceptions of legitimate international organizations emerge and change as the result of discursive interaction.

Against this background, we study legitimation by examining the normative justifications actors give for their evaluations of international organization (see also Reus-Smit 2007: 159; Steffek 2003). These justifications, which together constitute the justificatory order that prevails at a given time, may vary across actors, across policy fields, and over time. To investigate change, we reconstruct, in each case study, the contests around the norms that underpin the organization's legitimacy. We consider such legitimation contests to be shaped by three kinds of actors: the organization as a collective actor; its members; and external actors like non-member states, other international organizations, non-state actors, or the media.

Aiming to examine what these three kinds of speakers contribute to the legitimation contests of a given international organization over a period of forty years confronts us with an almost limitless range of possible primary sources. The primary text corpus on which we base our analysis includes over 150 annual reports, studied either in their entirety or with a focus on recurring segments; the verbatim or summary records of member states' statements made in eighty sessions of governing bodies of international organizations; and close to 2,000 media articles and over 200 reports, position papers, and other documents that contain statements from external actors. Finally, we complement these textual documents with interviews with staff members or other stakeholders. This allows us to fill remaining gaps in the textual analysis, to gain a better understanding of the institutional context that shapes how legitimation contests play out, and to develop an understanding of the specific legitimacy challenges each organization saw itself confronted with (see Appendix). As we elaborate further in Chapter 2, we draw on a combination of qualitative content analysis and interpretive methods to describe and make sense of the normative change we identify in our material, and on causal process tracing to reconstruct what made normative change possible in the various cases we examine.

KEY ARGUMENTS

Our reconstruction of the legitimation contests of five different international organizations leads us to conclude that the traditional legitimation narratives, that characterized the 'national constellation' of the post-1945 world, have not been replaced after the Cold War. Yet, they have been complemented by the rise of an equally powerful 'post-national' legitimation narrative from which international organizations may deviate only at their own risk. As we show, the combined force of both sets of norms occasionally allows international organizations to cherry-pick the standards that suit them particularly well. In general, however, they confront international organizations with a longer and more demanding list of normative expectations that contributes to the perception of a legitimacy crisis.

Describing our results in more detail, we break down this broad conclusion into four specific observations:

- International organizations have come *under pressure* as they need to respond to a longer and more diverse list of legitimacy standards.
- International organizations increasingly need to justify their efforts in terms of what they do, not only for their member states but also for 'the people'.

- While legitimation contests have traditionally focused on the *performance* of international organizations, *procedural demands* have become a second terrain of contestation in more recent decades.

- The rise of people-centred and procedural legitimacy principles occurs along *multiple paths*. These paths include but go significantly beyond the politicization of international authority.

International Organizations under Pressure

First, and most generally, we observe that *international organizations have come under increasing pressure since they need to respond to the demands of ever more heterogeneous constituencies and match an ever longer and more diverse list of normative expectations.* Not only do responses to the question, *'what* and *how* international organizations should govern', become more diverse but the question *for whom* they govern also receives greater attention. If we think about a generic form of a typical legitimation statement from one of the early years of our period of investigation, it would roughly read as follows:

> We help our member states to reap mutual gains through cooperating for the purposes set forth in our constitution, with special attention to the needs of our developing country members.

This generic form largely corresponds to institutionalist IR theory which identifies mutual gains as the main justification for the establishment and maintenance of international institutions (Keohane 1984), but also emphasizes the need to constructively deal with the tension between the fiction of sovereign equality, on the one hand, and the reality of vast power disparities, on the other (Koppell 2010). International organizations thus need to give states an incentive to join, usually in the form of mutual benefits accruing from cooperation (Abbott and Snidal 1998).

In doing so, they need to pay tribute to a reality in which some states are more powerful than others—hence the need to generate specific incentives for powerful states to join a cooperative scheme. The latter incentives commonly come in the form of privileges in either substantive or procedural rules. World trade rules that are tilted towards the interests of the US and EU are an example of the former. Weighted voting in the World Bank and IMF, or the veto right permanent members hold in the UN Security Council exemplify the latter. At the same time, the privileges granted to major powers must still be acceptable to less powerful states whose governments need to be able to domestically defend their membership in an organization that, while paying lip service to the sovereign equality norm, often assigns them a marginal role in practice (Koppell 2010; Viola et al. 2015). This challenge provides the context for the explicit acknowledgement of the special needs of developing countries.

In contrast, a typical legitimation statement from the end of our period of investigation would inevitably be a bit longer, reading something like this:

> We are an inclusive, transparent, and accountable organization. Our goal is to help our member states—and the citizens in our member states—to reap mutual gains through cooperating for the purposes set forth in our constitution, with special attention to the needs of the least developed countries. To ensure coherence, we follow best practice in coordinating our activities with relevant international and transnational organizations.

As can easily be seen, the core of the traditional legitimacy claim is still very much present. Yet, it is surrounded by a number of additional expectations like inclusive and transparent procedures, or the accountability of those 'in charge'; the idea that gains are to be reaped not only—or even primarily—for the member states but for the individuals inhabiting them; or the notion that the value of an international organization is not to be seen in isolation but rather in how well it fits into and aligns with the broader scheme of international cooperation that states have been weaving since the late nineteenth century.

In short, we do not argue that new standards of legitimacy have replaced the existing normative yardsticks but that they have been added to the menu. What results is a menu that fits the diverse tastes of a heterogeneous audience—a menu that has something to offer for everyone—but also a menu that keeps the *chef de cuisine* and her team busy. Catering to the diverse needs and demands of their clients, international organizations are thus no longer analogous to a small diner that offers two simple dishes a day. They are more like full-blown restaurants that require considerable management: places that need to stockpile the ingredients for a broad variety of dishes, simultaneously prepare many of them, keep their books in order, serve discerning customers that have developed a habit of evaluating the restaurant's performance in light of rapidly changing criteria, and—aided by a healthy competition in the market—of threatening to choose a different location next time.[5]

In our case studies, we thus see the WTO catering to the traditional norms of multilateralism, progressive liberalization or development, and seeking to meet demands of sustainability, human rights, or democratic decision making. Similarly, we see the AU seeking to respect the sovereignty of its member states while intervening or threatening to intervene in them and developing links with African citizens. We also see how IUCN's goal of conserving nature is

---

[5] For the latter point of the analogy, see Julia Morse and Robert Keohane's description of 'contested multilateralism' (Morse and Keohane 2014).

increasingly complemented by development goals and demands for democratic decision making that have people rather than nature as their primary reference point. Yet, seeking to comply with a longer list of legitimacy standards not only makes tensions more likely but also enhances the risk of failure in relation to at least one important standard.

The Rise of the People

Our second major observation builds on the first. It states that *'the people' have become a central reference point in the legitimation of international organizations.* In general, we understand people-centred legitimacy standards as norms that tie the right to govern at the international level not to the interests or the consent of states, but to the interests of the individuals or social groups within or beyond nation states. We examine this rise in relation to three dimensions: Who governs? How? And for whom?

On the question of who governs, international organizations continue to stress that the roots of their legitimacy lie in the support of their members. Yet many of them expand the range of relevant 'stakeholders'. They portray themselves as 'open', 'inclusive', and 'people-based'. They emphasize the greater role that consultations with NGOs and other non-state actors play in the organization. Or they suggest that the policies they make should be 'owned' by those affected. Individual organizations also stress the role of parliamentary assemblies (the AU) and a need to engage with national parliaments as representatives of 'the people' (the WTO); or they point out that indigenous knowledge will be used to formulate new programmes (IUCN).

On how international organizations should be governed, our record is more ambiguous. As predicted by those who identify a general trend towards the application of democratic norms to international organizations, we observe that norms of transparency and accountability are on the rise, combined with norms asking for stronger coordination with other relevant actors. However, requests for transparency or accountability often relate to the management of the organizations and hence to the possibility for member states or other important donors—but not necessarily for societies—to effectively control international bureaucracies. Only in some instances, notably the WTO and the AU, does transparency and accountability *towards the public* become a strong legitimacy standard. Similarly, the coordination of an organization's activities with other organizations is commonly linked to norms of efficiency and coherence. It therefore constitutes a 'people-centred' norm only where—as in the UNHCR case—coordination with societal actors becomes a standard for evaluating the quality of an international organization.

Finally, on the question for whom international organizations govern, the emphasis on regulating 'for the people' gains strength over time. Evidence for this change is clearest in our case study on the OAU/AU where the idea that continental integration should be 'driven by [African] citizens' has gained currency and altered the very purpose of the organization. But it is also at the heart of the major shift in the legitimation of IUCN where conservation for the sake of nature has increasingly been replaced by conservation for the sake of human well-being; in references to 'citizens' or to 'our people' at WTO ministerial conferences; and in the stronger emphasis the IAEA puts on its development-related activities in recent years. The only case in which the rise of individuals as a major category of beneficiaries is less pronounced is thus the UNHCR where the protection of refugees and their rights has been a cornerstone of legitimation ever since.

The Rise of Procedures

Our third observation is that procedural standards have gained importance in the evaluation of international organizations. Following the distinctions introduced above, this means that the question *how an international organization is governed* becomes more relevant over time. Again, procedural standards are not entirely novel but gain strength; and they do not replace but complement performance standards.

In several of the studied cases, constituencies increasingly tie the legitimacy of an organization to principles like 'transparency', 'inclusiveness', or 'participation'. In the case of the OAU/AU, for example, procedural standards come as demand for the direct inclusion of civil society actors, while in both IUCN and UNHCR legitimacy becomes more closely linked to the inclusion of 'those concerned' by a specific policy. Yet, greater concerns for inclusiveness and participation emerge not only where new constituencies are taken on board. In the GATT/WTO as well as in IUCN, the rise of procedural norms refers to a greater concern for rebalancing the relationship of traditional members, notably between those from the Global North and South. Moreover, managerial norms of 'accountability', 'coherence', and 'coordination' gain prominence in several of our case studies, including the UNHCR, the OAU/AU, and the WTO.

Evidence for the observation that procedural standards do not replace but complement performance standards also comes from cases we do not consider in this book. Debates over whether the policies of the IMF are sound and just, for instance, have been central for the social acceptance of the organization (Guastaferro and Moschella 2012); and the charge that the OSCE is effectively relegated to inactivity as a result of disputes between Russia and Western member states still looms large in evaluations of that organization (Peters 2013). Yet where contests over how an international organization is governed are added to the menu, procedural standards become a second major terrain of contestation for defining the terms in which international organizations are legitimated.

Finally, the two trends—the rise of people-centred standards on the one hand, procedural standards on the other—can also help us to make sense of the stronger but varying role which 'democratic' standards have come to play in the legitimation of international organizations, in recent decades (Grigorescu 2015; see also Biegoń 2016; Dingwerth et al. 2018; Nullmeier et al. 2010). Located at the intersection of both trends, international organizations can use democratic values such as inclusiveness, transparency, and accountability to explain how they relate to 'the people', as well as to explain how their decision making is based on sound procedures. The recent prominence of democratic norms in the legitimation of international organizations, for which some of our case studies provide further evidence, might stem from the fact that democratic norms fit well with both secular trends we observe, more so than alternative norms that international organizations may invoke.

The Multiplicity of Paths

Finally, we observe that *the processes that spur the rise of people-centred and procedural legitimacy standards are diverse* and they usually combine influences inside as well as outside of international organizations. The academic literature conventionally sees the politicization of international institutions in the wake of newly gained competences as the strongest force for the rise of people-centred norms (Zürn et al. 2012; Zürn 2018). Looking at our cases, such an explanation is plausible for the WTO where the politicization of supranational authority does indeed lead to the rise of democratic norms (see Chapter 3). Overall, however, our case studies suggest that politicization is neither a necessary nor a sufficient condition for the rise of people-centred legitimacy standards. For example, we observe a rise of people-centred legitimacy standards in organizations without large gains in international authority (IUCN; see Chapter 6) or without much public pressure (AU; see Chapter 4), and we also observe instances of politicization that lead to only a weak shift towards people-centred norms (IAEA; see Chapter 5).

In addition, we identify a range of causal pathways *beyond politicization*. In the OAU/AU case study, for example, we show how the organization's bureaucracy uses a people-centred discourse to build up a 'second audience' and boost the organization's international reputation. In IUCN, the conscious choice to frame the organization's central purpose in a more development-friendly manner sets in motion a self-reinforcing dynamic towards a more people-centred legitimation. And in most organizations we study, the rising share of members from the Global South is a key factor in strengthening a 'development' agenda which, combined with the dominant understanding of 'human development', lends further support to people-centred legitimacy standards.

BROADER IMPLICATIONS

The observations we make in this study have implications beyond the cases we examine. While we discuss these implications in more detail in our concluding chapter, we can sketch the major theoretical, practical, and normative implications the following way.

In theoretical terms, our study attests to the significant power international bureaucracies wield in shaping our conceptions of 'what is' and 'what has value' (Boltanski 2011). More precisely, our results attest to the role international bureaucracies play in defining the terrains on which the legitimacy of international organizations is negotiated as well as the terms of legitimation that constitute those terrains. While the rise of post-national legitimacy standards thus fits with the general expectations of the world culture scholars, several of our case studies highlight the role of international bureaucracies as agents of normative change and stability. Moreover, while world culture facilitates some homogenization across very different organizations, our study also traces major differences in the ways post-national legitimacy standards manifest—or 'localize' (Acharya 2004)—themselves in different policy fields. Finally, we observe that layering—a process in which 'the new does not replace the old, but is added to it' (Van der Heijden 2011: 9)—is the default mode in which normative change occurs. As we discuss further below, this has practical implications since layering feeds the expanding list of normative expectations to which international organizations are subjected. Yet, it also has theoretical implications because, like the 'normative path dependence' we see at work in various cases, it suggests that the vocabulary of historical institutionalism might be apt to study not only 'hard' institutional dynamics to which it is conventionally applied, but also the 'softer' discursive changes we are interested in.

For the practice of international organizations, our results have three main implications. First, the inclusion of post-national legitimacy standards adds another source of pressure that contributes to the 'gridlock' (Hale et al. 2013) contemporary international organizations face. Second, the expansion of the list of normative expectations means that conflicts between such expectations become more likely in specific situations. Hence, they require international organizations and the societies they serve to cope with greater complexity, and to develop a tolerance for such complexity as well as a capacity to differentiate—two demands international organizations will find particularly difficult to match in the increasingly polarized political climate of contemporary democratic societies. Third, our results show that efforts to resolve a legitimacy crisis often work in the short term but come at significant unintended costs and constraints in the longer term.

Finally, the shifts we observe are ambivalent from a normative perspective. On the one hand, the rise of people-centred and procedural legitimation norms holds a potential to more fully realize the 'right to justification' (Forst 2012) in global governance, and some of the developments we sketch clearly match this aspiration. This holds, for instance, for the WTO's recognition of democratic norms itself, or for the inclusion of local knowledge in IUCN's assembling of conservation expertise. At the same time, the WTO case illustrates that the emancipatory potential of post-national legitimacy standards is limited when powerful actors manage to appropriate the new, but relatively open linguistic terrain of 'democracy'. Unsurprisingly, then, post-national legitimacy standards are no panacea. Instead, approximating the normative ideal will depend on a continuous struggle for a better global political order—a struggle for which post-national legitimacy standards may, however, provide a fertile ground.

PLAN OF THE BOOK

In Chapter 2, we present the theoretical framework that informs our five case studies. International organizations, we argue, are legitimated in processes of contestation in which a plethora of actors seeks to define what distinguishes a 'good' from a 'bad' international organization. In doing so, the actors draw on—and shape—the normative environments in which international organizations are embedded. These environments, in turn, depend on the world political contexts of their time. Change in what we call the *terms of legitimation* therefore comes from two ends: first, from the dynamics of interaction among those who take part in legitimation contests ('change from within'); and second, from material or ideational developments that support or challenge the persuasiveness of individual normative frames ('change from the outside').

In Chapters 3 to 7, we apply our framework to five international organizations, starting with the three organizations that have seen the largest authority gains during our period of investigation. In Chapter 3, we re-examine the history of legitimation contests around the GATT and WTO. In descriptive terms, we reconstruct how, in the early 1990s, environmentalist and trade unions successfully challenged the 'GATT gospel' that had long served as a stable legitimation basis for the organization. Since its creation in 1947, the GATT was traditionally valued as a 'bulwark against protectionism' that provided growth—and later also development—through an orderly but continuous liberalization of international trade. However, the public protests ensured that so-called 'non-trade values' and 'democracy' became major reference points in the legitimation contest. The GATT and WTO dealt with the challenges in different ways. It delegated labour standards to the International Labour Organization, awarded environmental values quasi-constitutional status, and turned democracy into a core norm around which to rebuild legitimacy after the Seattle protests. Overall, the chapter thus confirms the relevance of politicization: protests in the wake of enhanced international authority provoked a recalibration of the legitimation discourse, in the context of which several new standards were added to the 'GATT gospel'. At the same time, the politicization of the GATT and WTO results not merely from enhanced authority but also from a more heterogeneous membership. Finally, the chapter reveals how the post-Seattle decision to rebuild legitimacy around the notion of 'democracy' severely constrains the options for answering the most recent legitimacy challenge the WTO confronts.

In Chapter 4, we adopt a legitimation lens to reconstruct the turbulent history of the OAU and its successor, the AU. Established in 1963 to assist African states in their efforts to liberate themselves from colonial rule, the purposes of the organization changed once such rule had formally been overcome. With the end of the Cold War, a series of macro-developments—among them the intensification of civil wars on the continent, and the low level of attention an inward-looking group of major powers paid to Africa—also spurred two major changes in the way the OAU and the AU sought to legitimate themselves. On the one hand, the focus shifted from merely facilitating cooperation to demonstrating that the work of the OAU and later the AU actually made a difference 'on the ground'; that it led to peace and development, to integration, and to a stronger representation of African interests in global institutions. On the other hand, the AU sought to build its legitimacy on the notion of working not only for and with African states, but also for and with the African people. Legitimation thus increasingly focused on the principles of 'democracy', 'human security', or 'human development'. As the case study reveals, various dynamics in the organizational environment facilitated these changes, but norm entrepreneurship was central. In this case, it involved the OAU/AU bureaucracy, in particular the respective executive heads, and external donors like the EU, which brought their own normative expectations to the OAU/AU.

In Chapter 5, we turn to the IAEA. Created in 1957 to promote nuclear energy, strengthen nuclear safety, and verify that states use nuclear sites for peaceful purposes, the changes we observe primarily occur in view of the proper relation among these pillars. Overall, the legitimation basis of the IAEA is thus not only more stable than in other cases but it also remains almost exclusively tied to performance standards. Nevertheless, two normative developments are noteworthy. First, the nuclear accident in Chernobyl in 1986 meant that the safety pillar gained relevance not only in the policies but also in the legitimation of the Agency. Second, after the verification pillar was strengthened and then politicized in the wake of a post-Cold War expansion of IAEA authority, the organization sought to depoliticize its work. Notably, it stressed that verification was only one of its many activities and showcased how its work also contributed to address development challenges in poorer member states. Analytically, the relative stability of the IAEA's legitimation discourse in a highly turbulent political environment confirms our suspicion that field-specific legitimation cultures matter, and that international security governance remains more stable than most other fields (see also Tallberg et al. 2013). At the same time, the case study illustrates how exceptional circumstances like the Chernobyl accident can create windows for change. Finally, the case study shows how politicization is closely linked to the emergence of a second legitimation audience next to states—in this case the media—but that responses to politicization may vary.

In Chapter 6, we reconstruct how the IUCN has been legitimated since the 1970s. Established in 1948 as a hybrid international organization that includes states as well as non-state actors, IUCN is best known for the *Red List of Threatened Species* it publishes each year. While the organization has not gained new competences vis-à-vis members, the terms of its legitimation have changed incrementally, yet profoundly in two waves. In the 1980s, its focus shifted from conserving nature for nature's sake to conserving nature for the sake of the people. This rise of human well-being norms was subsequently reinforced by changes in the organization's self-understanding as a 'democratic conservation forum' that increasingly works with local stakeholders, and as a science-based organization ready to include local and traditional knowledge in the design of its conservation projects. A second wave of change set in with the rise of economic thinking in the early 2000s. This rise is manifest in an increased—and increasingly normalized—cooperation with multinational corporations and in the organization's cooperation in efforts to determine the economic value of ecosystems. In theoretical terms, the case study shows that change in membership structures as well as in the ideational environment of international organizations provides windows for change; that normative shifts, like other forms of institutional change, can be self-reinforcing; and that institutional design facilitates the norm entrepreneurship of international bureaucracies.

Finally, Chapter 7 examines the legitimation of the UNHCR, first established in 1950. Again, we present two cases of normative change. On the one hand, we observe a strengthening of individuals and their rights as reference points of the organization's activities. On the other hand, managerial norms gain relevance in the representation of UNHCR as a 'good international organization'. While the former change attests to the rise of people-centred legitimacy standards, the latter provides further evidence for the increasing importance of procedural expectations which international organizations are asked to fulfil. Somewhat paradoxically, then, the turn towards 'results-based management' implies that the legitimacy of UNHCR is measured just as much by how it works as it is measured by the outcomes it produces. Theoretically, the study confirms that multiple ingredients combine to generate normative change. The organizational environment matters because the 'new wars' of the 1990s present the organization with unforeseen challenges that require a more interventionist approach. Moreover, 'non-traditional' audiences gain relevance since, as a former senior staff member sums up, 'the media can make or break a case'[6] for funding. This strong role of the media further testifies the importance of institutional design: the UNHCR needs the media because almost its entire budget consists of voluntary contributions from the member states. Finally, the chapter reveals how exceptional circumstances can make a difference as the financial crisis, in which the organization found itself in 1989/90, provided a window of opportunity for actors to push for stricter oversight thereby facilitating the rise of New Public Management norms.

In Chapter 8, we weave the different threads together to draw the bigger picture. Taken together, the five case studies reveal a considerable dynamic in the normative structure of global governance. They point to a variety of case-specific developments but also to a common trend towards people-centred and procedural legitimacy standards, even though the moves different organizations make towards these standards do not necessarily have the same origins or are experienced in the same ways. Yet they have at least one consequence in common, namely that the addition of post-national legitimation norms to the menu of normative standards international organizations are expected to fulfil, contributes to the pressures the latter already confront.

---

[6] Personal communication with a former senior manager of UNHCR, September 2016.

2

Legitimation Contests

A Theoretical Framework

Klaus Dingwerth and Antonia Witt

INTRODUCTION

Our primary interest in this study is to understand how the normative yardsticks actors invoke to legitimate or delegitimate international organizations have shifted over time. As indicated in Chapter 1, the 'how' in this question is deliberately ambiguous. On the one hand, we are interested in the changing *terms* that proponents and critics of international organizations use to legitimate international organizations and their activities, and in the *criteria* they apply in relation to these terms. On the other hand, we wish to examine the *processes* through which some terms, as well as particular meanings attached to these terms, become dominant legitimation frames. Thus, taking the two sides of our main question we ask: what do legitimacy standards for international organizations look like at different points in time? And what makes legitimacy standards change over time?

As these questions imply, our study presupposes that 'legitimacy' is a political concept that different actors fill with different meanings. This assumption may be neither controversial nor surprising. In fact, terms such as 'legitimate' or 'illegitimate' are widely used in everyday politics; and while they always express some kind of valuation, their precise meaning varies. Take for instance the following statements from practitioners of international politics:

- 'The legitimacy that the UN conveys can ensure that the greatest number of states are able and willing to take [collective action against collective threats].'[1]

---

[1] UN Secretary General Kofi Annan on 11 September 2002, cited in Hurd (2007: viii).

- 'The [International Monetary] Fund's ability to persuade our members to adopt wise policies depends not only on the quality of our analysis but also on the Fund's perceived legitimacy.'[2]

- 'A focus on practical outcomes is especially important in public organizations such as the World Bank, where checks and balances and procedures and committees can stymie initiative. Accomplishments build morale, support, accountability, and legitimacy.'[3]

- 'The Congolese government is the legitimate government of this country. Whatever we do is legitimate.'[4]

In this chapter, we elaborate how we understand legitimacy as well as the process of legitimation. The framework we present provides the conceptual and methodological backbone for the case studies in Chapters 3 to 7. In brief, we start from the assumption that international organizations are legitimated in *legitimation contests* in which a variety of actors seek to define what distinguishes a 'good' international organization from a 'bad' international organization. In defining the standards of appropriateness, the actors draw on—and also shape—the normative environments in which international organizations are embedded. Since legitimation contests always take place in a concrete world political context that can vary from case to case, change in what we dub the *terms of legitimation* comes from two ends. First, it results from the dynamics of interaction among those who take part in legitimation contests ('change from within'); and second, it originates from material or ideational developments in the world political context that make individual normative frames appear more or less persuasive ('change from the outside'). While the former highlights the role of agency, the latter emphasizes the role of structures.

To unfold this argument, we proceed in three steps. First, we draw on a broader social science literature to clarify core assumptions that underpin the concept of legitimation. Second, we develop in more detail the idea that processes of legitimation are best understood as discursive interactions that take place in structured social environments. Lastly, we explain how our conceptual framework translates into a common approach and structure that underpins the case studies that follow in Chapters 3 to 7.

LEGITIMACY AND LEGITIMATION

The social science literature offers a broad range of definitions of legitimacy and legitimation. Yet the general distinction between the two terms is widely

[2] IMF managing director Rodrigo de Rato in 2006, cited in Symons (2011: 2572).
[3] Former World Bank president Robert Zoellick (2012: 77).
[4] Kikaya Bin Karubi, spokesperson for the government of the Congo, October 2002, cited in Hurd (2007: 29).

shared. Whereas *legitimacy* refers to a property of rightfulness actors ascribe to an institution, actor, or activity, *legitimation* refers to the process through which the institution, actor, or activity acquires that property in the eyes of a particular audience. Our primary interest is in the changing terms of legitimation, so we investigate processes of legitimation rather than legitimacy as a property of international organizations. We understand legitimation *as a structured social process by which the rightfulness of a political order or a part of that political order is defined and contested.* Applied to international organizations, the concept thus refers to the structured social processes in which actors negotiate the rightfulness—the social acceptability—of international organizations, including their purposes, their performance, their procedures, and their 'personality'.

This definition is based on four conceptual dimensions that help us to disentangle our understanding of legitimacy and legitimation. These are a stress on *normative beliefs* in the rightfulness, 'truth', or appropriateness of an entity; the importance of a *social relationship* between those seeking to acquire legitimacy and those granting legitimacy; the role of the *audience* (or several audiences) as the collective entity with whose norms and values a 'legitimate' institution, actor, or action needs to be in conformity; and the idea of different *degrees of consensus* within the collective entities granting legitimacy.

Beliefs

The assumption that legitimacy has to do with *beliefs* goes back to German sociologist Max Weber's observation that 'every system [of rule] attempts to establish and to cultivate the belief in its legitimacy' (Weber 1978 [1921]: 213; see also Hurd 2007: 30; Steffek 2007: 179; Suchman 1995: 574). Taken literally, this 'belief in legitimacy' (*Legitimitätsglaube*) would seem to mean that an institution, actor, or action is legitimate to the extent that relevant actors perceive it as legitimate. In empirical social science research, this has inspired efforts at gauging the legitimacy of political institutions with the help of surveys. Hence, legitimacy understood as a belief is often treated as synonymous with trust (Edwards 2009; Torgler 2008). Similarly to the Eurobarometer we mentioned in Chapter 1, the 2014 *World Values Survey* thus revealed that half of the respondents in Africa had either 'not very much' or 'no confidence at all' in the African Union (AU).[5]

Such observations are often interpreted as signs of a 'legitimacy crisis'. Yet while trust may be related to legitimacy, it is not the same. In a much-cited phrase, David Beetham therefore suggests that 'a given power relationship is not legitimate because people believe in its legitimacy, but because it can be

---

[5] See World Values Survey 2010–14, http://www.worldvaluessurvey.org/WVSOnline.jsp; data were collected in Egypt, Ghana, Libya, Nigeria, Rwanda, South Africa, Tunisia, and Zimbabwe.

justified in terms of their beliefs' (Beetham 2013: 11, emphasis in the original). The problem with equating legitimacy and trust, Beetham argues, lies in the difficulty to comprehend how change in beliefs comes about, why people cease trusting at a certain point in time. Instead of studying 'legitimacy beliefs' directly, he thus proposes to study the 'congruence, or lack of it, between a given system of power and the beliefs, values and expectations that provide its justification' (Beetham 2013: 11). This suggestion ties the study of legitimacy less to survey research but more closely to the study of justificatory discourses. At the same time, it foregrounds how political and normative orders *become legitimate*, thereby connecting the study of legitimacy more closely to practices of legitimation and reactions thereto (Barker 2001; Bernstein 2011; Hurd 2007; Nullmeier et al. 2010; Steffek 2003; Zaum 2013a).

Social Relationship

A second dimension in the concept of legitimacy is that it denotes a social relationship. As a result, the practice of legitimation, too, has to be understood as an inherently *social* process (Reus-Smit 2007: 159). To give an example, the Secretary General of the UN can merely *claim* that his organization is legitimate but this claim does not *confer* legitimacy upon it. Legitimacy, instead, is conferred by others, be it UN member states or relevant external audiences. To state that an organization has legitimacy is thus identical to stating that others accept an organization as rightful.

Yet the kind of social relationship that legitimation establishes may differ across contexts. For political scientists, legitimacy is commonly restricted to relationships of power, authority, or rule. From this perspective, legitimacy equals a 'right to rule', thus licencing and delimiting a particular system or mode of governance and demanding obedience from those subject to its rule (Bukovansky 1999: 198; see also Bernstein 2011: 20; Hurd 2007: 30; Reus-Smit 2007: 158). In organizational sociology, a broader notion of legitimacy prevails. It builds on the idea that all organizations—whether or not they exercise power, authority, or rule—seek acceptance from at least their most immediate environments, and it defines such acceptance either in terms of the 'congruence of an organization with social laws, norms and values', or in terms of the cultural comprehensibility of an organization's identity or behaviour (Deephouse and Suchman 2008: 50–1).

With respect to our object of study, scholarly and public debates increasingly recognize international organizations as entities that exercise rule or authority. They formulate binding rules and decisions; they set global agendas; collect, synthesize, and disseminate authoritative knowledge; and in some cases, they also deploy physical force and replace national systems of governance (Avant et al. 2010; Barnett and Finnemore 2004; Chesterman 2004).

Yet international organizations usually lack resources other than legitimacy to prop up such delegated or self-acquired authority. Unlike national governments, international organizations usually cannot draw on coercive power. International Relations (IR) scholars thus usually conclude that, where decisions of international organizations run against the narrow interests of member states, the legitimacy of an organization can serve as a resource to make states accept and implement such decisions. By implication, increasing authority renders international organizations particularly dependent on legitimacy (Zürn et al. 2012: 70; Hurd 2007: 50, Zaum 2013b: 7–8).

While this may be true, it nonetheless makes sense to work with a conception of legitimacy that accommodates different degrees of authority. Max Weber (1978: 953), for example, discusses legitimation not only in relation to formal bureaucratic rule, but also to situations in which difference in status or other valued goods requires justification. He argues that,

> Men differ in their states of health or wealth or social status or what not. Simple observation shows that in every such situation he who is more favoured feels the never ceasing need to look upon his position as in some way 'legitimate', upon his advantaged as 'deserved', and the other's disadvantage as being brought about by the latter's 'fault'.

From this perspective, legitimation thus delineates and justifies a particular relationship of power, be it that between ruler and ruled, between boss and employee, or between teacher and student. For the purpose of our study, speaking about legitimation therefore does not necessarily entail a claim concerning the binding nature of the decisions taken by international organizations or the degree of rule they exercise. International organizations exert rule to different degrees. They generate more or less binding policies and rules; they act as stronger or weaker implementation agencies; and they can be more or less authoritative sources of knowledge that structure social relations. International authority may vary across organizations (the World Trade Organization (WTO) versus the International Union for Conservation of Nature (IUCN)) as well as across fields of activity (the International Atomic Energy Agency (IAEA) in non-proliferation versus nuclear safety). Similarly, it may differ across institutional bodies (the WTO dispute settlement body versus the WTO trade negotiation committees) as well as over time (the Organisation of African Unity (OAU) versus the AU). As a result, international organizations may be subject to different patterns of legitimation and delegitimation which only a broader notion of legitimation allows us to uncover.

In all cases, however, legitimation serves to justify a particular relationship that attributes a right to decision, command, or action to some actors, and a need for obedience to others; that draws the boundaries of acceptable scope of action; and that renders alternative courses of action either incomprehensible or inappropriate. As a result, legitimation is inherently connected to power, not only—as most liberal IR scholarship would hold it—because power *needs* legitimacy (Franck 1990), but also because legitimacy always *produces* power (Beetham 2013: 104; Forst 2015; Mulligan 2004: 482; Reus-Smit 2007: 162).

Audience

A third element shared by different conceptions of legitimacy is the need for a legitimacy-granting audience.[6] The audience condition refers to the notion that the understandings of appropriateness against which an institution, actor, or action is evaluated are 'social facts'. They develop not in isolation but in discursive communities bounded in space and time (Bernstein 2011: 24; Bukovansky 2002: 7–12; Reus-Smit 2007: 163).

Which audiences are relevant in terms of granting and withholding legitimacy is a matter of much debate and, as we discuss further below and illustrate in the case studies, subject to change. For a long time, member states were assumed to be the sole legitimacy audience of international organizations. Yet as a general observation, it seems increasingly clear that international organizations have expanded the range of audiences from which they actively seek legitimation. This also has implications for how they do so, and for what kinds of arguments they put forth to acquire such legitimacy (cf. Zaum 2013b: 16–19). We should therefore think about the audience dimension of legitimacy in its plural: as a multitude of possible audiences that are constantly reshaping and repositioning themselves vis-à-vis the organization. For instance, when the World Health Organization (WHO) increasingly relies on financial contributions from philanthropic foundations, such foundations become a legitimacy-granting community, and their visions of what is a 'good' WHO therefore become an additional normative yardstick by which the organization and its activities will be measured (Hanrieder 2009). As our case studies confirm, changes in the scope of audiences often lead to change in the ways international organizations seek to legitimate themselves.

Degrees of Agreement

Finally, the fourth element relates to the degree of normative agreement within legitimacy-granting audiences. It would come to constitute a difficult threshold if it meant actual consensus, defined either as the consent of all

---

[6] For one of the few definitions that do not include this element, see Hurd (2007: 30), whose definition of legitimacy as 'the belief by an actor that a rule or institution ought to be obeyed' is followed by the explanation that 'such a belief is necessarily normative and subjective, and not necessarily shared with any other actor'.

members of a community or as the absence of sustained opposition to a majority opinion within a community. In practice, both events would be very rare so that a strong consensus condition could only refer to 'perfect legitimation', understood as 'perfect theory, complete (i.e. without uncertainty) and confronted by no alternatives' (Meyer and Scott 1983: 201). In real-world terms, it is more appropriate to expect normative conflicts, within as well as among constituencies, with frictions between different normative concepts used to legitimate an organization more likely than not to occur. For example, Jonathan Koppell has shown how global governance institutions are caught between providing incentives to the most powerful actors and preserving the idea of equality among members. Elsewhere, Koppell has reconstructed how different conceptions of 'accountability' pose a serious challenge for the leaders of the Internet Corporation for Assigned Names and Numbers in addressing demands raised towards them (Koppell 2005, 2010). In turn, Patrick Cottrell (2016: 41) argues that for many international organizations, attempts to improve their procedural legitimacy, for instance through more inclusive deliberations, has had negative effects on the organization's performance—a possible dilemma we pick up in our discussion of the legitimation of the General Agreement on Tariffs and Trade (GATT) and WTO in Chapter 3.

It is therefore useful not to take the requirement of normative consensus literally, but to think of different 'degrees of agreement'[7] on political values as marking the discursive realm in which legitimation takes place. Thus, international organizations are more likely to acquire the legitimacy they seek if they can refer to normative principles that the audiences they care about share while those of others will be neglected. As a result, we can assume that the degrees of agreement in relation to a particular normative yardstick will affect how international organizations seek to legitimate themselves.[8] By implication, studying legitimation implies rendering visible just how normative consensus is established, sustained, or transformed within or across legitimacy-granting audiences, and by what means actors seek to portray an organization and its activities as either conforming to or violating the normative principles that prevail within relevant communities.

---

[7] We owe this term to Alex Grigorescu.

[8] Note, however, that what matters most in this respect is agreement on the *importance*, but not necessarily on the precise *meaning* of a principle. Vague principles that different audiences may interpret differently can thus also serve as normative 'containers' to which a variety of communities can subscribe for different reasons. Agreement on the importance of, say, 'democracy' as a normative yardstick therefore primarily determines the boundaries for the legitimation contest in as much as it requires actors that wish to make legitimacy claims to frame these claims *in terms of* 'democracy'.

THE DISCURSIVE INTERACTION MODEL

What do we imagine the process of legitimation to look like? Understanding legitimation as a social and discursive process requires accepting at least some ideas central to constructivist scholarship, notably the assumption that discourses—the practices that signify the world—also *give shape* to the world (Kubálková et al. 1998; Onuf 1989). In the following, we describe a heuristic framework that builds on this assumption but also takes agency and actors' (strategic) interactions seriously. With this, we seek to reach a perspective that acknowledges agency as well as structures, and that serves to understand the contests over international organizations' legitimacy within their broader ideational, material, and institutional contexts. As a model of legitimation, ours is thus based on a somewhat eclectic perspective; it differs from theoretically more 'purist' approaches that view either power or persuasion as the primary drivers of legitimation processes.[9]

The discursive interaction model starts from the assumption that framing contests lie at the heart of politics. Studying 'how normative principles are deployed in public debate' is therefore key (Krebs and Jackson 2007: 57). As Ronald Krebs and Patrick T. Jackson (2007: 36 and 44–5) argue, discursive interaction can be studied as 'observable rhetorical contests' in which the participants seek 'to maneuver each other onto more favorable rhetorical terrain and thereby to close off routes of acceptable rebuttal'—a state the authors call *rhetorical coercion*. In line with this argument, we can compare legitimation contests to a game of chess in which each player seeks to win the game by making the other's move impossible or unprofitable.

In this model, rhetorical coercion is successful when the claimant's moves 'deprive...[its opponent] of materials out of which to craft a reply that falls within the bounds of what [the public] would accept' (Krebs and Jackson 2007: 45). Discursive interaction is thus a continuous process of broadening or narrowing the possibilities for alternative articulations. In contrast to liberal versions of constructivist scholarship, however, the primary mechanism through which change occurs is not persuasion, but defeat in public discourse. Such a defeat occurs because 'political actors can rarely take tangible steps or advance policy positions without justifying those stances and behaviors' (Krebs and Jackson 2007: 45). Because legitimacy claims require a justification, shared causal and principled ideas shape the exchange of competing claims (cf. Cottrell 2016: 46–7; Reus-Smit 2007: 163). Hence, 'speakers may not say just anything they would like in the public arena: rhetoric is not infinitely elastic but is structured' (Krebs and Jackson 2007: 44–5).

---

[9] For the first, see for instance Coicaud (2010); Cox (1983); Rai and Waylen (2008); Zelditch (2001). For the latter, see for instance Steffek (2003).

On this account, structures matter in three important ways. First, the particular constellation of interests as well as the power relationship among those who participate in the legitimation contest shape legitimation contests. Second, the broader discursive environment, to which these actors can refer in order to justify their positions or challenge those of their opponents, acts as a constraint. Changes in the content of legitimation discourses can result from both sources: from the 'rhetorical game' itself (e.g. when actors seek to shift the contest to a more favourable terrain), as well as from changes in the discursive environment to which the actors refer (e.g. when particular frames acquire a new meaning or when new frames are added to public discourse). Finally, the institutional context in which legitimation contests take place matters—for instance by the allocation of speech time, or the formal and informal rules that determine who has access to meetings and documents (Cottrell 2016: 52–3; Holzscheiter 2010: 58).

What distinguishes this model from those based either on power or on reason, as main drivers for the changing (or not) terms of legitimation? Let us take the proliferation of women's suffrage in the nineteenth and twentieth centuries as an example. *Power*-based approaches would interpret this proliferation a marginal concession by dominant elites to defend liberal democracies against alternative visions of political order. On this account, the change in the principles legitimating domestic political order would have been preceded either by the rise of communism and socialism as competitors to liberal democracy, or by the process of industrialization that gave women a greater role in the production process, thereby also enhancing their political power as a social group. At the same time, the shift towards formal voting rights may have done just enough to leave a plethora of informal gender hierarchies in place. Discursive references to gender mainstreaming would then be seen as a strategy to legitimate a political order that rests on sustained inequalities among men and women.

Proponents of a *rational-legal approach* would instead argue that the movement managed to turn a 'normal' practice—namely the fact that women were barred from voting—into its opposite because of the superior quality of the ideas promoted by the women's rights movement, notably their appeal to reason. It is this quality that made 'votes for women [move] from unimaginable to imaginable, and then become standard state policy' (Keck and Sikkink 1998: 58).

The *discursive interaction approach*, in contrast, would emphasize how the social movement for women's suffrage aligned its demands with major tenets of liberal democracy such as equality or human rights, thereby pressuring opponents to either deny the validity of these liberal principles, or their applicability to the case of women's rights (cf. Ramirez et al. 1997). Denying liberal principles essentially shifts the discourse to one of liberalism versus conservatism and thereby enables the women's suffrage movement to forge a coalition with other powerful actors. In contrast, denying the applicability of the principle of equal political rights to women may have worked for some time but became a more difficult rhetorical strategy; initially as a result of the codification of human rights in the second half of the twentieth century, and then in response to the proliferation of women's suffrage in ever more societies.

In sum, all three readings agree on the power of ideas as well as on the centrality of discourse as the realm in which contestation over ideas is played out. At the same time, they model legitimation discourses differently. The power model expects legitimation contests to reflect either material or—as in post-structuralist approaches that focus on knowledge formations—immaterial power structures. It stresses that legitimation is an exchange among unequal parties, and that it is therefore important to understand *on whose terms* legitimation takes place. The rational-legal approach puts a high premium on reason and—at least in the long run—on the 'force of the better argument'. It thereby points to the particular power that scripts of rationality and objectivity have acquired in modern societies (Meyer 2009; Steffek 2003). Finally, the discursive interaction model holds that the outcomes of the 'legitimation game' are influenced not only by the interests and power of those who take part in that game, but also by the social structures in which legitimation takes place. This environment structures which legitimacy claims are likely to be successful, which strategies are available to actors, and which legitimating practices will be considered (in)appropriate.

While all three models offer a useful starting point to investigate legitimation contests, the discursive interaction model has a number of advantages in relation to our study. First, the focus on the interaction of competing claims allows us to take legitimacy claims as what they are, at least initially, and 'merely' engage in a reconstruction of the dynamics of interaction among competing claims advanced by different actors. This, as we will see in Chapters 3 to 7, is challenging enough indeed. However, it requires the observer neither to decide whether a claim is more or less 'reasonable', nor to predetermine whether an actor advances it to support a hegemonic order. Second, a focus on discursive interaction is ontologically less demanding and normatively less prescriptive. Thus, we do not need to presume that the institutional script of rationalization is a central force in modern political systems—if it is, arguments that fit the script will figure prominently in the legitimation contests we trace in our case studies. Similarly, our approach neither requires a normative background theory that informs us what is or is not appropriate, nor does it make us blind when it comes to inequalities among actors. For example, if local refugee organizations criticize how the Office of the United Nations High Commissioner for Refugees (UNHCR) runs a refugee camp, their voice may not carry the same weight as when the agencies' most powerful donors decide to withdraw their funding. But again, if the voices of local organizations do carry weight, we will recognize them in our data; conversely, we can highlight their exclusion if they do not.

SPEAKERS, AUDIENCES, AND THEIR ENVIRONMENTS: THE ELEMENTS OF A DISCURSIVE INTERACTION MODEL

A more precise elaboration of the discursive interaction model leaves us with the task of specifying the role and relations of the actors that engage in legitimation contests, as well as the ideational, material, and institutional structures that shape and result from such engagements. In simple terms, our model assumes that actors in legitimation contests engage in discursive interactions in order to applaud or challenge an international organization's processes, performance, and personality. In doing so, the 'speakers' in a legitimation contest draw on a set of more or less established normative frames to describe and evaluate international organizations and their activities. The collective of such frames determines the boundaries of a legitimation discourse at a given time, but these boundaries are flexible rather than fixed. Finally, we assume that legitimation contests are always embedded in a wider world political context that is itself subject to change. This context renders some discursive frames more acceptable than others, and it structures the ways in which they can be used (see also Cottrell 2016: 47).

Figure 2.1 summarizes this model. Applied to our research question, we can imagine Figure 2.1 as a dynamic motion picture: for each organization, we examine new bubbles (the *normative frames*) to enter the picture at some point in time, while others leave the terrain, pale, merge with neighbouring bubbles, separate again, or change in size (i.e. relative importance) or colour (i.e. their particular meaning). What drives this dynamic is, on the one hand, the actors in the inner circle who seek to promote specific frames or understandings. In the motion picture, the bubbles with new terms thus do not appear out of nowhere. Instead, we can imagine actors who carry banners with 'gender equality', 'democracy', or 'sustainable development' written on them to introduce new bubbles into the legitimation contest. On the other hand, the world political contexts in a given issue area affect the constellation of bubbles in as much as they 'soften' or 'harden' specific aspects of the legitimation contest, and thereby facilitate or complicate actors' attempts to alter the normative terrain on which the legitimacy of an international organization is negotiated.

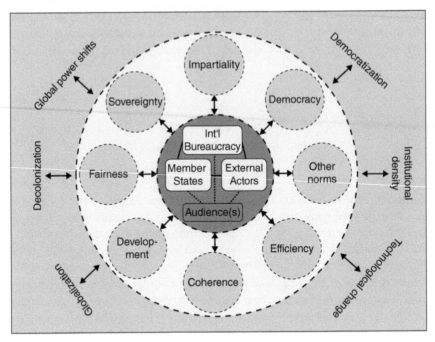

Figure 2.1. The bubbles model: international organizations, normative environment, and world political contexts

The Inner Circle: Who Speaks to Whom?

In our empirical reconstruction, we distinguish between three groups of speakers whose discursive interactions make up the legitimation contest. As a first group, the *international organization as a whole* communicates through its secretariat, its governing board, or its decision-making body.[10] Regular communications of this speaker include annual reports, press statements, public speeches of the executive head, or decisions of the general assemblies. While all of these documents would lend themselves to identify how the organization describes itself and justifies what it does, our reconstruction mainly relies on annual reports. They are accessible, have a relatively clearly defined audience—usually the member states and other donors—and cover a broad range of organizational activities. Moreover, their recurrent structure allows us to trace change in justificatory patterns over time.

---

[10] The idea that the organization as a whole communicates through its resolutions may not be straightforward since it is the *members* who adopt such resolutions. In line with common conceptions of (international) organizations, we count communicative acts of the *collective of members*—as opposed to communications of *individual members*—as 'organizational' statements. The corporate analogy would be to describe resolutions by the board of directors or shareholder assembly as statements on behalf of the organization as a whole.

Yet, the legitimating principles the organization uses in its communications need not reflect the principles on which its *members*—let alone each of them individually—base their legitimacy claims. As a result, the analysis of what members publicly state about their organization provides us with further insights into the dynamics of legitimation contests. In particular, it allows us to trace whose normative yardsticks are taken up and whose legitimating principles are side-lined at the organizational level. Moreover, examining how members publicly describe and evaluate an organization can help us to identify where and how different speakers fill the same terms—for instance references to 'sovereignty', 'fairness', or 'development'—with different meanings. Practically, we therefore reconstruct members' contributions to legitimation contests through the statements they make in general assemblies or executive council meetings of the respective organization.

Third, a diverse range of *non-members* publicly communicate about international organizations. Over the past decades, this group has become not only more relevant, but also more diverse. It includes non-governmental organizations (NGOs), the media, interest groups, philanthropic foundations, national political parties, other international organizations working in the same policy field, and in some cases also states that are not members of the organization. In relation to this broad group of speakers, the sheer number of statements makes it impossible to aim at an exhaustive analysis. Our selection thus initially focuses on the statements that accredited non-members make in formal bodies of the organization. Yet, these statements are often only available for the two most recent decades, and they tend to reflect the views of only a particular subset of non-members. As a result, we complement our analysis with statements from other relevant speakers identified via international media archives, secondary literature, and through interviews and archive visits at the organizations' headquarters.

Finally, actors always articulate their legitimacy claims *in front of an audience*. Unlike national governments, however, international organizations do not confront a ready-made and clearly discernible public as the main addressee of their claims to legitimacy. Rather, the speakers in the legitimation contests we examine usually have multiple relevant audiences. These audiences may include other speakers in the contest, for instance the governments of member states as well as segments of world society, and their composition varies across organizations as well as over time (Clark 2007c; Symons 2011; Zaum 2013b: 16–19). To whom an international organization speaks therefore depends on 'where [it] seeks to act' (Reus-Smit 2007: 164), but it also shapes how legitimacy claims will be framed. As our case studies show, the heterogeneity of the audiences that international organizations address has expanded dramatically since 1970, and this heterogeneity also has consequences for how international organizations seek to gain and maintain their legitimacy.

The Outer Circle: What Do Speakers Refer To?

When actors claim or challenge the legitimacy of an international organization, their statements form part of the inner circle depicted in Figure 2.1. Although we assume that actors seek to advance their positions based on principles that best reflect their own values and interests, we also acknowledge that legitimation discourses are always embedded in a broader discursive environment that pre-structures what kinds of arguments are likely to be accepted by target audiences. While this broader discursive environment extends beyond norms, our focus is on the latter. To use Friedrich Kratochwil's example, 'if someone says "This is a good car"...he always opens himself to the further question "Why do you say so?"'—and only some answers to this question will likely find acceptance as being based on an appropriate 'standard of goodness' for things such as cars (Kratochwil 2006: 305). The legitimation of international organizations, too, 'is always norm-referential' (Reus-Smit 2007: 162–3). Stated differently, a legitimation statement includes an evaluation paired with a justification for that evaluation, combined with the claim that this justification reflects an appropriate 'standard of goodness' for things such as international organizations. The main interest of this study is to answer how the standards that underlie evaluations of international organizations, as well as their public justifications, have changed over time and across issue areas.

So, what are the normative yardsticks to which participants in legitimation contests refer in their communications? To a large extent this is an empirically open question. In Kratochwil's example, cited above, the response 'Because it is yellow' is unlikely to find much acceptance since people do not generally view yellowness as an appropriate quality standard for cars. Consequently, as Kratochwil notes, we know that the person who invokes this standard 'is either pulling our leg or is acting like an "idiot"' (Kratochwil 2006: 305). Yet, political institutions are appraised on many different grounds, and the answer to what constitutes a shared normative standard for international organizations at a given point in time is, therefore, to be found in our data rather than in our theories.

In principle, almost anything can serve as a normative standard as long as target audiences accept it as corresponding to the rules of the legitimation game. As summarized in Table 2.1, preceding theoretical and empirical research shows a plethora of possible normative yardsticks. This once more underlines the necessity to determine them empirically rather than front-load the analysis with normative presumptions. For analytical reasons, we can nevertheless distinguish between evaluations that relate to the *performance*, to the *procedures*, and to the *personality* of international organizations.

Table 2.1. Legitimation principles: categories used in the literature

Study	Legitimation principles
Beetham 2013	Adherence to rules—Justifiability of rules—Voluntary public expressions of consent
Clark 2005	Legality—Morality—Constitutionality
Hurd 2007	Correct procedures—Fairness—Favourable outcomes
Junne 2001	Correct procedure—Representation—Justice—Effectiveness—Charisma
Nullmeier et al. 2010	Democratic input—Non-democratic input—Democratic output—Non-democratic output
Scholte 2011	Legality—Democracy—Morality—Efficiency—Charismatic leadership
Van Rooy 2004	Representation—Rights—Expertise—Public interest—Consistency—Austerity—Independence—Purity
Zürn and Stephen 2010	Expertise—Community—Legality—Accountability—Participation—Public debate

Evaluations of Performance

In the traditional view, states as major stakeholders evaluate international organizations primarily based on the quality of the solutions they offer for collaboration or cooperation problems (Keohane 1984). More generally, one may say that international organizations are seen as positive to the extent that they are perceived to generally promote the values and interests of the evaluating entity, and/or to the extent that they fulfil the functions that member states have assigned to them. Thus, the World Bank is good if it promotes development, the International Monetary Fund (IMF) if it contributes to financial stability, and the UN if it helps to maintain peace. Yet, the precise content of functional expectations may be heavily contested, and thus vary over time, even where the key terms remain identical. While most commentators agree that the World Bank should promote development in order to eradicate poverty, they tend to argue over what 'development' means and how exactly poverty gets eradicated (Vetterlein 2012). The UNHCR, in turn, was established with the mandate to seek 'durable solutions' to refugee crises, mainly referring to granting asylum and resettlement of refugees in host countries. Yet, over time, 'durable solutions' became 'permanent solutions' and instead of asylum or resettlement they meant repatriation of refugee populations in the countries they had originally come from (Barnett and Finnemore 2004: 99). And while the OAU/AU is frequently evaluated for its contributions to promote peace and security on the African continent, the notion of peace and security itself has changed in the course of the past two decades. Today, it is no longer restricted to the prevention of interstate war but includes a mandate to promote human development and peaceful social relations within states (see Chapter 4; see also Jolly et al. 2009: 163).

In sum, claims to an organization's effective fulfilment of its purposes entail references to efficiency and effectiveness, but they commonly do so in relation to a valued good. Based on the existing literature, plausible candidates for such valued goods include the *justice* of outcomes produced by an international organization and goods such as *peace, welfare, human rights, freedom, human development*, the *protection of the environment*, the *rule of law*, the *promotion of democracy* in member states, or *respect for national sovereignty*. Changes in the terms of legitimation can thus refer to changes in the hierarchy of different values or principles (as in 'Is economic development more important than the conservation of nature?') as well as to changes in the meaning of individual terms (as in 'What is sustainable development?'). Challenges to such claims, in turn, take two different forms. They can either argue that performance fails to meet the functional expectation (*performance challenges*), or claim that the underlying values are immoral or inadequate to achieve a desirable end (*value challenge*) (Deephouse and Suchman 2008: 51).

Evaluations of Procedure

In addition to performance criteria, evaluations of organizational processes also refer to the norms and values that guide how an organization develops, conducts, and evaluates its policies—in other words, how an organization is governed and how it governs. In terms of the common normative frames, used to evaluate the procedural side of international organizations, the literature offers a variety of principles that actors can and do invoke to define 'right process' criteria (see Table 2.1). David Beetham, for instance, argues that the first response by someone whose legitimacy to do or have something is questioned, usually comes as a reference to conformity with established rules (*adherence to rules*). He thus identifies the phrase 'I obtained it by the rules, and am therefore entitled to it' as 'a standard claim in all societies' (Beetham 2013: 64–5). This is echoed in the introductory quote to this chapter, according to which 'the Congolese government is the legitimate government of this country' and that, as a result, 'whatever [it does] is legitimate'. It is also echoed in distinctions made by other authors, for instance in Ian Clark's category of *legality*, or Gerd Junne's category of *correct procedure*. Yet, any evaluation of the adherence to established rules is subject to the possibility that different actors interpret these rules differently. As a result, we can expect contestation over the legitimacy of institutions, actors, and activities to centre on the question: what is the right interpretation of a given rule to which actors claim or demand an international organization to adhere?

Taking this argument further, Beetham notes that 'rules cannot justify themselves simply by being rules, but require justification by reference to considerations which lie beyond them' (Beetham 2013: 69). The justifiability of rules, and hence the response to the question 'what has value', is therefore central in legitimation contests (cf. Boltanski 2011). To the extent that justifications focus on the procedural rather than the substantive side of international organizations and their activities, references to *fairness* as well as to a whole bundle of *democracy-related terms* such as inclusiveness, representation, responsiveness, transparency, and accountability are common terms of legitimation debates (Grigorescu 2015; Zaum 2013c: 222). In addition, common normative frames include *rights-based claims*, claims to *independence and neutrality*, and claims referring to the *authoritative knowledge* upon which decision making rests (Barnett and Finnemore 2004; Haas 1992; Keck and Sikkink 1998).

Neutrality in the handling of a perceived conflict, for instance, becomes relevant if we take the potentially conflictive relationship between an organization's centralized structures and the sovereignty concerns of member states into account. One instance in which neutrality has become part of legitimation discourses is by reference to expert knowledge (Sending 2017). Here, speakers applaud or challenge an organization on the basis that its activities are congruent (or incongruent) with best available knowledge in a given field. This is for example an important yardstick in the legitimation of the IMF (see e.g. Barnett and Finnemore 2004: 45–72) and, among our case studies, the IAEA, as well as the IUCN. Both portray themselves as scientific and technocratic entities and justify their work through appeals to scientific authority. Finally, independence, for example from the particular interests of powerful states, is often invoked as a source of legitimacy. For example, the Shanghai Cooperation Organization is praised for not bowing to pressures from Western donors (Prantl 2013: 176). In contrast, some challenge the legitimacy of the UN by claiming that it is little more than a 'puppet' of the United States (Morris and Wheeler 2007: 216).

Evaluations of Personality

While performance and procedure can be linked to the categories of 'output' and 'input', our third category is informed by what Mark Suchman has termed the 'essence' of an organization. In adding this category, Suchman wished to distinguish 'between the organization's *operating* in a desirable, proper, and appropriate manner and the organization's *being* desirable, proper, and appropriate, *in itself*' or '[having] good character' (Suchman 1995: 583; emphasis in the original). Other authors refer to the concept of organizational identity as something that transcends the concrete claims to performance or due process (He and Brown 2013). Examples would include the UNHCR as an agent of 'humanitarianism', the UN as embodying the idea of an 'international community', the AU as representing values such as 'Pan-Africanism' and 'African solidarity', or the World Intellectual Property Organization seeking 'to refine and promote the Organization's corporate image as "an organization for the future"' (WIPO 2001: 36). Yet, evaluations of an organization's *personality* do not necessarily have to be positive: as elaborated in Chapter 1, former World Bank director Robert Zoellick (2012) was forced to note that 'one problem of the World Bank is that it is called a bank'. Neither procedural reforms nor shifts in the Bank's stated goals will change this in the short run.

Suchman also observed that such evaluations often lead to personifying organizations, treating them as 'autonomous, coherent, and morally responsible actors'. He thus concludes that 'constituents are likely to accord legitimacy to those organizations that "have our best interests at heart," that "share our values," or that are "honest," "trustworthy," "decent," and "wise"' (Suchman 1995: 578).

In terms of plausible candidates for personality-based norms, we can also expect to find traces of some of the norms Alison van Rooy (2004: 103–26) identifies in her study on the legitimation of international NGOs. *Organizational austerity* is thus a common argument in domestic debates about the budgets of international organizations; the *(in)consistency of words and deeds* has been a frequent concern of critics of the World Bank and other international organizations (Bukovansky 2010; Weaver 2008). We can further imagine *purity*—which Stephen Hopgood (2006) identified as a central frame in the self-understanding of Amnesty International—to be a standard against which international organizations, notably those engaged in protecting human rights or promoting development, are measured.

The notion of purity points to the possibility that 'good character' is not only found in personalized accounts of the organization as a whole, but can also be ascribed to individuals acting on behalf of the organization, notably their publicly visible executive heads. As a result, the personal qualities and professional qualifications of organizational leaders, identified as an important legitimation source for international NGOs, can also be used to publicly support or discredit international organizations (see e.g. Chesterman 2007; Harman 2011). The integrity of former UN Secretary General Kofi Annan, for example, figured prominently in the (de)legitimation strategies of UN supporters and critics (Johnstone 2007).

Finally, the symbolic *association with or dissociation from others*, notably other organizations that are perceived as good or bad, is used in legitimation contests over international organizations, too (Avant et al. 2010: 17). The WTO, for example, describes itself as a 'rules-based and member-driven organization' and as 'the most democratic international body in existence today'. Thus, it draws a boundary between itself and other multilateral economic institutions like the World Bank or IMF which are commonly criticized for giving its wealthy members larger voting shares (Moore 2002).

As Julia Black argues, we can thus speak of 'systems of mutual legitimacy enhancement' or 'legitimacy networks' that refer to the efforts of organizations to bandwagon on the perceived successes of their peers, or the better or complementary reputations of other types of organizations (Black 2008: 147). The UN Global Compact can illustrate how an international organization seeks to legitimate itself through the association with another kind of organization, in this case large multinational corporations—an attempt that critics used to accuse the Global Compact of allowing corporations to engage in 'bluewashing' without actually changing any of their harmful practices (Gregoratti and Slob 2015). Similarly, the International Organization for Standardization is keen to note that its standards carry the weight of explicit recognition by another international organization, the WTO. And whether they like it or not, the UN's special agencies are almost inevitably bound up with the UN itself. Likewise, we discuss in Chapters 5 and 7 that the legitimacy of the IAEA is linked to the legitimacy of a particular international regime, the Treaty on the Non-Proliferation of Nuclear Weapons, while the UNHCR's legitimacy is intimately tied to that of the international refugee regime, based on the 1951 Refugee Convention. As these examples illustrate, how and to what extent 'legitimacy networks' matter is not always defined by the organizations themselves but can also be established by their audiences. Moreover, legitimacy networks do not only serve as systems of mutual legitimacy *enhancement* but can also mutually *undermine* their members' legitimacy. Finally, legitimacy gained through association with others can stand in marked tension with the normative frame of *independence* discussed above.

Inherent in all three dimensions of legitimacy—performance, procedure, and personality—lies the question *in whose name* claims to effectiveness, democracy, justice, fairness, representation, or expertise are made. Underlying each legitimacy claim is always an assumption about the rightful beneficiaries. The question of who is supposed to benefit is hence key to understanding legitimation contests. Claims to democracy may, for example, refer to democracy *among states*, to the adequate representation *of individuals*, or to the adequate representation of *social groups or communities*. Similarly, justice or equality can be framed in relation to states, in relation to social groups (e.g. gender, class, or some other dividing line), or in relation to individuals. This is an important distinction that applies to many of the frames discussed above, even though some are more closely linked to the state (e.g. respect for sovereignty) or the individual (e.g. human rights) as their primary beneficiary. Overall, conventional IR narratives would lead us to expect both contestation and change in relation to the question for whom international organizations ought to act. As the traditional normative framework of state sovereignty increasingly erodes, the rise of non-state actors in particular is said to have rendered legitimacy contests more pluralist (Clark 2007a; Frost 2013: 35). Notably, the rise of cosmopolitan political ideas, international human rights, and notions like the 'responsibility to protect' suggest a parallel rise of discursive frames in which individuals rather than states figure prominently.

Finally, in terms of normative change, we can imagine several ways in which actors may seek to affect the constellation of legitimation frames. For instance, they could seek to add new frames (e.g. the rise of gender), change the meaning of existing frames (e.g. what constitutes 'development' or 'democracy'), (re)combine existing frames (e.g. 'sustainable development'), or alter the hierarchy, relative importance, or scope of application of principles commonly used to evaluate an international organization and its activities. Which strategy actors use will depend on their specific interests and resources as well as on the context of the legitimation contest. For example, the alter-globalization movement, which describes itself above all as a movement for 'global justice', campaigned against the WTO in Seattle by calling for 'democracy' and 'ecological integrity' since these frames resonated better with the claims of other groups also protesting against the WTO (see Chapter 3).

Beyond the Outer Circle: in Which World Political Contexts Do Speakers Speak?

Legitimation contests do not take place in vacuum, but in a particular 'world time'. They are embedded in a social structure on which they draw and which they affect in turn. Consequently, changes in the causal and principled ideas on which an organization's foundation rests can, at least in part, be attributed to 'political time' defined by external shocks or fundamental changes in the organization's policy field. While not an automatic trigger, such moments serve as windows of opportunity that may allow actors to alter the terms of an organization's legitimation (Cottrell 2016: 55).

As a result, we expect at least some major transformations in this world political context to affect the parameters of the legitimation contests around international organizations. In the following, we discuss the implications of five such transformations since the 1970s:

- the *democratization of member states*;
- *economic globalization*;
- *political globalization*;
- *major power shifts in the international system*;
- *the revolution in communications technology*.

Waves of Democratization

For most international organizations, the democratization of their member states after 1989/90 is an undeniable fact. It is therefore plausible to assume that the spread of a democratic political culture at the national level also affects the evaluations of international organizations, in particular where the latter is perceived as a threat to—sometimes newly gained—domestic democratic systems. Broadly in line with this idea, Alex Grigorescu (2007, 2010) finds that transparency rules within and oversight of international organizations are positively correlated with the extent of democratic membership. As for the mechanism at work, Grigorescu (2010: 875; see also Weise 2015) suggests that, 'the spread of IGO [international governmental organization] oversight mechanisms is partly due to the application of domestic democratic norms, such as the norm of accountability, to the supranational realm'. He further argues that key to this are state representatives who have internalized democratic norms:

> For those socialized in domestic democratic norms, the potential of not holding officials accountable for mistakes may simply be unacceptable, even if the costs of oversight are high. Such norms may tip the balance of the aggregate member-state preferences in favor of adopting the mechanism.

If this mechanism of 'uploading domestic norms' applies to the organizations in our study, the democratization of member states can be expected to trigger shifts in favour of one particular set of values, namely those associated with democratic governance.[11] Which values these are may differ from case to case: in addition to notions of transparency and accountability, one may think of responsiveness, participation, equality, or the rule of law. In addition to state representatives that have internalized democratic norms, normative pressure may also come from domestic audiences that expect *all* political institutions, whose decisions significantly affect them, to adhere to democratic norms.

As Table 2.2. reveals, the membership of the international organizations we examine has become more democratic over time. As a consequence, we would also expect a strengthening of democracy-related principles in their legitimation over time, in particular after 1990. Furthermore, we would expect such claims to be of greater relevance in organizations whose member states score highest on conventional indicators of democratic governance (see Table 2.2). Third, we would expect democratic frames to be used primarily by speakers from states or societies that score particularly high on conventional democracy indices, or by speakers from countries that have only recently undergone a democratic transition.[12]

Economic Globalization and the Rise of Global Capitalism

In the second half of the twentieth century, virtually all indicators of cross-border social relations show a steep rise. The number of international air travellers grew from 25 million in 1956 to 400 million in 1996. The volume of

---

[11] On a corresponding mechanism of downloading, see for example Pevehouse (2005). Both mechanisms could be imagined as mutually reinforcing.

[12] But see Eisentraut (2013), who argues that, at least in UN General Assembly debates, democracies and non-democracies do not differ in their use of democratic yardsticks for evaluating the UN.

Table 2.2. Mean Polity IV scores for organizational members[13]

	1975	1985	1995	2005
OAU/AU	−6.00	−5.95	−0.41	1.50
IAEA	−1.25	−0.16	3.24	4.18
UN	−2.11	−1.29	2.03	2.87
GATT/WTO	0.01	0.63	3.95	4.17

international bank loans rose from 9 billion US dollars (USD) in 1972 to 1,465 billion USD in 2000. Daily foreign exchange turnover increased from 15 billion USD in 1973 to 1,900 billion USD in 2004. The volume of international trade went up from 629 billion USD in 1960 to 7,430 billion USD in 2001 (Scholte 2005: 117). One result of economic globalization is a heightened pressure on domestic producers to remain or become internationally competitive. At the same time, the growing interdependence among national economies limits the possibility for autonomous economic decision making at the domestic level. While international agreements about the 'right' level of regulation cannot be reached, limited autonomy, paired with competitiveness concerns of domestic producers, provides incentives to national governments to deregulate their economies. By and large, and despite many differentiated views, most scholars seem to agree that economic globalization in the second half of the twentieth century has shifted the balance of power between states and markets in favour of the latter (Held et al. 1999; Scholte 2005; see also Strange 1996).

In line with this observation, many commentators associate economic globalization with the rise of neoliberal market ideas. On some accounts, this rise has not left international organizations unaffected; it required them to submit to pressure and become market-like actors. Junne (2001: 10) thus holds that, 'in an effort to bolster their competitiveness, international organizations have increasingly sought to streamline and restructure their internal operations, as well as to adopt and apply corporate management philosophies and techniques in the organization and management of their businesses'. He cites stakeholder consultations as 'the most recent form of organizational

---

[13] Our calculations are based on membership information contained in the Correlates of War Database on Intergovernmental Organizations (Version 2.3) and on Polity IV Data for the level of democratization of each member state at a given point in time. The Polity IV index combines separate measures for autocracy (−10 to 0) and democracy (0 to 10) by simple addition; values for individual countries thus range from −10 (most autocratic) to +10 (most democratic). We exclude the IUCN in this table as it includes both state and non-state members and thus does not lend itself to the same measurement. Moreover, UNHCR does not have formal members, and measuring the level of democratic membership based on membership in the organization's executive committee (from thirty-one members in 1975 to sixty-eight in 2005) would only inadequately reflect the composition of the states that contributed to the work of UNHCR. As a result, we use UN membership as a proxy.

activity based on corporate analogies' (Junne 2001: 11). Moreover, in the logic of unbound growth and progress, global media coverage often nourishes expectations of international organizations to contribute to the solving of global problems—or instead laments their 'failure' to do so. As performance challenges dominate over value challenges, international organizations would thus be expected to bolster their legitimacy through associating themselves with the corporate sector. Examples would be the UN Global Compact, or the humanitarian sector's more recent turn to 'transformation through innovation' and partnerships with private corporations (Betts and Bloom 2014). Alternatively, international organizations may also choose to adapt their legitimation discourses towards corporate language and analogies: stressing for instance their 'fitness', 'flexibility', and 'comparative advantages'. In a similar vein, the rise of neoliberal market ideas may also affect the framing of policy planning and evaluation processes and thus the yardsticks against which international organizations' procedures are assessed (Moretti and Pestre 2015).

Whether one perceives the rise of neoliberal political discourse as a prerequisite for or an effect of economic globalization, the discursive and the material world are closely intertwined. Depending on differing perceptions about the strength and scope of neoliberal ideology, we would expect pressures to conform to market ideas to be either restricted to international economic organizations (e.g. the IMF, the regional development banks, the WTO), or to affect all international organizations in a similar fashion. Changes that would be consistent with a 'power of markets hypothesis' would include a reinterpretation of existing norms (e.g. sustainability) in a more market-friendly way, the shift from more value-based legitimating norms (e.g. justice and democracy) to more performance-based legitimating principles (e.g. effectiveness and efficiency), as well as the rise of procedural norms that resonate with new public management ideas (e.g. transparency and sound project management). As for the actors pushing for normative change, we would expect representatives of states that subscribe to a neoliberal policy agenda, together with business representatives, to be in the driver's seat in the initial years (i.e. the early 1980s). In later stages, a common narrative would suggest a normalization of neoliberal discourse with strong opposition coming only from internationally marginalized states and social movement actors. Moreover, we would expect the voices of business representatives to gain centrality in the legitimation contests over time.

Political Globalization and the Authority and Density of International Organizations

A third contextual influence on legitimation contests is political globalization (Avant et al. 2010; O'Brien et al. 2000; Zürn et al. 2012). Political globalization mainly comes in two forms: first, in the growing authority that states have either delegated to or pooled in international institutions (Hooghe et al. 2017). Second, in the increasing density of international institutions which scholars have variously described in terms of 'regime complexity' (Alter and Meunier 2009), fragmentation (Biermann et al. 2009), or 'contested multilateralism' (Morse and Keohane 2014).

In the first case, delegation and pooling makes decisions taken by international organizations binding even for member states that have not consented to them. This expansion of authority, some argue, has also led to a *politicization* of international institutions, understood as their discussion and contestation in public. As Michael Zürn, Martin Binder, and Matthias Ecker-Ehrhardt (2012: 70) observe, over the last decades a range of such institutions have 'developed procedures that contradict the consensus principle and the principle of non-intervention'. The International Criminal Court, for instance, supersedes national jurisdiction in case the latter is unable or unwilling to investigate cases which involve a limited number of the most severe international crimes. The OAU/AU, in turn, has adopted a strong anti-coup norm. The norm prohibits governments that come to power unconstitutionally to participate in the organization, and it mandates the AU to re-establish 'constitutional order'. Finally, when the GATT became the WTO, its member states not only broadened the scope of agreements to include trade in services and intellectual property rights, but they also significantly hardened the legal quality of these agreements. In short, international institutional arrangements increasingly create direct, 'behind-the-border' effects for individual citizens in member states (Zürn 2004: 268–9). In a context like this, the 'legitimacy chain' that connects international institutions with the citizens of their member states becomes not only long, but also fragile (Dahl 1999).

In the absence of systematic efforts to measure the authority of international organizations comparatively and over time, the notion of a growth in international authority necessarily remains somewhat impressionistic.[14] Yet, the impression of expanded authority may be as important as its factual basis in triggering a change in demands vis-à-vis international organizations. In accordance with this insight, the politicization literature observes that 'internationalized governance has reached a reflexive stage in which progressively more societal actors pay attention to and reflect on political order beyond national borders' (Zürn et al. 2012: 72; see also Zürn 2018). Substantively, the authority that international organizations have acquired frequently translates into demands for greater responsiveness by these organizations to societal demands, and accountability towards those directly affected by their policies.

---

[14] But see the recent publication by Liesbet Hooghe et al, *Measuring International Authority*, which contains empirical data for seventy-four international organizations 'with standing in international relations' (Hooghe et al. 2017).

Public critique is thus mainly voiced in the language of democracy and points to the many 'democratic deficits' from which international organizations are said to suffer. Empirically, we would therefore expect a close connection between either factual growth in authority or a widespread impression that such a growth has taken place, on the one hand, and the increasing relevance of democracy-related legitimacy claims, on the other.

Beyond calls for a democratization of international institutions, a second response is to ask governments to refrain from transferring further competences to the international level—or as the 'Leave' campaign proposed, ahead of the United Kingdom referendum on membership of the European Union, to 'take back control' from the international level. According to this view, the expansion of international authority creates negative societal attitudes towards it, and thus leads to a 'national backlash' against international institutions rather than to calls for their democratization. Accordingly, reform demands may focus not so much on enhanced participation or transparency, but on enhanced state oversight over international institutions to ensure that they do not undermine national sovereignty claims (Zürn et al. 2012: 79–80).

Beyond politicization resulting from authority transfers, a second major way in which political globalization affects the legitimation of international organizations is via the *proliferation* of international institutions. Over the course of the past decades, this proliferation has led to a dense web of international cooperation in which international organizations face a stronger need to find and defend their 'ecological niche', on the one hand (Abbott et al. 2016), and cooperate or at least coordinate with other international organizations for the sake of 'coherence' (Bernstein and Hannah 2012), on the other. States, in turn, have realized the opportunities this offers and selectively engage in 'forum shifting' to pursue their interests in alternative institutions. Enhanced competition—dubbed as 'contested multilateralism' (Morse and Keohane 2014) by some—presents international organizations that have long been focal points for international cooperation in their particular fields not only with a new situation, but also with a new legitimation challenge.

Among the cases we study, we expect these dynamics to play out differently across cases as well as over time. Calls for democratization are to be expected in those organizations that have expanded their authority and in times after particularly clear authority transfers. The shift from the GATT to the WTO, the new competences the AU gained in the field of security and democratization, and the expanded role of the IAEA in inspecting nuclear sites in member states are the most likely candidates in this regard. In contrast, we would not expect similar dynamics of politicization to unfold in IUCN or the UNHCR.[15]

---

[15] Precise measures of the authority of international organizations have long been difficult to come by for the organizations we study. The newly published measures developed by Liesbet Hooghe and colleagues includes the IAEA (delegation score: 0.13 (1957–2010); pooling score:

Moreover, with a view to institutional density, we would expect demands for coordination and coherence to become stronger where and when the density of international organizations grows in a way that leads to significantly overlapping areas of activity.

Global Power Shifts

Fourth, we expect shifts in the power structure of the international system to leave a trace in discourses about what constitutes good international governance. Between 1970 and 2010, decolonization, the decline of communist states, the rise of Brazil, China, and India, and the rise of transnational actors are the most prominent cases in this regard.

The progress of decolonization affected many international organizations in two crucial ways. On the one hand, the growing number of newly independent states joining international organizations changed their membership, shifted more voting power—at least numerically—to the Global South, and set new cleavages along the North/South divide. On the other hand, the growing number of members from the Global South also pushed questions of global justice, equity among members, fairness, and 'development' irreversibly onto the agenda of many international organizations (Frey et al. 2014: 8–9; Helleiner 2014b; Buzdugan and Payne 2016). The decline of communism has largely discredited normative frames that had hitherto been pushed for by the Soviet Union and its allies, including socialist and communist ideas, but also notions of solidarity and equity, or references to particular social classes as the 'right' beneficiaries of international organizations and their activities.

The effect of the second development is more difficult to predict, not least since the rising powers lack a common political ideology. Michael Zürn and Matthew Stephen argue, for instance, that so-called old and new powers hold 'differentiated notions about the appropriate sources of legitimacy of international institutions' (Zürn and Stephen 2010: 96). They tend to promote a transnational yet also sovereignty-based form of global order (Stephen 2014a and 2014b). Thus overall, new powers do not seek to 'overhaul the existing international institutions; rather, they want to be co-opted and to reform them from the inside' (Zürn and Stephen 2010: 99). In a similar vein, Oliver

---

0.61 (1957–2010)), the WTO (delegation score: 0.41 (1995–2010); pooling score: 0.11 (1995–2010)) and the OAU/AU (delegation score: from 0.02 (1963) to 0.25 (2010); pooling score: from 0.13 (1963) to 0.35 (2010)); see Hooghe et al. (2017). Zürn (2018: 107–11) also includes measures for thirty-four international organizations, with the AU ranked fourth and the WTO ranked eighth. The older and simpler 'structure' score in Ingram et al. (2005) distinguishes between 'minimalist', 'structured', and 'interventionist' international governmental organizations and lists the IAEA, the WTO, as well as the OAU in the latter category. UNHCR is included in none of these studies, but is described as a weak international organization in Rittberger and Zangl's textbook overview of international organizations (2006).

Richmond and Ioannis Tellidis (2014) observe that while Brazil, China, and South Africa increasingly shape the global peacebuilding and development agenda, they do not serve as 'critical states' to change the overall normative foundation of the international peacebuilding regime. Overall, this leaves us with two fairly open expectations. First, we expect that the normative principles rising powers invoke in the contest over the legitimation of an international organization—principles that may vary across issue areas as well as over time—have become more visible elements of legitimation contests in the final years of our period of investigation. Second, we expect that international organizations have become more likely to take the values and norms propagated by these countries on board in their own communications.

Technological Change

Finally, the revolution in information and communication technologies, in combination with the expansion of skills among citizens, has greatly facilitated the organization of collective identities and interests outside state institutions. In relation to our key question, the rise of the world-wide web, email, and social media primarily results in an expansion of audiences that take note of the communications of international organizations and, in turn, raise their own demands (Castells 2008; Florini 2000; Rosenau 1990, 1997). On the one hand, international organizations increasingly invest in public relations campaigns, internet appearance, and a diversification of publication outlets. In Chapter 1, we have already hinted at the dissemination of 2,500 stories through the Organization of the Petroleum Exporting Countries (OPEC)'s news agency in 1983 (OPEC 1983: 60). At the OAU, we observe the Secretary General noting in 1994 that the new fax machine had enabled the OAU to 'reaching out to the international media through briefings, press releases, booklets, leaflets and brochures' (OAU Secretariat 1994b: 90). Today, things have changed considerably: the OAU's successor has its own media strategy, *Twitter* account, *YouTube* channel, and its press conferences can be followed and joined live on the internet, while the OPEC's welcome page offers access to at least seven different publication formats informing about the organization's work. At the same time, this turn towards more diverse public(s) also means that, for many international organizations, the audiences of communications become more diverse and that the norms, values, and interests they hold become more likely to differ and contradict each other.

Yet, while the revolution in information and communication technologies significantly reduces the costs of organizing and communicating collective interests, it does not remove them entirely. The audiences of international organizations can be assumed to expand most rapidly where transnational civil society resources are abundant. Thus, we expect the content of legitimation discourses to shift—starting in the 1990s—towards the norms, values, and interests that predominate in well-resourced European and North American civil society networks. Which norms, values, and interests these are is likely to vary across issue areas. However, insights from preceding empirical research would suggest that rights, democracy, and social justice are likely to figure prominently (Keck and Sikkink 1998; O'Brien et al. 2000). In contrast, references to the norms, values, and interests that prevail among non-Western civil society networks would be expected to either enter the legitimation discourse only much more recently—namely as such networks grow in terms of their resources, density of contacts with Northern civil society networks, and presence at international meetings—or to remain weak altogether.

Table 2.3 summarizes the general direction in which we expect the various structural trends we have discussed above to push legitimation contests. Evidently, the directions we formulate are broad, and different concretizations will be compatible with the expectations we sketch. Moreover, the influences

Table 2.3. Expected general effects of macro-trends on legitimation contests

Macro-trend	Expected effects on legitimation contests
Decolonization	Strengthening of development norms since the 1970s
	Strengthening of justice and fairness norms since the 1970s, based in particular on equality and supported in particular by newly established states
	Strengthening of democratic norms since the 1970s, based in particular on equality and supported in particular by newly established states
Democratization	Strengthening of democratic norms after 1989/90, supported primarily by particularly democratic or newly democratized member states
	Strengthening of democracy promotion norms after 1989/90, supported primarily by newly democratized member states
	Challenges of hypocrisy after 1989/90, in particular from economically or politically weaker democratic or newly democratized states
Economic globalization	Strengthening of norms that are closely linked to neoliberal ideology since the 1980s, supported primarily by member states that subscribe to a neoliberal policy agenda and opposed—in particular in later decades—only by internationally marginalized states
	Strengthening of the voice of business representatives in legitimation contests
Political globalization	Strengthening of democratic legitimation frame since the second half of the 1990s, in particular in contexts where international authority has expanded
	Strengthening of sovereignty frames since the second half of the 1990s, in particular in contexts where international authority has expanded
	Strengthening of coordination and coherence in response to growing institutional density since the late 1990s
Power shifts	Strengthening of legitimation frames supported by rising powers after 2000 (combined with defence of existing frames by traditional powers)
Technological change	Strengthening of the voices of and frames supported by relatively resource-rich Western civil society organizations since the second half of the 1990s

of the various trends may well cancel each other out, and they may also be overshadowed by issue-specific developments that matter in one, but not in other policy fields. As a result, Table 2.1 should not necessarily be read as a list of hypotheses in a narrow sense, but rather as broader theoretical expectations that inform our analysis in Chapters 3 to 7. This is all the more important because we expect normative change to result from the interaction of world political forces—sketched above—and the particular and often contingent dynamics of legitimation discourses.

THE FRAMEWORK IN BRIEF

In a nutshell, our study is guided by the following assumptions:

1. Legitimation contests are discursive interactions in which actors exchange claims and justifications about what constitutes a 'good' international organization. Those who compete over the power to define the appropriate standard of legitimacy for an international organization include the international bureaucracy which speaks on behalf of the organization as a whole, the members of the organization, and finally a range of non-members that have an interest in the organization and its activities. The composition of these groups, their interests, and their relations vary across organizations as well as over time.

2. The legitimation contest is norm-referential and hence embedded in a discursive environment in which the norms to which speakers refer are developed, defined, and defended. Individual statements that seek to legitimate or delegitimate an organization or its activities make reference to normative frames, drawn from the discursive environment in which legitimation contests take place. The reference to a particular normative frame may demand compliance with principles that large shares of the audience already accept as valid for the organization ('if you care about justice as you say, then you have to care about the things that we care about'). Alternatively, it can attempt to shift the terms of the debate from one particular principle to another ('what really counts are human rights, not justice').

3. The precise contours of the pool of norms upon which legitimation contests draw is variable in two important ways. First, which normative frames are present or absent at a given time, which ones are inserted or eliminated, and how strong they are relative to each other varies over time as well as across organizations. Second, what a particular 'term of legitimation' means at a given time and in relation to a given international organization is subject to constant (re)negotiation.

4. Normative change emanates both from the interactions and strategies of those who take part in the legitimation contest (i.e. the inner circle of our 'bubbles model') as well as from the influences of the world political context (i.e. the outer circle of our 'bubbles model'). Change from within occurs when a particular group of speakers is rhetorically manoeuvred onto a territory where it can no longer defend its initial position in a legitimation contest. A prominent example in the history of international organizations is the success of civil society activists who, in the late 1980s and early 1990s, forced the World Bank to take environmental concerns on board (Park 2010). Change induced by shifts in the world political context occurs when particular developments render individual normative frames more or less persuasive or when they add to or reduce the strength of those who promote such frames. Justice claims that gain currency in the face of evidence about growing gaps between the rich and poor serve as an example of the former; an example of the latter are the legitimacy claims of civil society networks that gain strength as a result of their enhanced capacity to organize across borders (O'Brien et al. 2000; Keck and Sikkink 1998).

5. As these examples illustrate, the separation of 'internal' and 'external' dimensions of our model is analytical. In practice, the contextual transformations discussed in this chapter enhance or reduce the strength of some actors in the legitimation contest (and hence, also of the frames these actors use to advance their positions), lead actors to redefine their own interests in the context of a changing world, or give impetus to particular normative frames such as democracy. Yet, in all these cases, the trace they leave on the terms of legitimation is mediated by those who speak about international organizations as well as by the expectations of those to whom they speak.

Taken together, these assumptions suggest multiple pathways of normative change. Some may be relatively straightforward. For instance, when the heterogeneity of values and interests among members increases, this makes consensus on substantive values more difficult. It might therefore lead organizations to search for legitimacy based on consensus about procedures instead. The WTO's insistence on its 'democratic' one-state, one-vote policy is a case in point (see Chapter 3). Other pathways are more complex, but emphasize the importance of strategic considerations. 'Democracy' has thus come to play an important role not only in the WTO but also in the AU. Yet, the rise of democratic principles results less from open critique or strong citizen demands, but rather from the bureaucracy's efforts to build up a complementary legitimating constituency among civil society organizations (CSOs) and AU citizens, and to thereby gain a modicum of autonomy vis-à-vis member state governments (see Chapter 4). As the two examples illustrate, what looks like similar developments at first becomes different at a closer look. It is this close perspective on the legitimation of international organizations which we seek to provide in the chapters that follow.

CASE STUDY APPROACH AND STRUCTURE

To put our framework to work, the case studies we present in Chapters 3 to 7 closely reconstruct justificatory discourses from a variety of texts. In our efforts to make sense of these discourses, we follow a common structure as well as a common approach to data collection and analysis.

In terms of structure, each chapter includes five substantive sections. Following a brief introduction to each case, a first section situates the international organization 'in time' (Hanrieder 2015). For each organization, we reconstruct those parts of the organizational history that are relevant to understand and contextualize the norm changes we discuss; discuss how the policy field in which the organization operates has changed since 1970; and identify major obstacles to the organization's legitimation during that period. In a second section, we then describe the 'normative baseline' in or around 1970, the starting point of our empirical analysis. Once we have clarified this baseline, two further sections describe the major normative shifts that have taken place in the contests over the legitimacy of the organization. This is bound up by a short discussion as to how the normative changes we describe continue (or not) to affect the organization today. Finally, each chapter traces the processes that have led to these changes, and discusses how internal as well as external developments have contributed to shape the organization's changing terms of legitimation. The chapters close with a discussion of what the main results of the case study imply for our theoretical framework.

In terms of data collection and analysis, the case studies seek to strike a balance between coherence, on the one hand, and attention to relevant particularities, on the other. In line with the three main speakers in legitimation contests—the organization as a whole, its member states, and external audiences such as NGOs or the media—each case study rests on a comparable set of primary documents that we analysed according to a common interpretive scheme. Inspired by the 'legitimation grammar' that informs the major content analytical study in the field (Nullmeier et al. 2010), the most basic level of our interpretive scheme distinguishes between the following elements:

- different *objects of legitimation*—e.g. the actions of an organization, specific bodies of an organization, specific rules of an organization, and the 'essence' of an organization;

- the *direction* or *tonality* of a legitimation statement—i.e. whether it expressed that the legitimation object *is* something, *should be* something, or is *deficient* in some important ways;
- the *reference point* of legitimation statements—i.e. whether a statement included states, particular social groups, or individuals as its main reference point, or remained general in that regard;
- the *value basis* that underpins a legitimation statement—i.e. whether a statement refers to the *functionality* of an organization, *development*, *justice*, *democracy*, *legality*, or some other value.

While this scheme provides a first and general orientation about the normative yardsticks most relevant for each organization, we add case-specific codes and subcodes to arrive at a more nuanced picture about the literal meaning and significance of the norms. For instance, while 'democracy' may be a crucial, normative yardstick in legitimation contests in the AU and the WTO alike, it has meant something different in the contests over the legitimacy of these organizations.

The main function of the common interpretive scheme is to ensure consistency and comparability across our cases. To recall our bubbles model depicted in Figure 2.1, has *justice* become a more relevant value in the legitimation of the international organizations we study? If so, is it used in roughly comparable ways across our case studies, or does it mainly serve as a container that each organization fills differently? And if justice is on the rise, which other values are declining relative to it? At the same time, the structure of our scheme allows us to trace discursive dynamics. Do, for example, emerging countries like Brazil, China, and India advance a particular set of normative arguments? And do other actors increasingly adopt these arguments as these countries become economic powerhouses?

When applying the interpretive scheme, however, a strong commitment to coding—as the standard method in content analysis—also has its limitations. Notably, it misses how concepts gain meaning in context; it cannot uncover what makes contests over meaning particular in each case; and it fails to shed light on how the meanings associated with particular concepts travel or change across different contexts and time (Fierke 2004). In many ways, however, this is precisely what we seek to get at in this study. Ultimately, therefore, we base our analysis less on counting the frequency of specific concepts or arguments— although such counts can help us to test the plausibility of different interpretations—but rather on an interpretative approach that examines specific *terms of legitimation* in the context of the broader legitimation discourse. This interpretative and, in a way, more holistic approach includes the task of reconstructing how and by whom meaning is made in a particular institutional context, and how actors seek and manage to change the meaning and functions of the *terms of legitimation* we identify (Milliken 1999: 231;

Schwartz-Shea and Yanow 2012). It also involves shifting back and forth between different interpretations until we can identify a reading that is sufficiently plausible in view of the primary sources and secondary texts that each of our case studies considers. Coding can help because it allows us to cross-check our subjective readings against 'hard' data. But ultimately, it is the interpretations which allow us to 'dig deeper' in our efforts to understand individual statements within their contexts, and to reconstruct organizational discourses as the complex 'webs of meaning' which they are. Last but not least, it is our interpretive work that enables us to turn the patterns we observe into—more or less coherent—storylines, that help us to 'make sense of' the legitimation contests we study.

Based on this approach, we reconstruct ten stories of normative change that have occurred in five international organizations. The histories we present in Chapters 3 to 7 necessarily remain cut-outs. They are limited by the possible vicinity of what we are able to grasp. They are shaped by the circumstances in which they were researched and written. And they are naturally constrained by the fact that—despite seemingly limitless textual resources—our ultimate objective was to write a book about international organizations, and not five organizational histories. For all their limitations, thus, this is what each case study is: a piece of a mosaic depicting international organizations that are puzzled by ever more complex and pluralist contests about the norms that define their role in the world.

3

From the GATT Gospel to Democratic Global Governance

Legitimating the GATT and the World Trade Organization

Klaus Dingwerth

As the trading world moves ahead, the WTO cannot stand still.

WTO Annual Report 1996, p. 8

INTRODUCTION

Among the organizations we study in this book, the General Agreement on Tariffs and Trade (GATT) and its successor, the World Trade Organization (WTO), enjoy a degree of authority that is matched only by the African Union (AU)'s authority to intervene in member states in situations of a threat to regional peace and security. Moreover, over the course of the past four and a half decades, the scope and depth of authority commanded by the GATT and the WTO have expanded dramatically. With the shift from the old GATT to the new WTO in 1995, the organization is no longer only in charge of international trade in goods, but its legislative arm also extends to trade in services and the protection of trade-related intellectual property. In addition, the new Trade Policy Review Mechanism institutionalized compliance monitoring. By requiring all WTO members to undergo regular compliance checks, it adds to the executive arm. Finally, the new Dispute Settlement Understanding has significantly strengthened the judicial arm of the organization. If member states believe that policies of other members violate WTO law, they can request a panel; and while panel rulings may be appealed, the decisions of the new appellate body are binding regardless of whether or not a state shares the particular interpretation of the law that informs the ruling. As a result, the intergovernmental GATT has become a supranational WTO.

In cases like this, politicization theory predicts trouble; and trouble there is. Not surprisingly, the WTO has become one of the publicly most contested international organizations of our time. But in the wake of powerful public protests, it has also become the one global organization that most emphatically accepts the critics' challenge: an international organization that wields power can only be legitimate if it is democratic. Nowadays, therefore, the WTO puts a lot of effort into defending the argument that it is a 'democratic' organization— a claim that played little role in the past. Considering this rise of democratic norms in external evaluations as well as in the organization's self-descriptions, the 'authority–legitimacy nexus' seems to hold. Where authority expands, those subject to it will challenge it and demand to have a say; and where audiences are sufficiently powerful to keep the organization from fulfilling its functions, the organization will listen.

In this chapter, we argue that this interpretation is correct but incomplete. Tracing the evolution of legitimacy standards in the Tokyo (1973–9), Uruguay (1986–94), and Doha Rounds (2001–present), we argue that until about the early 1990s, the legitimation of the GATT is founded on a relatively stable set of core values which we identify as the 'GATT gospel'. Yet, over the course of our period of investigation two normative shifts occur. First, 'non-trade' values like environmental concerns and labour rights enter the legitimation contest during the Uruguay Round. Second, democracy rises after public protests in the 1990s. Both shifts build on the view that the traditional GATT gospel is too narrow. From about 2005 onwards, we observe a different dynamic: more observers ask whether the WTO can remain legitimate in the absence of further multilateral trade deals. This leads to a widely shared feeling that the GATT gospel, rather than being too narrow, no longer provides a viable normative foundation for the organization. As a result, the norms of liberal- ization, multilateralism, and consensus on which the legitimacy of the GATT is historically founded have come under pressure. Our findings contribute to the bigger picture we paint in this study in two ways. Concerns about labour rights and the democratic deficit add people-based norms to the legitimation menu of the GATT and the WTO. Meanwhile, the shift towards democratic legitimation also puts an emphasis on the procedural legitimacy standards, something we also see in other cases. Moreover, while the politicization of growing international authority is a key driver initially, we also observe further pathways of normative change—notably the self-reinforcing dynamics that we identify as normative path dependence.

To unfold these central arguments, the following section sketches the major historical developments in world trade governance that provide the back- ground for the legitimation contests we study. We then describe the normative foundations on which the GATT is traditionally legitimated, and in two further sections reconstruct the two major norm shifts we observe. The first shift refers to the addition of 'non-trade values'; the second to the rise of 'democratic legitimation'. Finally, we examine the pathways along which normative change occurred and discuss the implications of the GATT and the WTO case for our broader theoretical framework.

THE HISTORICAL CONTEXT OF TRADE LIBERALIZATION: FROM HAVANA TO DOHA

Our objective in this chapter is to examine how the norms used to justify or criticize the GATT and the WTO have shifted since the 1970s. Understanding these changes—which we primarily trace in the normative language major actors use during the Tokyo Round (1973–9), the Uruguay Round (1986–94), and the Doha Round (since 2001)—requires an understanding of the political and institutional contexts in which actors form their judgements. The following paragraphs seek to provide the relevant contextual information. In relation to the early institutional history, we discuss the role of protectionism as the common enemy that GATT members seek to fight; the failure to set up an International Trade Organization (ITO) after World War II; the resulting need for the GATT to work in the absence of a written constitution; and the rising demands among developing countries for a *New International Economic Order* (NIEO), combined with the rise of the United Nations Conference on Trade and Development (UNCTAD) as a competitor to the GATT. In relation to more recent decades, we stress the rise of neoliberalism, the Seattle protests, and the failure to conclude the Doha Round as the relevant contexts in which legitimation of the GATT and WTO takes place.

The Founding Years

Established as a result of trade negotiations among the governments of twenty-three countries in 1947, the GATT is first and foremost a post-World War II institution.[1] It reflects the distribution of power, and hence the interests of the United States (US) (and in part the United Kingdom) as its most powerful member, at the time of its establishment. US interests were driven by political as well as economic concerns. Politically, the US saw the

---

[1] The founding members of the GATT were Australia, Belgium, Brazil, Burma, Canada, Ceylon, Chile, China, Cuba, Czechoslovakia, France, India, Lebanon, Luxembourg, Netherlands, New Zealand, Norway, Pakistan, Southern Rhodesia, South Africa, Syria, the United Kingdom, and the US.

GATT as a 'weapon of the free world' (Strange 2013: 41–5). A multilateral liberalization of trade, it was argued, served to organize and strengthen the American sphere of influence in its ideological competition with the Soviet Union. Economically, the US then produced more than half of the world's manufactured goods, providing it with a keen interest in gaining access to foreign markets (Wilkinson 2006: 23–4). As a result, the GATT was primarily designed to '[facilitate] trade-led US growth and Allied reconstruction' (47).

These hard interests were backed up by the idea that the protectionism of the interwar years—seen as an outburst of 'nationalism'—had played an important part in the lead-up to World War II. Consequently, it had to be overcome by a 'multilateral' approach (Strange 2013: 30; Wilkinson 2006: 31). The US administration campaigned for an ITO, arguing that 'if goods can't cross borders, soldiers will' (Marceau 1994: 61). Moreover, references to 'the 1930s' as the dangerous Other, which the multilateral approach of the GATT would help to avoid, were vital to justify the need for an international organization, and they have continued to be part of the discursive repertoire ever since.[2]

Nonetheless, building the ITO was not a straightforward endeavour. Some European states, Australia, and India were concerned about mass unemployment, whereas the US mainly sought to protect some of its industrial sectors from competition; at the same time, the US administration feared that social unrest in Europe could play into the hands of the Soviet Union. In the Bretton Woods institutions as well as in the Havana Charter for the ITO, this resulted in a 'mixed economy' where capital mobility—and hence also private property rights—was limited, and where economic liberalism was 'embedded' in the sense that domestic interventions to tame the disruptive effects of market liberalization remained acceptable (Abdelal and Ruggie 2009; Buzdugan and Payne 2016: 33; Gill 1998: 29; Ruggie 1982).

The GATT was never envisaged to become the core institution of world trade regulation. Instead, it emerged as a fall-back option when the US Senate declined to ratify the ITO Charter (Demaret 1995: 126). The peculiarity of the GATT was, as its organizational provisions were minimal, that it remained very much 'an organization without a charter' (Curzon and Curzon 1973:

---

[2] See for example GATT (1993: 3) which warns that 'the alternative to making the multilateral system operate effectively through a good Uruguay Round settlement could, too easily, be the kind of situation which some very old lessons of history will have to be learned again'. See also WTO (1999: 2) which applauds member states for refraining from protectionist measures in the wake of the Asian financial crisis, stating that 'rather than becoming part of the problem, as it did in the 1930s, trade made a crucial contribution to paving the way for recovery'. Finally, see WTO (2017: 3) where Director General Azevêdo displays satisfaction that the global financial crisis has not led to 'a significant rise in protectionism' and that 'we certainly have not seen a repeat of the 1930s where escalating tariffs and unilateral actions helped fuel the downward spiral that wiped out two-thirds of global trade and ultimately led to the Great Depression', and claims that identifies the WTO as 'now more important than ever' in global efforts to avoid such a peril.

300). Nonetheless, member states managed to use the GATT as a basis for constructing the post-war international trade order, with powerful members taking advantage of the informal nature of the regime. Substantively, the core principles of the GATT were the most-favoured nation (MFN) principle which required states to extend a concession granted to one member to all members; the principle of non-discrimination of foreign products once they passed the border; the principle of reciprocity in making tariff concessions; and a commitment to dispute settlement (Curzon and Curzon 1973: 299; Wilkinson 2006: 36). Procedurally, the commitment to reducing trade barriers in consecutive multilateral trade negotiations shaped the development of the GATT in the following decades (Ruggie 1982: 394). Moreover, the consensus principle became the primary decision-making rule of the GATT even though informal consultations among major trading nations remained a common practice throughout the organization's history.

The Growth of the GATT

Beginning in the late 1950s, the nominal focus of the GATT on multilateralism and equality made the institution attractive for newly independent states. Through the insertion of a new Article XVIII and an expert report known as the *Haberler Report* in 1958, the GATT sought to acknowledge the specific problems faced by these new GATT members. The concept of 'equality' was now rearticulated as 'special and differential treatment', and 'development' became a central normative reference point in the legitimation contest. In response, the GATT set up a Committee on Trade and Development and adopted a new Part IV on Trade and Development as a part of the Kennedy Round (1964–7), exempting developing countries from the requirement of reciprocity (Strange 2013: 45–8).

In 1964, however, the establishment of the UNCTAD signalled an increasing capacity of developing countries to coordinate their positions on economic issues; they already gave an early flavour of that at the 1955 Bandung Conference (Acharya 2016). In subsequent years, UNCTAD—which also gave rise to the creation of the Group of 77 in 1964—became the focal point for Third World countries to organize their challenge to the global economic structures, leading them to call for an NIEO.

In their Declaration on the New International Economic Order, which the Sixth Special Session of the UN General Assembly adopted in May 1974, developing countries demanded better terms of trade for commodities in particular, stressed their right to exercise control over natural resources on their territories in the face of increasing foreign direct investment, and asked for 'the full and equal participation of the developing countries in the formulation and application of all decisions that concern the international community' (UN General Assembly 1974: §1; see also Buzdugan and Payne 2016: 74 and 78–87; Helleiner 2014a: 273–6; Wilkinson 2006: 69). Confronted with this first wave of politicization, the concessions GATT members granted to developing countries remained largely symbolic (Curzon and Curzon 1973: 308–10; Steffek 2013). Commitments were thus either voluntary or consisted of promises to address major concerns like trade in agricultural goods and textiles in future trade rounds.

The Tokyo and Uruguay Rounds

From the second half of the 1970s onwards, the GATT operated against the background of prolonged economic crisis. The oil price shock not only slowed down economic growth, but it also led to the surge of protectionist sentiments in the US and elsewhere. In the US in particular, multilateralism was further questioned because many felt that the Kennedy Round had brought little for the country; moreover, closer integration in the European Economic Community seemed to pose yet another challenge to US competitiveness. In this political climate, the Tokyo Round (1973–9) had acquired 'great symbolic importance as a last bastion against economic chaos' (Graham 1979: 52), and the US in particular sought to regain some of its territory as a trading nation in that round.

The negotiations themselves proved cumbersome, but they eventually resulted in a number of plurilateral agreements on issues previously excluded from the purview of the GATT. Since members could freely pick and choose from agreements, based on whether they had deemed them economically attractive, the result differed significantly from the previous rounds. It led to an expansion of the GATT agenda into new fields but also generated selectivity and fragmentation, described by some as 'GATT à la carte' (Demaret 1995: 128). This fragmentation subsequently led to a 'push for the unification of GATT-negotiated trade law under a single body' (Wilkinson 2006: 82)—the 'single undertaking' formula of the subsequent Uruguay Round for which the US began to press under the new Reagan administration, already in 1982.

Lasting from 1986 to 1994, the Uruguay Round became yet another arduous affair. Negotiation dynamics were altered by the emergence of the Cairns Group, a coalition of agricultural producers that brought together fourteen industrialized and developing countries, as a fourth major player besides the US, the European Communities, and Japan (Braithwaite and Drahos 2000: 198).[3] But when governments finally reached agreement, they agreed on a fundamental

---

[3] The original members of the Cairns Group were Argentina, Australia, Brazil, Canada, Chile, Colombia, Fiji, Hungary, Indonesia, Malaysia, New Zealand, the Philippines, Thailand, and Uruguay.

overhaul of the institution. By adding a General Agreement on Trade in Services, an agreement on Trade-Related Intellectual Property Rights, and an agreement on Trade-Related Investment Measures, they redefined and significantly broadened the notion of 'trade' that had formed the basis of the GATT (Braithwaite and Drahos 2000: 178–81). In institutional terms, the single undertaking formula meant that states could no longer sign up to individual agreements that resulted from the round, but had to buy either the whole package or remain outside the WTO. Moreover, the 1994 Marrakesh Agreement on the Establishment of the World Trade Organization put an end to the informal and provisional nature of the GATT by creating a strong organization with important supranational elements (von Bogdandy 2001).

The Doha Round

Following the end of the Cold War, the WTO's 1997 Annual Report notes 'the emergence of a virtual global consensus on the fundamental contribution to economic progress made by open trade policies' (WTO 1997: 2). This ideological consensus motivated the launch of a further round of multilateral trade talks at the end of the 1990s. For several reasons, the launch of the 'Millennium Round' failed at the 1999 ministerial conference in Seattle. Seattle, as well as the ministerial conference held in Cancún in 2003, also marked an important moment in view of the legitimation of the WTO. It put the organization on the front pages of the global media and turned it into a major target for a rising alter-globalization movement. The latter accused the WTO of selling out on democracy, harming the environment, and violating the rights of workers.

While the Seattle impasse merely postponed the launch of new negotiations, the WTO sought to deflect some of the criticism by labelling the round a 'development' round. Thus, the Doha Development Agenda (DDA) agreed at the 2001 ministerial conference included a number of issues called for by developing countries, among them agriculture, special and differential treatment, technical cooperation, and capacity building. Yet, even though the WTO (2002: 2) called the conference 'a turning point in the history of the WTO and in relations between developed and developing countries', the DDA did not necessarily prioritize developing country interests. Instead, the commitment to open negotiations on investment, on government procurement, on competition policy, or on trade facilitation meant that 'the balance of potential gains from the work programme remained firmly in the interest of the industrial states' (Wilkinson 2006: 124).

Structurally, the legalization of the WTO had reduced the flexibility associated with previous agreements (Goldstein and Martin 2000). Moreover, the heterogeneity of now 162 WTO members and the shift towards a more multipolar economic order meant that members have found insufficient common ground for concluding the Doha Round. As a result, states have concluded bilateral and regional trade agreements at an increasing pace since 2005. This regionalization of trade policy making has put the WTO under increasing pressure, with governments and the media increasingly questioning its role—and occasionally also its survival—in the future. The question 'whether we still need the WTO' was thus on the agenda.

LEGITIMATING THE GATT AND WTO: THE NORMATIVE BASELINE

A close reading of the annual reports of the GATT and of the statements GATT members have delivered in meetings of the contracting parties reveals that from the early 1970s to the early 1990s, the legitimation of the GATT and WTO rested on a relatively stable set of norms. This set defines the 'issue area culture' of global trade governance we have introduced in Chapter 1. During the above-mentioned period, the legitimation contests mainly revolved around two questions. First, to what extent does the GATT live up to the set of values on which it was built? And second, what role should 'development' play in the organization's value system? Despite its stability, however, the legitimation contest during this time comprises a number of cracks and hooks on which critics could build to gradually alter the terms of GATT/WTO legitimation in later years.

In official GATT communications, the joint activities of the member states take centre stage. The organization thus figures primarily in its character as a *forum*—for instance referring to the GATT *as a place* or, in more recent WTO publications, *as a 'table'* (WTO 2015: 8–9)—with further references also emphasizing its character as an *instrument* for member states, for instance referring to the 'GATT machinery'. Appearing in every single annual report from 1970 to 1979, the metaphor of an 'institutional machinery' also attests to the fact that a 'normal' way of doing things had developed and became widely accepted among GATT members.

Moreover, the annual reports prepared by the GATT begin with a summary of major developments in international trade of the preceding year. In these sections, the GATT itself is rarely mentioned. In a way, we could read this as providing the background for the report of the GATT's activities in the chapters that follow. Yet, the prominent place in which the summaries appear renders a different interpretation more plausible, namely that the GATT assumes responsibility for—that it is in charge of—the 'multilateral trading system', a term the actors in world trade politics regularly use as a synonym for the GATT. Taken together, the GATT *as an actor* that regulates and monitors the conduct of its members thus remains invisible most of the time, while the GATT *as a common institution* of its members is legitimated in view of its central role as a manager of world trade.

This role, in turn, is captured in a variety of ideas that appear repeatedly in annual reports and member state statements, and that serve as the main basis for legitimating the GATT throughout both the Tokyo and Uruguay Rounds. Applying our 'bubbles model' developed in Chapter 2, we thus see a relatively stable set of speech bubbles that move around slowly and only moderately change their size (= relevance), constellation (= relation to each other), or colour (= substantive meaning). Substantively, the notion of 'orderly liberalization' (A. Dunkel, cited in GATT 1974b: 43) captures much of the content of these bubbles, and hence of the traditional 'issue area culture' of global trade governance. On a first level, it combines a number of performance standards focused on *anti-protectionism*, *stability*, and *liberalization*, with procedural standard focused on *multilateralism* and *consensus*. In brief, it suggests that,

- the GATT is legitimate to the extent that it fulfils its function as a *bulwark against protectionism* that helps to restrain its members' appetite for creating new trade barriers;
- the GATT is legitimate to the extent that it generates *progressive liberalization*—that is, that it induces members to advance with *multilateral* trade negotiations and open up their markets—and thereby facilitates an *expansion of international trade*;
- the GATT is legitimate to the extent that it provides *stability* and *order* which, via the enhanced *predictability* and *reliability* of trade rules, are depicted as important preconditions for trade expansion;
- the GATT is legitimate because its decisions are *based on the consensus of its member states*.

Many of the values alluded to in these legitimacy standards are commonly presented as ends rather than means. In other words, the ideas that *protectionism* is bad and *liberalization* is good are largely presented as self-evident—they do not require further justification. The *GATT Activities* exemplify this when they state that the GATT exists 'to deter member countries...from succumbing to protectionist pressures and temptations', declare that 'preparations for the next *assault on barriers to international trade* are therefore GATT's central preoccupation at this time' (GATT 1970: 5–6, emphasis added), or emphasize 'the grave dangers that a general lapse into protectionism...would represent' (GATT 1975a: 5).[4] References are either to 'growth',

---

[4] See also GATT (1978a: 7): 'The potential benefits to the world community, in terms of new trading opportunities and a strengthened and updated set of rules to govern and foster

'progress', and 'living standards', or to the experience of 'the 1930s' which serves as justification for the principled stance against protectionism. In short, the GATT is applauded when its rules work to deter 'protectionist temptations'; and even where a 'protectionist threat' (GATT 1972: 5; see also GATT 1973: 7) is detected, this only confirms the relevance of GATT. Yet, which practices actually count as 'protectionism' becomes a major terrain of contestation. Critics, for instance, soon begin to challenge the apparent contradiction between a principled stance on protectionism, on the one hand, and a factual liberalization limited to trade in manufactured goods, on the other (Winslett 2019).

This, among other factors, leads to a second set of performance standards that gain relevance as the GATT develops. Two common features unite these standards: first, that member states tie the continued legitimacy of the GATT to the organization's ability to meet a number of challenges; and second, that these challenges are formulated in relatively open terms. In brief, they hold that,

- the GATT is legitimate to the extent that it *delivers on its promises*—in other words to the extent that its members put words into deeds and sincerely implement decisions;
- the GATT is legitimate to the extent that it is *comprehensive* rather than selective in efforts to liberalize trade;
- the GATT is legitimate to the extent that it *responds quickly and adequately to changes and challenges in the world economy*.

As all three frames are multifaceted, they contain a modicum of change within them. The *need to deliver* can be compromised by the failure to implement decisions taken in previous negotiations, but also by the failure to deliver on any of the standard promises of preventing protectionism, providing predictability, and progressing with multilateral liberalization. *Comprehensiveness* was originally conceived as the need to cover a broad range of sectors but has more recently paved the way for integrating 'non-trade values' in the legitimation discourse. And the *ability to respond to a changing world*, originally used to refer to the ability of the GATT to cope with economic crises, has more recently been employed to signal a need to acknowledge the changing membership of the WTO as well as global power shifts in WTO decision making.

Finally, as indicated in the previous section, the legitimation of the GATT is regularly tied to the *recognition of the specific needs and interests of developing*

---

international trade relations, are generally recognized. So too are the great dangers of a relapse into economic nationalism which a failure of the multilateral trade negotiations would signal, and probably entail.'

countries. This frame is central—and it remains so today—because it marks the North–South divide as a primary cleavage among GATT members (Buzdugan and Payne 2016; Steffek 2013; Wilkinson 2006). In the GATT and the WTO, this cleavage becomes particularly relevant as the organization manages to keep two further global conflicts at bay—namely US–Soviet bipolarity and the Middle East conflict—that lead to a strong politicization within many other international organizations (Steffek 2013). At the same time, the early rise of the development frame is critical because it offers 'redistributive multilateralism' as a more radical alternative to the 'embedded liberalism' on which the GATT traditionally rests (Steffek 2006). Eventually, the compromise formula of 'special and differential treatment' requires a number of other core values of the GATT to be redefined. *Equality among members* thus comes to mean that members are *not* treated equally, but according to capacity; *reciprocity* remains a key norm of the GATT, but developing countries are exempt from the general expectation the norm expresses; and the *MFN* principle is limited as the so-called generalized system of preferences allows industrialized countries to grant preferential treatment to developing countries on a bilateral basis.

Overall, the core values we identify based on member state statements, annual reports, and other GATT and WTO documents thus constitute a solid basis for legitimating a complex organization which, as a result of its particular founding history, lacked a written constitution. In many ways, the 'GATT gospel' we have described above fulfilled the function of an unwritten constitution. Substantively, it was formulated in broad terms to include anti-protectionism, stability, and liberalization as the goals to be pursued; and multilateralism, consensus-based decision making, and attention to the specific needs of developing countries as procedural standards that guide the pursuit of these goals. The 'GATT gospel' remains of fundamental relevance for the legitimation of the WTO today. But as we discuss in the following sections, its norms also provided the basis for two major additions to the legitimation contest that began to take shape in the 1990s.

AFTER THE GOSPEL: THE RISE OF NON-TRADE VALUES

With the Uruguay Round drawing to a close, the legitimation contest took a different shape. As public interest in the project of establishing a broader and stronger WTO grew, the audience as well as the range of speakers expanded. The *New York Times*, for example, included four times as many articles dealing with the GATT in 1993 and 1994 than in the preceding years.[5] In addition, non-governmental organizations (NGOs) regularly voiced their opinion in media stories about the GATT. In 1990, only ten GATT-related articles included in the Factiva Database mentioned organizations like Friends of the Earth, the International Confederation of Free Trade Unions (ICFTU), Oxfam, or Public Citizen. This number rose to ninety-two (1992) and 198 (1994)—in other words, by a factor of twenty—in subsequent years.[6] Finally, not only public attention, but also public protest became manifest, as a *Reuters* news report on the GATT negotiations in December 1990 illustrates (Kaluzynska 1990):

> The final stage of the four-year Uruguay Round of GATT talks opened on a pessimistic note, bogged down by a transatlantic row over farm subsidies and heckled in the streets by farmers worried about falling income. Para-military police fired tear gas and used water cannon to control an estimated crowd of 30,000 mainly European farmers, who tore down trees and traffic signs, burned tyres and overturned a public works cabin in protest against the talks.

Public interest in and protest against the GATT also affected the terms of legitimation. Most importantly, protesters held the institution accountable in relation to a host of 'non-trade values' such as environmental concerns, food safety, or labour rights. In its *Annual Report 2007*, the WTO unequivocally accepts these new values as a part of its legitimation basis. Under the label of 'humanizing globalization', it thus states (WTO 2007: 3):

> To address global questions, problems, threats, fears, at the appropriate level, requires a system of governance at the global level which is responsive to emerging global challenges. The international trading system and its benefits belong to everyone—they are an international public good. It is in accordance with this principle that the WTO and the multilateral system recognize different values, including a consensus on the benefits resulting from market opening or the right to protect the environment. It is clearly recognized in the WTO that non-trade values can supersede trade considerations in some circumstances.

In the following, we trace how these new values have entered the legitimation discourse of the GATT and the WTO. We discuss environmental concerns and labour rights in this section, and focus on the 'democratic deficit' challenge, to which the WTO has responded in a particularly strong manner,

---

[5] Based on Factiva data for 1988 to 1995, using the operator ('GATT' OR 'WTO' OR 'World Trade Organization') and 'New York Times—All Sources' as the source. Absolute numbers range from twenty-one reports in 1990 to 119 reports in 1993.

[6] Based on Factiva data for 1990 to 1994, using the operator ['GATT' AND ('Friends of the Earth' OR 'ICFTU' OR 'Oxfam' or 'Public Citizen')] and 'All Sources' as the source. An additional query using the word 'is' as a search term suggests that the overall number of articles in the Factiva source 'all sources' grows by a factor of slightly below 1.6 in the same period of time.

thereafter. Throughout our discussion, three contextual aspects need to be recalled. First, 'non-trade values' were strongly voiced not only—and sometimes not even primarily—from within the GATT community itself, but also by NGOs, journalists, and other domestic actors. Second, civil society voices gained relevance in media debates on the GATT and the WTO only from the late 1980s onwards. And third, a relatively small number of civil society organizations (CSOs)—groups like Friends of the Earth, Oxfam, Public Citizen, or ICFTU—dominated in global media debates while Southern groups like the Third World Network had a more difficult time to make their views heard.[7]

Environmental Concerns

The protests at the 1990 GATT meeting in Brussels, that we have alluded to above, remain in a traditional frame. They are explicitly justified in terms of the protection of economic interests, usually of a specific domestic industry. In contrast, the introduction of non-trade concerns means that actors successfully invoke legitimacy standards that are not primarily economic in nature.

With regard to environmental concerns, the conventional narrative holds that they entered the GATT in the wake of the Tuna-Dolphin case in 1991 (see also O'Brien et al. 2000: 134–53). In that dispute, Mexico challenged the legality of a US regulation that prohibited imports of tuna from Mexico. The US argued that the nets used on Mexican fisher boats allowed for the possibility of incidental killing of dolphins and that an import ban was thus required under the US Mammal Protection Act. The report of the dispute settlement panel ruled that the US regulation was illegal. On the one hand, it had failed to treat like products alike, and on the other hand, states could not prohibit imports based on foreign producers' lack of compliance with domestic laws of the importing countries (GATT 1991b).

Although it was never formally adopted, the ruling came as 'a major blow to conservationists around the globe' (Associated Press 1991). Environmentalists used it to campaign against the GATT, with trade advocates dismissing their response as 'a blitzkrieg of condemnatory ads and anti-GATT propaganda' (Bhagwati 1993). American NGOs, for example, stated that 'the GATT decision declares open season on allowing dolphin-deadly tuna into the U.S.', and asked 'how many of these gentle creatures will have to die in the name of free trade' (PR Newswire 1991). More importantly, however, there were broader implications beyond the case itself. On these, Charles Arden-Clarke (1991),

---

[7] On the latter point, a search in the media database Factiva, for instance, leads to slightly more than 6,000 articles mentioning the GATT or WTO in combination with Oxfam for the period of 1980 to 2012, while the Third World Network appears just under 800 times.

a senior policy advisor with World Wide Fund for Nature International, argued that the GATT rules had been 'interpreted as if trade liberalisation [were] the only objective that matters', and that the dispute had been 'settled with wholly inadequate reference to the consequent impacts on the environment, or on the legislation established to protect it'. His organization consequently called for an 'immediate audit of GATT's impact on the environment... to provide the basis for reform'.

GATT members responded by putting the environment on the agenda. They revitalized the Committee on Trade and the Environment (CTE) that had been dormant for long and actively addressed environmental concerns in official communications. Published in the year in which the dispute arose, the *GATT Activities in 1990* is the first annual report to mention the environment in its introductory chapter. In the report, GATT officials give the impression that their institution seeks ways to carefully balance legitimate environmental policy goals with trade policy interests. At the same time, they resolve the issue in conformity with traditional GATT values when they argue that *growth* will help to finance environmentally friendly technologies (GATT 1991a).

Three years later, when environmentalists raised their opposition to strengthening the organization, the GATT Secretariat came back to the theme, and presented itself as a learning organization (GATT 1994a: 2): 'We have already built up a substantial understanding of the issues which need to be dealt with, concerning the interplay between trade and environmental policies'. The *GATT Activities in 1993* continues: 'our future work will determine carefully whether, and if so what, changes may be needed to avoid damaging clashes between these two important policy areas'. Member state delegations, in contrast, rarely raise the issue at all, and if they do, their statements indicate that the audience they address is as much a domestic as an international one. One of the few environment-related statements during the Uruguay Round comes from the Canadian delegation in the 1994 meeting of the contracting parties. 'We are well launched in our consideration of the trade/environment relationship,' it says, 'and the Canadian delegation will continue to be active in addressing this issue to ensure that sustainable development and trade liberalization remain compatible and mutually reinforcing' (GATT 1994b: 2).

With the establishment of the WTO in 1995, and the major structural change it implied, public attention increased once more and so did the discussion over what the new WTO meant for domestic environmental regulation. The debate was most pronounced in the US where Ralph Nader and his colleagues at the NGO Public Citizen ran a strong campaign against the WTO based on the argument that it would undermine US environmental and food safety standards. Yet, while industrialized countries were open to giving environmental concerns a platform in the WTO, developing countries feared protectionism (Fickling and Hufbauer 2012). Eventually, the compromise formula was to include 'sustainable development', rather than 'environmental protection' as a goal in the preamble to the *Marrakesh Agreement on the Establishment of the World Trade Organization*. The preamble now asks the WTO to work towards the expansion of trade in goods and services, 'while allowing for the optimal use of the world's resources in accordance with the objective of sustainable development' (WTO 1994: 1144).

In terms of our bubbles model, this turned sustainable development into an 'official' part of the discursive terrain on which actors negotiate the legitimacy of the WTO. However, sustainable development has sparked gradually less controversy over time.[8] On the one hand, organizations like the Geneva-based International Centre for Trade and Sustainable Development gathered considerable expertise on trade issues, leading the environmental movement to increasingly attempt to change the WTO 'from within' rather than from the outside (O'Brien et al. 2000). On the other hand, expertise and sensitivity within the WTO have increased, and dispute-settlement bodies have learnt from the experience of the GATT's *Tuna-Dolphin* and the WTO's *Shrimp-Turtle* (1998) cases. By exercising a bit of self-restraint on environmental questions, they have avoided the trap of further arousing public opinion.

Finally, as the Doha Round has come to a halt, environmental NGOs have increasingly turned away from the WTO and focused their lobbying activities on other international forums. Ultimately, however, the inclusion of sustainable development in the WTO's constitutional document has failed to anchor this principle enough for a lasting public debate over a more environmentally friendly world trade regime. At the same time, it is evident that a 'normative pressure' in Grigorescu's term has been established. To remain legitimate, the WTO can no longer afford to be perceived as deviating too overtly or too strongly from the principles of sustainable development. It is in this spirit that the 2009 Annual Report of the WTO confirms environmental protection as one of the 'principles [which] are the foundation of the multilateral trading

---

[8] The *Shrimp-Turtle* dispute was structurally similar to the *Tuna-Dolphin* case in many ways. In the case, India, Malaysia, Pakistan, and Thailand disputed the legality of a US law that prohibited the import of shrimps, unless the harvesting nation introduced measures comparable to those for domestic fishermen in the US against the incidental killing of sea turtles, or unless 'the particular fishing environment of the harvesting nation did not pose a threat to sea turtles' (see the WTO's summary of the case, retrieved from https://www.wto.org/english/tratop_e/envir_e/edis08_e.htm, last accessed 10 March 2017). In its ruling, the Appellate Body generally permitted a regulation like the US law in question, thus amending the process versus product standard upheld in the earlier Tuna-Dolphin case. The US lost the case nonetheless because it had provided technical and financial assistance, and granted transition periods to some but not to all WTO members. As a result, some groups used the ruling to underline their argument that the WTO, despite its nominal commitment to 'sustainable development', failed 'to correct its bias against the environment' (World Wide Fund for Nature statement, cited in *Bridges*, Vol. 2, No. 40, 19 October 1998).

system' (WTO 2009a: 3), and in which the WTO, together with the UN Environment Programme, sees a need to actively shape the debate over trade and climate change (Tamiotti et al. 2009; see also Fickling and Hufbauer 2012). Taken together, the inclusion of sustainable development in the preamble to the Marrakesh Agreement thus provides a new normative corridor within which world trade law counts as legitimate.

Labour Rights

Like environmental concerns, the issue of core labour standards entered the GATT and the WTO in the early 1990s when member states negotiated the scope and design of a new WTO.[9] Overall, labour unions in industrialized countries mainly argued that the GATT and the WTO ought to protect workers' rights against a 'race to the bottom'. The fundamental critique of the GATT was that it prioritized growth at the cost of exploiting workers and infringed upon their basic rights; the proposed solution was to '[add] muscle to the decisions of the ILO [International Labour Organization]' by introducing a 'social clause' in the GATT and the WTO. This clause would have allowed states to withhold trade preferences when other states do not respect basic ILO conventions (O'Brien et al. 2000: 67–108, quotation at p. 71).

Like with environmental concerns, member state coalitions on this issue were clear-cut. While many industrialized countries pushed for a social clause, virtually all developing countries fought against it. The Indian delegation, for example, called the 'tendency on the part of some developed countries to seek linkages between trade in goods and other matters', including fair labour standards, 'the most serious development in the trade policy area in recent years'. To underline its claim, the Indian delegation cited the support of the 'international community' which, in the form of the Final Act of UNCTAD VII (1987), had recognized that 'observance of multilaterally agreed commitments with respect to trade in goods should not be made conditional on receiving concessions in other areas'. In an explicit effort at subordinating the GATT to UNCTAD, the Indian delegation asked the contracting parties of the GATT to adhere to this commitment 'in the course of negotiations in the Uruguay Round' (GATT 1987: 4).

Similarly, the Colombian delegation took issue with the term 'social dumping' that some proponents of a social clause used to describe developing country practices. Building its argument on the notion of comparative advantage,

---

[9] But see the statement from the US delegation at the end of the Tokyo Round that it 'would have liked to have added more new projects to the work programme', including minimum international labour standards (GATT 1979c: 67).

the Colombian delegate essentially pitted core labour standards against development options (GATT 1994c: 2):

> The belief that labour costs are lower in developing countries as a result of deliberate policies to exploit workers and of unfair competition creates a smokescreen hiding the reality of international inequalities in development. Labour is cheaper for the simple reason that these are less affluent societies with very different structural patterns. By closing the door on imports of goods, using the hysterical argument based on cost differences, you bar the way to the basic theories of comparative advantage and reduce the development options open to the less privileged countries of the world. For this reason it disturbs us to hear Europe's major leaders voice such reactionary ideas, which are inconsistent with . . . the efforts put into economic and social progress by the peoples of the developing world.

Eventually, labour standards were not included in the Marrakesh Agreement, but moved on to the first WTO ministerial conference in Singapore in 1996. The meeting saw a heated debate on the issue, with the Singapore Declaration adopted at the end of the ministerial conference resolving the issue in what has been termed a 'classic compromise that was interpreted differently by opposing parties' (O'Brien et al. 2000: 82–108, citation at p. 91). The declaration states:

> We renew our commitment to the observance of internationally recognized core labour standards. The International Labour Organization (ILO) is the competent body to set and deal with these standards, and we affirm our support for its work in promoting them. We believe that economic growth and development fostered by increased trade and further trade liberalization contribute to the promotion of these standards. We reject the use of labour standards for protectionist purposes, and agree that the comparative advantage of countries, particularly low-wage developing countries, must in no way be put into question. In this regard, we note that the WTO and ILO Secretariats will continue their existing collaboration.

Statements made in later years confirm that developing countries interpret this paragraph as putting an end to the discussion. When some states sought to reopen the debate at the 2001 ministerial conference in Doha, the Indian delegation made it very clear that it 'firmly [opposes] any linkage between trade and labour standards'. It maintained that 'the Singapore Declaration had once and for all dealt with this issue and there is no need to refer to it again' (WTO 2001b: 2). Labour standards, the Government of India argued, were to be dealt with at the ILO, not the WTO.

In contrast, industrialized countries interpret the declaration differently. Canada, France, Italy, and Norway used the 2001 ministerial conference in Doha to push for the inclusion of labour standards as well as for closer collaboration between the WTO and the ILO. The Norwegian delegation even demanded that the 'Ministerial Declaration must include a reference to the international efforts to secure core labour standards' (WTO 2001c: 2). The reference was indeed added to the declaration in the end, but only to 'reaffirm [the] declaration made at the Singapore Ministerial Conference', and to 'take note of work under way in the International Labour Organization (ILO) on the social dimension of globalization' (WTO 2001d: article 8). In subsequent ministerial conferences as well as in all but one introductory chapter to the WTO's annual reports, labour standards no longer play a major role, indicating—like in the case of environmental values—a declining relevance of the issue among member states.[10]

What lessons can we draw from the rise of these different 'non-trade values' for efforts to shift the terms of legitimation more generally? Comparing environmental and labour concerns, two things are striking. First, environmental concerns and labour rights entered the legitimation discourse of the GATT and the WTO around the same time. They were both pushed by strong coalitions of Northern civil society groups, and the civil society groups that fought for them found support among GATT members from the industrialized world. Opposing this coalition, developing countries battled hard against 'greening the GATT' or adding a social clause to it. Nonetheless, the WTO responded differently in the two cases. It reframed environmental norms in the language of 'sustainable development', and reserved a constitutional status for them in the preamble to the WTO agreement. Labour issues were less successful. The WTO acknowledged them in a mere 'declaration', and effectively outsourced the issue to the ILO. This difference seems striking, if we take into account that labour issues resonated more strongly with the 'embedded liberalism' narrative on which the GATT was originally built.

Second, environmental concerns and labour standards were not the only 'non-trade' values. Other concerns included the fear that the WTO would undermine domestic food safety standards and hence consumer protection, and the worry that a liberalization of trade in agricultural goods would force WTO members to give up 'policy space' in a particularly sensitive field. The former challenge was eventually resolved in the decision to recognize measures based on 'international standards' as being compliant with WTO rules. This decision linked the WTO to the work done at the International Organization for Standardization and other international standard setters; the decision also required the latter to organize their standard-setting processes in an open, transparent, and inclusive manner.[11] The agricultural challenge, in contrast, was not resolved at all; it was put on the agenda of the Doha

---

[10] The Norwegian delegation continues to refer to labour standards in its 2005 and 2009 statements, the delegations of Italy and Hong Kong in 2005. Among the WTO's annual reports, only the Annual Report 1996 includes a reference to labour standards in its summary of the Singapore Declaration.

[11] Agreement on the Application of Sanitary and Phytosanitary Measures (SPS Agreement), article 3 and Agreement on Technical Barriers to Trade (TBT Agreement), annex 3.

Round for further negotiation. Yet, with their focus on open and consensual procedures as well as the need for 'policy space', both additional 'non-trade values' prefigured the second major legitimation challenge the GATT and the WTO was to confront: the challenge associated with 'democratic' governance.

AFTER POLITICIZATION: THE RISE OF DEMOCRACY

We can narrate the rise of democracy as a new term of legitimation in two broad steps. First, even though protests in the 1990s did not give birth to the democratic frame, they added significant strength to it and turned it into a central legitimacy standard for the WTO by the early 2000s. Second, after its stellar rise in the 1990s and early 2000s, the democratic frame has receded to the background again after 2005. Even though official WTO communications refer to them less frequently, democratic standards remain important in two ways. On the one hand, just like the 'non-trade values' discussed in the previous section, they add yet another standard of legitimacy which the WTO is expected to meet, thereby further complicating the conclusion of the Doha Round. On the other hand, the rise of democracy in the 1990s and early 2000s has led to a redefinition of the consensus norm. While consensus was originally not linked to a 'democratic' claim, the WTO's efforts to repair its legitimacy after Seattle built primarily on reinterpreting—and thereby also strengthening—the consensus norm as a 'democratic' norm. In the most recent crisis the WTO confronts, this leads to a dilemma. Tinkering with the consensus norm would diminish the credibility of the democratic legitimation claim, while leaving the consensus norm untouched threatens the viability of a WTO that has grown from twenty-three to 162 states and is living through a period of sustained 'gridlock' (Hale et al. 2013: 154–62).

The Democratic Legitimation Frame after Seattle

At the Seattle protests against the 1999 ministerial conference of the WTO, democracy made headlines when activists managed to turn one of their banners into a symbol for the alter-globalization movement.[12] The banner showed one arrow pointing to the left, and one pointing to the right. The former had 'WTO' written on it; the latter read 'Democracy'. Following the

---

[12] This section draws on Dingwerth (2019: 83–5 and 87–9).

path of the WTO, the banner said, leads us away from democracy. Following the road to democracy, in contrast, requires us to leave the WTO behind.

Prior to these events, the 'democratic' quality of the GATT had not been a prominent term in legitimation contests around the GATT (for two exceptions see GATT 1974a: 5 and GATT 1988: 2). By the early 2000s, however, speeches by the WTO Directors General, annual reports issued by the WTO, and member state statements made in WTO governing bodies regularly included references to democracy. Developed as well as developing countries, and democracies as well as non-democracies invoke the language of democracy. France, for example, 'favours a strong, legitimate, and democratic WTO' (WTO 2001e: 1); it also applauds Director General Pascal Lamy for 'making our organization more open and more democratic' (WTO 2013b: 1). The Chinese delegation, in turn, is 'ready to work together with other members towards building a more democratic, more efficient, more just and more balanced multilateral trading system' (WTO 2009b: 2). And the Government of Pakistan expresses its hope that delegations 'will succeed through an open and democratic process, in evolving a genuine consensus at Doha' (WTO 2001f: 3).

Conventionally, the rise of the democratic frame is ascribed to the Seattle protests. In fact, however, the protests have not invented the democratic frame but merely added *strength* to it. Historically, the democratic challenge thus gained relevance in the early 1990s when CSOs began to question whether a new WTO could be legitimate, if it undermined democracy. A prominent example of this challenge is the straightforward claim by Lord Frank Judd, former director of Oxfam, that the 'GATT is an undemocratic and closed institution' (Reuters News 1992; see also Strange 2011). Discursively, those who introduced the frame could build on two historical legacies that refer to the two different ways in which 'democracy' has been used to both challenge and defend the legitimacy of the WTO.

The first use of democracy in legitimation contests ties democracy to sovereignty. This use refers to the GATT and the WTO as organizations that undermine the national democratic process. In the history of the GATT this argument pops up early. When the US Congress failed to ratify the ITO, concerns that this new organization would 'infringe on national sovereignty' played a central role (Reis 2009: 44). Choosing the GATT instead of the ITO gave member states the option to interpret the agreements in accordance with their national preferences and laws (Zangl 2008). Moreover, members could resolve disputes through consultations or, where this failed, in a formal yet diplomatic dispute-settlement process. Informally, the recognition of the need for 'policy space' thus provided an important foundation for the legitimacy of the GATT (Ruggie 1982). Unsurprisingly, then, it also became the cornerstone of domestic protests in the US and elsewhere, when the Uruguay Round negotiations led to the proposal for creating the WTO.

The second use ties democracy to transparency and consensus-based decision making. In the Uruguay Round, negotiations on trade in services led several developing countries to frame their concerns in terms of national sovereignty, as well. The Peruvian delegation maintained that it would 'follow closely the negotiations on trade in services, to ensure that...the general policy objectives of national legislation and regulations on services are observed' (GATT 1986a: 4). Others demanded that negotiations 'observe a maximum of transparency' (GATT 1986b: 1), asked that consultations be 'carried out in a most transparent manner' (GATT 1986c: 2), or criticized, like the Chilean delegation, that 'there has not been a single open and formal discussion in which the contracting parties could express their views concerning general matters relating to the organization, plan and procedures of the negotiations' (GATT 1986d: 1). In doing so, they introduced the call for *transparency* as a further element of the democracy frame. Their remarks also prefigured elements of the 'Green Room' argument that became central to the legitimacy crisis after Seattle.

This use of transparency as a democratic value was novel in as much as it did not view the GATT as undermining the domestic democratic process. Instead, it suggested that the operation of the GATT did not itself meet a standard of democratic governance. Like the first use of the democracy frame, however, it resonated with earlier arguments from the broader GATT discourse. While the specific call for transparency may be novel in this regard, member states already invoked the standard of 'adequate representation' during most years of the Tokyo Round.[13] Similarly, the claim that developing countries should become 'effective participants', 'full participants', or 'full partners' in negotiations was frequently articulated, and it also constituted a key justification for the GATT's technical-assistance programme during the Uruguay Round.[14] In sum, the seeds for raising the profile of democratic standards in the GATT and the WTO legitimation discourse were planted earlier. In particular, the presence of frames had resonated with new normative demands for a more democratic organization the task of building discursive coalitions around such demands.

Compared to this baseline, however, the immediate post-Seattle years present a fundamental shift. The WTO now explicitly accepted democratic normative demands as an appropriate standard of legitimacy, and it sought to convince its audiences that it was well positioned to meet the standard. The 2000 and 2001 annual reports, for example, strove to '[demonstrate] the truth that the WTO is firmly based in democratic legitimacy' (WTO 2000: 4).

---

[13] See GATT (1974a: 32; 1974b: 43; 1975b: 2, 1975c: 42; 1976: 39; 1978b: 40; 1979a: 35–6; 1979b: 49; 1979c: 75 and 77–8).

[14] See for instance Sri Lanka (GATT 1986h: 3), Chile (GATT 1986i: 2) and Federal Republic of Germany (GATT 1986j: 1).

They also 'emphasize the importance of conducting public debates on trade policy—essential in any democratic process—on the basis of an accurate understanding of the policies being considered by the negotiators' (WTO 2001a: 2). The organization stressed that its consensus-based decision making 'gives negotiating agendas a solid basis in democratic legitimacy and accountability' (WTO 2001a: 3). Finally, Director General Mike Moore directly confronted the critics and argued that 'opponents of the World Trade Organization who sometimes claim that the system is "undemocratic" start from a basic fallacy'; that the consensus rule 'embodies...the right to sovereignty, free choice, self-government—in other words "democracy" in its most basic sense'; and that the WTO was, in fact, 'the most democratic international body in existence today' (Moore 2002).

The Doha Deadlock and the Long Legacy of Seattle

By the early 2000s, the emerging consensus suggested that only a 'democratic' WTO could be a legitimate WTO.[15] At the same time, references to democracy became less frequent after 2005 (see also Dingwerth et al. 2018; Rauh and Zürn 2018), not least because the deadlock of the Doha Round meant that the WTO confronted a different challenge by then. Addressing readers in the organization's 2011 annual report, WTO Director General Pascal Lamy thus claims that 'the World Trade Organization is about much more than just the Doha Round' (WTO 2011: 10). A comparison of member state statements at the 2005, 2009, and 2013 ministerial conferences gives a good impression of the normative pressures Lamy sought to deflect with his remark. It indicates the growing importance actors attach to the conclusion of the round. In 2005, a typical statement would have been one that starts with noting the 'need to move forward' in the first paragraph, concludes on the same note in the final paragraph, and discusses substantive or procedural points in between. Only few delegations set the bar higher when they equated failure with 'the start of the total disintegration of the multilateral system' (Norway, WTO 2005: 1).

Four years later, delegations already used a stronger language. Many of them stated that the 'credibility' of the WTO depended on progress in multilateral negotiations. They called upon other delegations to 'show that the WTO is alive and relevant' (Switzerland, WTO 2009c: 2). They asked members to 'demonstrate to the world that the system still works and merits our continued support' (Hongkong, China, WTO 2009d: 1). And they expressed hope that members would 'prove to the world that the WTO is a

---

[15] This section draws on Dingwerth (2019: 89–92).

vibrant institution to reckon with, that lays the foundation for international trade' (Tanzania, WTO 2009e: 1).[16]

The 2013 ministerial conference continued the theme of 'credibility' and 'relevance' but also included more explicit warnings that 'the world is watching closely' and that 'if we fail here, we will have to face grave consequences' (Republic of Korea, WTO 2013c: 1). US trade representative Michael Froman used particularly strong language. He introduced his statement by commenting that 'by the time we leave here this week, the WTO will have entered a new era—one way or another'. Subsequently, he called upon delegations 'to prove to a sceptical world that the WTO is a vital, vibrant institution, capable of producing important results for trade and development, worthy of our future confidence, attention and resources' (US, WTO 2013d: 2).

Beyond government statements, media comments provide a similar sense of urgency, with metaphors frequently revolving around life and death. They argue that incoming WTO Director General Azevêdo needs to 'reanimate' an organization that is in a 'death struggle'. They quote WTO spokesperson Keith Rockwell, who expects a 'dangerous situation for the organisation', should the 2015 ministerial conference in Nairobi fail to produce meaningful outcomes, and Swiss federal councillor Johann Schneider-Ammann who declares 2015 the 'year of credibility' for the WTO. And they see the WTO as a 'phase-out model' stuck in a 'blind-alley', a 'construction site with no end', or a 'pile of broken glass', with more factually minded observers noting an 'erosion of confidence', a 'loss of credibility', or simply a 'crisis'.[17]

Taken together, the widespread sense of crisis is easy to spot. But what is the standard based on which the WTO is failing? In a sense, one could speak of the *end of the liberalization challenge*: the legitimacy of the WTO is in jeopardy because its promise to liberalize international trade no longer seems to hold. In general, the idea that 'if the institution...fails in concluding a Round, its overall legitimacy is at stake' (Elsig and Dupont 2012: 624) is not itself new. It derives from the notion of 'progressive liberalization' that has been a central motive in the legitimation of the GATT ever since: the GATT was good if— and only if—it moved on (see e.g. GATT 1994a: 1; GATT 1980: 6). Standstill, in turn, implied a breakdown in the common imagination of the world trade

---

[16] For similar references, see also the statements issued by the delegations of Cambodia ('the conclusion of the DDA Round by 2010 is a MUST'), Israel ('that the WTO is indeed relevant'), Kenya ('relevance and credibility of WTO is closely tied to conclusion of the DDA'), Suriname ('restoring the credibility of our organization'), and Taiwan ('to restore the world's confidence in the multilateral trading system') in 2009; and the statements made by the delegations on Bangladesh ('credibility'), Rwanda ('to send a strong signal that this system—our system—is still needed'), the Central African Republic ('credibility of our Organization but also the Doha Development Round'), and Norway ('with a decision in Bali, the negotiating arm of the WTO will start rebuilding its credibility') in 2013.

[17] *Business Times*, 28 July 2015; *Neue Zürcher Zeitung*, 26 January 2015, 2 August 2014, 26 June 2014, 10 September 2013, 11 May 2013, 4 August 2012, 20 December 2011, 11 June 2011.

community, and the impression that the WTO may have reached the end of multilateral liberalization constitutes a major challenge for an organization with a mandate formulated in dynamic terms.

Thus, in contrast to the 1990s, the contemporary crisis does not build on the impression that the GATT gospel is too narrow, but rather that it is *no longer viable*. The WTO is seen to be unable to pursue the three core norms of multilateralism, liberalization, and consensus-based decision making at the same time. But if multilateralism, liberalization, and consensus no longer go together well, which one should be dropped or made to fit? Could the WTO relinquish its legislative function—and hence the promise of *liberalization*—and focus on monitoring compliance with existing agreements and helping states to settle trade disputes instead? Could it leave the *consensus* principle that has been said to 'blockade the WTO' behind?[18] Or should the WTO recalibrate its *multilateral* identity and make room for plurilateral agreements?

In response to the option of dropping liberalization, GATT officials made strong efforts in earlier situations to convey the relevance of the organization's day-to-day work for the world trade system. In their opening remarks to the 42nd session of the contracting parties, the chairman thus stressed that 'the regular work of GATT must, and will, proceed alongside the Uruguay Round' (GATT 1986e: 4), and member states underlined 'the importance that we shall continue to attach to the day-to-day functioning of GATT and to observance of GATT obligations' (GATT 1986f: 3; see also GATT 1986g: 2). These statements might suggest that those seeking to defend the WTO 'at the end of liberalization' could draw on an existing discursive repertoire, focused on the importance of the day-to-day activities that help to guarantee the currently existing liberalization levels. In accordance with such an idea, for instance, the annual reports published under Director General Roberto Azevêdo's leadership stress the 'notable rise in the interest' (WTO 2017: 2) non-traditional stakeholders take in the WTO, or emphasize how the 'regular use of the WTO's dispute settlement system by both developing and developed countries is a clear indication of the . . . confidence' (WTO 2017: 3) members attach to it. On the other hand, member state statements from 1986, quoted above, also make the limitation of such a strategy apparent as speakers consistently present monitoring, surveillance, and dispute settlement as relevant *for the negotiations*. In line with this interpretation, Azevêdo made it clear from the very start of his term in office that he does not see a viable alternative to further *liberalization* for the WTO:

> Our negotiating arm is struggling. We all know that this is just one part of the work that we do here. We all know that. But the WTO, as we know, has been defined by what we have been doing in the negotiating front. This is how the

---

[18] *Neue Zürcher Zeitung*, 2 August 2014 and 5 December 2013.

world sees us. There is no escaping that. It doesn't matter how much we say that we do more than negotiate, that we have a number of other things going on here, which are extremely important to the world even though the world doesn't know it. People only see us as good as our progress on Doha. That is the reality. And the perception in the world is that we have forgotten how to negotiate. The perception is ineffectiveness. The perception is paralysis. Our failure to address this paralysis casts a shadow which goes well beyond the negotiating arm, and it covers every other part of our work. It is essential that we breathe new life into negotiations. We must send a clear and unequivocal message to the world that the WTO can deliver multilateral trade deals.

But while *liberalization* cannot be compromised, much the same seems to hold for the *consensus* norm which has become the main pillar of the WTO's claim to be a 'democratic' organization since the Seattle protests. The mantra at the time was that 'the WTO functions on the basis of consensus' and that, 'along with being essential for the acceptance and enforcement of its rules, [consensus] also gives negotiating agendas a solid basis in democratic legitimacy and account-ability' (WTO 2001a: 5; 2002: 3). This notion continued to be supported in the subsequent reports in which the WTO emphasizes that 'virtually all decisions in the WTO are taken by consensus among all member countries', and that 'equal treatment is one of the basic principles of the multilateral trading system' (WTO 2012: 2; WTO 2013a: 2). Even though the most recent reports published under the leadership of Roberto Azevêdo omit this phrase, there is a clear sense that tinkering with the consensus norm would once more make the WTO vulnerable to the democratic deficit challenge. The traumatic experience of the Seattle protests suffices as a reminder for WTO members and officials to want to avoid that challenge. But the observation that recent protests against regional trade agreements (e.g. the Comprehensive Economic and Trade Agreement between Canada and the European Union (EU); or the Transatlantic Trade and Investment Partnership between the EU and the US) strongly rely on demo-cratic frames, is likely to strengthen the resolve against becoming vulnerable on the democratic front. Consequently, WTO officials and members seek to avoid giving the impression that the consensus norm is up for negotiation.

Instead, they interpret even small steps—among them the limited agree-ments reached at the 2013 and 2015 ministerial conferences in Bali and Nairobi—as proofs of a regained ability to deliver on the promise of multi-lateral, consensus-based liberalization. When fifty-four WTO members reached an agreement on the reductions of barriers to trade in IT goods in July 2015, Azevêdo saw 'the first major tariff-cutting deal at the WTO in 18 years' as proof 'that the multilateral trading system can deliver'.[19] What is

---

[19] *Financial Times*, 24 July 2015; see also WTO (2016: 3). The 'multilateral' character of the agreement is secured by the fact that fifty-four WTO members that agreed to eliminate tariffs on specified IT products will do so on the basis of the MFN clause and hence for all WTO members.

interesting in this statement is that the agreement itself is plurilateral since only fifty-four WTO members signed up to it. Even though signatories also extend the benefits of the agreement to non-signatory WTO members, the agreement is not multilateral in the sense the term is commonly used in GATT-speak, namely an agreement to which all WTO members subscribe. So, in fact, Azevêdo's statement seeks to solve the trilemma by redefining the meaning of multilateralism in the legitimation contest around the WTO.

In sum, democratic norms have become a central legitimacy standard for the GATT and the WTO in the 1990s and early 2000s. Their presence in legitimation contests has decreased in recent years, but the legacy of Seattle implies that the democratic frame nonetheless remains a part of the contemporary legitimation repertoire. While the acceptance of the democratic legitimacy standard has allowed the WTO to respond to the challenge of Seattle, it constrains the reform options the organization might want to consider today.

PATHWAYS OF NORMATIVE CHANGE

In the early decades, major shifts in the norms that underpin the legitimation of the GATT can be traced to changes in the organization's membership. As the number of developing countries rises, the development norm gains prominence and the discursive ground is prepared for the rise of notions like *comprehensiveness, coherence,* and *full participation.* In comparison, the normative changes we observe since the 1970s occur along a more diverse set of paths. In the following, we focus on four such pathways. The first connects to the politicization and popularization of the GATT and the WTO that follows in the wake of its growing authority; it is thus linked to the 'political globalization' variable of our bubbles model. The second path is tied to changes in the ideational environment in which the GATT and the WTO are embedded, among them the rise of environmental awareness and neoliberal economic thinking. The third path emphasizes the role of exceptional circumstances that open windows for change; in our bubbles model, such circumstances would not necessarily be linked to secular trends or systematic transformations, but rather to 'singular events'. Finally, the fourth path identifies self-reinforcing dynamics as a driving force behind the changes we observe, a factor we do not explicitly theorize in Chapter 2 but which also becomes relevant in our case studies on the AU (see Chapter 4) and on the International Union for Conservation of Nature (see Chapter 6).

Politicization and Popularization: The Rise of a Second Audience

That a significant part of the normative change we observe in the GATT and the WTO follows in the wake of politicization should not come as a surprise. Along with the EU, the International Monetary Fund (IMF), and the World Bank, the WTO has served as an empirical building block for the literature on the politicization of international institutions, and its politicization is thus well documented (O'Brien et al. 2000; Steffek 2013; see also Zürn et al. 2012). According to Michael Zürn (2014: 52), the politicization of international institutions refers to 'a process by which the technocratic behind-closed-doors logic of decisions and decision-making processes...is challenged'. For the GATT and the WTO, Zürn (2014: 52, referring to the works of Schmitter and de Wilde) observes:

> Although the Geneva round and the Dillon round of the General Agreement on Tariff and Trade in the early 1960s led, for instance, to significant reductions of tariffs worth billions of dollars, they remained almost exclusively the business of executive negotiators and economists. Four decades later the situation has changed. The battle of Seattle...was a sign of politicization and a challenge to executive multilateralism. Operationally speaking, this seemingly paradoxical 'politicization of world politics' comprises a 'widening of the audience or clientele interested and active' as a consequence of the increasing 'controversiality of issues' leading to three indicators...: awareness, mobilization, and contestation.

The evidence we have presented in the previous sections confirms the plausibility of this interpretation. The protests in Brussels (1990), in Geneva (1998), and eventually in Seattle (1999) certainly constitute a 'politicization' of the GATT and the WTO as they reveal the contestation of the institution and make visible that it is a 'political' as well as a 'technical' institution. Moreover, the claims put forth at these protests are indeed marked by a fear that an increasingly powerful international organization—perceived not only as 'neoliberal' in substantive terms, but also as suffering from a 'democratic deficit' in its procedural dimension—had come to shape or even trump domestic politics. The concern was that the WTO would be able to overrule laws and decisions that societies had arrived at in a democratic process, thus supporting the 'authority-legitimacy link' (Zürn 2018) stressed in the politicization literature.

In addition, the popularization of the WTO is key. It is exemplified by rising media attention but also by a wealth of cartoons that spell out the various charges against the WTO in newspapers, magazines, and on the web. On the one hand, the cartoons make visible on which values critics ground their critique: in addition to democracy, these values commonly include fairness, justice, and human rights. On the other hand, they also show that protests have raised popular awareness of the WTO. Further evidence for this awareness comes straight from Hollywood. Written and directed by Stuart Townsend, and featuring Woody Harrelson and Charlize Theron among others, the *Battle in Seattle*—quite unlikely for a meeting of an international organization—made it onto the big screen in 2008. Besides considerable drama, the movie script also includes a neat summary of what the protests ultimately achieved: 'A week ago, nobody knew what the hell the WTO was,' it lets its protagonist sum up. 'Now they still don't know what the WTO is, but at least they know it's bad.'

Popularization is relevant because it implies a need to seek legitimacy from a new and much broader legitimation constituency. Non-trade values, for instance, do not primarily owe their rise to the intergovernmental legitimation discourse, but mainly to CSOs claiming to speak on behalf of 'the public'. As the GATT and the WTO became highly visible in the media around 1993 and 1994, this *second audience* became increasingly relevant. The Seattle protests then demonstrated the potential of this second audience to significantly disrupt the workings of the trade policy community; the success of protesters to impede delegates from entering the conference centre became a strong symbol of that power.

Institutionally, too, the biennial ministerial conferences provide a focal point for attention that regularly guarantees the WTO—as well as its critics—a prominent place in the international news media. For the legitimation discourse, this presented a challenge insofar as the broader public had never been socialized into the GATT gospel in the same way as governments and trade diplomats had been. For the WTO, this implied a need to recalibrate its legitimation narrative to take the expectations of new constituencies on board. Where these new audiences hold strong beliefs, the WTO can disregard them only at its own peril. In contrast, where new audiences may not yet have a clear idea about what the WTO is, or ought to be, their normative expectations may still be moulded, thus providing discursive space for a variety of norm entrepreneurs to introduce their own frames.

In hindsight, 'reformist' Northern environmental activists, trade unions, and consumer groups have been relatively successful in filling this gap with democratic and justice frames, providing the necessary unity to turn heterogeneous movements into a force for change. At the same time, power disparities within civil society become apparent, too. In the context of the Doha Round, Oxfam International has gained a particularly strong recognition as an 'NGO voice' in media reporting. Between 2003 and 2006, Oxfam appears in around twenty times more news reports on the WTO than the most prominent Southern voice, the Third World Network.[20] This has implications not

---

[20] The figures are based on searching the media database Factiva for 1995 to 2012. For the Third World Network, annual hits from 2003 to 2006, that include the WTO as well as the organization's name, range between 45 and 71; for Oxfam, they range from 663 to 1,493 per year.

only in terms of who speaks but also in terms of what is said. In the case at hand, the Third World Network, for instance, puts a clear emphasis on development needs while Oxfam combines environmental and development concerns in a sustainable development frame; the Third World Network speaks out more strongly against Northern protectionism framed as concerns for nature, workers' rights, or 'fair trade'; and it puts a stronger emphasis on the 'institutional imbalances' in a world trade regime in which developing countries may formally have equal status but are informally subordinated to their industrialized counterparts.

Discursive Coalitions in Favourable Ideational Climates

Looking beyond politicization, the observation that environmental concerns managed to leave a stronger trace in the legitimation discourse of the GATT and the WTO than labour standards remains puzzling. Considering the stronger resonance of labour standards with the 'embedded liberalism' narrative that was so central to the legitimation of the GATT, and considering the common wisdom that new norms need to be 'grafted upon' existing norms (Price 1998), the opposite outcome would have seemed just as likely.

What could explain the relative success of environmental concerns? Among the background conditions we discuss in Chapter 2, the *ideational environment* of the 1990s and 2000s seems particularly relevant (cf. Buzdugan and Payne 2016: 119–44). International environmental policy making blossomed after 1990. In 1987, the Brundtland Report paved the way for 'sustainable development' as a compromise formula behind which Northern and Southern actors as well as environmentalists and business representatives could rally (Bernstein 2001; Pattberg 2007; see also Chapter 5). In 1992, the Earth Summit in Rio de Janeiro not only further increased environmental awareness but also led to the adoption of Agenda 21, the UN Framework Convention on Climate Change, and the Convention on Biological Diversity; their legal provisions were further specified by additional protocols in subsequent years. In a decade when the international community launched a concerted effort to protect the global environment, environmental activists could legitimately hope that their voices would also be heard in the GATT—not least because a part of the sustainable development agenda had always been about the need for innovation and, to spur such innovation, for markets for environmental goods. In comparison, labour standards, as well as trade unions as the primary actors pushing for their inclusion in the GATT, had a more 'socialist' flair that fitted much less with a world in which socialist economies had just collapsed. In many ways, environmental concerns could be portrayed as 'progressive', while labour rights appeared as a thing of the past.

If *normative fit* with the broader discursive environment is indeed a relevant factor, the argument also holds for democracy which had become the 'gold standard' in the post-1990 world, and to which almost all political organizations sought to relate in one way or another. But in comparison to environmental concerns and labour standards, the democratic legitimation frame could also count on the support of a *broader coalition of actors spanning the North–South divide*. As indicated in the previous sections, those calling upon the WTO to respect 'democracy' included Northern social movements as well as the governments of China, Indonesia, or Pakistan. As an observer to the 2001 ministerial conference, the Pacific Islands Forum for instance refers to an unhappy history of 'obligation without representation', and declares that 'the WTO will only be a truly democratic institution when it ensures that all Members are represented in Geneva and in the WTO process'. Furthermore, the delegation also explicitly references the WTO's own aspirations when it states that 'the present situation is clearly not consistent with the fundamental democratic ideals proclaimed by the WTO', and recalls 'the lack of transparency and democratic decision-making process' at the Seattle ministerial conference as 'one of the region's greatest disappointments' (Pacific Islands Forum, WTO 2001g: 2). Many other developing states—small ones like Mauritius, but also large ones like Indonesia—join the call for greater democracy within the WTO, either using the term democracy itself or referring to the FIT formula of 'full inclusiveness and transparency' instead.

Combining both factors, we arrive at something like a 2 × 2 matrix. Democratic norms had a clear *ideational fit*, and they had *broad support*. Both characteristics facilitated their rise, and democratic norms left a strong trace in the legitimation discourse. Environmentalist claims fitted with the ideational environment of their time but they had to overcome developing country concerns. To succeed, environmental activists were thus forced to settle for the more development-friendly notion of 'sustainable development'. Finally, trade union demands neither fitted particularly well with the intellectual climate of the 1990s, nor received support from stakeholders in the developing world. As a result, they faced the strongest impediments among the newly introduced 'non-trade values'.[21]

---

[21] This interpretation can also be extended to the observation that another major challenge of the alter-globalization movement, namely the critique that liberalization harms rather than benefits economic growth and living standards in the Global South, never entered the GATT and the WTO discourse in the same way as other legitimation challenges did. On this reading, it is the fundamental misfit of the argument with the basic paradigm on which the GATT is built, which impeded it from playing a more prominent role.

'No Crisis, No Change': Quasi-Constitutional Moments as Windows for Change

A third pathway of normative change is linked to *exceptional circumstances* that provide norm entrepreneurs with an opportunity to introduce new norms, or redefine existing norms in light of their own normative vision or strategic interests. Over the period we investigate in this study, two moments are particularly significant.

First, the shift from GATT to WTO provides a rare constitutional moment in the history of the world trade regime, comparable in its significance only to the founding years of the GATT. Between 1947 and 1994, the GATT changed incrementally as a result of eight multilateral negotiation rounds that drove down tariffs, institutionalized trade relations, and covered an ever larger share of the global economy. Yet, the Uruguay Round presented a rupture in terms of its effort to simultaneously and fundamentally change both the substantive rules that guided international trade, and the institutional design of the organization that made and overlooked these rules. A look at primary and secondary sources confirms that the scope of this shift played a key role in raising awareness and mobilizing business associations, CSOs, and the mass media to engage in a heated debate over the contours of a future 'multilateral' or—as it was ultimately labelled—'World Trade Organization'. While cartoons depict the WTO as a Nazi-like figure that tells Uncle Sam that he had 'signed away [his] constitutional rights back in 1995', environmentalists visualized the fears of an excessively powerful international organization with the help of 'thousands of anonymously produced posters littering the streets of Paris, Tokyo and Washington, featuring a monstrous Gattzilla devouring the globe, smashing the Capitol building, spilling DDT with one hand and squeezing a dolphin to death with the other' (Dunne 1992).[22] Arguably, such imagery would have had little traction under normal circumstances. In times when the world trade regime was to be set on a new path, however, it counted as sufficiently relevant to feature in the *Financial Times*, with the reporter seeing the US greens as 'leading a growing lobby worried about the loss of sovereignty' (Dunne 1992).

Second, the Seattle protests constitute a moment of shock for the WTO. After Seattle, it became apparent that the WTO could not go back to business as usual—too massive the protests had been, too many images of fierce and widespread opposition to the WTO had been conveyed to a global TV audience, and too many people seemed to be happy that the organization had finally been taught a lesson. Simply blaming the protesters, and calling the

---

[22] For the cartoon, see: http://images.slideplayer.com/15/4723938/slides/slide_20.jpg (last accessed 29 August 2016; author and precise date of cartoon unknown).

failure of Seattle a missed opportunity to start a new Millennium Round seemed insufficient to regain legitimacy with an audience that had hitherto mattered little to the WTO, and whose expectations the WTO had known little about. So, while it was apparent that something needed to change, it was unclear what exactly that should be. Faced with this vacuum, the terms of WTO legitimation were once again up for renegotiation.

Eventually, WTO officials proved to be proactive norm entrepreneurs in their effort to accept the democratic legitimation frame and tie the organization's 'social licence to operate' to the credibility of its democratic claim. Executive heads like Mike Moore and later Pascal Lamy, but also WTO spokesperson Keith Rockwell, who serves the organization in this function since 1996, played key roles in this regard, thereby exemplifying the importance of bureaucratic leadership in redirecting and channelling the political discourse. Seen in this way, the acceptance of the democratic legitimation frame is a creative act that provided WTO leaders with the opportunity to put forth their own definition of democracy at the international level. As we have discussed above, the banners that carried the term 'democracy' remained unspecific. Consequently, they managed to shift normative contestation to a new conceptual terrain, but they could not define the terms of that terrain at the same time (Strange 2011).

In this context, linking 'democracy' to the consensus norm allowed WTO officials to compare their organization to the IMF and the World Bank, which were both based on a one dollar, one vote scheme. Director General Mike Moore, for example, made implicit use of this comparison when he characterized the WTO as the 'most democratic international body in existence today'. At the same time, the 'democratic' label WTO leaders sought to attach to their organization remains sufficiently vague to encompass different understandings of 'democracy'. While technical assistance programmes for delegations from least-developed countries thus resonate with notions of interstate democracy, the practice of hosting annual dialogues with civil society speaks to cosmopolitan conceptions, in which 'world society' constitutes a second tier for democratic global governance next to an international society of states.

Normative Path Dependence

Finally, the previous section has already hinted at the relevance of path-dependent developments. The responses of the WTO to the alter-globalization protests of the 1990s are central in this regard, as they inspired two developments. First, by accepting the democratic challenge, environmental concerns, and to some extent also labour standards as relevant measures of the organization's legitimacy, the WTO added further standards to the menu. Notably, however, the Doha Round takes place in a context in which the stronger legalization of the WTO has made new trade deals less flexible and hence more difficult to arrive at (Goldstein and Martin 2000); in which the membership of the WTO has become larger and more heterogeneous than ever before (Hale et al. 2013: 154–62); and in which any new deal will need to take the growing economic power of Brazil, China, and India into account (Zangl et al. 2016). All three factors contribute largely to the standstill we observe. But when the protests of the 1990s added environmental concerns, labour standards, and democracy to an already comprehensive GATT gospel, the expectations this expansion generated only added to the complexity of the multilateral trade talks that were to follow in the organization's future. So, while the Doha deadlock has many causes, and while the relative force of each individual cause will be difficult to measure, the expansion of the legitimation menu constitutes yet another piece in this larger puzzle.

Second, the deadlock of negotiations led to a widely shared impression that the WTO is no longer viable in its current form. To remain a valuable international organization, it needed to reform. Here, a further legacy of Seattle lies in the WTO's decision to build its defence to the 'democratic deficit' challenge on its consensus norm. Redefining consensus in terms of democracy, however, changed the meaning as well as the role of the consensus norm within the WTO discourse. Most importantly, it limits the range of 'legitimate' reform proposals in times when the need for reform often appears as the strongest consensus among members and observers. Like other case studies we present in this volume, the GATT and the WTO case thus illustrates that shifts in legitimation strategies often occur to deflect acute legitimation pressures. But even where they accomplish this short-term goal, altering the terms of legitimation implies that the newly introduced terms can generate new kinds of pressures in the long term.

CONCLUSION

In conclusion, the GATT rested on a fairly stable set of legitimation norms—the GATT gospel—from the 1970s to the early 1990s. These norms valued the GATT as a 'bulwark against protectionism' that provided stability and enabled economic growth—and development—through consensus and rule-based processes, geared at progressive liberalization and a continuous expansion of international trade. Towards the end of the Uruguay Round, however, two additional sets of standards—or two new speech bubbles in our bubbles model—entered the legitimation contest. On the one hand, environmental and labour standards became relevant as 'non-trade values'; on the other hand, democracy became a central procedural standard for the legitimation of the GATT and the WTO. The WTO addressed all three challenges in different ways.

While the proposal to tie the legitimacy of the GATT and the WTO to the latter's promotion of labour standards was effectively rejected, environmental concerns attained quasi-constitutional status. Finally, WTO leaders responded to the democracy challenge by embracing it and forcefully defending their organization as the 'most democratic international body in existence today'. This response is strong not only because the democratic legitimation frame is invoked frequently, but also—and more importantly—because it ties democratic norms to the very identity—the *personality*—of the WTO.

In terms of our two overarching trends—the *rise of the people* and the *rise of procedures*—labour standards are most evidently people-based norms: their primary reference point is, at least nominally, the individual worker and not the national economy. The response to environmental concerns, in contrast, also includes a strengthening of procedures and hence both substantive and procedural elements. In addition to asking the GATT and the WTO to consider what their rules imply for the substantive objective of environmental protection, it strengthens the position of the CTE. Moreover, it requires the organization to better coordinate its activities with relevant international environmental agencies, thereby tying the legitimacy of the WTO more closely to how it is governed. Finally, it demands that the WTO provides sufficient 'policy space' for member states, hence linking environmental concerns to concerns for preserving *popular sovereignty* within (democratic) member states.[23]

Third, people-centred and procedural legitimacy standards intersect in the prominent place the WTO has given to respect for *democratic norms* at the domestic as well as the international level. Yet, while the rise of democratic norms inevitably renders adherence to the 'right procedures' more important, the extent to which people-based legitimacy standards are strengthened depends on how democratic norms are understood. Where the democratic deficit is framed in terms of unequal access for member states, the 'people' do not play a prominent role. Where it is understood in more cosmopolitan terms, to include access for NGOs and transparency and accountability to the wider public, they do. The legitimation contest we describe in this chapter primarily reveals that the conceptual terrain on which the WTO is legitimated has shifted towards 'democracy', but it does not prejudge which interpretation of democracy will prevail. Overall, the normative logic that guides the semantic field of 'democracy' helps to boost people-based legitimacy standards, while the traditional issue area culture of global trade governance constrains the

---

[23] This argument would seem to hold for democratic member states only; yet the WTO discourse does not normally make a distinction between democratic and non-democratic members. The argument for 'policy space' thus essentially strengthens the role of *sovereignty* in the GATT and the WTO discourse, with the concept being interpreted as 'popular sovereignty'— and hence strengthening democratic legitimation norms—among democratic members.

extent to which cosmopolitan norms may succeed (Tallberg et al. 2013). Heated debates over the decision of the Argentinian government to deny access to sixty-four NGO representatives the WTO had already accredited for the 2017 ministerial conference in Buenos Aires illustrate that this tension continues to mark the WTO until today. Unsurprisingly, NGOs challenged that the decision—unprecedented in the history of the WTO and including some NGOs that had interacted with the WTO since the Marrakesh meeting in 1994—would '[curtail] democratic participation in an arena where matters of global concern that affect all of society are discussed' (Third World Network 2017).

Finally, our discussion points to several causal pathways that have made normative change possible. On the one hand, *politicization* clearly matters as the Seattle protests led to a recalibration of the legitimation discourse in which values like inclusiveness, transparency, responsiveness, and accountability were strengthened. At the same time, the politicization of international organizations is not merely a function of greater competences, but also of the popularization of the WTO and the organization's increasingly heterogeneous membership. Moreover, our study reveals relevant dynamics *beyond politicization*. In particular, the broader ideational climate as well as the exceptional circumstances—fundamental reform in 1994/5, the Seattle protests, and the deadlock of the Doha Round—have created opportunities for normative change and thereby shaped the legitimation discourse. Finally, when the WTO embarked on a 'democratic' path, that path became self-reinforcing in ways that constrained the organization's legitimation in subsequent crises.

Thus, in sum, the study of legitimation contests in the GATT and the WTO confirms a major argument of our book: the rise of people-based and procedural norms along multiple paths. The continued relevance of people-based and procedural legitimacy standards is maybe best exemplified in the closing remarks of Director General Azevêdo, at the most recent ministerial conference held in Buenos Aires, in December 2017. Against the backdrop of a disappointing conference that failed to make progress in most areas of multilateral trade negotiations, Azevêdo maintained that 'development and inclusiveness must remain at the heart of our work' and challenged that 'if we are not improving the lives of the poorest or giving the smallest a chance to compete, we are not doing our jobs' (WTO 2018).

At the same time, the study of legitimation contests in the GATT and the WTO helps to understand how the GATT and the WTO have come *under pressure* over the past four decades. In a sense, the definition of the organization's core objectives in dynamic terms—namely in terms of liberalization—already entails the possibility that this mission will become a liability once the endpoint of multilateral liberalization has been reached. But our study also shows how a rapidly changing political and economic environment, the increasing ability of diverse social groups to publicly stage their claims, and—closely linked—the emergence of additional legitimation audiences come to require speedy and far-reaching responses from an organization that, with ever more members and decision-making procedures based on consensus, has become more difficult to govern over time. This way, our study also confirms the more general suspicion that, in times when international organizations are needed most to help societies cope with the consequences of economic interdependence, the challenges associated with legitimating these organizations have become greater than ever.

4

Between the Shadow of History and the 'Union of People'

Legitimating the Organisation of African Unity and the African Union

Antonia Witt

INTRODUCTION

On 23 May 2013, the African Union (AU) celebrated its fiftieth anniversary under the theme of 'Pan-Africanism and African Renaissance'. The regular summit meetings of permanent representatives, foreign ministers, and heads of state were framed by a public celebration of the organization's history and achievements, and the event was supposed to be 'memorable, global, people-centric and multi-level' (AU Executive Council 2013: 7). Numerous high-ranking international state officials were invited; many—from John Kerry to François Hollande and Dilma Rousseff—accepted the invitation. The foreign guests praised the AU for its 'legacy of progress' and 'remarkable accomplishments' (Kerry 2013), and for reflecting 'Africa's own aspirations for pan-African institutions and development programmes' (AU 2013). All of them praised the AU's role for representing African voices globally, called for strengthening international cooperation with the AU, and promised financial aid (Kerry 2013; AU 2013; Hollande 2013). In the meantime, however, the hall had largely emptied. The 'people' who had been handed out tickets to attend the celebration had expected more than a chain of endless speeches. To their great disappointment, they were even asked to pay for their own drinks and food. By the time the last speech was delivered, the only remaining attendants were a few journalists and academics including myself, for whom the fiftieth anniversary celebration became a symbol of the contested efforts to legitimate the AU today (see also SABC 2013).

This snapshot epitomizes both new terms and core dilemmas in legitimating the continental organization. It shows on the one hand that people-centred norms as well as those referring to the organization's performance have become crucial terms for legitimating the AU. On the other hand, the event also reflects the changing and increasingly diverse audiences that participate in setting these terms of legitimation. In 1970, the AU's predecessor, the Organisation of African Unity (OAU), was dominated by its member states. Today, the AU's legitimacy is negotiated by both state and non-state actors as well as by international donors and partners. This chapter sets out to reconstruct how these new terms of legitimation emerged, and explains how they raised the pressure on the AU to realize an increasingly pluralist set of expectations.

In particular, we shed light on two changes in the OAU/AU's terms of legitimation that both set in with the beginning of the 1990s. The first is a shift from coordination to delivery by which outcomes and efficiency became increasingly stressed to prove that the OAU/AU was more than a 'talking shop'. Second, the idea that the OAU/AU is a 'people-centred' union gained ground, breaking with the organization's past as a 'Club of Dictators' (AU Commission 2004b: 24; AU Commission 2014: 30). At the level of performance, this meant *inter alia* a shift towards the promotion of democratic governance, election monitoring, and human rights whose purpose was to empower African citizens. At the level of procedures, it introduced the idea of broadening participation in the AU towards the inclusion of non-state actors. With this, the case of the OAU/AU underscores the first key observations made in this book: the rise of both *people-based* and *procedure-based norms* in the legitimation of international organizations.

In marked contrast to the General Agreement on Tariffs and Trade (GATT) and the World Trade Organization (WTO), the major institutional and normative reform projects that transformed the organization since the beginning of the 1990s were not a reaction to external protest or politicization (OAU Secretariat 1990a: 11). Instead, they resulted from changes in the organization's external environment—particularly the end of the Cold War, the rise of 'human security', and the spread of regionalism as a principle of international order—combined with the active contribution of a small set of norm entrepreneurs within the organization's bureaucracy whose leadership was decisive in bringing about the described normative changes. This altogether proves the third argument made in this book: that normative change takes place along multiple paths. However, both norm shifts also had their discontents. And so the AU became increasingly entrapped in its own expansive legitimation. Rather than appeasing critics and sceptics, the expansive claims and promises of a performance-oriented and people-centred organization rendered it even more prone to critique and deception. The AU thus shows that legitimation itself is not a panacea, but can instead be perilous and a source of increased hypocrisy. The unhappy turn of the fiftieth anniversary celebration was but one illustration.

To elaborate these arguments, this chapter is structured as follows: we first sketch out how the challenges of regional integration in Africa changed over time, which provide the background for the legitimation contests we study. We then describe the normative foundations based on which the OAU was traditionally legitimated. In two further sections, we reconstruct the two major norm shifts we observe: the change from 'coordination' to 'delivery' and the rise of the 'people-centred' union. Finally, we examine the pathways along which normative change occurred and discuss the implications of the OAU/AU case for our broader theoretical framework.

THE HISTORICAL CONTEXT OF AFRICAN INTEGRATION

Unlike the other organizations discussed in this book, the OAU/AU does not cover a single policy field, but a broad range of issues related to the integration and prosperity of the African continent. As a continental organization, the OAU/AU's mandate is to foster political, economic, and social integration on the African continent and to represent African voices globally (OAU 1963: art. II(b) and II(c); OAU 2000: art. 3(c) and 3(d)). While the preamble of the OAU Charter of 1963 referred to the 'general progress of Africa' (OAU 1963), to which its signatories committed, the 2000 Constitutive Act of the AU under-lined 'the multifaceted challenges that confront our continent and peoples in the light of the social, economic and political changes taking place in the world' (OAU 2000). Over the years, realizing the organization's goals therefore depended on changing political, economic, and social realities on the African continent, which also directly affected how the organization was perceived. As van Walraven (1996: 381) has summarized for the OAU, it 'assembles all the continent's ambiguities and contradictions, as well as hopes and frustrations of its people' which indeed was a 'heavy moral burden'. This became particularly visible in the early 1990s when economic decline, poverty, and rising numbers of violent conflicts were widely interpreted as signs that the OAU's integration project was a failure. At the same time, this 'heavy moral burden' meant that the organization's actual mandate was amenable and up for negotiation. What exactly counted as relevant to deepen African integration became the core terrain to define both the OAU/AU's overall purpose and its terms of legitimation.

Three developments in particular reflect changes in the organization's environment that rendered the terms and processes of legitimating the AU in 2010 different from those in 1970. First, when the OAU was founded in May 1963, parts of the continent were still under colonial or white minority rule. The eradication of colonialism and minority rule were hence among the OAU's primary purposes as well as a precondition to attain continental integration (OAU 1963: art. II (d)). This changed gradually with the liberation of former Portuguese and French colonies in the early 1970s, the independence of Zimbabwe (1980) and Namibia (1990), as well as the end of apartheid rule in South Africa (1994). With this, one of the primary purposes of the OAU, the eradication of all forms of colonialism from Africa, was attained. Anti-colonialism and the memories of the liberation struggle still play an important role in the politics of the AU (see AU Assembly 2013; Welz 2013). Yet, the gradual decolonization of the continent meant that coordinating and intensifying African states' 'efforts to achieve a better life for the peoples of Africa' (OAU 1963) required *other* means than rallying international and continental support for national liberation movements. What exactly that implied, however, remained open.

Second, the economic and political situation on the continent had changed dramatically over the past forty years and with it also the focus and priorities of the continental integration project. In contrast to the initial euphoria at the eve of independence, from the 1970s onwards the majority of African national economies declined, foreign debt levels increased, and so did food insecurity, inflation, and dependence on foreign aid. The International Monetary Fund (IMF) and the World Bank's answers in the form of structural adjustment programmes in most cases only aggravated the severe socio-economic situation. The economic crisis was coupled with increasing political instability and in some cases the outbreak of violent conflict. In 1990, then OAU Secretary General Salim Ahmed Salim noted that 'the absence of sound and realistic socio-economic policies and poor economic management in addition to an adverse International Economic Environment have converged to hamstring efforts at recovery'. He also stressed that 'the political situation in Africa today is bedevilled by various conflicts that threaten not only human rights and social order but also prospects for the survival, economic development and even the sovereignty of some states' (OAU Secretariat 1990b: 5 and 10).

The beginning of the 1990s thus marked a crucial moment: on the one hand, many African states underwent a phase of political liberalization with the introduction of multiparty elections and the fall of many of the continent's most brutal regimes. By 2010, only Eritrea and Swaziland had not held multiparty elections (Cheeseman 2015: 86). Yet on the other hand, political realities in many African states were increasingly shaped by intra-state armed conflicts (Cilliers and Schünemann 2013: 2). In 2000, the World Bank estimated that 1 billion United States dollars (USD) in Central Africa and 800 million USD in West Africa were annually diverted from 'development uses' as a consequence of violent conflict (World Bank 2000: 59). This novel economic and political landscape did not only alter what counted as priorities for African integration. Rather, the negative trend the continent had taken also heavily affected the overall image of the organization and deepened the perception that the OAU had failed to deliver on its promise (van Walraven 1996: 305–6).

Third, the African integration agenda was not only shaped by continental developments, but also by how the latter related to its outside world. In 1970, OAU member states struggled committing to the OAU Charter's 'affirmation of a policy of non-alignment' (OAU 1963): most of them effectively sided with either of the Cold War rivals. With the end of the Cold War, these alliances broke away. On the one hand, this initially brought a greater sense of insecurity and fears that 'the emergence of a new geo-political balance of forces as well as a new international economic order…could further debilitate and marginalise Africa' (OAU Secretariat 1990b: 22). On the other hand, the global transformations that have taken place since—particularly the increasing relevance attributed to processes of political and economic regionalization—also created new opportunities to adapt the OAU/AU to changing rules and players in the international system. As a result, the OAU/AU gradually broadened its international cooperation. In 2017, the AU was part of nine continental partnerships with other regional organizations or individual donor countries, none of which had been in place prior to the 1990s. The number of officially accredited non-African states and organizations rose from fifty in 2004 to 118 in 2017 (AU Commission 2007: 11; 2018: 185–8). What is more, external partners today fund more than 90 per cent of the AU's annual programme budget, while a division within the AU Commission was established in 2012 to manage the organization's 'strategic partnerships' (AU Commission 2017: 182; 2013: 13).

At the end of our period of investigation, African integration and the need to represent African voices globally were thus by no means less important than in 1970. What that entails exactly, however, remains up for negotiation. Integration tasks have become more complex and comprehensive, ranging from peacekeeping in order to end violence to fostering intra-African trade, from managing migration to promoting women's rights. Moreover, today's regional integration takes place within a much denser international environment. It responds to and is similarly shaped by discourses, norms, and interests outside of the continent that have their own imprint on what kind of integration project gets implemented.

LEGITIMATING THE OAU/AU: THE NORMATIVE BASELINE

The OAU was founded as a weak organization that depended on the norms of an international order, based on the ideals of *state sovereignty* and *non-interference.* Despite its potentially broad mandate, the OAU was not endowed with the structures, resources, and human capital necessary for its fulfilment. This was one of the core dilemmas that shaped the relationship between the organization and its members, and which therefore set the (restricted) terms for legitimating and realizing the African integration project (see generally Naldi 1989; van Walraven 1996). The highest decision-making organ was the Assembly of Heads of State and Government, whose ordinary sessions were held once a year. The Secretariat in Addis Ababa, headed by an Administrative Secretary General, was small, constantly underfinanced, and understaffed (OAU Secretariat 1974b: 6; 2000: 88). Its mandate was to encourage cooperation, supervise implementation, but not to initiate policies (see van Walraven 1996: 169; Wolfers 1984: 89). In 1979, the 'administrative' was dropped from the chief bureaucrat's job description, but a lack of financial means and human capacities continued to delimit the actual powers of the Secretariat (OAU Secretariat 1982: 2; 1994b: 9).

In line with the principles of continental *solidarity* and *unity*, decision making was usually based on consensus. Even if diverging interests among OAU member states had shaped the organization from its first day onwards, concealing such conflicts from the broader public remained an important aspect of the organization's internal culture (van Walraven 1996: 367). As a consequence, OAU meetings were neither recorded nor open to participants other than member state representatives. Policy making and implementation remained the purview of states, their diplomats, and national bureaucracies. This gave the organization a taste of secrecy and exclusiveness that contradicted the charter's appeals to solidarity and to the well-being and 'legitimate aspirations of the African peoples' (OAU 1963).

Legitimating the OAU therefore required addressing the tension that emanated from the organization's exclusive dependence on its member states on the one hand and the latter's often ambiguous commitment to the principles and purposes defined in the OAU Charter on the other hand (see OAU Secretariat 1970b: 21; see also OAU Secretariat 1970a; Amate 1986: 170). In 1970, a typical legitimation statement would therefore refer to the service the OAU rendered to member states in supporting coordination and integration in a few selected policy fields. This often required portraying a particular issue area as an integration problem: from the promotion of intra-African trade to the protection of natural resources and the cultivation of African languages. It also implied convincing member states that coordination was actually in their interest (OAU Secretariat 1974a: 19; 1978: 21; 1982: 40). In 1970, *solidarity* and *unity* were hence seen as the result of deepened cooperation between member states, which would ultimately lead to the 'general progress of Africa', as promised in the charter (OAU 1963). The role of the OAU was thus mainly that of a platform or forum.

In the same vein, the representation of member states' voices globally—for instance in negotiations with the European Economic Community, the UN Conference on Trade and Development, the United Nations Development Programme, and the WTO—was a service offered by the OAU as forum (OAU Secretariat 1974a: 5; 1974b: 23; 1998: 41). The organization of numerous ministerial conferences and workshops was said to 'help formulating general guidelines for arriving at a common African position' (OAU Secretariat 1974b: 27) while in the face of the European Union (EU)'s regional partnerships on economic cooperation, the OAU Secretariat for instance 'monitored closely the evolution of events in order to guard against... disruptive trends that could jeopardize Africa's interests' (OAU Secretariat 2000: 75). Here, too, member states often had to be reminded that coordinating their voices in global affairs is actually to their benefit (OAU Secretariat 1974b: 27; 1990a: 19; 1998: 37).

In both cases, however, it was not the organization's special knowledge, expertise, or capacities that justified its mandate to integrate Africa. Rather, continental integration was treated as an almost self-evident goal for 'Africa' and the OAU as its similarly self-evident embodiment (OAU Secretariat 1970b: 24).

In short, at the beginning of our period of investigation, legitimating the OAU was directed towards states, and appealed to the organization's service providing both *coordination* and *representation* in global affairs. *Solidarity, unity,* and *justice* were important normative references, but they were appeals to the organization's overall 'personality' rather than to norms defining the OAU's actual performance or procedures.

By 2010, the organization's structure and its terms of legitimation changed dramatically compared to the 1970s. In 2002, the OAU was transformed into a new organization which was given a more comprehensive mandate and a more powerful administrative arm, and its founding norms transgressed the previous focus on state sovereignty and territorial integrity.

Today, the AU's mandate ranges from the protection and promotion of human rights and democracy to gender equality, sustainable development, and the prevention of conflict within its member states. The AU has also been authorized to sanction member states by intervening in cases of genocide, war crimes, crimes against humanity, unconstitutional changes of government, or if members fail to comply with their financial obligations or decisions and policies of the union (OAU 2000: articles 4(h), 23 and 30).

In line with this normative adjustment, the establishment of the AU also came with a number of institutional innovations. The Pan-African Parliament (PAP), composed of 235 members of forty-seven national parliaments, was inaugurated in 2004. Moreover, the Economic, Social, and Cultural Council (ECOSOCC), which comprises 150 representatives of social and professional groups, non-governmental, cultural, and diaspora organizations, was set up as an advisory body to the AU Assembly. With the African Court of Justice, the AU also introduced a supra-national judicial organ (AU Assembly 2008). And finally, with the establishment of a fifteen-member Peace and Security Council (PSC) as the central decision-making organ in the area of peace and security, the AU abandoned the hitherto central procedural norm of consensual and inclusive decision making (AU 2002a). Thus, while the AU remained an intergovernmental organization, the normative and institutional changes already suggest that the organization's former state-centric focus on sovereignty and the principle of equality were slowly shifting (van Walraven 1996: 380).

Finally, there has also been a gradual redefinition of the structure, mandate, and powers of the organization's bureaucracy. This can be seen in an increase in the approved budget from 6 million USD in 1974 to 31 million USD in 2002 and 140 million USD in 2008, reaching its hitherto highest point with an approved budget of 782 million USD in 2017. The budget increase is also paralleled by an, albeit more moderate, rise in the organization's staff structure (from 247 in 1970 to 715 permanent staff in 2017) as well as an enlargement of the bureaucracy's departmental portfolios from four to eight (see AU Commission 2018: 84).[1] These structural changes were accompanied by an official redefinition of the role of the organization's bureaucracy. While the OAU Secretariat was mandated to merely coordinate and supervise policies, the AU Commission's mandate includes initiating policies, implementing, coordinating, and monitoring decisions, resource mobilization, as well as the proactive promotion of AU policies in the areas of peace and security, democracy, and socio-economic development (AU 2002b: art. 3; Engel 2013).

In 2004, the AU Commission presented its Strategic Plan for the years 2004–7 and coined a new vision for the continental organization: to 'build an integrated, prosperous and peaceful Africa, an Africa driven by its own citizens and representing a dynamic force in the international arena' (AU Commission 2004b: 26). The terms of African integration thus largely stayed the same, but were expanded and translated into a new institutional, norma-tive, and world political context. Facilitating coordination among African states as well as representing African voices globally remained important legitimation principles (AU Commission 2004a: 68; 2006: 50; 2008a: 143; 2010: ii). However, in 2010, the 'African people' had become a new point of reference for justifying both what the AU does and how it operates. Moreover, the fact that it was the AU Commission—rather than member states—who formulated a strategic plan for the entire organization underlined a major shift with regard to who sets the terms for legitimating the AU. And finally, that the

---

[1] Together with short-term employees, the AU Commission in 2017 had a staff structure of 1,688 (AU Commission 2018: 84). This is nevertheless a small number compared to 32,546 employees the EU Commission count in 2017 (http://ec.europa.eu/civil_service/docs/hr_key_figures_en.pdf, last accessed 13 April 2018).

Commission in fact worked according to a strategic plan was an innovation in itself that pointed to new standards set for how to assess good performance. As formulated by the drafters themselves, the strategic plan was meant to introduce 'a paradigm shift in the way that the Union conducts its business' (AU Commission 2004a: ii). With regard to our bubbles model explained in Chapter 2, this means that while the existing bubbles remained in place, both their colour (= meaning) and size (= relevance) changed over time as new speech bubbles were gradually added. The following two sections reconstruct how exactly this change came about and explore the contestation and dilemmas this generated.

AFTER THE 'TALKING SHOP': FROM COORDINATION TO DELIVERY

From the early 1990s onwards, the OAU was increasingly pressured to prove that it was more than a 'talking shop' (Nujoma 2002) or a 'nominal organization', as Eritrea's president Isayas Afewerki had put it in 1992 (Legum 2000: A33; see generally AllAfrica 2002; *East African* 2002; van Walraven 1996: 305).

In 1990, OAU Secretary General Salim Ahmed Salim noted 'enthusiastic support' for the idea that 'Africa should re-size the initiative and play a central role in finding realistic solutions to African problems', which also implied putting the 'OAU at the center and in the service of the continent' (OAU Secretariat 1990a: 11–12). He had noted that 'our credibility and legitimacy have come as a result of the seriousness with which we have approached the affairs of our continental organisation' (quoted in Lulie and Cilliers 2016: 83). As a result, proving outcomes was decisive to maintain that legitimacy.

Initially, this shift implied that apart from stressing the OAU's coordinating functions, it became crucial to underline the difference these efforts made. Implementation thus became a key demand, for instance with regard to children's rights (OAU Secretariat 1990a: 21), women's empowerment (OAU Secretariat 1994b: 81), the OAU's role in facilitating peace processes (OAU Secretariat 1998: 11), and land and resource management (AU Commission 2006: 89). With the transformation of the OAU into the AU and the latter's expanded mandate, this trend intensified further. Rather than merely enlisting coordination activities and demanding its member states to implement them, the AU today is held to show its *own* proactive contribution to the continental integration project and presents itself as a results-oriented organization (AU Commission 2010: 134; 2004c: 8). As we will discuss further below, and in line with this, new norms of public management, project planning, and budgeting also became important in order to show that the AU was more than the 'talking shop' it once succeeded (AU Commission 2008a: 109; 2010: 119). This shift towards a proactive organization is most evident in the field of peace and security (see also Lotze 2013).

The Rise of Peace and (Human) Security

Peace has always been an important normative reference in the self-portrayals of both the OAU and the AU. Yet, in line with the OAU Charter this was initially confined to resolving disputes *between* states (OAU 1963: article III (4)). The OAU's neglect of *intra-state* conflicts and large-scale human rights violations within its own member states meant that the organization's overall sincerity became heavily questioned. As an African journalist observed in 1980 (quoted in Červenka and Legum 1981b: 65; see also Mustapha 1980: 20):

> When threatened with internal political revolt, no matter how justified, our leaders look to the OAU for protection. Yet, when it suits them they conveniently ignore the authority of that organization. The practical political implications of this sad anomaly is that it jeopardizes the human rights of the ordinary citizen in many an African state while the OAU remains an impotent spectator.

This critique pointed to the hypocrisy with which the OAU's principles were applied, notably that by ignoring human rights violations and violence against civilians in its member states, the OAU has largely served to protect incumbent governments (Williams 2007: 266; van Walraven 1996: 305). Beginning in the late 1970s, a few African leaders and bureaucrats from the OAU Secretariat more openly called for changing the OAU's policy of non-interference (see Novicki 1983; Červenka and Legum 1981a; Okoth 1987). Tanzania's president Julius Nyerere and later on also Nigeria's president Olusegun Obasanjo repeatedly demanded a new charter for the OAU, which would address human rights abuses and injustices committed by Africans themselves (Červenka and Legum 1980: 38). However, this critique did little to change the overall image of an organization that failed to protect its own people from massive violence and human rights violations (van Walraven 1996: 308).

This situation changed from the 1990s onwards when, in line with their general rise in number and destructiveness, internal conflicts increasingly became a concern for the OAU. In 1990, Secretary General Salim Ahmed Salim reported that he 'intends to take more seriously and enhance OAU's role as active partner in efforts to resolve inter-African disputes'. This followed the rationale that the OAU 'cannot be indifferent to the internal conflicts that spread death and sorrow and ruin member states and sway them away from their efforts to foster their socio-economic development' (OAU Secretariat 1990a: 7 and 12). Increased efforts to create a peaceful continent thus included two things: a general rethinking by which peace and security came to be seen as the preconditions for economic development and integration, as well as a necessary enlargement of the organization's legal, financial, and other capacities to pursue this newly entrusted role.

In 1993 the OAU Mechanism for Conflict Prevention, Management, and Resolution was set up, whose Central Organ was mandated to monitor conflict situations on the continent. This normative impetus was supported by a new generation of African leaders including Yoweri Museveni of Uganda, Isayas Afewerki of Eritrea, and Meles Zenawi of Ethiopia, whose governments, originating from armed opposition movements, had themselves fallen victim to the OAU's silence on the internal situations in member states (see also Kioko 2003: 813). For them, supporting a normative shift within the OAU also meant ex-post legitimating their own, often violent struggle against their predecessors. In light of these reform efforts, African member states also used the UN General Assembly as a forum to stress the OAU's positive achievements in peacemaking. They hence increasingly evaluated the OAU in terms of what the organization delivered.[2] In 1993, the delegation of Zimbabwe, for instance, summarized (UN General Assembly 1993b: 18):

> The OAU has initiated peacemaking efforts and has complemented the efforts of the United Nations—most notably, in recent times, in South Africa, Somalia and Rwanda. The OAU has undertaken peace missions in the Congo, Angola, Liberia and Burundi. It is our hope that, with further concerted cooperation between the United Nations and the OAU, these conflicts will be speedily resolved.

However, as the report of the International Panel of Eminent Personalities (IPEP), which assessed the OAU's role in the Rwandan genocide, frankly reflected, a genuine shift in focus was facing serious obstacles. The panel particularly criticized the ambivalence in member states' commitment, the large dependence on external military and financial support, as well as insufficient instruments and overall limited financial resources allocated to the OAU's peacemaking role (Masire et al. 2000: chapter 21). In section III: C. 22 of its report, the panel recommended that,

> Since Africa recognizes its own primary responsibility to protect the lives of its citizens, we call on: a) the OAU to establish appropriate structures to enable it to respond effectively to enforce the peace in conflict situations; and b) the international community to assist such endeavours by the OAU through financial, logistic, and capacity support.

---

[2] In contrast to the 1980s, OAU member states pointed positively to intra-OAU developments such as the OAU Mechanism (see for instance UN General Assembly 1994a: 10, 13–14; 1995: 16). However, it is noteworthy that many described the role of the OAU as *complementary* to that of the UN and underlined the UN Security Council's *primary* responsibility (see for instance UN General Assembly 1993a: 17; 1997a: 12; 1998: 6; 2004b: 16).

Many of the panel's concrete recommendations became reflected in the so-called African Peace and Security Architecture and the normative and institutional transformations that accompanied the establishment of the AU (Engel and Gomes Porto 2010; 2013). The resulting explosion in AU's peace and security activities—today ranging from peacekeeping to preventive diplomacy, early warning, mediation, and post-conflict reconstruction (IPSS 2017)—meant that peace and security matters arose to the organization's central concern and a crucial resource for its legitimation (Lotze 2013). In AU member states' statements about OAU/AU–UN cooperation at the UN General Assembly, the PSC has been the single most mentioned AU institution. It was praised for tackling issues of peace and security 'systematically' (UN General Assembly 2006: 6); for working in a 'more focused' and 'proactive' manner (UN General Assembly 2004a: 21); and for being a 'useful tool to increase cooperation between the United Nations and the African Union' (UN General Assembly 2004c: 7). Moreover, the largest chapters of the Commission's reports to the Assembly as well as the Commission's staff structure reflect that proving outcomes in this policy field is of high relevance to the AU.[3] Finally, peace and security challenges on the continent usually dominate summit debates and thereby also divert attention from the summit's respectively official thematic focus.

As indicated in the assessments of the IPEP, the rise of the peacemaking role of the OAU/AU was inextricably linked to a changing international context. Because the UN as well as the former colonial powers became increasingly reluctant to intervene in support of peace and security on the African continent, 'African ownership' and 'responsibility' became convenient external narratives (UN General Assembly 1992: 63–5; Franke and Esmenjaud 2008). In the UN General Assembly, the change in the organization's image and mandate therefore also enjoyed acclamation from non-African actors—such as the EU or Japan—who applauded the OAU's role in peacemaking activities and offered financial and technical support (UN General Assembly 1996: 3; 1997a: 14; 1999a: 4).

African states, in contrast, also used the opportunity to call for international financial assistance to enable the OAU/AU to realize its newly enlarged functions (UN General Assembly 1994a: 14). Despite invoking the rhetoric of African 'ownership', for them African responsibility also implied financial responsibility of international partners. Tunisia, for example, declared in 2006 (UN General Assembly 2006: 7), 'The African Union, which has proven its effectiveness when it has received support, does not have sufficient resources to confront all situations. Hence the needs for the United Nations and the international community to further enhance its support.' Thus, from the very

---

[3] Interview, AU staff, 19 May 2013, Addis Ababa.

beginning, proving the AU's proactive contribution to a peaceful continent was also a means to promote the organization to an *external* audience. This external audience was not only important in order to pressure OAU/AU member states to equally support the organization's enlarged peacemaking activities. Rather, external actors themselves became an active part of this development by financing much of it (see also Lotze 2013: 123).

...and Its Critics

The various ways to prove that the OAU/AU was more than a 'talking shop' did not evolve without contestation. Two lines of critique can be identified. Firstly, by stressing more proactive policies, outcomes, and effectiveness in various issue areas, the AU was soon exposed to the critique of *not delivering what it had promised*. This is particularly the case in the field of peace and security, where enduring conflicts, increasing levels of violence, human rights violations, the failure to implement a rigorous African criminal justice system, as well as negative consequences of AU peacemaking efforts themselves exposed the AU to the critique of not doing enough (CCP-AU 2008b: 4; OSIEA 2008; Various 2010; HRW 2010).

Secondly, and more fundamentally, the hitherto set *priorities were questioned*. For instance, there has been a repeated, yet still marginal critique that the organization's predominant focus on issues of peace and security sidelines the continent's demand for (socio)-economic development. In 2009 Tanzania's President Kikwete (2009) argued that,

> Unfortunately, we use a lot time in conflict resolution and for political issues especially power sharing among politicians or for some of us to give ourselves more powers or more popularity. I appeal to my colleagues to change. Let us define well our priorities and give prominence to issues pertaining to economic development.

Other member states similarly pointed out that violent conflicts in fact only concern the minority of OAU/AU member states (UN General Assembly 1996: 5–6; 1997a: 12). The almost exclusive focus on peace and security thus also threatens the idea that they are all equals in shaping the priorities for continental integration. Others—mainly civil society actors—criticized that the dominant, often short-term focus on peace and security hinders addressing the real conditions for long-term and sustainable peace. They argued that it neglected addressing the just distribution of resources, the reduction of relative deprivations (for instance Various 2010), or of Africa's marginalized position in the global economy more generally (Shivji 2007). These critical voices underline that apart from being merely a question of priorities, what is at stake is the conflictive readings of how transformative the African integration project ought to be, and how socio-economic and broader global conditions either facilitate or hinder attaining the AU's promise of an 'integrated prosperous and peaceful' Africa (AU Commission 2004b: 26).

The Promise of Better Management and Efficiency

The OAU/AU's increasing focus on outcomes also forced the organization to pay more attention to procedural efficiency, sound project management, and financial accountability. Since the 1970s, a recurring theme in the Secretary General's reports had been improving the Secretariat's internal structures, financial endowment as well as human resources (OAU Secretariat 1970b: 10; 1974b: 3–4). According to the Secretariat, the OAU should be the home of an 'administrative elite in the technical, professional, and moral sphere— hence an Administration of which Africa could be justly proud' which provided 'the best guarantee for the rapid and effective implementation of [OAU] decisions' (OAU Secretariat 1970b: 12). Yet, despite repeated calls, the 'Administration of which Africa could be justly proud' never materialized. With the transformation of the OAU into the AU there was consequently a much greater need to 'demonstrate towards all its constituencies that the AU is a different type of institution than the OAU' (AU Commission 2004c: 16; 2010: 119–23; see also OAU Secretariat 1998: 55–9).

'Institutional transformation' was therefore the first out of three priority areas in the first Strategic Plan of the AU Commission. Among others, it entailed the reorganization of the commission's structures, the enhancement of human resources and the general work environment at AU headquarters, as well as the introduction of a results-based and outcome-oriented management culture, geared to promote 'responsibility, team spirit, devotion to the ideal of African integration, performance, and integrity' (AU Commission 2004c: 20). Thus, a plethora of tools and initiatives in the realm of strategic planning and budgeting, evaluation and monitoring, staff performance and productivity, and 'continuous improvement' were employed to turn the AU into a 'learning' (OAU Secretariat 2002a: 135), 'modern, efficient, transparent, and accountability-driven' (AU Commission 2010: i), as well as 'focused and disciplined' organization (AU Commission 2004a: 1; 2011).

Two factors supported this rise of new management norms. Firstly, in 2007, a comprehensive audit of the AU had dedicated a major share of its recommendations to the AU Commission in order to tackle the 'institutional incoherence and disarray' it had found (Adedeji et al. 2007: 189). The commission thus used this impetus as official confirmation of the need to structurally strengthen its own role (see AU Commission 2008b; 2010: 9). Secondly, institutional transformation was also in the interests of major AU donors for whom a more efficient, effective, and transparent AU Commission became a key precondition to turn the AU into the 'strategic partner' they were seeking. On the one hand, this support resulted in a series of externally funded capacity-building projects by the AU's major donors (see for instance Laporte and Mackie 2010; UNECA 2014). On the other hand, external capacity building itself increased the demand for effectiveness and transparency. The commission thus justified the need for better management, transparency, and accountability with demands from the AU's international donors (AU Commission 2008a: i–ii; 2010: i; see also OAU Secretariat 1990a: 6). In this sense, the AU chairperson Jean Ping concluded in 2008 that (AU Commission 2008a: 109), 'administrative and financial management systems reforms [*sic*] under the auspices of the Institutional Transformation Project have played a great role in enhancing the credibility of the Commission and it is expected that this will result in increased resource inflows for the AU's priority programmes.' Thus, in sum, the OAU/AU's turn away from the 'talking shop' did not simply introduce a greater focus on outcomes and implementation of regional policies. It also shifted attention towards the concrete procedures—referring to managerial capacities, institutional cultures, and rationalities—by which this change was supposed to materialize.

Summary and Outlook

Since the beginning of the 1990s, the OAU/AU gradually moved away from the initial focus on facilitating interstate cooperation and its role as a forum for heads of state and government. Instead, proving outcomes and effectiveness in its contributions to African integration took centre stage. This also required the organization itself to become more proactive in both policy formulation and implementation and to expand its thematic portfolio. We demonstrated this by zooming into the policy field of peace and security which is today still the most important area of AU engagement (see also Lotze 2013).

This normative broadening, however, also faced clear challenges and in several regards itself increased the need for *more* legitimation on the side of the OAU/AU. First, the sheer limitless wish list of themes and issues relevant for establishing an 'integrated, prosperous and peaceful' Africa (AU Commission 2004b: 26) meant that the organization soon confronted the critique of not doing enough, choosing wrong priorities, or following erroneous strategies. Second, the more general challenges that had, thus far, hindered a more proactive and efficient continental integration became even more visible: in particular the lack of commitment among member states when it came to financing the OAU/AU and implementing its policies (OAU Secretariat 2002a: 2; AU Commission 2006: 17). In 2008, AU chairperson Jean Ping therefore noted that (AU Commission 2008a: 1; see also 2010: 134),

It is thus necessary that, beyond adopting scores of often bold and far-reaching decisions that touch all areas of the continent's life, the Commission should be strengthened in terms of providing it with the financial and human resources to carry out its policies and that a reliable follow-up mechanism be established at the level of all stakeholders, especially to ensure greater involvement by each Member State, so as to ensure that these decisions are effectively implemented, before further decisions are adopted along similar lines. This is a crucial issue of credibility for the Union, the entire body of Member States and for the organs of the Union, including the Commission.

That the AU's credibility depends on the seriousness with which its decisions are actually implemented had also been a concern for the organization's international donors who increasingly demanded sound project and financial management as well as more rationalized organizational structures. The rise and growing importance of such procedural norms thus once again underlined that merely claiming to leave the 'talking shop' behind was not enough. In fact, it required a much more profound and difficult institutional transformation and hence the introduction of yet new terms of legitimation.

Even after 2010, the described turn towards concrete outcomes and sound management of continental policies remained both key to the legitimation of the AU and heavily contested. In fact, realizing the envisaged institutional transformation towards an organization that delivers is as relevant today as it is at the end of our period of investigation (AU Commission 2013: i; 2015: 63; 2016: 88–90 and 100; see also ICG 2018). In 2016, Rwanda's president Paul Kagame was mandated by the AU Summit to launch an institutional reform debate with the aim 'to put in place a system of governance capable of addressing the challenges facing the Union' (AU Assembly 2016a). Kagame's (2017: 2–3) first frank report diagnosed that, 'Africa today is ill-prepared to adequately respond to current events, because the African Union still has to be made fit for purpose... Without an African Union that delivers, the continent cannot progress, and we face the likelihood of yet another decade of lost opportunity.' More concretely, he noted that 'The Assembly has adopted more than 1,500 resolutions. Yet there is no easy way to determine how many of those have actually been implemented.' In short, 'we have a dysfunctional organisation in which member states see limited value, global partners find little credibility, and our citizens have no trust' (Kagame 2017: 5). As a consequence, Kagame proposed reforms in four main areas: to limit the organization's operational focus to a few policy areas only, to realign its diverse institutions, to improve managerial capacities at the level of the AU Commission and member states, and to finance the AU sustainably and with greater independence from external donors. This latter aspect has been on the AU's agenda for quite some time: acquiring financial 'self-sufficiency' is seen as a key principle and precondition today for turning the AU into an effective and delivering organization (AU Commission 2015: 47; 2016: 77;

AU Assembly 2016b). Yet, despite far-reaching reform proposals in this area as well, the unreliable financial commitment of member states to the organization remains a key obstacle to effective continental integration (AU Commission 2015: 5; 2016: 77 and 88). Thus, while effective implementation of these reforms remains an issue for the future, the ongoing debate on institutional and financial reform underscores that the ideal of an efficient and effective continental organization, that works for bettering the lives of Africans, still serves as an important legitimation principle. Thus, the organization's described turn towards delivering concrete outcomes and showing effectiveness remains both highly relevant and unattained.

BEYOND THE 'CLUB OF DICTATORS': THE RISE OF THE 'PEOPLE-CENTRED UNION'

Even though the 1963 OAU Charter referred to the 'wellbeing of the African peoples', the OAU was soon decried as a club of presidents whose interests and decisions ignored the actual living realities of Africans (van Walraven 1996: 305–6). Against this background, a normative shift set in at the beginning of the 1990s with which the OAU, and later the AU, sought to become a more 'people-centred' organization. This took place along two lines: firstly, with regard to the beneficiaries of the OAU/AU's *policies*; secondly, with regard to the organization's own *procedures*.

Like in the GATT/WTO case, it is nevertheless important to underline that people-based norms did already figure among the OAU's main terms of legitimation before the 1990s. Yet they were confined to justifying the OAU's support for the liberation of Africans under colonial rule (OAU Secretariat 1974b: 10; 1978: 5).[4] In the early 1990s, the meaning of empowerment and self-determination changed once Africans were no longer under formal colonial rule.

Promoting Participation and Inclusive Governance through the OAU/AU

With the early 1980s and the spread of the idea of 'participation in development', the meaning of empowerment was gradually broadened beyond its initial link to self-determination from colonial rule (OAU 1980; 1990). With

---

[4] The strict focus on only recognizing the right to self-determination of those people under colonial or minority rule has, however, also been an early source for critique, for instance from armed liberation movements (see van Walraven 1996: 303).

this, the internal governance of OAU member states also came into the organization's focus. From the 1990s onwards, democratization was said to be a necessary precondition for reversing the economic decline that most African states had started to face since the late 1970s. It was also said to provide the ingredients for a peaceful continent in light of the growing number of armed conflicts (Salim 1998: 250). In this sense, the OAU's mandate to 'achieve a better life for the peoples of Africa' was interpreted as also involving the promotion of democratic governance in its member states. Secretary General Salim Ahmed Salim, for instance, repeatedly reminded member states that (OAU Secretariat 1994a: 9–10),

> our countries also ought to move equally with greater determination in dealing with issues of political governance... The overriding objective must be to ensure that people are placed at the centre of any national endeavour. To do so most effectively, we need to pursue with vigour, politics of inclusion in which every segment of society is permitted and enabled to participate... Likewise, we should sustain the process of further democratization which is now underway with many democratic multiparty elections which have been held in the Continent.

With this call, good governance, human rights, and the promotion of inclusive politics became an increasingly important issue on the organization's agenda. In this sense, the OAU/AU gradually developed norms and policy scripts *inter alia* in the areas of election observation, human rights, the banning of coups d'état, and anti-corruption. The AU Constitutive Act explicitly mandated the organization to 'promote democratic principles and institutions, popular participation, and good governance' (OAU 2000: art 3(g), art. 4 (m)). Likewise, it was decided that 'governments which shall come to power through unconstitutional means shall not be allowed to participate in the activities of the Union' (OAU 2000: art. 30). In 2002, the *AU Declaration on the Principles Governing Democratic Elections in Africa* was adopted, which set continental standards for the organization and monitoring of electoral processes. In 2007, the *African Charter on Democracy, Elections, and Governance* combined all hitherto made declarations in the area of governance into a legally binding document.

The growing attention paid to the governance of its member states also altered the relationship between the latter and the organization as a whole. While in 1994, the Secretariat offered 'to be of better service to the Member States' (OAU Secretariat 1994a: 10), OAU Secretary General Amara Essy (OAU Secretariat 2002a: 83) in 2002 demanded that in turn, 'the OAU/ African Union should get more involved in concrete actions to backstop the democratic and electoral process thereby guaranteeing the credibility and transparency of elections in keeping with the criteria and standards mutually acceptable by our societies.' Thus, although the majority of OAU member states had signed and ratified the Constitutive Act within a rather short time, agreement on paper did not necessarily mean normative conviction (Witt 2013). Reverses in democratic achievements, coups d'état, and contested elections continued to mark the AU's agenda, and the AU was increasingly forced to implement its more intrusive mandate based on only reluctant support, and sometimes even open resistance, from member states. Yet for Jean Ping, the AU Commission nevertheless 'plays and will continue to play its rightful role in the promotion of democracy and democratic elections in the Continent' (AU Commission 2006: 54).

An additional indication of reluctant support by member states for this normative shift is that in their speeches at the UN General Assembly, only a few of them actively praised the organization's mandate and achievements in promoting democracy (see for instance UN General Assembly 1994a: 17; 2002: 25). And even if so, they describe democratization as a state-led process. For Togo, for instance, the UN and AU's democracy-promotion efforts represented 'a useful support to the efforts made in this area by African States . . . [and] part of the efforts undertaken by African countries themselves in setting up stable and representative Governments' (UN General Assembly 2000a: 11).

In contrast to member states, the OAU's international partners as well as civil society organizations (CSOs) actively applauded these new legitimation principles. Since the early 1990s, the EU for instance repeatedly reminded the UN General Assembly that the OAU 'has an influential role—and indeed a responsibility—to foster and support' a debate on democracy and how to make it 'more directly relevant to the people themselves' (UN General Assembly 1996: 3; see also 1997a: 10). In a similar vein, external guests to AU summits often positively stressed African states' latest initiatives in democratization and good governance, and offered more support. At the same time, democratization together with development and peace were also those areas in which AU's partners—especially the UN, IMF, and the UN Economic Commission for Africa—demanded more from the organization for the future (see for example Annan 2001; Köhler 2003).

Promoting Participation and Inclusion in the OAU/AU

Since the beginning of the 1990s, participation in the organization's own structures increasingly became a matter of concern for the OAU. As with the democratization agenda in general, this process was initially driven by the OAU Secretariat. In 1994, Salim Ahmed Salim reiterated in his report that (OAU Secretariat 1994a: 9),

> Ultimately, the people of Africa will find the Community relevant, only if they are involved and made to have a stake in it. This is why I believe that in the days

ahead, our countries should move more resolutely, both in broadening the areas of cooperation between them and in sensitizing the people of Africa on the African Economic Community. Taking the Community to the people of this Continent, and placing them at the centre of its development must now be the primary objective and the theme of the future.

As reflected in this quote, from the very beginning, 'taking the Community to the people' was framed as a self-evident consequence of the organization's integration agenda. Rather than an intrinsic value, this 'partnership' with the people was described as a functional necessity, because the envisaged integration requires other partners than only member states (see also OAU Secretariat 1994b: 37; 1998: 40). In 2000, Salim Ahmed Salim for instance justified the 'working relations with African Non-Governmental Organizations', the Secretariat was about to foster, by appealing to (OAU Secretariat 2000: 60),

the growing realization and acceptance within the Continent that the African Civil Society has a special role and should be developed and strengthened to enable it to supplement the efforts of the governments and inter-governmental organizations, in the pursuit of the African Agenda for Peace, Democracy and Development.

As a result, the promotion of participation and inclusive OAU/AU institutions meant two things at the same time. On the one hand, it referred to a greater concern for 'popularizing' the OAU/AU and 'sensitizing' African citizens about continental policies, hence making them aware of the continental organization and its integration agenda (OAU Secretariat 2002a: 5). On the other hand, it meant that the OAU/AU itself should become more responsive to citizens' demands, actively listen to their concerns, and include them—where possible—in policy planning and implementation (OAU Secretariat 2002b: 37).

Initially, the OAU's novel attention to participation and inclusion led to numerous ad hoc ways in which CSOs, women, youth, and the private sector were sought to be integrated into OAU policy making and implementation (Murithi 2005: 115–18; OAU Secretariat 2002b: 37). After the transformation into the AU and its principle of 'participation of the African peoples in the activities of the Union' (OAU 2000: art. 4(c)), more formalized structures for non-state participation were set up. Apart from the PAP and the ECOSOCC, the so-called African Citizens' Directorate (CIDO) was created within the AU Commission, mandated to establish a permanent entry point for civil society and diaspora groups to participate in the institutions of the AU (AU Commission 2004a: 29).

That, as mentioned above, even the Secretariat officially promoted a rather functional understanding of participation and inclusive governance suggests that once again not all members wholeheartedly supported this agenda. While member states only rarely mentioned the AU's participatory institutions in their speeches at the UN General Assembly or AU summits (for an exception see UN General Assembly 2004b: 22; Dlamini-Zuma 2003), consecutive heads of the organization's bureaucracy specifically welcomed the institutional developments and stressed that they represented a normative shift for the organization (Essy 2002a; 2002b). In practice, over the past years, debates on the reform of the PAP, its transformation into an effective legislative arm, the inclusion of CSOs in meetings of the PSC, or the composition of ECOSOCC have repeatedly been delayed, complicated, or dismissed for interfering too much into politically delicate territory.[5] In addition, even though the Secretariat's reports were clear in their call for a more inclusive and participatory organization, situations in which the organization already cooperated with CSOs are rarely specifically highlighted as such. Rather, CSOs are usually mentioned as one among several 'partners' or 'stakeholders' (see for instance AU Commission 2009: 12; 2010: 72). Thus, despite the aim of a 'people-friendly' and 'people-oriented' AU (AU Commission 2006: 95), where non-state actors already have access and voice, they are portrayed as not threatening member states' *primary* powers over the OAU/AU's policy-making and implementation process.

Over time, the initially programmatic statements generally vanished and altogether gave way to more pragmatic descriptions of consultations with civil society actors (AU Commission 2008a: 10–33; 2010: 7). In this sense, even the AU Commission's portrayals of the 'people-centred Union' today seem to describe an almost natural fait accompli rather than a programmatic call for reforming and ameliorating the organization's structures and procedures (AU Commission 2010: 69).

...and Its Critics

Like the narrative of an OAU/AU that 'delivers' rather than 'coordinates', the narrative of the 'people-centred Union' was contested, too. Contestation revolved around both the *policies* to which the narrative gave rise, and the *procedures* it envisaged.

In terms of *policies*, many non-governmental organizations (NGOs) applauded the AU's pro-democracy agenda yet also demanded more tangible effects. Moreover, they also promoted a different *meaning* of democracy. Contrary to the external partners' recurring but vague references to 'democracy' and 'good governance', newspaper articles and documents from CSOs often refer to a more rights-based approach to democracy. Here, democracy is

---

[5] Interview, member African NGO, 14 May 2013, Addis Ababa; interview, member African NGO, 22 May 2013, Addis Ababa.

substantially defined as an individual right of citizens to vote and to choose their own government. In addition, it guaranteed basic political freedoms, protection against abuses of power and state violence, the fight against impunity, access to information, fairness of political competition and electoral campaigns, as well as prosecution of acts of corruption.

In these portrayals, the AU epitomizes the hope of a potential ally—even a saviour—in the struggles against violations of fundamental rights and democratic standards (see Fahamu 2008: 60; *Reporter* 2007; Various 2007). CSOs, for instance, frequently demand stricter and more consequential monitoring mechanisms at the continental level and the unconditional implementation of the *African Charter on Democracy, Elections, and Governance* (AU Monitor 2010; GIMPA 2007: 5; State of the Union Project 2010: 2); they ask for more forceful AU policies against perpetrators of coups and incumbent presidents who seek to prolong their terms in office (CCP-AU 2009: 3; *East African* 2002); and they call for more powers for the AU's judicial arms (see for instance GIMPA 2007). Some also demand that membership should be earned by adherence to democratic norms, regular elections, and a general commitment to economic development, instead of being automatically granted on geographical terms (see *Daily News* 2002; Githongo and Gumede 2008).

The promise of more people-centred *procedures*, too, soon came under critique. Although demands for 'a continental architecture...rooted in peoples' popular participation' (Fahamu 2008: 60) abound, the AU's character as a 'people-centred' organization is still seen as mainly cosmetic in nature and insufficient to render the AU truly receptive towards the will of ordinary African citizens. Overall, critics formulate five major challenges.

Their most overt point of critique is that, despite officially setting up participatory institutions, member states had constrained their actual mandates, functions as well as financial and human resources. Without actual powers, the critics maintain, none of these institutions will allow African citizens to actually shape continental politics (GIMPA 2007: 4; GiMAC 2007 3).

A second point of critique refers to the lack of transparency in the selection of those few who have access to these institutions. With regard to ECOSOCC, a joint review report by several CSOs observes that (AFRODAD et al. 2007: 37),

> a lack of transparent processes and poor communications strategy leads to perceptions of ECOSOCC as a 'club of friends' and that it is packed with government supported organizations with little legitimacy in the wider civil society movement. In particular, there is no clarity on the definition of organisations that should be on the 'electoral roll' of voters nor on the election processes that must be followed to choose the national representatives to the General Assembly.

ECOSOCC eligibility criteria, which include that CSOs shall not be financed by international sources, are seen as a subtle measure to exclude those organizations that work in politically sensitive areas such as human rights and democratization. Some therefore claim that (CCP-AU 2010: 4),

> Despite the rhetoric on creating a Union of peoples rather than governments, CSOs on the continent continue to operate in an atmosphere of suspicion and mistrust linked to external funding. Accusations continue to be levied on CSOs regarding their pursuit of a foreign agenda. This is doublespeak, particularly coming from governments and a continental institution that have more than half their funding from the same external partners.

Similarly, the criteria upon which CSOs are accredited to participate at the official pre-summits organized by CIDO are said to remain non-transparent, selective, and subject to political considerations (AFRODAD et al. 2007: 3; CCP-AU 2010: 5).

A third point of critique is that despite these participatory mechanisms, the organization altogether remains exclusive, non-transparent, and inaccessible to the wider public. Journalists' access to summit events, for instance, is a recurring problem. African media representatives point out that, unlike Western media who are accredited without any difficulty, African reporters often have to stay outside (*Herald* 2007).[6] This is echoed by reports of CSOs being hindered to participate at AU summits because of unclear accreditation rules and difficulties encountered in obtaining visas (AFRODAD et al. 2007: 3; CCP-AU 2008a). In the context of the 2007 summit in Accra, Ghana it was observed that (*Foroyaa* 2007),

> Such summits are usually held under closed doors and there is no independent news agency that is capable of getting vital information until a final communiqué is issued. The AU Commission needs to look into the problem of access to information during such important summits. One cannot close summits to the media without any consistent briefing and expect the African people to be properly informed.

A fourth point of critique refers to the question as to whose voices are represented within AU structures. Who constitutes the 'African people'? Who can claim representation? And with what weight? Among those repeatedly demanding a stronger representation within the AU are the diaspora (see This Day 2007; Araya 2007), women (GiMAC 2007), and youth (PAYLF 2007). However, requests for representation also came from traditional leaders, business organizations, chambers of commerce, and trade federations (see *Business Day* 2002; *BuaNews* 2007). In 2010, AU member states also hindered the South African Coalition of African Lesbians from attending the AU

---

[6] Interview, member of African NGO, 22 May 2013, Addis Ababa; author's conversations with African journalists on the side of the fiftieth anniversary celebrations.

summit in Kampala: claims to represent the 'African people' had apparently reached a clear boundary here (see *New Vision* 2010).[7]

Finally, the AU's current approach to 'corporate' representation—as women, youth, and business actor—is also criticized, because it raises the barriers for participation and introduces a bias towards organized and formalized structures. This excludes large parts of those who are claimed to be addressed because they lack such formal organization.[8] Moreover, this bias towards formality also stands in sharp contrast with the otherwise practised informality in most CSOs' daily encounters with the AU (CCP-AU 2010: 5).[9]

Summary and Outlook

Since the early 1990s, empowerment, participation, and inclusive governance became important normative references to justify the policies and procedures of the OAU/AU. In terms of our bubbles model presented in Chapter 2, this meant that—although not entirely new for the legitimation of the OAU/AU— these norms had gradually changed both their relevance (size) and their meaning (colour) over time. While the AU's bureaucracy, external partners, and non-state actors actively supported this shift, AU member states remained more reluctant and occasionally even resistant. Moreover, the emblem of a 'people-centred organization' also provided limitless fodder for critique, as it invited critics to expose the gap between self-portrayal and reality. This has most starkly been the case with regard to the AU's own internal structures and procedures, which are said to remain non-transparent and exclusive.

In 2002, then OAU Secretary General Amara Essy (2002a) observed that, 'Even the complaints from the people about inadequate involvement as conveyed through the media and other channels, are all evidence of an Africa that is keen and eager to launch into a new orbit.' In Essy's understanding, exposing the gap between words and deeds hence underscored the organization's relevance as spearhead of a journey into the 'new orbit'. Yet, a more sceptical take would be to point to the fact that the critical voices, summarized in this chapter, are actually those who already *have* access to the AU. Thus, they are in a privileged position compared to the majority of African citizens for whom the AU remains a distant and largely unknown organization (see also Murithi 2012: 667). What the latter want remains hidden from both academic inquiry and those claiming their representation.

---

[7] The African Commission on Human and Peoples' Rights in 2010 similarly declined to grant CAL observer status (see http://pambazuka.org/en/category/features/68946, last accessed 22 March 2017).

[8] Interview, member African NGO, 22 May 2013, Addis Ababa.

[9] Interview, member African NGO, 22 May 2013, Addis Ababa.

Even after 2010, the described new terms for legitimating AU policies and procedures remained both highly relevant and contested. The AU's appeal to the 'people-centred' organization continues to be a dominant principle in the organization's self-presentation of its policies—as for instance the 'Africa that belongs to all its citizens' of the Agenda 2063 (AU Commission 2013: 2 and 16; 2015: 12 and 15; 2016: 6 and 25)—and its procedures (AU Commission 2013: 121; 2015: 49; 2016: 81). However, efforts towards actually realizing this claim continue to face crucial obstacles. In his above-quoted 2017 report on the ongoing institutional reform project, Paul Kagame listed second the 'perception of limited relevance [of the organization] to African citizens' (Kagame 2017: 4; see also AU Commission 2013: 122) as a key shortcoming of the way the AU operates today. The solutions he proposes, however, also underline the above-observed growing pragmatism with which questions of participation and inclusive governance are debated today. In order to 'increase the AU's relevance to citizens' Kagame suggested introducing women and youth quotas, establishing an African Volunteer Corps, making available the African passport, and providing clearly identifiable 'common services valued by member states and citizens' (Kagame 2017: 11). In light of our bubbles model and the preceding section, this means that while still highly relevant, the meaning of the 'people-centred' organization today refers to pragmatic rather than programmatic understandings, as some of the above-quoted critics would have preferred to see.

PATHWAYS OF NORMATIVE CHANGE

In 2011, AU chairperson Jean Ping observed that 'change is often not a choice. It is a matter of survival' (AU Commission 2011: 1). The two broad normative shifts that underpin the OAU/AU's history of legitimation contests—from coordination to delivery and towards a 'people-centred' organization— exemplify this observation. Both were reactions to two very fundamental critiques levied against the OAU: that it was a mere 'talking shop' and that it was a 'club of dictators' serving the interests of heads of state and political elites only. Both shifts thus promised to reconcile the organization with its initial mandate to 'achieve a better life for the peoples of Africa' (OAU 1963).

Yet both instances also show that normative change has come incrementally rather than in the form of sudden ruptures. They therefore represent, as van Walraven (2010) observes, a moment of heritage and transformation. Moreover, they underline that normative change has always resulted from a combination of external and intra-organizational dynamics: developments in the organization's environment, such as broader normative and structural changes in the world political context, as well as concrete efforts of norm entrepreneurs within the institution itself. In the following, we highlight three of these contextual changes—the end of the Cold War, changes in the political and economic situation of the African continent, and the rise of regionalism— as well as the contribution of the bureaucracy and its respective head in particular as norm entrepreneurs.

Changing World Political Context

Both normative changes started with the beginning of the 1990s, indicating that the *end of the Cold War* and the global political changes that followed in its wake had affected the OAU/AU in important ways. Apart from the temporal contiguity, two further reasons explain the influence of this event on the changing terms of legitimating the OAU/AU. First, at the end of the Cold War, the African continent risked losing the attention of former colonial powers, international donors, and other international organizations (OAU Secretariat 1990b: 12–14). This, in turn, compelled some to argue for a more proactive role of the OAU in shaping and managing African integration, particularly promoted by then OAU Secretary General Salim Ahmed Salim. This included the rationale that if 'Africa' does not react adequately to these changes, the continent will face even further marginalization (OAU Secretariat 1990b: 22). The result was a greater urgency for intra-African cooperation, and a greater need for reforming and strengthening the OAU. The gradual institutional and normative transformations that ultimately led to the establishment of the AU is, in fact, the answer African heads of state gave to this diagnosis (OAU 2000: preamble; AU Commission 2004b: 16).

Second, the end of the Cold War was also a crucial driver behind the rise of popular participation and good governance principles. On the one hand, international donors increasingly attached political conditions to their development cooperation with African states (OAU Secretariat 1990b: 14). On the other hand, the number of democracies among OAU member states had grown steadily since the beginning of the 1990s. Among those vocal proponents of a reformed OAU, that would matter for the people rather than merely to presidents, were those regimes that had only recently come to power. For them, promoting a different continental organization also became a matter of self-legitimation. The same can be said for Nigeria and South Africa, two key formulators of reform proposals that ultimately paved the way to transform the OAU into the AU (see Tieku 2009). Yet, the so-called 'third wave' of political liberalization and democratization did not just spread democracy among African states, as some had initially hoped. Rather, its effects were both ambiguous and threatened to be reversed (Cheeseman 2015: 1). This, in turn, also explains the ambiguous reflection the 'third wave' had on the

continental organization: despite great normative and institutional transformations, the change towards a genuinely 'people-centred' organization remains
contested and unattained.

A second driver behind the observed normative changes resulted from the
changing economic and political situation on the continent. This also affected
the *perception of what constitutes the main problems* for which the OAU/AU
should take responsibility. On the one hand, the end of formal colonial rule
had forced the OAU to adapt its mandate and purpose as one of its initial
purposes had vanished (OAU Secretariat 1990b: 10). On the other hand, the
changing nature and proliferation of violent conflict revealed the OAU's
failure to actually contribute to better the lives of Africans. However, the
growing attention the OAU/AU paid to its role as peacemaker also built on
a different way to *think about* and *approach* conflict. This shift was aided by a
global discourse about 'human security' and 'development' in which peace,
security, and development were thought of as interconnected, and in which
individual lives and perceptions of security had become more central (Jolly
et al. 2009: 163; OAU Secretariat 1990b: 23; Lulie and Cilliers 2016: 73–4).

Finally, a third driver behind the normative changes was a more general
global discursive shift by which regional integration and regional organizations
were increasingly valued as building blocks for a new global order (Fawcett
2005). In the realm of peace and security, the UN promoted regionalization
and deepened its cooperation with regional organizations. In his Agenda for
Peace, then UN Secretary General Boutros Boutros-Ghali argued that regional
organizations 'possess a potential that should be utilised serving . . . preventive
diplomacy, peace-keeping, peacemaking and post-conflict peacebuilding'.
Moreover, closer cooperation with and support for establishing regional
organizations could lead to 'a deeper sense of participation, consensus and
democratization in international affairs' (UN Secretary General 1992: 18
and 22). Likewise, the EU started to cooperate with, build, and finance regional
organizations worldwide (UN General Assembly 1994a: 20).

The impact of this regionalist discourse is evident in at least two regards.
First, external actors were vocal supporters of both normative changes. Unlike
many member states, external donors used the summit meetings to praise the
AU's turn towards 'delivery' and towards a more people-centred organization,
and they also called for more coherence in implementing these new normative
principles. Second, international donors supported concrete policies, including capacity building and institutional reforms, that served to inscribe these
new legitimacy principles into the structures and procedures of the AU
(Laporte and Mackie 2010; UNECA 2014).

At the same time, this belief in the efficiency of regional organizations also
inspired a more general proliferation of regional organizations. Over the past
decades, the African continent has seen a virtual explosion in the number and
activities of regional and subregional organizations that all gained from this

global trend. That the AU is increasingly measured according to what it *does* itself—rather than what it helps its member states to do—may thus also be accelerated by a growing number of rival institutions, competing to offer solutions to the challenges the continent is facing (Hartmann 2016: 276).

Bureaucrats and Leadership as Drivers of Change

However, the change towards a more results-oriented and people-based organization was not merely a reflection of changing contextual features. Rather, these changes required active framing and an elaboration of what they meant for the continental organization. Similar to the GATT/WTO case, the role of the bureaucracy and its leaders was crucial here. In the OAU Secretariat, former Secretary General Salim Ahmed Salim, who headed the OAU's bureaucracy from 1989 until 2001, played a particularly important part (see Lulie and Cilliers 2016). At the beginning of the 1990s, Salim formulated a reform agenda for the OAU which comprised three main pillars: a comprehensive understanding of the peace and security challenges on the continent and the resulting necessity to develop OAU instruments to effectively address them; a more constructive involvement of non-state actors in shaping continental integration; and a transformation of OAU institutions and structures that led to a more comprehensive mandate and to more tangible outputs (see Novicki 1983; 1992; Adotey 1991). Thus, both normative changes discussed in this chapter are reflected in this 'roadmap' which altogether laid the 'legal and structural foundation for a more proactive organisation' (Lulie and Cilliers 2016: 72).

Within the institutional set-up of the OAU, the bureaucracy's powers have always been limited, particularly with regard to its financial and human resources-related capacities. There are nevertheless three reasons that explain the specific role the Secretariat, and its respective head in particular, played in shaping the changing terms of OAU/AU legitimation. First, although officially not vested with outstanding powers, the OAU Secretary General skilfully used his reporting mandate to introduce new ways of thinking and doing continental politics. The 1990 *Report on Fundamental Changes Taking Place in the World and Their Implications for Africa* is a good example (OAU Secretariat 1990b; see also Lulie and Cilliers 2016: 70). It set much of the novel terms of legitimation following the observation that (OAU Secretariat 1990b: 11), 'the OAU member states and the secretariat ought to exert more rigour and discipline so as to ensure that the organization is more efficient and responsive to the problems facing the continent and to the aspirations of the African people.' Despite fierce debates, Salim Ahmed Salim managed to subsequently convince OAU member states to adopt a declaration which recognized the need for 'Africa' to become more proactive, and he acknowledged the importance of 'popular participation of our peoples in processes of government and development', as well as the need for 'human-centred and sustainable development' (OAU Assembly 1990; see also Lulie and Cilliers 2016: 71).

Second, the role of the Secretariat was also enhanced by the Secretary General's skilful use of external critique. The report of the IPEP on Rwanda, for instance, had suggested a redefinition of the OAU's role in peacemaking that supported Salim Ahmed Salim's reform agenda (Masire et al. 2000: chapter 24 C). Later on, then AU Commission chairpersons Alpha Konare and Jean Ping used the results of an external audit of the AU to promote the envisaged Institutional Transformation Programme. This aimed at placing greater attention on the AU's institutional efficiency and effectiveness (AU Commission 2005: 1). Konare in particular had regularly argued that the norms and values the organization promoted *externally*—such as good governance, transparency, and accountability—also needed to be reflected in the organization's *own* structures (AU Commission 2004b: 3).[10] In 2007, the AU audit noted that (Adedeji et al. 2007: 77),

> for the Commission to carry out its mandate to meet the aspirations of the peoples of this continent...good governance, probity, accountability and transparency must be institutionalised. The panel remains seized of the urgent need to address the management and leadership capacities at all levels of the Commission with respect to its role as the driving force of all the activities of the Union. Unless it develops its capability to play this role, the objective of Africa's political and economic integration will not be realised.

These recommendations were regularly weaved into the chairperson's reports, for instance when Jean Ping observed that (AU Commission 2010: 122),

> We all agreed on the rationale for the urgent need to review and make adjustments to the organizational structure of the Commission...The Commission has...progressively become the agenda setter for Africa providing leadership in policy and programme development and advocacy...All this comes after the Report of the Audit of the African Union by the High-Level Panel which among other things called for immediate steps to be taken to adapt and transform the Commission's structures, processes and procedures for greater efficiencies and effectiveness.

He also noted that the commission 'gives priority to the promotion of a results-driven culture, internal good governance and meticulous and transparent management of the organization's modest resources...as contained in...the Report of the High-Level Panel on the Audit of the Union and other relevant documents' (AU Commission 2010 134; see also 2008a: 136; 2008b). The strategy of using external reports, audits, and assessments as 'backup' to

---

[10] Interview, long-term serving OAU/AU staff, 21 May 2013, Addis Ababa.

introduce new terms of legitimation, or strengthen existing ones, thus proved ubiquitous and successful.

Third, the role of the Secretariat as norm entrepreneur was facilitated by the establishment of alliances with other actors, particularly non-governmental and other international organizations. The second normative shift towards a 'people-centred' organization in particular has been shaped by a constant interaction between the bureaucracy's head, African and international NGOs, as well as other international organizations (OAU Secretariat 2000: 60–2; see also Tieku 2009: 76). In 2002, for instance, Amara Essy explained that he used the powers member states had 'entrusted' him with to build a broader network of non-governmental contacts, 'to popularize the African Union so that it may... become the undertaking of all Africans' (OAU Secretariat 2002a: 5). Moreover, international donors increasingly supported the AU's turn to become a more efficient and more people-centred organization.

Finally, the Secretariat's room for manoeuvre was facilitated by the fact that member states had only invested little in their embassies in Addis Ababa. Moreover, in the early 1990s, participation in OAU meetings gradually decreased (OAU Secretariat 1990b: 11). Disengaged member states thus left a vacuum which the OAU/AU Secretariat and its head in particular could use to shape the terms of legitimation.

In sum, the OAU/AU's changing terms of legitimation were the result of an incremental process. This stemmed from developments in the world political context on the African continent and beyond, as well as from the ways they were framed as shaping the 'moment in time', and with this the role and place of the continental organization. What is more, change in one area, for instance towards valuating 'outcomes' and 'effectiveness', also facilitated change in other areas, for instance by introducing new procedural norms on sound management or participation. In all this, the organization's bureaucracy, especially the individuals heading it, and their respective alliances with non-state and international actors were crucial. As their powers were limited, however, change too was a matter of negotiation, gradual adaptations, and remaining ambiguity. And it continues to be so.

CONCLUSION

Of the five international organizations covered in this book, the OAU/AU together with the WTO have undergone the most fundamental transformation over the past forty years. In this sense, the establishment of the AU in 2002 was in itself an attempt to relegitimate a continental integration project that had been facing its own demise. And yet, as elaborated in this chapter, the institutional change alone cannot account for the OAU/AU's changing terms of legitimation.

These terms have shifted in two important ways. First, the terms for assessing the organization's performance changed from an initial focus on facilitating coordination between member states to an emphasis on the organization's own active contributions to better the lives of Africans. We underlined the observation that proving outcomes and effectiveness increasingly mattered with the example of the policy field of peace and security. Since it was embedded in normative changes beyond the OAU/AU—in particular the rise of paradigms such as 'human security' and 'human development'—the shift towards outcomes and effectiveness also came with a growing attention towards African societies and the individual as beneficiaries of continental integration. At the same time, it directed attention towards questions of institutional procedures, sound project management, and financial accountability. In sum, this first change in the terms of legitimation thus underlines both the rise of *people-based norms* and the growing importance of *procedural norms*.

The second normative shift we observe expands this development. Here, the individual was not merely a beneficiary, but became itself an active agent in fostering integration. From the early 1990s onwards, people's right to democratic governance, participation, and inclusive politics shaped the agenda of the OAU and later the AU. At the same time, democracy and participation also became discussed in relation to the organization's own procedures. The emblem of the 'people-centred union' (AU Commission 2004b: 24) hence served to epitomize the AU's novel approach to popular participation. Like the first shift, this second change supports our general observation that both *people-based* and *procedural legitimation principles* are on the rise.

With regard to the pathways of change, the OAU/AU case highlights how changes in the world political context and the skilled efforts of norm entrepreneurs combined to produce normative change. Despite key events such as the end of the Cold War or the Rwandan genocide, these changes nevertheless evolved incrementally rather than abruptly; and they preceded the official transformation of the OAU into the AU. Although both normative innovations were formulated as a break from the organization's past—the 'talking shop' and the 'club of dictators'—the traces of history did not vanish overnight (see also van Walraven 2010). Contestations around these changes thus remain, as do open challenges to their realization.

Consequently, the AU's struggle for legitimacy has not become easier: member states continue to show only ambiguous commitment to the continental integration project, the AU is still financed mainly by external sources, and the more expansive mandate has not been matched with the necessary institutional capacities (Lotze 2013: 120; AU Commission 2016). The ongoing debate on financing the AU and Paul Kagame's (2017) above-quoted critical report on institutional reform vividly underline this assessment.

In addition, however, this chapter showed that the increasingly comprehensive integration agenda also set expectations high, and that these come from a much more diverse audience today. Hence the AU, unlike its predecessor in 1970 but like other organizations we study in this book, has to broker between demands from states and non-state actors, as well as between those from African constituencies and external financiers or partners.

Thus, in both instances of norm change, the AU sees itself threatened by an increasing level of hypocrisy that exposes the organization's failure to deliver on the ever expanding list of promises (see also Kagame 2017: 7). While the *what* and *how* of African integration have increasingly become addressed, the question *for whom* the AU ultimately works remains a bone of contention. In this sense, the OAU/AU's history of expanding normative claims and broadening audiences for legitimation also underlines the potential for self-entrapment. Investing in legitimation, in other words, is not a panacea. It may help to meet short-term needs, but at the risk of creating new expectations and hence stirring rather than settling the longer-term struggle over what it means to establish an 'integrated, prosperous and peaceful' Africa (AU Commission 2004b: 26).

5

The Involuntary Watchdog

Legitimating the International Atomic Energy Agency

Tobias Weise

INTRODUCTION

The International Atomic Energy Agency (IAEA) is an intergovernmental organization with a mandate in the areas of security and development, and thus with a broad legitimation discourse. Located in Vienna, with 170 member states, a staff of more than 2,500, and with close ties to the United Nations (UN), the Agency is active in three areas.

The first of these *three pillars*, as the Agency calls them, is peaceful nuclear technologies, which the Agency brings to member states as a development actor. The IAEA funds research and developmental programmes when nuclear applications like energy, health, or food and agricultural industries are used in development contexts. The second is safety. The Agency is the main producer of international standards for the safe use of nuclear technologies, and it organizes peer reviews and safety assessments of national nuclear power regulations. The Agency's safety pillar has become significantly more important for the legitimation of the Agency since the nuclear disaster in Chernobyl in April 1986, and also received public attention after the Fukushima Daiichi incident in March 2011. Especially in the technical nuclear community—as opposed to the more critical anti-nuclear non-governmental movement—the Agency has a high standing as a broker of nuclear information, and as a coordinating body of nuclear knowledge and safety-related standards. The mainstream of public attention, as e.g. witnessed in media reporting on the IAEA, however, is directed towards the Agency's activities under its third pillar: verification. Regulated by safeguard agreements with its member states and under the broader framework of the Treaty on the Non-Proliferation of Nuclear Weapons (NPT), the IAEA regularly inspects nuclear facilities to verify the peaceful use of nuclear materials and thus prevents the proliferation of nuclear weapons. Starting in the 1990s, the verification pillar has received particularly high attention since the UN Security Council mandated the IAEA to inspect nuclear facilities in Iraq and later in North Korea, Libya, and Iran, thereby significantly enhancing the reach of the IAEA into the domestic affairs of these states and increasing the Agency's role as an important actor in international (nuclear) security politics.

Overall, the IAEA's legitimacy mainly rests on its perceived performance under those three pillars of activities: nuclear promotion, nuclear safety, and verification of nuclear non-proliferation. Over the period of observation, many aspects of the legitimation contest we reconstruct remain relatively stable. In the context of this book, this is a surprising finding: in the other case studies, we find considerable normative change. In contrast, the IAEA's legitimation remains largely functional over the period of observation—despite considerable turbulence in its institutional environment, including a growing nuclear scepticism, heated public debates about the future of nuclear energy after Chernobyl and Fukushima, and the growing security relevance of nuclear non-proliferation in states in the Middle East and Asia.

Notwithstanding the overall stability, we also identify two shifts in the legitimation discourse of the IAEA. The first of these shifts illustrates the strong effect of external events on the IAEA's legitimation. After the Chernobyl nuclear accident, the safety pillar received considerable upgrades while the promotion pillar became less important. This changed the discourse about the functional goals the Agency should achieve and thus altered what states and external audiences expected of a 'legitimate' IAEA. The second shift happened in the early 1990s and was connected to changing IAEA verification activities. In the 1990s, IAEA authority rose when it started to take over special inspection activities that were different from traditional NPT verification missions as they were legitimated by UN Security Council resolutions. This caused a politicization of IAEA activities by a wider range of actors and an expansion of legitimation audiences, in particular with the addition of a critical world news media. As a result, normative issues such as political imbalances, an alleged pro-Western bias, and the status of the Agency's political independence were raised by the Agency's extended legitimation audiences. This contestation of IAEA legitimacy on political grounds strongly clashes with the self-understanding of the Agency as an expertise-driven, apolitical, scientific organization. The IAEA responds to those challenges by increasingly referring to its work under the development pillar in its self-legitimation, thus expanding its founding myth of *Atoms for Peace* to *Atoms for Peace and Development* (on the history of the IAEA see e.g. Bechhoefer 1959; IAEA 1977; Scheinman 1987; Fischer and IAEA 1997; ElBaradei and IAEA 2007; Schriefer et al. 2007; Olwell 2008).

In the context of this book, the IAEA represents a case of relative stability in legitimation discourses despite strong external influences (Three Mile Island

(TMI), Chernobyl, Fukushima), growing politicization (of special inspections), and an extension of legitimation audiences (mainly the news media). Over the years, the IAEA actively maintains its image as a technical, expert-driven, apolitical, and independent organization. Not surprisingly for such an organization, the overwhelming share of legitimation efforts focuses on the organization's performance and much less on its institutional procedures. As we will discuss in more detail below, the two shifts in the legitimation discourse have created greater diversity and complexity in the Agency's legitimation environment. Yet, its self-understanding and the legitimation statements of its main audience, its member states, have changed only little over time. While external shocks and a growing politicization added new aspects of performance-based legitimacy to the discourse, the core idea of a technical IAEA remained in place.

In the following, we first discuss the world political developments in the nuclear non-proliferation regime, setting the context of IAEA legitimation. Second, we present the main ideas and concepts that IAEA legitimation is built upon. Third, we discuss in more detail the stability and the two largest, yet relative, changes in the Agency's legitimation: the expansion of safety after Chernobyl, and politicization since the 1990s. Finally, we provide an analysis of the *causal pathways* that led to both broad stability and nuanced changes in the Agency's legitimation discourse.

THE HISTORICAL CONTEXT: THE IAEA
IN WORLD POLITICAL TIME

The legitimation contest we reconstruct in this chapter is closely linked to the broader development of the policy field in which the IAEA acts. Three specific developments are particularly relevant in this regard. They relate to the close tie that developed between the IAEA and the wider non-proliferation regime; the rise of nuclear scepticism after the TMI and Chernobyl nuclear accidents; and the growing intrusiveness of the IAEA's verification missions in the post-1990 world.

In the aftermath of the first use of nuclear weapons in Hiroshima and Nagasaki in August 1945, the international community was both shocked and fascinated by the potential and dangers of nuclear fission. Next to the nuclear arms race during the first phase of the Cold War, voices for cooperation between states for peaceful uses of nuclear technology were also growing. After the failure of the United States (US)-led *Baruch Plan*, which proposed an international agency to control all aspects of nuclear technology, the most prominent efforts to assure peaceful uses of nuclear energy came with the Atoms for Peace Program. Again, developed under US leadership and proposed to the world community in President Eisenhower's December 1953 UN address, it laid the foundation for peaceful nuclear cooperation between states under the control of the IAEA. Further, it marked a significant change in attitudes towards nuclear technology exchange and export controls, and set in motion the diplomatic process that led to the creation of the IAEA in 1957 (Pilat et al. 1985).

In those early years, there was widespread optimism regarding the positive effects of nuclear applications for development (Kasperson et al. 1980; Gamson and Modigliani 1989). Consequently, during its early years, the IAEA was primarily occupied with developing scientific knowledge about nuclear technologies and with providing nuclear development opportunities to its developing member states. There was a high demand for the Agency's expertise from a large number of freshly decolonized states which also demanded participation in the benefits of nuclear technologies. The IAEA's activities under the third pillar, verification, were less controversial during the time as those were largely limited to verifying the peaceful use of nuclear technology transfers to the developing world.

While non-military applications were beginning to flourish, progress on the limitation of military uses of nuclear fission was slower. Following Eisenhower's speech, many efforts, especially in the institutional framework of the UN General Assembly, were made to limit the spread of nuclear weapons and the nuclear arms race. Calls for a binding international treaty on nuclear disarmament were strong, but negotiations were dependent on credible commitments by the two largest nuclear powers, the US and the Soviet Union. In 1968, a basic agreement for the NTP was reached and it was opened for signature. The NPT established an international regime built on four core shared assumptions of its signatories: the need to stop the spread of nuclear weapons; the need to regulate the valuable use of nuclear technologies; the need to enforce a taboo on the use of nuclear weapons; and the consideration of nuclear weapons as a part of military arsenals used as a deterrent (Cottrell 2016: 147). For non-nuclear weapon states, the treaty was basically an exchange of the right to keep nuclear weapons for development aid in nuclear technologies (see e.g. Müller et al. 1994: 49–50). With the entry into force of the NPT in 1970, the verification pillar of the IAEA was upgraded. All signatory states with nuclear installations became subject to IAEA *safeguards*, that is, to regular inspections verifying the peaceful nature of nuclear programmes. The introduction of mandatory safeguards meant a significant increase of IAEA authority because the Agency could now act as an independent, intergovernmental accountant of national nuclear programmes.

At the same time, early challenges to the non-proliferation regime arose when its shortcomings became visible. Already in 1974, the first Indian nuclear explosion made sceptics wonder how effective international safeguards could be in stopping nuclear proliferation. Thus, to some extent, the legitimacy of the IAEA was now also bound by legitimacy perceptions of the larger nuclear non-proliferation regime. This had at least two implications. First, the IAEA profited from associating itself to positively connoted norms of the non-proliferation regime—peace, cooperation, and the nuclear taboo— and including these in its own institutional legitimation discourse. On the other hand, fundamental criticism of the nuclear non-proliferation regime— e.g. accusations of 'nuclear apartheid' and discrimination in favour of the nuclear haves—was now also reflected in IAEA discourse. Inside the IAEA, the significant growth of the verification pillar caused some unease in the group of developing states. They constantly reminded developed nations to uphold their promise of technical support and to make the benefits of nuclear technologies available for all. For the IAEA, this meant an increased demand for support missions to establish national nuclear power programmes (Scheinman 1987: chapter 1).

The end of nuclear optimism came relatively quickly. The nuclear melt- down at TMI, and even more the nuclear disaster at the Chernobyl nuclear power plant, marked the beginning of a growing nuclear scepticism. Numer- ous studies have since shown how public support for nuclear power dropped immediately after the Chernobyl accident (Eiser et al. 1990; Van Der Pligt and Midden 1990). Public scepticism focused on the creation of new reactors, especially in those publics that were affected by the radioactive fallout of the Chernobyl reactor. While opposition to nuclear power receded after some months, public support never recovered to pre-accident levels. This is in contrast to the TMI accident where the effects on public support for nuclear energy were less long-lasting (Rosa and Dunlap 1994). Next to public support, many states re-evaluated their nuclear power programmes and discussed phasing out nuclear energy (Renn 1990). At the same time, Chernobyl marked the growth of notable anti-nuclear movements at regional, national, and international levels. However, the IAEA and its staff at the time was already deeply embedded in an epistemic community of technical nuclear experts. Since its founding days, the Agency has taken pride in the level of its staff's nuclear expertise: many section heads and deputy directors are scientists by training, often having a long-standing career in national nuclear administra- tions, research centres, and institutions. Similarly, state representatives at the IAEA often have a scientific or technical background. Many delegations are headed by technical experts, not by diplomats.

This growing nuclear scepticism had strong effects on the IAEA and the general non-proliferation regime. Given the transboundary nature of nuclear accidents, as painfully noted by the international community after Chernobyl, the international community realized that it was necessary to build a regime that contained mechanisms for early warning and damage limitation, and stronger safety standards. The IAEA, due to its technical character and existing community of experts, was well equipped to expand its existing tasks in that direction (Young 1989: chapter 6). The Agency responded by investigating the Chernobyl accident, drawing key lessons, and stepping up its work on technical safety norms. Immediately after Chernobyl, the board of governors pushed for the creation of two safety-related conventions. Both the Convention on Early Notification of a Nuclear Accident of 1986 and the Convention on Assistance in the Case of a Nuclear Accident or Radiological Emergency of 1986 seek to assure better cooperation and better information in the case of future accidents where nuclear radiation is released. Both conventions were adopted at a special session of the general conference, the highest policy-making organ of the IAEA comprising all member states, in September 1986. It took place only a few months after the Chernobyl accident, highlighting the exceptional commitment of member states and the Agency's expertise and support to the issue. Still, nuclear cooperation was in decline and the frustration of developing states with the deal they got out of the NPT was growing.

The main problem of access to nuclear technologies for developing states is often based on the reluctance of developed states to provide those technologies and a supply of nuclear material for the independent use of developing states, often rhetorically justified by security and safety concerns. Since the IAEA's early years, nuclear possessor states feared that exported technologies could be used for military programmes. Here, the IAEA fails to some extent to provide a trusted framework for the exchange of technologies and materials. Instead, possessor states created independent institutions such as the Nuclear Suppliers Group to decide among themselves about the criteria and guidelines for technology transfer (Braithwaite and Drahos 2000: 300). At the IAEA, developing member states thus increasingly demand stronger Agency activities under the assistance pillar.

With the end of the Cold War in 1990, new challenges arose. Notably, many smaller conflicts with possible nuclear dimensions began to escalate, putting stress on the nuclear non-proliferation regime. The discovery of clandestine nuclear programmes in the Middle East shifted the discourse towards non-proliferation, at the expense of disarmament and cooperation in nuclear technologies (Cottrell 2016: 152–3). Often, the IAEA was asked to function as an independent investigator of allegations of military use of nuclear technologies. In contrast to routine safeguard inspections that are guided by agreed inspection schedules and routines, the Agency has also been asked to conduct special inspections in situations of political conflict by the international community since the 1990s. The first important instance of this new development was the inspections in Iraq, mandated in 1991 under UN Security Council Resolution 687. After the first Iraq War, as part of an international mission tasked with removing all weapons of mass destruction, the IAEA had the mandate to dismantle the Iraqi nuclear programme. In a tense political climate, the IAEA needed to reconstruct how the Iraqi programme had been created and to make sure that instruments and materials were removed from

Iraq to prevent new work on nuclear weapons. During this time, the term *nuclear watchdog* was coined, giving the Agency a new image in public perceptions (Harrer 2014)—an image that almost entirely focused on non-proliferation. While the Iraq inspections continued for many years, new special inspection tasks emerged for the newly appointed nuclear watchdog. For example, in North Korea, IAEA inspectors discovered irregularities, leading to demands for special inspections by the international community and the expulsion of IAEA inspectors and, eventually, to the North Korean withdrawal from the NPT and the IAEA. Later, the Agency was asked to verify this regime's agreement with the US to freeze its nuclear programme. In parallel, the IAEA also supervised the dismantling of South Africa's nuclear programme. Later, similar tasks emerged in Libya (Wing and Simpson 2013). Since 2003, inspections in Iran have dominated the public discourse and perception of the IAEA. Here, IAEA reports on inspections in Iran have become highly political documents because of the conclusions that can or cannot be drawn from the inspections.

Today, the international nuclear non-proliferation regime is under strong pressure. A growing number of states have acquired military nuclear capabilities, and nuclear disarmament proceeds only slowly. Furthermore, cheap and safe nuclear energy is still far from reality for most developing countries, because nuclear technologies and know-how remain in the hands of a few developed countries. Due to its close connections to the non-proliferation regime, the IAEA today thus faces many challenges. While many see it as an international agent that, with its limited capacities, helps to maintain world peace by verifying non-proliferation, others are disappointed that the IAEA has failed to fulfil the promise of economic development based on nuclear energy. Not surprisingly, then, legitimation efforts for the IAEA are more complex today than they were in the early days of scientific nuclear optimism, yet the contents of the legitimation discourse have not changed dramatically. The Agency speaks to larger audiences with varying interest in the activities of the Agency. Whereas most developed member states remain highly concerned about technically assuring nuclear non-proliferation through safeguards and about nuclear safety, developing states keep pushing for more benefits from nuclear technologies, and the global news media is mainly interested in the politics and conflicts of nuclear proliferation.

LEGITIMATING THE IAEA: THE NORMATIVE BASELINE

In this section, we discuss the main normative foundations of IAEA legitimacy. Overall, they are based on four distinct functions: the promotion of nuclear science, the development of nuclear safety measures, the promotion of nuclear applications, and nuclear non-proliferation. Over time, to a large extent, there is continuity in the legitimation discourse about the Agency's main functions. Yet, there is a gradual shift from the image of the IAEA as a science-based nuclear technology provider to a safety and non-proliferation actor. The shift is relative and not fundamental, as all four functions remain important elements of IAEA legitimation. Before engaging with these relative normative changes, we will briefly describe those four baselines of IAEA legitimation.

Since its inception in 1957, the IAEA has based its legitimation on a self-image of *scientific progress* and on the idea of *spreading nuclear technologies* to support the development of its member states. The science-based image portrays the Agency as a place where knowledge is collected, organized, and created. This scientific function of the IAEA is also embedded in its Statute (1956). Article III, A1 empowers the Agency to 'encourage and assist research on, and development and practical application of, atomic energy for peaceful uses throughout the world'. Article III, A2 mandates the IAEA to 'foster the exchange of scientific and technical information on peaceful uses of atomic energy'. Consequently, over the years, the Agency has developed several instruments to serve the scientific community and to promote the advancement of nuclear sciences (Scheinman 1987, chapter 3; Göthel et al. 2007). In addition, and closely connected to the science-based legitimation, the Agency is widely perceived as an international promoter of nuclear energy in the wider context of the non-proliferation regime. During its early years, nuclear energy was widely seen as a most promising technology, assuring safe and cheap electricity for the growing world economy, that all states should have the chance to benefit from. The promotion of nuclear energy is also inscribed in the Agency statute as an important pillar (IAEA 1956, art. II), indicating the enthusiasm for nuclear applications at the time of the Agency's foundation. The Agency runs many programs to promote nuclear energy (Doub and Dukert 1975: 757–8).

The importance of science and nuclear promotion also becomes visible in the legitimation discourses of the Agency and its main constituencies. For example, in its annual reports, the values of science (IAEA 1971: 8; 1979: 31) and promotion (IAEA 1979: 19; 1987b: 7; 2003: 13) appear in many settings. When referring to itself as a scientific and nuclear promotion organization, the Agency invokes norms of *independence, objectivity, development,* and *scientific progress.* The same normative evaluations are present in the legitimation statements of member states (IAEA 1970: 8; 1978b: 2; 1982c: 20; 1990f: 38). They only rarely contest the scientific promotion function. Non-governmental organizations (NGOs) and the media hardly ever speak about the IAEA and there is very limited public discourse about those IAEA functions in expert communities.

Next, *nuclear safety* is the third important normative baseline of the IAEA's legitimation. When the Agency describes itself with the language of safety (Scheinman 1987: chapter 3), it relies on norms like *expertise, international cooperation*, and *independence*. The IAEA is very active in the safety field and finances many activities to fulfil its statutory safety function, the establishment of 'standards of safety for protection of health and minimization of danger to life and property (including such standards for labour conditions)' (IAEA 1956, art. III A6; see also Niehaus 2007). In addition to safety guidelines, the IAEA provides safety assistance to its member states (Washington 1997).

The Agency has widely embraced the importance of it being a safety provider, which again becomes visible in the legitimation discourse. In its annual reports, the Agency frequently stresses its contributions to safety (IAEA 2003: 8; 2008: 15). Here, it is especially the collaborative, consensus-based, and multilateral character of the safety-related activities that get highlighted. Member states are strong supporters of the Agency's safety functions and often demand even more efforts for nuclear safety (IAEA 1986b: 37–8; 2006a: 19). Public contestation of safety-related work is only rarely present, in part because social movements and NGOs challenge nuclear technologies and their safety primarily in domestic debates and rarely target the international level directly.

In contrast, the *non-proliferation activities* of the IAEA evoke somewhat stronger normative contestation amongst the Agency and its main audiences. At the core of its non-proliferation activities are the norms of *peace* and *international cooperation*. This was also a core intention of the Agency's founders that gave it the competence 'to establish and administer safeguards designed to ensure that special fissionable and other materials, services, equipment, facilities, and information...are not used in such a way as to further any military purpose' (IAEA 1956: art. III A5). In this regard, the Agency figures as the only international body in the non-proliferation regime where non-proliferation, and thus a significant contribution to world peace, is achieved through partnership and cooperation between states in an *independent*, i.e. free from single-state influence, IAEA. This notion is also very present in self-descriptions (IAEA 2007: 65) and in the legitimation statements of member states (IAEA 1998c: 5; 2002: 30).

However, as we will discuss in more detail below, there is contestation of the Agency's effectiveness in assuring non-proliferation (IAEA 1994b: 18–19). Such scepticism is often voiced regarding the Agency's system of nuclear safeguards (Szasz 1970: chapter 21; Fischer 2000). Even more fundamental criticism is voiced regarding the Agency's *independence*. For some observers, the Agency's non-proliferation activities have become biased and politicized, i.e. following political instead of rational motives. Both kinds of criticism are also common in the news media about the Agency and in the criticism by

NGOs. In comparison, normative evaluations and contestation based on non-proliferation have increased the most over the years.

Finally, there is one underlying conflict that has influenced the legitimation baseline of the Agency since the entry into force of the NPT. It is the question of the right *balance of Agency activities*. Developing members have continuously called for increasing funds and attention to the development pillar of the Agency. At the IAEA, questions of development are closely linked to safeguards because most of the safeguarded facilities are situated in highly developed countries. If the Agency were to focus only on safeguards, its developing members would have little interest in supporting an organization that is only active in the developed world. Thus, technical assistance is a major reason for developing states to join and support the IAEA. For the Agency to remain legitimate in the eyes of its large membership, it needs to carefully balance both pillars. Certainly, with the deeper embedding of the Agency in the global nuclear non-proliferation regime, the balance has shifted more towards inspections, and the public perception of the Agency as a political actor has increased the weight of the verification pillar in the legitimation discourse.

AFTER CHERNOBYL: THE RISE OF NUCLEAR SAFETY

How has the IAEA managed to not only survive the effects of the Chernobyl disaster but also to refocus its work on safety aspects, thus strengthening its position as a useful organization for the international community of states? Furthermore, has the more recent Fukushima Daiichi nuclear accident in March 2011 altered the Agency's legitimation efforts? The nuclear accidents at TMI and at Chernobyl have significantly shaped public opinion and state policies on nuclear energy. While the TMI accident had already increased the Agency's focus on safety, the qualitative shift in the Agency's normative foundations came with the Chernobyl accident and its 'political fallout'. Previously a facilitator of safety cooperation between states, the IAEA began to take up a more active role as a legal and technical norm setter in matters of the safe use of nuclear technologies (Barkenbus 1987: 490). As a consequence, normative evaluations of the Agency's functionality shifted towards an effective provision of safety, mainly understood as efforts to increase international cooperation among states. This shift in legitimation prepared the Agency well for the discussions evolving after Fukushima, where the IAEA further built upon its standing as an intergovernmental forum of expertise and regulation, and not as a 'nuclear safety watchdog' (IAEA 2011c).

The following paragraphs discuss changes in the underlying norms that structure the IAEA's struggle for legitimacy. Like in the other chapters, we trace the changes in discourse and the underlying legitimation norms by relying on material from three kinds of sources: self-descriptions in annual reports published by the IAEA, member statements from the general conference, and external evaluations from the media and NGO statements. Overall, the Agency's *terms of legitimation*, as already noted above, remain surprisingly stable despite a rather marginal shift towards people-based norms. Yet, when looking at the processes of legitimation, key developments resemble those we observe in other organizations, too: the range of relevant actors expands as rising powers gain influence in the legitimation contest and the media emerge as a second legitimation audience in addition to governments.

Chernobyl, Nuclear Scepticism, and IAEA Responses

The nuclear accident at the Chernobyl nuclear power plant changed public perceptions and discourses of nuclear energy and nuclear technologies. As a consequence, it also increased calls for more safety-related work of the IAEA. As David Fischer (Fischer and IAEA 1997: 109) puts it, the Chernobyl accident:

> was by far the worst blow ever inflicted on nuclear power; it put an end to nuclear power programmes in several countries and left a deep sense of unease amongst the population, even in many of those countries that continued to build new nuclear power plants. It also led to an immediate surge of support for a major extension of the IAEA's work relating to nuclear safety.

Since its creation, in the area of nuclear safety, the Agency 'has never had the firm charter it has enjoyed from the outset in respect to safeguards' (Doub and Dukert 1975: 766). After TMI, there were only modest increases in the IAEA's safety-related work. Chernobyl, however, changed the political landscape in as much as the cross-border implications of nuclear safety became more apparent. The fact that nuclear fallout from Chernobyl spread to several European countries underlined the need for international regulation and cooperation on nuclear safety. In the eyes of its member states, the IAEA was the right forum to address this need. This is also highlighted in political analyses of that time. For example, in 1987, Jack Barkenbus (1987: 485) argues:

> The Chernobyl accident will probably impact IAEA's safety mandate even more than the TMI accident. IAEA has been the focus of international response to the accident. The legitimacy of IAEA's safety program was surely enhanced when the IAEA director-general and the safety director were the first foreign experts invited by the Soviets to assess the damage at Chernobyl. Moreover, the Soviets chose IAEA as the proper forum for a detailed account of the Chernobyl accident.

Looking at changes in the activities of the IAEA, there is no large-scale increase in spending in the Agency's regular budget related to nuclear safety:

the relative share of the safety budget shrank after TMI from about 7 per cent to approximately 5 per cent of the total. Regular and extra-budgetary funding for safety already grew before Chernobyl to about 10 per cent of the total budget. In the immediate years after Chernobyl, relative safety expenditures slightly increased. Yet, already in the early 1990s, their share fell again to pre-Chernobyl levels. Thus, there appears to be no strong, long-term commitment by the member states to transform the Agency into a stronger safety actor on the budgetary dimension.

Also, other activities, such as the creation of safety standards, did not increase in the immediate aftermath of Chernobyl. For example, the number of newly published safety standards has increased strongly after TMI with the publication of about twelve new standard documents per year. Yet, after Chernobyl, there was no such strong trend towards reviewing existing safety standards or creating new ones. In addition, the number of IAEA peer-review safety missions slightly increases but only for a few years. Thus, overall, there are no strong and sustainable effects of the Chernobyl accident on the IAEA's safety budget or activities.

Discursive Strengthening of the Agency's Safety Pillar

Despite the limited change in the safety-related activities and budget of the IAEA, the legitimation contest changed. In the following paragraphs, we discuss how the actors in the IAEA's legitimation discourse reacted to their changing environment. We argue that the safety pillar became a universal functional legitimation demand of the Agency's members after the Chernobyl accident.

First, the *legitimation rhetoric of the Agency* in its annual reports changed relatively little in the four years after Chernobyl. There was thus no immediate, fundamental impact of Chernobyl on the self-legitimation discourse. Overall, the Agency continued to describe safety as an important aspect of its functional work for the peaceful uses of atomic energy. In the annual reports before 1986, safety only played a minor role in the self-descriptions of the Agency. If it was mentioned at all, it was referred to as an important task that is especially geared towards assisting member states (IAEA 1975: 5; 1979: 6; 1983: 40). When describing its activities, the Agency first put an emphasis on how it provides high-quality information on nuclear safety to its member states. Second, it illustrated how it fosters the creation of new safety knowledge through expert consultations. Third, it underlined how it directly supports its members through advisory and expert missions. Also, there was already some reporting on the Agency's safety standards. These patterns did not change significantly in the annual reports of 1986 and 1990.

Similarly, when addressing the general conference, the language of the Director General changed only marginally. When discussing nuclear safety, he highlighted the IAEA's contribution, especially in the form of safety standards and technical advice to member states. Direct references to the Chernobyl accident were rare. For example, in 1986, Director General Hans Blix referred to Chernobyl only twice: first, when discussing the limited effects of the accident on the viability of nuclear energy as an energy source of the future, and second, when discussing possible IAEA involvement in the design of safer reactor types (IAEA 1986g: 7). In the following years, most of the statements about Chernobyl pointed out that the main impact of the Chernobyl accident for the IAEA was a strengthening of the Agency's role as a facilitator of international cooperation (Blix, IAEA 1987a: 9, emphasis added):

> the accident had stimulated powerful efforts to prevent any repetition of such a misfortune and to ensure that if, despite all the precautions taken, a serious accident were to happen again, its consequences would be minimized. A particularly important point was that the accident had shown that collective action at the international level was essential to bring about much of the analysis, assessment and action that governments believed to be necessary. *The fact that full use had been made of the Agency showed that Members had confidence in the Agency as a common forum and instrument for action.* That confidence in the mechanisms and traditions of the Agency, and in its Secretariat, was an asset which had been gradually built up during three decades of fruitful co-operation. It was something that the governments of Member States and the Secretariat could alike be proud of.

Compared to the IAEA Secretariat, *IAEA member states* reacted more quickly to Chernobyl, and safety became a more important issue in their legitimation statements. References to safety increased for states both with or without a nuclear programme.[1] When looking at the detailed statements of both groups of states, there are however some differences in how they saw the future of nuclear safety at the IAEA.

First, the development of *safety standards* by the IAEA was an important issue for all member states. Before Chernobyl, members emphasized the quality of safety standards and generally appreciated their development (see e.g. IAEA 1974c: 12; 1978a: 2; 1982b: 32). Also, especially in the years immediately before TMI, there were already some demands for stronger and internationally accepted safety standards. For example, as the Canadian

---

[1] According to the IAEA's Power Reactor Information System, the following member states have operational nuclear power programmes: Argentina, Armenia, Belarus, Belgium, Brazil, Bulgaria, Canada, China, Czech Republic, Finland, France, Germany, Hungary, India, Iran, Italy, Japan, Kazakhstan, Republic of Korea, Lithuania, Mexico, Netherlands, Pakistan, Romania, Russia, Slovakia, Slovenia, South Africa, Spain, Sweden, Switzerland, United Kingdom, Ukraine, United Arab Emirates, US.

representative noted in 1974, 'a great deal remained to be done to prepare an adequate set of international standards and guidelines quickly for all countries using or planning to construct nuclear power plants' (IAEA 1974b: 5, see also 1974a: 7; 1974c: 5). After Chernobyl, critique of the safety standards was more common among member states. For example, the representative of Iraq (IAEA 1986b: 42) argued that,

> The Three Mile Island accident...had led to extensive discussions and studies on nuclear power plant safety. The reassuring data on the share of nuclear power plants in the total irradiation dose received by the population had not stopped the continuation of efforts to improve safety, and the Agency had undertaken a number of programmes in that area, including the Nuclear Safety Standards Programme (NUSS). However, it had not been possible to prevent the Chernobyl catastrophe, which in terms of its scale and its consequences had been much more dangerous than previous accidents.

Other states joined in demanding stronger standards (IAEA 1990d: 36; 1990b: 7). However, for most states, and especially for the IAEA Secretariat, safety standards were to remain guidelines, with the main responsibility for safety staying with the states and not an international organization. As Director General Blix put it in 1988, 'inspection of safety was a national function—for the simple reason that no one could be more interested in the safety of a plant than the authorities of the country in which it operated' (IAEA 1988: 17).

On other issues, the stance of nuclear power states and states that do not use the technology for energy production differed. Already before Chernobyl, in the aftermath of TMI, nuclear power states were interested in the IAEA's contribution to the *safe design of nuclear reactors* (IAEA 1982b: 16; 1982d: 10). After Chernobyl, demands broadened and calls for more *safety cooperation* in general were voiced. For example, the Belgian representative underlined that 'international co-operation must obviously be intensified: in the first stage, a common approach to evaluating the safety of nuclear facilities and the probability of serious accidents should be worked out' (IAEA 1986a: 4). Similarly, the United Kingdom's delegate noted that 'there would be an unrivalled opportunity to establish international safety collaboration on a wider scale than ever before, and it was essential that the Agency should show itself ready to grasp that opportunity and carry the task through' (IAEA 1986a: 33). Moreover, he urged that 'it was imperative to maintain the momentum of the co-operative activity which had developed under the impetus of Chernobyl' (IAEA 1986a: 34, see also 1986f: 2; 1986b: 7 and 34). Parallel to the discussion on safety standards, increased safety cooperation was often linked to the primary responsibility of states. For example, the Swiss delegate points out that safety was 'the responsibility of each State, whereas the Agency must play the pivotal role in the vital area of international co-operation' (IAEA 1990d: 17, see also 1990b: 20).

For the non-nuclear power states, a number of different issues were of importance for evaluating the IAEA. After Chernobyl, these states were quick to applaud the signing of the international conventions on nuclear safety and early warning. As states without nuclear programmes, they often missed strong national radiation-protection facilities, and thus remained dependent on the Agency's support in the case of nuclear accidents and radiation leaks in other states. For example, in highlighting that the conventions were only a first step in the right direction, the Ghanaian representative argued that 'it was to be hoped that, in view of their evident shortcomings, the two conventions would be subsequently re-examined and modified to meet the legitimate concerns of many States—the problems of nuclear safety knew no boundaries' (IAEA 1986d: 2, see also 1986c: 25). In the following years, demands for stronger safety conventions were brought up from time to time (IAEA 1990c: 12; 1990a: 28). This underlined the general concern of a number of non-nuclear states to force more binding safety standards on nuclear power states. Their success, however, was limited in a context where nuclear power states and the Agency repeatedly highlighted national, and not international, responsibility for safety over strong international standards (again, see IAEA 1988: 16).

Non-nuclear power states were more successful in their call for safety peer-review missions, which are now a common activity of the IAEA. Those missions were considered to provide an additional layer of safety for nuclear reactors despite their voluntary and non-coercive nature. For example, this notion was highlighted by the Irish delegate in 1990 (IAEA 1990a: 43, similarly e.g. 1990b: 7):

> there was also an urgent need for peer reviews. A new and real openness was needed to improve safety and verify that it was in keeping with present and future requirements...In requesting such reviews, the regulatory authorities of Member States with nuclear power programmes would clearly demonstrate to the international community their commitment to nuclear safety.

Finally, non-nuclear power states were strong supporters of a generally increased safety role of the IAEA. In 1986, there was a debate on the amount of increase in the budget for nuclear safety. Many non-nuclear power states backed a growing safety budget (IAEA 1986a: 8; 1986f: 38 and 28; 1986d: 21). As the group of non-nuclear power states to a large extent overlapped with the group of developing member states, their concerns were also reflected when discussing the general safety functions of the Agency. For example, the representative from Zaire demanded that safety become an integral part of the small reactors programme, which 'represented the only chance of giving nuclear power a foothold in the majority of developing countries' (IAEA 1986a: 23, also see 1990c: 23). Other states joined in to demand the connecting of safety and development (IAEA 1986d: 18, also see 1990e: 6). However, when looking at the discursive material as a whole, there was little contestation about the need for increased safety action by either non-nuclear power states or developing states—they differed on the level of authority the Agency should be given in this field.

In summary, the Chernobyl nuclear accident thus led states to reaffirm as well as expand the performance standards they had applied to the IAEA. Before Chernobyl, technical aspects like safety standards and reactor design were of some importance for IAEA members. After 1986, the goal of many states was to increase all aspects of nuclear safety by encouraging the Agency to become a stronger forum for multilateral consultations and standards development in the nuclear safety area. What does this shift towards safety tell us about the legitimation of the IAEA at the time? How did the IAEA 'survive' Chernobyl?

The nuclear accidents at TMI and Chernobyl were significant external events with the potential to delegitimize the future use of nuclear energy and thereby a key purpose of the Agency. However, the effects of Chernobyl remained surprisingly limited in this regard. Already after TMI, the Agency began to increase its regulatory work, thus building the defence of its legitimacy on the notion that nuclear energy did, in fact, imply severe risks and that it was, therefore, important to control such risks. State demands for change were modest. Members that already had nuclear power programmes mainly argued for stronger IAEA safety standards, without transforming them into binding obligations. In addition, developing members and states without nuclear power programmes failed to build a sufficiently strong coalition to transform the IAEA into a stronger international safety regulator. This is not too surprising as many of those states still played with the idea of establishing their own nuclear power programmes in the future, when small-scale nuclear reactors and adequate power grids would be feasible. Consequently, their demands for safety were connected to their development interests. In addition, public criticism from social movements, NGOs, or the press was rarely directed at the IAEA but mostly at national governments. This made discussions at the IAEA easier for the member states as large parts of their legitimation audiences, their national publics, did not actively participate in the 'After Chernobyl and the IAEA' discourse.

Overall, the IAEA Secretariat and its Secretary General Blix thus found a comfortable position for legitimizing their work after Chernobyl. The Agency could highlight its standard-setting activities and echo the nuclear power state position that primary responsibility for safety lay with the operating states, while promising its developing members to include safety considerations in their technical-assistance programmes. This successful legitimation strategy also carried the Agency through the next major nuclear accident, Fukushima.

The Fukushima Daiichi accident caused considerably less release of nuclear materials, however, its effect on public perceptions and policy was considerable

(Kim et al. 2013). The immediate response of the IAEA highlighted its efficient distributing of information on the event to its member states and other international organizations. Yet, the next days also highlighted how the Agency and its leadership clung to the Agency's role as a technical analyst, instead of adopting 'a more proactive, holistic, "political" response attuned to member states' expectations' (Findlay 2012: 27). The Agency refrained from releasing independent information or their own analyses of the situation, bound by the established image as a technical agency, not a political information broker. Again, the Secretariat and its executive head Yukiya Amano highlighted state responsibilities, and emphasized the IAEA's role as an independent, technical analyst and adviser without direct involvement. The imagery of IAEA reporting and self-presentation after Fukushima further underlines this detached, expertise-driven approach of the Agency. For example, the IAEA's YouTube channel documented the Director General's visit to Fukushima on 25 July 2011 (IAEA 2011b), showing him and his team in white radiologic protection suits and respirators, touring the Fukushima site—scientists, not politicians. Responses at the 2011 IAEA general conference were again comparable to the debates after Chernobyl. The member states agreed upon the IAEA Action Plan on Nuclear Safety (IAEA 2011d), asking the Agency to strengthen safety standards and peer review services and collecting information on the accident. In their statements, member states underlined the importance of safety standards and their application, yet steps towards more IAEA authority on safety aspects were not taken. In summary, the Chernobyl accident, and many years later the accident at Fukushima, primarily shifted attention to the safety aspect of the Agency's functionality without fundamentally questioning the functional benefits of the organization. Functionality was redefined, but the larger normative framework of legitimation of the Agency was not challenged.

AFTER POLITICIZATION: THE RISE
OF DEVELOPMENT NORMS

A second notable shift in the Agency's legitimation discourse lies in the increasing focus the IAEA has put on its development work since its work became politicized. This emphasis can be interpreted as a response to the politicization of the IAEA. Thus, this section illustrates an alternative response to politicization: rather than embracing new political functions and growing authority and legitimating those in a language of democracy, the IAEA tries to deflect normative pressures and remain a non-political agency, committed to making nuclear applications work for peaceful purposes.

Since the 1990s, the IAEA has continuously tried to counter public and internal politicization of its work. It has done so by increasingly highlighting its achievements in the development sector. This is also where *society-based* norms come into play. These norms highlight the Agency's impact not only on its member states, but also on communities and individuals directly.

In the following paragraphs, we first discuss how political inspections have changed the work and especially the public perceptions of the IAEA. Further, we show how internally, a growing number of member states voice their concerns about growing politicization. Often, their criticism is connected to demands for a better balance between the Agency's verification and promotion pillars, leading to some contestation from within. The rhetoric employed by the IAEA Secretariat seeks to alter the legitimation contest by directing attention to its development achievements, as opposed to its inspection work, thus balancing its sources of legitimation.

The Contestation of IAEA Inspections and Balancing the Agency's Pillars

The IAEA's non-proliferation-related legitimation discourse is characterized by the following points. First, reporting on political conflicts tops the agenda of the global news media when it comes to the IAEA. Over the years, the IAEA saw its highest global news coverage when it was conducting special inspections. Second, there are large differences in how the Agency's main audiences describe the organization in those situations. The news media largely represents the Agency as a *nuclear watchdog*, i.e. as a resourceful, political guardian of nuclear non-proliferation. The Agency's other activities are hardly ever a topic of global news reporting. The watchdog image, however, is only evoked by certain groups of members and hardly ever by the Agency itself. It is especially those states themselves affected by political inspections and their allies that actively politicize the IAEA. Others argue that the Agency's work should remain technical and strictly non-political, and thus, they call for a more nuanced public portrayal of the IAEA.

Also, the growing imbalance of the Agency's activities becomes visible when looking at the organization's spending on verification and development assistance. Inspections account for large parts of the Agency's budget, rising from an average of 10 per cent before 1980 to 37 per cent on average since 1990. In the 2016–17 budget plan, 38 per cent of funds are spent on verification activities (IAEA 2015). This increase over time is mainly caused by the growing number of regular inspections in a world with more nuclear facilities. Special inspections, on the other hand, are usually funded by extra-budgetary contributions. At the same time, funding for technical assistance grew much slower between the 1980s and the 2000s. The 2016–17 plan reserves 18 per cent of the budget for technical cooperation and nuclear technologies for development. In addition, large sums for technical assistance are channelled through the Technical Cooperation Fund, amounting to 84 million euros for 2016, which is equivalent to 19 per cent of the total budget. Yet, this extra-budgetary form of financing the development pillar is less reliable as states often fail to pay their contributions on time. Given this increasing gap between the Agency's verification and promotion pillars, the underlying conflict on the right balance of IAEA activities becomes more acute. Fuelled by the public perception of the IAEA as a verification agent and by the continuously increasing verification budget, a growing number of developing states have increased their demands for more development work. This debate is embedded in the context of the general non-proliferation discourse, where non-proliferation receives more attention at the cost of technical cooperation and nuclear disarmament.

In the next section, we show how this growing gap between the pillars has caused contestation about the right balance of the IAEA's activities. Further, it has provided the Secretariat with the opportunity to use its development work as an alternative story about the organization, a story in contrast to the politicized one that the media tells.

Deflecting Politicization by Highlighting Development

How exactly have the IAEA members positioned themselves in questions of politicization since the 1990s? The strongest statements to uphold a non-political IAEA come from the members of the non-aligned movement (NAM). They criticize the introduction of political topics at the general conference, such as resolution drafts singling out individual states, or the establishment of a nuclear weapons-free zone in the Middle East. For example, in 1998, India (IAEA 1998e: 14):

> stressed the importance of restoring the original scientific and technical character of the Agency. It must not be allowed to degenerate into a shadow political forum merely duplicating the debates in the General Assembly. The vast scientific and technical knowledge accumulated by the Agency should be disseminated in an unbiased fashion to meet the objectives of its Statute.

Similarly, in 2010, others joined the call for 'balanced, impartial and non-political activities by the Agency' (Kenya, IAEA 2010b: 18) that 'should continue without the hindrance of any political considerations, which undermined the good name the Agency had earned' (Costa Rica, IAEA 2010d: 3). Also, 'the principles guiding the Agency should be respected and not used for political purposes or to promote geopolitical confrontation' (Ecuador, IAEA 2010d: 15). Furthermore, inspections and the Agency's inspectorate 'must be shielded from undue interference or pressure' (Algeria, IAEA 2010c: 21). Other states are silent on the issue or use other communication channels to voice their concerns.

The special inspections the Agency conducts are less controversial. Most states either do not mention them in their general conference statements or signal their support. The only exception is the statements of affected states, like Iran or Iraq, that use the venue of the general conference to justify their mode of cooperation with the IAEA. The politicized debate in media reports on special inspections is thus reflected in the Agency's official member state discussion only to a limited extent. Most states continue to underline that they view the IAEA as a non-political organization, and only rarely voice strong demands for the Agency to handle its public perception differently. If such demands appear, they are linked to the question of balancing the Agency's activities, as discussed below. For example, the Italian representative hopes 'that the general public would learn to see the Agency as an institution which not only carried out verification work but also helped less developed countries to achieve better living standards' (IAEA 2010f: 4).

Questions relating to the balance between the Agency's pillars are more salient. Developing member states in particular call for more development activities from the IAEA. For example, India demands that 'the Agency need [ed] to maintain a balance between its promotional and safeguards-related activities' (IAEA 2010a: 7). Many other states demand the same adjustments to Agency activities (e.g. Mexico, IAEA 1994a: 22; Cuba, IAEA 1994c: 19; Turkey, IAEA 1998a: 12). The developing state demands, however, are rarely justified in more detail. Most delegations simply refer to the fact that both pillars are essential parts of the Agency's statute. Thus, the intergovernmental discourse is not presenting many alternative views to the status quo, but mainly demands more resources for the development work of the IAEA. Developed states hardly ever voice opposition to the balancing demands. They are the main cause and beneficiaries of increased safeguard activities, and they are the ones which could improve the situation directly, by increasing their extra-budgetary contributions. Yet, in the debates, they choose to remain silent on the issue.

As a result, it falls to the IAEA Secretariat to integrate—at least at the rhetorical level—the different demands. It has done so since the mid-1990s by underlining its development work in its communication. For example, the Agency's annual reports dedicate more space to report about development work. Standard verification activities like inspections, in contrast, are discussed only briefly in the annual reports. In addition, the Agency only dedicates one or two paragraphs to its special inspections, describing its activities in a neutral style and drawing conclusions very carefully. In contrast, development activities receive more space. The Agency describes them in more detail, highlights individual projects, and reserves boxes in the reports to present success stories of IAEA technical assistance. The reports also contain a growing number of photographs that portray development projects (e.g. 12 of 39 in the 2010 annual report, 7 of 17 in 2005, 1 of 2 in 2000).

As another example, in public information materials that target the general public more directly, technical assistance is frequently made a top issue. For example, between 2000 and 2016, seventeen of the forty-four issues of *IAEA Bulletin*, a journal that presents IAEA activities to a wide readership, have development-related titles, while only four dealing with safety and security and only two with verification as their cover story. Moreover, on the Agency's website, the news section prominently features technical-assistance projects, and on social media, the Department of Technical Cooperation hosts its own Twitter channel through which it distributes information directly to interested audiences.

These examples illustrate how the Agency's communication has shifted towards development topics despite the fact that it spends a declining share of its budget on these activities. Also, when reporting about its development activities, the Agency's language, both visual and textual, is very close to the reporting by other development organizations in the UN family, thus evoking a UN family resemblance for its legitimation efforts. For example, the Agency describes its achievements in the context of Millennium Development Goals (IAEA 2007: 12), highlights its commitment to sustainable development (IAEA 1995: introduction; 1999: 16; 2003: 1), and tells stories by introducing individual beneficiaries to the public. Those stories illustrate, for example, how the IAEA has helped farmers to overcome pests (IAEA 2008: 40), how the Agency assists the development of better crop varieties (IAEA 2011a: 42), or how it builds local capacities through training events (IAEA 2003: 31; 2007: 40).

Analysing the IAEA's communication, it appears to be targeted at 'correcting' the public perception of the Agency as a watchdog. In 2010, when addressing the general conference, Director General Amano claimed that he 'was trying to change the widespread perception of the Agency as simply the world's "nuclear watchdog", which did not do justice to its extensive activities in other areas, especially in nuclear energy, nuclear applications and technical cooperation' (IAEA 2010b: 5–6). Similar wordings can be found in many of Amano's speeches since 2009, indicating a substantive shift in the legitimation contest in which the Agency itself seeks to highlight its development work.[2] Before politicization of its work, public communication focused primarily on the IAEA's contributions to the scientific promotion of nuclear energy and to nuclear safety. The changes we observe thus suggest that public interest in the IAEA has caused a challenge for the ways in which the organization was traditionally legitimated.

---

[2] See https://www.iaea.org/about/dg/statements (last accessed July 2018).

To summarize, this struggle is perhaps best captured in the 2005 joint award of the Nobel Peace Prize to the IAEA and its Director General Mohamed ElBaradei. On the one hand, the award is firmly based on the Agency's role in verification. The Nobel citation thus stipulates that the recipients are awarded the prize 'for their efforts to prevent nuclear energy from being used for military purposes and to ensure that nuclear energy for peaceful purposes is used in the safest possible way' (Norwegian Nobel Committee, reprinted in IAEA 2006e: 3). More precisely, the decision is justified as follows:

> In the nuclear non-proliferation regime, it is the IAEA which controls that nuclear energy is not misused for military purposes, and the Director General has stood out as an unafraid advocate of new measures to strengthen that regime. At a time when disarmament efforts appear deadlocked, when there is a danger that nuclear arms will spread both to states and to terrorist groups, and when nuclear power again appears to be playing an increasingly significant role, IAEA's work is of incalculable importance.

The committee thus builds on—and further reinforces—the public image of the IAEA as a 'nuclear watchdog'. In contrast, Director General ElBaradei sets a different tone in his Nobel lecture. As the overarching value, he invokes 'the security of the human family' (ElBaradei, reprinted in IAEA 2006e: 5). And while briefly mentioning the threats of armed conflict, terrorism, and weapons of mass destruction, large parts of his discourse are about something else: about the gap between 'the wealthy of world' and those 'living on an income of less than \$2 per day', about the 'imbalance in living conditions' and the 'inequality of opportunity', and about the hopes for 'a world order that would be equitable, inclusive and effective'. Suggesting that 'our priorities are skewed, and our approaches uneven', ElBaradei acknowledges that protecting nuclear material, strengthening verification, controlling the fuel cycle, and accelerating disarmament will all be essential in a comprehensive non-proliferation pillar. But he spends just as much effort on describing what the IAEA and nuclear energy do 'for the benefit of humankind', and ends by calling the Nobel Peace Prize 'a powerful message for us—to endure in our efforts to work for security *and development*' (IAEA 2006e: 5-6, 7, and 10, emphasis added).

What ElBaradei's lecture reveals, thus, is the ambivalence that comes with the Nobel Peace Prize. On the one hand, 'this most worthy of honours' (IAEA 2006e: 5) bestows legitimacy on the IAEA. On the other hand, it does so for the same reasons that have led to a politicization of the Agency's work in the post-1990 world in which its authority to inspect nuclear sites within states and make judgements about military dimensions of nuclear programmes has grown. Moreover, it puts an agency in the international spotlight that cultivates an identity of being 'technical', 'independent', 'neutral', and 'impartial'—but not 'political'—and that traditionally prefers to fly below the radar of public attention. The response the Agency presents, once more, is not to negate its role in non-proliferation and nuclear safety but to emphasize the relevance of its development-related work.

PATHWAYS OF NORMATIVE CHANGE

What has caused stability and the shifts in the balance of legitimation norms in the IAEA case? We argue that the main drivers of change are developments in the Agency's environment, notably singular events, and an expansion of authority combined with a related expansion of legitimation audiences. Stability, on the other hand, can be traced back to limited public contestation, strong epistemic communities of nuclear experts inside and outside the Agency, and the lack of strong member state formations inside the IAEA pushing for change.

Singular Events: Discursive Effects of Chernobyl

The emerging nuclear scepticism in the wake of TMI, Chernobyl, and Fukushima was a potential danger for the IAEA that had promoted nuclear applications as promising and safe technologies since its foundation. Yet, strong contestation of the Agency and its promotion pillar was absent during those times of crisis. We argue that this was caused by the lack of contestation of the IAEA in the wider public discourse, a strong pro-nuclear community, and by strong member state support for the Agency's promotion pillar. Changes in the institutional context of the Agency (public nuclear scepticism) were not used by speakers in the discourse to fundamentally alter the legitimation discourse of the IAEA.

Looking at the member statements of the 1986 general conference, held five months after the disaster, there was only marginal contestation of the organization's core functions. Nuclear power states like France and Germany saw the accident as an opportunity for the IAEA to show its relevance and to embrace nuclear cooperation on the international level (IAEA 1986e: 24, 30, 34). Further, those states discussed the growing nuclear scepticism in their national publics. Yet, there was no connection made between those public demands and a possible IAEA reform. During the 1986 general conference, nearly all states with nuclear power programmes voiced concerns about a growing public debate about the risks of nuclear technologies. Often, they spoke of 'public misconceptions' about the safety of nuclear technologies, about a 'lack of confidence' and 'fears' that needed to be overcome to use the full potential of nuclear technologies. At the same time, they considered the dialogue with nuclear sceptics as a national task and not one that should be delegated to an international organization. This again highlights the special group of people that make up IAEA staff and many state representatives, a technical community of nuclear scientists or technical political officers, not activists or politicians. Consequently, a large majority of member states saw only a limited need for the IAEA to adapt and help restore public confidence in nuclear energy. Instead, it was supposed to continue its important work of facilitating international cooperation while respecting national responsibilities.

With little contestation from its members, was there stronger public discussion about the usefulness of the IAEA and its pro-nuclear programme? Public criticism was present, but directed against nation states and their nuclear power oversight and regulation policies. In the eye of the public, the IAEA was not seen as responsible in any way for the nuclear disasters. This was also due to the low publicity of the IAEA in the general public.

In sum, as Chernobyl had shaken confidence in the quick, easy, and safe distribution of nuclear power technologies around the globe, the IAEA was to play its part in rebuilding trust in existing nuclear power applications and in developing safe nuclear technologies, especially for developing member states. For nuclear power, this meant that the Agency had to expand its role as an international standard setter in the field of nuclear safety and give more weight to this second 'pillar' of IAEA legitimation. For other applications, the challenge was to propose and support technologies that developing members, in particular, could benefit from. Surprisingly, however, this latter issue did not materialize in the legitimation contest of the time. It would be plausible to assume that Chernobyl effectively destroyed the hopes developing countries had for growth driven by cheap nuclear energy and that, as a result, the IAEA had to find new ways of satisfying developing country demands. Yet, the development frame only became more central much later in the IAEA legitimation contest. In the late 1980s, hopes for finding the right tools for safe nuclear power remained high.

Further, we could imagine a fundamental challenge to the IAEA, based on its support for a technology which the Chernobyl accident had largely discredited. Yet the decisive epistemic community, which included scientists and the 'nuclear' bureaucracies in the nuclear power member states which the IAEA bureaucracy had helped to build and was a part of, remained united by the shared belief in the possibility of a safe nuclear energy. This provided little space, let alone a platform, for anti-nuclear ideas. Nuclear power users remained eager to not give up on nuclear power as a source of energy, a technology that states had already invested in heavily. Instead, they used the IAEA platform to increase international cooperation through conventions and safety standards. In sum, forums for developing a nuclear safety regime also existed at the Organisation for Economic Co-operation and Development and elsewhere. Yet, the IAEA and the epistemic community that supported it positioned the Agency prominently when it came to negotiating 'clear-cut safety standards' and providing monitoring services for ensuring compliance through the pooling of scientific expertise (Young 1989: 153 and 162).

Politicizing Internationalized Authority: The Relevance of Special Inspections

Compared to the moderate changes in the legitimation discourse after Chernobyl, IAEA legitimation is currently in flux due to politicization after 1990. As most international organizations in the past, the IAEA 'has had its share of contentious issues and conflicts—East–West confrontations in the early years, and North–South tensions more recently' (Scheinman 1987: 209). However, two factors are important for the shift in politicization-related legitimation we witness after 1990. First, change in the legitimation contest starts once the special inspections open a window of opportunity to promote normative change. Second, power shifts in the constellation of member states give those who might want to contest the prevailing legitimation norms a stronger voice.

After the end of the Cold War, there were a number of relevant power shifts in global governance that challenged the non-proliferation regime and the Agency. First, the Agency's ongoing politicization is an effect of the growing power of non-traditional nuclear weapon states. States with nuclear programmes outside the NPT (India, Pakistan, North Korea) and those with suspected military nuclear programmes (Israel, Libya, Iraq, Iran, South Africa) are important actors in the today's IAEA legitimation game. Often they take the role of delegitimizers, attacking core norms of the Agency's self-conception like independence and effectiveness. They now bring politics into the general conference, a place previously appraised for its apolitical and technical character of discussion (Scheinman 1987: chapter 7).

The first telling examples that mark the beginnings of politicization are the treatment of South Africa and Israel in the general conference. For example, the issue that the general conference took with apartheid South Africa resulted in the denial of a quasi-permanent seat on the IAEA board of governors, and exclusion from other IAEA committees and working groups. The Middle East issue, however, brings world politics even more strongly into the general conference. While the East–West conflict was rarely invisible in IAEA debates, the Middle East problem has been present since the 1980s. Since then, there are regular efforts of member states to suspend Israel, to deny the credentials of Israeli representatives, or to pass resolutions asking Israel to disarm and create a nuclear weapons-free zone in the Middle East.

An example of the long-lasting conflict between a nuclear Israel and the states of the Middle East is the general conference discussion in 1982 about a draft resolution (IAEA 1982a) proposing to suspend Israel's IAEA membership for attacking the Iraqi Osirak nuclear power reactor. Here, it was especially Western states that tried to defend the non-political character of the Agency. For example, the US delegation highlighted that 'it would be a tragedy for succeeding generations if we permit this organization to be weakened or undermined by political issues and concerns which are extraneous to the technical purposes for which the Agency was founded' (IAEA 1982e: 15, also see 1982b: 17; 1982c: 15).

Topics with a political character have further proliferated in the general conference debates since the 1990s. For example, special inspection activities have increasingly become an issue in member state statements. Yet, most of the members highlight the important task of supporting those inspections (IAEA 2006d: 15, 17, 18; 2010b: 22). Furthermore, some states underline the responsibility of the IAEA for negotiating nuclear issues. Often they set the IAEA in contrast to the UN Security Council and argue 'that the only appropriate forum for finding a peaceful negotiated solution to that issue was the Agency' (see China, IAEA 2006b: 7; South Africa, 2006b: 12; Malaysia, 2006c: 3; Venezuela, 2010c: 25). This support commonly happens in the spirit of finding technical, non-political solutions to political conflicts. Thus, some states continue to defend the possibility of the IAEA as a *technical, non-political* arbiter in contrast to the *political* Security Council.

More active contestation of special inspections and of the non-political nature of the Agency is limited to a small number of states, mostly the inspected ones or their allies. For example, Iran strongly and repeatedly criticizes injustices in the non-proliferation regime, thereby also accusing the IAEA. Discussing the difficult access to nuclear power technologies, the country, for example, argues that it 'had been one of the victims of such gross injustices and, although its nuclear activities had always been approved by the Agency, it had been subjected to strong pressure from the United States and certain other Western countries' (IAEA 1994d: 7). Further, it highlights that the 'notion of political interference had regrettably left its mark in the field of technical cooperation as well' (IAEA 2010b: 14). As a result of this form of politicization, Iran feels excluded from important safety- and development-related Agency activities. This critique also extends to Agency inspections, the core of its technical legitimation basis. For example, Cuba underlines that the 'climate of lack of confidence that had arisen with respect to the Agency's verification activities in the Islamic Republic of Iran and the Syrian Arab Republic, as a result of geopolitical interests and double standards, was a cause for deep concern' (IAEA 2010e: 5). Instead, verification activities need to value 'sovereignty and national interests' as well as 'impartiality and professionalism'. The Iraq issues were discussed in a comparable way when Iraq was subjected to special inspections. Here, the country itself underlined the 'technical mandate' of the general conference (IAEA 1990f: 8) and that the 'Agency's essential role, as laid down in its Statute, was to expand the peaceful uses of nuclear energy' (IAEA 1990a: 34). Similarly, it highlighted the danger of involving the Agency 'in political issues unrelated to its mission which ran contrary to its principles and its Statute' and thus the effects of politicization (IAEA 1994a: 8, similarly 1998d: 7; 1998b: 12).

In summary, we see that the content of legitimation-relevant language rises due to special inspections. The Agency thus faces more legitimation challenges today than when it did not run those more intrusive kinds of inspections. Yet, we also notice that such limited forms of member state contestation alone are not powerful enough to cause large-scale shifts in the legitimation discourse of the Agency.

The Rise of a Second Audience: Media Reporting about Verification

In public perception, the growing political authority of the Agency in special inspections means that the Agency is primarily viewed as a political, non-proliferation actor. This perception and the underlying (de)legitimation efforts are particularly strong in media representations of the IAEA. Thus, with the growing perception of the IAEA's political power, the media directs more attention to the Agency's verification pillar. In contrast to other organizations we discuss in this book, however, this growth in power does not translate into demands for stronger democratic control of the Agency and its activities.

How exactly do media representations cause disturbances in the IAEA's legitimation discourse? Large parts of media reporting on the IAEA remains uncritical within the time frame of this study.[3] Most mentions of the Agency relate to a factual presentation of its inspection work. Also, political inspections are usually discussed from a state perspective, where the IAEA is often presented as an independent actor or as a source of information. However, and this is where the media has a strong effect on the legitimation discourse, this reporting is most of the time focused on the Agency's verification activities, describing it as the UN's *watchdog*, a label rising in popularity since 1992 (e.g. *Herald* 1993; Linzer 2004; *Daily Yomiuri* 2009; *Japan Times* 2009). As a result, the IAEA is primarily described as a security actor. Furthermore,

---

[3] For this study, we searched the *Lexis-Nexis* world major newspapers corpus, containing international English-language newspapers. We extracted all articles containing the organization's name. The first articles were from 1977. This resulted in an annual article corpus with a maximum of 3,193 annual articles in 2003. Of this corpus, all 669 articles with the organization's name in the headline were qualitatively coded for analysis.

routine inspections are rarely mentioned while special inspections draw much attention. Thus, the public perception of the IAEA is dominated by an image of an international watchdog that is active in situations of political crises like in Iraq (1991), North Korea (1993–4), and Iran (in particular since 2011); these were also peaks in media attention to the Agency.

Further, the media contributes to politicization by reporting state or non-state criticism, thereby transmitting delegitimation statements to wider audiences. For example, articles highlight the IAEA's 'uneven record in tracking down nuclear cheats' (*Nation* 2007), and that the Iraq inspections in the 1990s 'exposed in particular a serious flaw in the workings of the International Atomic Energy Agency' (Toups 1995; Steinberg 2007; also see *Korea Times* 2004). Second, next to these kinds of criticism, the media gives voice to states affected by special investigations. For example, in 2001, North Korea holds that in its inspection activities, 'the IAEA is playing into the hands of the U.S., dancing to its tune' (*Korea Times* 2001b, see also 2001a). Similarly, Iranian diplomats are cited, arguing that 'the controversy over Iran's nuclear program is "100 percent political" and that the IAEA is "under pressure from foreign powers"' (Warrick 2011), while Iranian president Mahmoud Ahmadinejad argues that the IAEA's 'treatment of Iran is politically motivated and influenced by western powers' (*New Straits Times* 2006), and that the Agency has yielded to 'political pressure of a few countries and without any legal justification' (Anderson 2006).

In summary, the rising political importance of states like Iraq and Iran in the 1990s has given them a stronger voice in the news media about the Agency and in the Agency's general conference. Moreover, the growing authority and contestation of the IAEA in relation to its special inspections mean that public perceptions centre on a *watchdog* image, which the Agency itself seeks to balance by highlighting its activities under the development pillar. Both developments—the rise of the watchdog image and the rise of the development pillar in IAEA communications—serve to qualify the rise of the safety pillar we observe in response to the Chernobyl accident. Taken together, both developments also illustrate the degree of fluidity that persists even where the normative grounds for contesting the IAEA's legitimacy remain more stable than in other cases we study in this book.

CONCLUSIONS

Since the Agency's founding year, its *terms of legitimation* have shifted only gradually in response to changes in its discursive environment. First, the nuclear disaster at Chernobyl did not cause the Agency to abandon efforts of promoting nuclear application, instead it has transformed the IAEA into a stronger international forum for nuclear safety. Second, since the 1990s, when the Agency began to take over inspections in political conflicts, its work has become largely politicized, raising legitimacy challenges for the traditional self-understanding of the organization as technical and apolitical. Yet, even under these circumstances, the Agency is still capable of satisfying its basic legitimation audiences by shifting communicative attention between its pillars—the adoption of new normative reference frames like democracy or other procedure-based norms is hardly visible. In this chapter, we have analysed these two developments, highlighted the effects of changing environments and external events on the legitimation of the IAEA, and discussed the sources of relative normative stability. Like in the General Agreement on Tariffs and Trade (GATT) and the World Trade Organization (WTO) case, we find that singular events open windows for change. However, lasting change is only realized when internal and external contestation of the traditional baseline of legitimation come together.

At the IAEA, the nuclear accidents have not caused large public debate on the usefulness of the Agency, as most public criticism was focused on national instead of international institutions. Similarly, internal contestation from member states was moderate because most members were unwilling to write off nuclear energy as a source for energy and economic development. Consequently, the nuclear accidents had only a moderate effect on the IAEA's legitimation discourse, with the IAEA's safety-related activities mainly helping to rebuild confidence in nuclear energy. In the second shift, the Agency's focus on development after politicization, we find both internal and external contestation. The politicization of the Agency's special inspection work gives power to affected state actors in the Agency's internal legitimation discourse. In addition, the media carries their voices to larger audiences. Consequently, the IAEA Secretariat is confronted with the public image of a *watchdog* that it tries to counter by highlighting its development work and arguing that it is *more than a watchdog*.

Compared to the other international organizations discussed in this book, the IAEA case illustrates two differences and one commonality. While the differences relate to the relative stability in the legitimation contest, and to the ways in which the IAEA responds to the politicization of its newly gained authority, a major commonality lies in the rise of a 'second audience'.

More precisely, we observe that the main mode of legitimation remains focused on functional attributes of the organization: nuclear security, nuclear safety, and science and technology for development. We observe shifts in the relative weights of the functional baselines of legitimation, but neither an addition of truly new legitimation norms nor a new focus on procedural legitimacy standards materializes. Moreover, the response to politicization is not 'democracy' as in the GATT/WTO (Chapter 3) and the Organisation of African Unity/African Union (OAU/AU) (Chapter 4) cases, but rather 'development'. This suggests that the politicization of international authority can occur along different paths, with the normative underpinnings of a policy field, the precise scope and function of internationalized authority, and the power constellations in an issue area all contributing to the dynamics that unfold in a given case.

Finally, like our studies of the OAU/AU and the GATT/WTO, the IAEA case further illustrates the importance of the widening of legitimation audience to affect change in legitimation discourses. The Chernobyl nuclear accident strongly affected the public interest in and attitudes towards nuclear energy in IAEA member states. Moreover, it led to the birth of powerful anti-nuclear movements in many societies. Yet, as these movements targeted national governments, they had little effect on the IAEA. In the immediate aftermath of Chernobyl, most member states remained committed to nuclear energy, and the IAEA continued to act as a facilitator for cooperation in questions of nuclear safety. This legitimation frame also remains stable after Fukushima, with the IAEA well positioned as a technical, independent, and expertise-driven actor in the nuclear field.

Change in the IAEA's patterns of legitimation did occur in the 1990s when world political contexts shifted. Here, the media, and thus an interested general public formed a new audience that was interested in hearing how the IAEA legitimates its activities. This new audience picked up arguments contesting the Agency's legitimacy from states affected by special inspections, and whose political power had increased because of their suspected military nuclear programmes. The interaction of these two groups challenged the Agency's standard of self-legitimation, leading the Agency to attempt to deflect its emerging public image as a political actor by underlining its development work.

To conclude, the IAEA represents an interesting case for legitimation research. On the one hand, its legitimacy is closely tied to the legitimacy of the global non-proliferation regime. On the other hand, it was founded and became active well before the entry into force of the NPT. It still builds upon its founding myth of *Atoms for Peace*, which allows it to shield itself from many political problems and cleavages that have structured the policy field over the years. When looking at the political discussion about the justice and effectiveness of the NPT regime, those debates are primarily held at the NPT review conferences, to which the IAEA as an organization only contributes marginally. This isolates the IAEA and its work to some extent from debates about the general design and implications of the NPT regime. Similarly, during special and standard inspections, the IAEA upholds its image as an 'accountant' rather than a 'police officer'. As with the NPT, political debates about inspections are usually discussed in other contexts, for instance, in the UN Security Council or other negotiation groups. Finally, even in the field of safety, the member states uphold their strong belief in national responsibility for nuclear safety, giving the IAEA the role of a coordinator and facilitator, and shielding it from criticism in the event of nuclear accidents. In many ways, this could lead us to applaud the clever design of the IAEA; an organization that remains an expertise-based bureaucracy in many aspects, a truly non-political organization. Yet, when looking at the decisions that are made and the activities that are performed at the IAEA on a regular basis, it might also make us wonder whether more public contestation would be necessary to scrutinize the normative quality of the IAEA and its work.

6

From Noah's Ark to 'Nature+'

Legitimating the International Union for Conservation of Nature

Ina Lehmann

INTRODUCTION

At the 1994 General Assembly of the International Union for Conservation of Nature (IUCN), a member of the Pakistani Sustainable Development Policy Institute (quoted in IUCN 1995: 4) complained:

> The Union continues to be dominated by what some of us see as Northern perspectives and Northern concerns...The most important [is] the disproportionate emphasis on what could be called the Noah's Ark approach to conservation, namely species survival, protected areas, and so forth. To us, sitting in the South, the Noah's Ark approach is incomplete and if it is pushed without adequate attention to other dimensions of sustainability, can be counterproductive and even dangerous.

This quote neatly summarizes where IUCN has come from: founded in 1948, it was a predominantly European and North American organization dedicated to the conservation of species around the world, a task that culminated in the organization's responsibility for the *Red List of Threatened Species* as the globally authoritative source of knowledge about the conservation status of animal, fungi, and plant species. Species conservation has for a long time remained the primary rationale and base of legitimation of IUCN.

In this chapter, we show how, from 1970 onwards, the bases of IUCN's legitimation have broadened in a way that it now describes its spectrum of activities as 'Nature+' (Cherny-Scanlon 2012)—meaning that a broad range of additional purposes have been attached to the nature conservation purpose. We argue that at the heart of norm change is IUCN's approach to economic considerations in their broadest sense. This is a remarkable development in so far as the 'culture' of conservation policies has historically been one that strongly promoted ideals of 'pristine' nature and rejected its 'exploitation' through economic use.

Against this background, at the beginning of the 1970s, a typical legitimation statement by IUCN would have expressed that it engages its members and scientific experts to save species as an activity in its own right. In terms of a first change, a typical legitimation statement would now clearly situate IUCN's work in the concept of sustainable development. It would point out that the Union undertakes species conservation in line with human needs to use natural resources for their economic well-being. In addition, it would emphasize how much effort IUCN undertakes to include a broad variety of members and stakeholders as well as their knowledge and experiences in its governance and activities. In terms of a second change, another typical legitimation statement today would highlight the economic value of nature and would stress how communicating this value helps to make the case for conservation among decision makers. Moreover, the statement would support cooperation between IUCN and businesses as a further tool to conserve nature.

More abstractly speaking, the main normative changes thus take place with regard to the questions *for whom* and *by which means* conservation policy should work. In both regards, species conservation remains the underlying core of IUCN's work but the spectrum of activities and normative orientations invoked for doing so broadens considerably over time. In short, a typical legitimation statement in 1970 would describe Noah's Ark; typical statements nowadays would epitomize 'Nature+'.

These changes reflect broader developments in the field of international environmental policy. But they manifest in IUCN later than in the environmental policy mainstream and only when additional driving forces emerge. In both changes, the IUCN Secretariat paved the way for the organization's uptake of new norms. In addition, the first change was pushed by an increasing institutional density in the field, the growing power of Southern and indigenous stakeholders, and, finally, a strong normative path dependence by which an initial turn to human well-being norms triggered further norm changes. In terms of the overall arguments we make in this book, the first broader norm change thus encompasses the move to both more *people* and more *procedure*-based legitimation, while both changes together reflect the multiplicity of pathways that norm change in international organizations can take.

To develop these arguments more fully, the following section provides the essential historical background of the environmental policy field in which the legitimation of IUCN takes place. Subsequently, we lay out the basic institutional features of the organization as well as the major constants of the legitimation discourse which provide the context for the normative changes we describe in this chapter. The main part of the chapter is then reserved for a detailed reconstruction of the two major changes in the legitimation discourse, and of the pathways that have led to these changes. In a final section, we conclude by situating the major findings from the IUCN case in the broader theoretical framework of this book.

THE HISTORICAL CONTEXT OF INTERNATIONAL ENVIRONMENTAL AND CONSERVATION POLICY

Despite a few earlier treaties on the protection of particular endangered species (see e.g. Andresen 2002 on the International Whaling Commission), environmental and conservation policy only emerged from the 1970s onwards to become one of the major areas of international cooperation. In addition to a growing institutional density in this field, three ideational developments in particular shape the context within which changes in the (de)legitimation of IUCN have to be understood: the emergence of the concept of sustainable development, according to which conservation and development need to go together; a turn towards the rights-based governance of protected areas which included an increased sensitivity for indigenous rights; and the proliferation of market-based environmental governance.

The beginning of widespread environmental interest in industrialized countries was marked by Rachel Carson's (1962) bestselling book *Silent Spring*, which documented the detrimental health and environmental effects of pesticide use, and by the world's first super tanker wreck, the Torrey Canyon, in 1967 (Johnson 2012: 11). Following such landmark events, major environmental pressure groups were founded, among others Friends of the Earth in 1969 and Greenpeace in 1971 (Radkau 2011: 128–33). Moreover, throughout the 1970s and 1980s, large-scale environmental research programmes were set up in industrialized countries, and scientists started to communicate their findings to larger audiences. Most notably, the ozone hole, global warming, and the loss of species and ecosystems made international headlines. Hence, policy makers came increasingly under pressure from the scientific community and the public to address environmental problems, and due to its transboundary character the environment became a burgeoning new field of international cooperation (Speth and Haas 2006: 62–6).

Consequently, a rising number of international environmental treaties has been adopted, and by the mid-1990s most major environmental problems were addressed by international agreements (Speth and Haas 2006: 61–5). Among the most influential and wide-ranging are the 1987 Montreal Protocol on Substances that Deplete the Ozone Layer (the Montreal Protocol), the 1992 United Nations Framework Convention on Climate Change (UNFCCC) with its 1997 Kyoto Protocol, and now its 2015 Paris Agreement, as well as the 1992

United Nations Convention on Biological Diversity (CBD). Moreover, several international environmental bodies have been established starting from the 1970s, including, notably, the UN Environment Programme (UNEP) in 1972 and the Global Environment Facility (GEF) in 1990.[1] Most multilateral environmental agreements now have treaty secretariats, some of which exert considerable influence over the ways these treaties are being implemented (Biermann and Siebenhüner 2009). Environmental concerns have furthermore been mainstreamed into various international organizations such as the European Union, the UN Development Programme, the World Bank, or the World Trade Organization (WTO) (on the uptake of environmental concerns in the latter see Chapter 3).

Moreover, especially after the turn of the millennium, the private sector has taken on an increasingly important role in global environmental governance. On the one hand, so-called public-private partnerships have proliferated. These are joint initiatives by international organizations or governments and the industry and/or civil society with the aim to achieve greater participation and hence more legitimacy and effectiveness in designing and implementing environmental policies. A prominent example was the World Commission on Dams which brought governments, the construction industry, and civil society representatives together under the auspices of the World Bank to develop guidance for the planning of large dams (O'Neill 2017: 176–8). On the other hand, many private actors undertake government-independent initiatives by setting voluntary standards for corporate behaviour and testifying compliance through eco-labelling, with the Forest Stewardship Council—a non-governmental organization (NGO)-business partnership—probably being the best-known example (Pattberg 2007).

This changing institutional context interacts with, and was partly enabled by, three main ideational developments that also significantly influenced the normative evolvement of IUCN. First, the rise of the concept of sustainable development represented a clear break with a long-standing belief in the incompatibility of sound environmental management and economic growth in Western Europe and North America (McCormick 1986: 177). This belief manifested most visibly in the *Limits to Growth* report (Meadows et al. 1972) and its largely positive reception throughout the Global North. Due to this underlying hostility towards economic growth, the industrialized countries' initial attempts at international environmental cooperation were received only reluctantly in the Global South (Johnson 2012: 12). After their historical experience of colonial exploitation the newly independent countries insisted on the right to have control over their natural resources and wanted to use them for economic development (Speth and Haas 2006: 57–8). Consequently,

---

[1] The GEF supports international financial cooperation in the areas of climate change, biodiversity, international waters, land degradation, ozone layer depletion, and persistent organic pollutants (see http://www.thegef.org/; last accessed 14 July 2018).

with the advent of the 1970s, the overall tone of the international debate started to change as former colonies entered the stage of international environmental politics. At the 1972 UN Conference on the Human Environment in Stockholm, for the first time in international environmental politics, they made their voices heard. By speaking together, they conveyed the message that Southern countries could not refrain from economic growth if they wanted to solve their social problems (McCormick 1989: 105; Najam 2005: 308–9).

By the mid- to late 1980s, a shared understanding had emerged in major international environmental policy circles that environmental policies can only gather Southern countries' support and thus be successful if they respect these countries' (economic) needs. This acknowledgement was coined in the formula of 'sustainable development'. According to its landmark definition by the 1987 World Commission on Environment and Development (WCED), development is sustainable when it 'meets the needs of the present without compromising the ability of future generations to meet their own needs' (WCED 1987: 43). The WCED thereby firmly promoted the equal significance of conservation and development purposes among international environmental policy makers and practitioners. These considerations have materialized politically, for instance, in the differentiated responsibilities in some of the main multilateral environmental agreements. Thus, the Montreal Protocol and the UNFCCC call primarily on the Northern countries to reduce their emissions and accept that Southern countries may even need to increase theirs in order to develop economically (Biermann 1998: 132–43 and 193–206). Moreover, 'sustainable use' of biodiversity has been firmly inscribed as an objective in the CBD (United Nations 1992: art. 1). With the 2015 adoption of the Sustainable Development Goals by the UN General Assembly (United Nations 2018) at the latest, the joint pursuit of environmental and development objectives has become the gold standard for global action in either of these fields.

Second, a related but more conservation-specific ideational shift was the turn towards more rights-based protected areas governance. This can only be understood against the background of the very early origins of species conservation in the nineteenth century which promoted the ideal of pristine wilderness and the assumption that nature is best conserved by large-scale national parks devoid of human habitation and resource use. The earliest example is the establishment of the Yosemite National Park in California in 1864. In the following century, this ideal was exported from the United States (US) around the world. Notably, it was mirrored in the European colonies leading to the mass exclusion of local people from their traditional homelands with the establishment of the Kruger National Park in South Africa in 1926, and the Serengeti National Park in Tanzania in 1951 being only the most prominent examples (Colchester 2004: 145–6; Hutton et al. 2005: 342).

Primordial wilderness remained an ideal for most European and North American conservationists well into the 1960s (Radkau 2011: 114–15), especially as local people in the Global South were generally presented as being unable to sustainably manage local resources (Martin 2017: 111). While protected areas have, since those days, remained the cornerstone of (international) conservation policy, and their coverage of the earth's surface has increased from 2.4 million km^2 in 1962 to 32.9 million km^2 in 2014 (Deguignet et al. 2014), their governance models now range from strictly exclusive national parks to community conserved areas managed by local people. This was the outcome of a confluence of several factors in the 1970s and 1980s. Among the most relevant were the wide endorsement of the concept of sustainable development; an enhanced visibility of the harm inflicted by exclusionary protected areas on local people; a growing body of research that documented well-working local resource-management systems; and a growing perception that conservation is more effective if stakeholders have a say in it (Adams and Hutton 2007: 150–1; Martin 2017: 112–13). 'By the 1980s,' Adams and Hutton (2007: 150) conclude, 'the whole conservation paradigm had changed to feature social inclusion rather than exclusion.'

A stakeholder group whose livelihoods have always been particularly affected by protected area policies are indigenous peoples. First, because they have traditionally lived in remote territories in and around protected areas (Dowie 2011: xxi; Stevens 1997a: 14), and second, because since colonial times they have had a weak legal position within states and have frequently been subject to marginalization (Anaya 2004). Ignoring their land and resource claims was particularly easy for conservationists, not least because indigenous peoples had been 'portrayed [as] backwards, primitive, and inferior' (Reimerson 2013: 996). But since the 1970s, an increasingly strong international indigenous rights movement has succeeded to improve the standing of indigenous peoples in international human rights and environmental law, notably, regarding access to and governance of lands and resources (Adams and Hutton 2007: 162; Reimerson 2013: 996). In this vein, the 1992 UN Conference on Environment and Development in Rio de Janeiro for the first time accepted indigenous peoples as a 'Major Group' that should participate in sustainable development. The CBD (United Nations 1992: art. 8j) demands state parties to 'respect, preserve and maintain knowledge, innovations and practices of indigenous and local communities embodying traditional lifestyles relevant for the conservation and sustainable use of biological resources'. Finally, the adoption of the UN Declaration on the Rights of Indigenous Peoples (UNDRIP, United Nations 2007) sets out their economic, cultural, and self-determination rights. And yet, tensions remain on the ground as many protected areas are still governed by an underlying ideal of untouched pristine wilderness (Martin 2017: 112; Reimerson 2013: 995).

Finally, a third ideational change with repercussions for IUCN is the promotion of the capitalist market system as the answer to conservation challenges by the major UN environmental conferences since Stockholm (Bernstein 2001; Mert 2015). Environmental protection now has to be compatible with what Steven Bernstein calls 'liberal environmentalism'. It epitomizes the idea that a liberal international trading and finance system is beneficial for environmental conservation because it promotes economic growth which, in turn, is thought to help with challenges of pollution and environmental degradation. In this sense, legitimate environmental policies should not only be firmly embedded in an open international trading system, but environmental policy makers should also actively support such a system. According to liberal environmentalism, market mechanisms can more effectively protect the environment than command-and-control approaches and therefore their application ought to bolster such a global liberal structure (Bernstein 2001: 211–14).

Market-based instruments attach a price to nature, but they take a variety of forms ranging from ecotourism to carbon markets or payments for ecosystem services schemes.[2] Their proponents expect that the economic rationale will encourage decision makers to foster conservation and that the approaches will promote efficiency and generate new funding for conservation. However, critics have raised doubts about the efficiency gains. Instead they argue that the value of nature cannot be captured in economic terms and that the benefits of market-based approaches are frequently captured by economic elites to the detriment of the local poor (Sandbrook et al. 2013). Despite such criticism, the application of economic instruments in conservation practice has proliferated from the 1990s onwards (Gómez-Baggethun et al. 2010). Many conservation organizations, both governmental and non-governmental, have adopted market-based approaches for their conservation projects praising themselves for the ability to bridge the historical cleavages between public and private interests (MacDonald 2010a).

In later sections of the chapter we show that the three ideational developments we sketch above became relevant for the (de)legitimation of IUCN—but later than in the broader field of international environmental politics and only through the support of additional driving forces. Sustainable development became a guiding principle for IUCN only when influential actors inside and outside IUCN simultaneously pushed for its consideration. Indigenous peoples' rights only became a serious concern for IUCN as a logical next step after it had already pursued a long path towards the better consideration of

---

[2] The latter can, for instance, include payments for the conservation of forests so as to create incentives to maintain them for their biodiversity and/or as carbon sinks (on such schemes more generally see e.g. Wunder 2007).

human needs in conservation. Finally, market-based conservation norms only attracted political support in IUCN when more business-friendly individuals took over high-level positions in the Secretariat that would grant them considerable leeway in steering IUCN's course.

LEGITIMATING IUCN: THE NORMATIVE BASELINE

In the overall landscape of international environmental politics, IUCN is the primary actor for the conservation of species and habitats. Traditionally composed of both governmental and non-governmental members, it is commonly characterized as a 'hybrid' international organization (Christoffersen 1997: 59 and 93). Members meet every four years at World Conservation Congresses (WCCs) to decide about the governance of the Union, and the conservation-related activities it should undertake until the next Congress.[3] Any decision has to be adopted by a majority in both voting chambers, one composed of governmental the other of non-governmental members, respectively (IUCN 2012a: part V). In 2016, a landmark decision was taken to add a new membership category comprising indigenous peoples (IUCN 2017: 2); however their votes will be counted together with those of other NGOs (IUCN 2016a: §30bis). As of July 2018, IUCN has almost 1,100 national and international NGO members, slightly more than 200 government and state agency members, and seventeen indigenous peoples' organization members. Most members come from Western Europe, followed by South and East Asia. Membership is very diverse and ranges from small and specialized national NGOs and government agencies like the Indian Gujarat Institute of Desert Ecology to major players on the conservation scene as some national chapters of the World Wide Fund for Nature (WWF).[4] In between Congresses, the Council and the Secretariat in Gland, Switzerland are responsible for keeping the organization running. While the Council provides strategic direction and policy guidance and has the oversight over all activities of IUCN, the Secretariat is responsible for implementing the organization's policies and programmes (IUCN 2012a: parts VI and IX). Beyond that, IUCN is highly decentralized, with staff in eleven regional and over fifty national offices.[5] A further specificity of IUCN are its commissions of scientific expert volunteers, which do not have

---

[3] Until 1994 these have been called General Assemblies which took place on average every third year. For the sake of brevity, we use the term 'Congresses' when generally referring to IUCN's membership meetings.

[4] See https://www.iucn.org/about/union/members/who-are-our-members (last accessed 14 July 2018).

[5] See https://www.iucn.org/regions (last accessed 14 July 2018).

decision-making powers but provide crucial scientific advice to guide IUCN's activities (IUCN 2012a: part VIII).[6]

Prima facie, IUCN looks like a rather weak organization with little formal powers, or enforcement and sanctioning capacities over its members. Moreover, its governance structure implies that the organization can only launch carefully balanced statements that are acceptable to its different membership categories.[7] Nonetheless, the Union can have profound policy impact through its focus on cooperation with governments and influence them from within (Holdgate 1999: 40). In line with its foundation in species conservation, it is active in three main areas. First, it gathers and provides scientific knowledge about species loss and natural resource management. Its most well-known 'knowledge products' are its *Red List of Threatened Species* and its *Protected Areas Categories System*, both of which are used by many international bodies and governments to define and record protected areas. Second, IUCN provides advice for national and international environmental policies and laws. This includes hands-on assistance for the conduct of conservation activities but also significant input into the drafting of national and international species conservation legislation. The latter is most visible in IUCN's expert contributions to many of the major multilateral environmental agreements, thereby 'weaving a web of environmental law' (Lausche 2008).[8] Third, IUCN plans and implements its own conservation projects around the world, an activity that has gained importance over time.

The changing normative expectations of what IUCN should do and how need to be understood against the background of three normative continuities, and one inherent normative conflict. The uncontested core of the legitimation discourse around IUCN can be summarized in the agreement among key actors that IUCN should contribute to the *conservation of nature* through *expertise* and *broad participation*. In contrast, the most fundamental conflict is over the question *for whom* nature conservation should ultimately be undertaken.

To begin with, promoting the norm of *conservation of nature* defines IUCN's *personality* as an organization expressed in the image of Noah's Ark, as invoked in the introductory quote. Nature conservation has always been the

---

[6] These are the Commission on Education and Communication, the Commission on Environment, Economic and Social Policy, the World Commission on Environmental Law, the Commission on Ecosystem Management, the Species Survival Commission, and the World Commission on Protected Areas (http://www.iucn.org/about/union/commissions/, last accessed 14 July 2018).

[7] Interview, IUCN staff, 15 May 2013, Gland.

[8] IUCN contributed inter alia to the Convention on International Trade in Endangered Species of Wild Fauna and Flora, the Convention Concerning the Protection of the World Cultural and Natural Heritage (the World Heritage Convention), the Convention on Wetlands of International Importance, Especially as Waterfowl Habitat (Ramsar Convention), or the CBD.

most fundamental rationale of IUCN's activities; it therefore constitutes a constant positive reference point in communications of the IUCN bureaucracy and of its members.[9] Throughout the years, the IUCN bureaucracy makes abundantly clear that conservation is the benefit IUCN provides to the world, and it puts a lot of effort into demonstrating its conservation-related activities and successes. Members agree that IUCN's focus on nature conservation is fundamental to the organization, and they sometimes use emotional language in support of this idea. To quote a government delegate from Zaire (IUCN 1975: 217; see also 1994: 91, government member Bolivia), IUCN 'is a Sacred Union because it has a noble mission: to protect the most valuable asset of mankind: Nature'. To the extent that this objective is contested, this relates to IUCN's lack of *effectiveness* in achieving it. Members time and again criticize a severe lack of funding that undermines IUCN's goal achievements.[10] However, this criticism does not undermine but rather supports the normative relevance of *conservation effectiveness*, and thereby IUCN's *performance*, in the legitimation discourse.

Furthermore, the fundamental importance of this yardstick is supported by the observation that other key norms in the legitimation discourse, notably democratic decision making and expertise, are tied to the realization of conservation effectiveness. In terms of the Union's particularly *democratic* character, the traditional two-chamber membership structure in combination with the Congresses, where thousands of state and non-state representatives meet for exchange and joint decision making, is constantly heralded as the Union's major strength. First, making new contacts, learning from each other, and discussing current issues are regularly praised for their instrumental normative value as they contribute to the *effectiveness* of IUCN's activities.[11] Second, there is widespread support for the intrinsic normative claim that its governance structure makes IUCN a particularly *democratic* organization, notably because it guarantees *inclusiveness*. Sometimes, this particular normative foundation is praised in very enthusiastic language such as descriptions of the General Assemblies as 'gratifyingly democratic' (IUCN 1975/6: 2).[12] *Process*-related legitimation of IUCN thus refers primarily to the question *who* governs and not *how* the Union is governed. This setting of priorities persists

---

[9] See for example for the Secretariat side: IUCN 1975: 5; 1990: 8; 2005a: 21; 2009: 18; 2017: 42; 2018: 42; for the members: IUCN 1975: 217, government member Zaire; 1990: 103, WWF; 1994: 91, government member Bolivia; 2001: 10, NGO member Earth Council; 2009: 22, government member US.

[10] See for example IUCN 1981: 18 and 22, government member Netherlands; 1984: 15 and 148, WWF; 1988: 187–8, WWF; 2001: 36, government member Sweden; 2005b: 17, NGO member World Association of Zoos and Aquariums; 2012b: NGO member Sierra Club.

[11] See for example IUCN 1971: 21; 1973: 68; 1975: 66; 2013: 11; 1977: 145, government member France; 2001: 10, government member Jordan; 2017: 2.

[12] See also IUCN 1997a: 5; 2003: 14; 2005a: 14; 2005b: 57, government member Thailand; 2017: 4.

over time, even as the dominant notion of who the relevant constituencies are broadens.

Comparable to the instrumental legitimation for IUCN's democratic character, norms of *scientific expertise* are always strongly valued because they are perceived essential in making IUCN a relevant and effective actor for worldwide conservation. Just as we observe in our International Atomic Energy Agency (IAEA) case study (Chapter 5), *scientific expertise* is throughout heralded in a very positivist and natural science-based understanding. For instance, reports praise that the Union has always 'provided impartial scientific advice needed by other conservation organizations' (IUCN 1975: 5; see also 1973: 6; 1997a: 4; 2009: 18; 2017: 4), or they acclaim the scientific reliability of IUCN's *Red Lists of Threatened Species* (IUCN 1971: 41; 2009: 6; 2016b: 16). Crucial demands from the membership include that IUCN should produce 'objectivity' in its assessments (IUCN 1997b: 15, government member Japan, see also 1997b: 16, NGO from the United Kingdom). In this sense, members approve that IUCN provides 'information and opinions about the threats to the natural environment and wild populations, and about the technical problems of their conservation' (IUCN 1988: 188, member WWF).[13]

However, from the beginning it is contested *for whom* IUCN should ultimately undertake conservation, namely whether nature should be primarily conserved for its own sake or primarily for *human well-being*. IUCN had originally been established under the name of the International Union for Protection of Nature (IUPN) (Olivier 2005: 17). Its founders wanted the organization to gather international support for species preservation and habitat protection (Christoffersen 1997: 60). On the one hand, former Director General Lee Talbot recalls that IUPN's founders referred to the wise use of nature in the preamble of the original IUPN statutes (Talbot 1983: 6–7). On the other hand, long-term Environmental Law Commission chair Wolfgang Burhenne recalls that IUPN founders promoted the unconditional protection of plants and animals and did not foresee provisions for resource use. Many of them were still influenced by the century-old ideal of pristine nature according to which conservation prohibited human interference with protected areas.[14] These views came to a first major clash at the 1956 General Assembly when the Union's leadership, with the backing of parts of the membership, pushed through the name change to International Union for *Conservation* of Nature, as 'conservation' was understood to be more reflective of human well-being concerns than 'protection'. However, this move was fiercely contested as some members insisted that protection of nature as such should remain the

---

[13] For further emphases of the importance of the scientific quality of IUCN's work see e.g. 1997b: 34, NGO from US, government members Canada and Norway; 2001: 28, government member US; 2008: 33, government member Japan.

[14] Interview, IUCN Environmental Law Centre, 22 July 2013, Bonn.

organization's prime goal (Holdgate 1999: 64; Lausche 2008: 18). As we elaborate in the following two sections, the solution to this conflict has affected the broader contest over the legitimation of IUCN in several important ways. In terms of our bubbles model presented in Chapter 2, this means that the size (= relevance) of the bubbles representing norms of conservation of nature, participation, and expertise was always considerable. Beyond that, the bubble representing human well-being norms was always present, but from IUCN's early years onwards some actors tried to squeeze it while others aimed to inflate it.

AFTER THE WILDERNESS MYTH: THE RISE OF HUMAN WELL-BEING NORMS

A first major shift in the ways in which IUCN has been legitimated is the rise of *human well-being* as one of the most central legitimacy standards. Both IUCN and its members have become increasingly sensitive to the need to integrate human economic resource use requirements into conservation policies and activities. In this sense, the change also affects IUCN's *personality* as a conservation actor: IUCN can no more simply be Noah's Ark and save species for their intrinsic value. As illustrated above, *human well-being* has always been a relevant norm for parts of IUCN's constituencies. Yet it has gained considerable traction over time and has also spurred further normative changes, notably a growing attention to *local participation* and *local knowledge* and, related to that, *indigenous peoples' rights*.

The Rise of Sustainable Development and Associated Human Well-Being Norms

Despite the 1956 commitment to 'conservation' instead of 'protection', the human well-being aspects of IUCN's work initially found few repercussions in the Union's network. Only after its 1969 General Assembly in New Delhi did IUCN start to pursue the path towards norms of *sustainable development* and conservation for *human well-being* more consistently. It adopted the 'sustainable quality of life' as a goal and noted that this includes the use of nature for human (economic) purposes and not merely species-oriented conservation largely for its own sake (Lausche 2008: 95; Talbot 1983: 8). The New Delhi General Assembly is therefore commonly considered a 'turning point' in IUCN's history (Holdgate 1999: 108; Talbot 1983: 8). Even after this date, however, IUCN's annual reports make only occasional references to the idea that conservation should take account of development needs (IUCN 1975/6: 2–3) or that species conservation contributes to human welfare (IUCN 1971: 51). But when they do so, they are very explicit in stating that 'central to IUCN's philosophy... is the insistence that development, far from being the enemy of conservation, can and must go hand in hand with it' (IUCN 1975/6: 16).

This understanding became much more publicly visible from 1980 onwards when IUCN, supported by UNEP and WWF, launched its *World Conservation Strategy* (WCS) with the subtitle 'Living Resource Conservation for Sustainable Development' (IUCN 1980). Becoming IUCN's core strategic framework for years, it had considerable programmatic weight. The document takes for granted that development ought to be 'sustainable', yet without defining this any further. Nevertheless, it conveys the message that conservation and development are mutually dependent (IUCN 1980: § 1.10), and it endorses the (sustainable) use of species and ecosystems as a legitimate objective (IUCN 1980: vi). In the light of IUCN's historical legacy this was a significant step, as the organization thereby acknowledged that a heavy focus on pristine wilderness was no longer appropriate and that human livelihood needs deserved more attention.

Compared to ideational developments in other international forums, however, the inclusion of development in the WCS represents only a minor step towards more openness for human well-being norms (McCormick 1989: 169–70). In contrast to the results achieved by Southern countries at the Stockholm conference in 1972, the WCS retains a strong focus on the conservation of species and ecosystems, and touches only briefly upon the need to integrate this with development concerns. It moreover engages relatively little with the political and economic drivers of resource overexploitation and potential consequences for a reorganization of the international economic system (see also Adams 1990: 49–50; Bernstein 2001: 59–60; McCormick 1986: 186). According to Steven Bernstein (2001: 59), this omission was the reason why the WCS had little lasting effect on international norm creation. Thus whereas, with the WCS, IUCN first introduced the term 'sustainable development' into the international conservation policy discourse (Holdgate 1999: 153; Lausche 2008: 206), its definition and discussion in a broader political and development-oriented context was only later taken up by the WCED (Bernstein 2001: 61).

And still, after the launch of the WCS, sustainable development became a prominent catchword and a matter of sustained debate within the IUCN network. The IUCN Secretariat consistently developed the organization's sustainable development orientation further. The annual reports of the time clearly present it as an integral part and objective of IUCN's activities that conservation should serve human well-being (e.g. IUCN 1981: 5; 1987: 7–12; 1993: 4). Moreover, IUCN further strengthened its view of the compatibility of conservation and human development by publishing the WCS follow-up document, *Caring for the Earth: A Strategy for Sustainable Living* (IUCN et al. 1991), in 1991. Building on the WCS, as well as the report of the WCED, *Caring for the Earth* stresses the importance of integrating anthropocentric sustainability principles with conservation requirements. All of this finds notable expression in the mission of a 'just world that values and conserves nature' to which the annual reports refer from 1998 onwards.

In parallel to these programmatic developments, members also started debating sustainable development and human well-being norms more intensely after the adoption of the WCS. While the majority of members agreed that human well-being concerns needed to be reconciled with nature conservation (as reported e.g. in IUCN 1993: 9),[15] the debate over how much emphasis IUCN should put on the social aspects of environmental conservation gained momentum (IUCN 1994: 44; 1997b: 26). As summarized in one of the annual reports of the time (IUCN 1995: 14; see also 1990: 18):

> Sustainable use of nature, whether of species or ecosystems, is one of the most challenging aspects of IUCN's work, since there are sharp differences of views among the Union's members. Some see sustainable use, such as of African mammals, as the only way to make conservation possible and acceptable to vast numbers of rural people in developing countries. In contrast, others see it as a betrayal of their fundamental conservation beliefs.

Government representatives, by and large, portrayed conservation and sustainable (economic) development as naturally linked (e.g. IUCN 1981: 78, government member New Zealand; 1990: 195, government member Mali). As a result, they did not spend much effort on justifying why IUCN should adopt a focus on sustainable use. Only some of them warned that IUCN should not lose sight of its main objective of nature conservation (see e.g. IUCN 1994: 14, government member New Zealand; 1994: 21, government member Netherlands). To the extent that there was a rift among membership over IUCN's role in sustainable development, this primarily occurred within the NGO community. Largely, the conservationist NGOs from the North were 'far from happy about the sign that IUCN was becoming a development-related operational agency' (Holdgate 1999: 159). In contrast, Southern NGOs were 'pushing hard to make sure that the social agenda [was] part of the actions of IUCN on the ground'.[16] A typical fear from their side was that IUCN still put too much emphasis on conservation approaches that prohibit economic activity (see e.g. IUCN 1994: 14, NGO from Botswana; 1994: 20, NGO from Pakistan).

---

[15] Telephone interview, former IUCN councillor, 5 July 2013.
[16] Interview, IUCN staff, 15 May 2013, Gland.

Since 2000, however, these debates have slowly abated. This parallels developments we also observe in the WTO where the commitment to sustainable development has sparked less controversy over time (Chapter 3). Today, criticism by members on this issue is almost exclusively voiced in private conversation.[17] This suggests that *human well-being* has become more and more accepted as a main motivation and benchmark for conservation, and that it is no longer considered appropriate to voice such criticisms publicly within the IUCN network. Indeed, the comprehensive illustration of all of IUCN's areas of work in the 2017 annual report with the icons of the Sustainable Development Goals (IUCN 2018) may be the most immediately visible sign how self-evident this framework has become for IUCN's work. In contrast, the criticism from Southern members that IUCN does not do enough to promote human well-being persists.[18]

Normative Implications of the Turn to Sustainable Development

This strong turn towards legitimating IUCN because it conserves nature *for the people* had wider repercussions for the contest over its legitimacy. In the wake of this shift, democratic norms have thus been strengthened, norms of scientific expertise have been recalibrated, and recognition of indigenous rights has gained traction.

The strengthening of *democratic* norms, especially *inclusiveness*, became a key characteristic of the legitimation discourse, starting from the late 1980s onwards and especially throughout the 1990s, and found notable expression in a shift of attention to Southern stakeholders' and members' needs and interests. A crucial manifestation of this was the increasing consideration of local people's involvement in conservation projects—a move that we also observe with regard to the empowerment of refugees in the work of the Office of the UN High Commissioner for Refugees (Chapter 7). IUCN reports, more explicitly than before the adoption of the WCS, acknowledged that 'people matter in conservation' (IUCN 1994: 25), and rhetorically supported this commitment by showing where it has included local people in its conservation projects (e.g. IUCN 1990: 27; 1993: 15 and 17; 1994: 25; 1997a: 24). An important reason for this new outlook was the acknowledgement that community involvement facilitates effective field projects (e.g. IUCN 1987: 9; 1993: 16; 1994: 20; 1995: 2 and 26). This emphasis on people's participation was a new development compared to the early years when the focus of IUCN's work was much more on scientific and legal advice to governments. After the turn of the

---

[17] Interview, IUCN staff, 13 May 2013, Gland. For a rare but prominent example of a publicly outspoken critic of IUCN's social agenda, see Terborgh (2004).
[18] Interview, IUCN staff, 13 May 2013, Gland.

millennium, several IUCN annual reports devoted short, separate sections to the equitable and/or democratic governance of its programmes, and actions on the ground (e.g. IUCN 2007: 27–30; 2008: 32; 2016b: 12; 2018: 36–7). Such consistent attention to inclusive governance of conservation action shows how much it has become a standard requirement of IUCN's operations.

In parallel to the growing sensitivity for local stakeholder participation in conservation activities, the inclusive governance of IUCN as an organization also became a matter of serious concern. In particular, Southern NGOs and governments attacked IUCN for being regionally biased. To some extent, this was also driven by the expectation that conservation would be more effective in its operational regions, if their needs were better represented in the Union (e.g. IUCN 1994: 13, NGO from India; 1997b: 18, government member US). However, a genuine interest in making IUCN more accessible to Southern concerns also seems to have played a role. Major demands from Southern members included (enhanced) North–South parity among IUCN leadership,[19] and the installation of regional offices so that stakeholders' concerns could be better taken on board in the set-up of regional activities.[20]

These concerns resonated strongly within the IUCN bureaucracy. After years of steering all of IUCN's activities from its headquarters in Switzerland, the first regional office was opened in East Africa in 1985 (Holdgate 1999: 207). From then on, the number of regional and country offices outside Europe rose to twelve in 1990 and forty-two by the late 1990s (Lausche 2008: 287). The Secretariat viewed responsiveness to members as a matter of the Union's democratic governance, and an important means for more effectiveness of conservation activities. Hence, it began to promote regional and national meetings to support members to develop regional programmes or to improve interaction between the regions and the Secretariat (IUCN 1990: 63; 1993: 12; 1994: 4; 1995: 4–5 and 7; see also Holdgate 1999: 207). A stepping stone in this development was the new IUCN strategy, adopted at the 1994 Buenos Aires General Assembly, which provided a significant push for further regionalization, and greater devolution of responsibility to the regions in deciding their own priorities (Holdgate 1999: 226–9).

Since the late 1990s the process of regionalization and decentralization has continued; by 2018 IUCN had eleven regional and more than fifty country offices.[21] National and regional forums have become important venues for the membership to discuss the challenges they experience in their work on the

---

[19] IUCN 1994: 25, NGO from Pakistan; 1997b: 8, state member Saudi Arabia, NGOs from Jordan and Pakistan; see also 1972: 203, USSR government and NGO representatives.
[20] Telephone interview former councillor, 5 July 2013.
[21] See https://www.iucn.org/regions (last accessed 14 July 2018).

ground, and IUCN tries to implement most of its projects through the members.[22] Attention to regionalization and decentralization has abated since the turn of the millennium, but it remains a challenge: on the one hand, IUCN reports throughout the 2000s and 2010s sporadically praise IUCN for its work with and through its members in the regions (IUCN 2005a: 9; 2013: 11), on the other hand, they admit that the promise of a membership-based organization has not yet been fulfilled (IUCN 2005a: 60; 2008: 8 and 22). Likewise, concerns about inclusiveness and regional balance of IUCN's governance occasionally surface among the membership (e.g. IUCN 2009: 13, NGO from Guatemala; 2016c: 10, NGO from Bangladesh; 2016c: 18, NGO from Cameroon; 2016c: 51, NGO from Pakistan). Together, these developments show that IUCN's inclusiveness has become a matter of serious concern among constituencies. In short, the demand is that if con-servation is meant to be *for the people*, then single projects as well as the Union as such should also be governed *by the people*.

A similar opening up towards local people can be observed regarding norms of *scientific expertise*. By and large, a traditional natural science-based under-standing of knowledge remains prevalent in the discourse.[23] But—in marked contrast to the IAEA (Chapter 5)—the positivist understanding of IUCN's scientific contributions has slowly been complemented with a greater sensi-tivity for local and practical knowledge. Throughout the 1990s, the participa-tion and knowledge of local communities was further presented as a key precondition for successful field projects (e.g. IUCN 1990: 23; 1993: 16; 1995: 20), or for the development of strategies more generally (IUCN 1995: 17). The logic behind this thinking found a vivid expression in a summary introduction of the 1988–90 IUCN Programme which sets out IUCN's activ-ities for that period (IUCN 1990: 8):

> The environment is moulded by people, including millions of the rural poor who have no access to science but do have traditions which are increasingly recognized as true reflections of environmental wisdom. The Programme emphasized the need to mobilize this wisdom and blend it with the teachings of science, so that the resulting proposals for action were tuned to the communities that it was hoped would put them into effect.

Whereas previously, the constant, science-related emphasis had been on the advice that IUCN could provide to others in order to solve (local) problems, this quote illustrates a relaxation of such a top-down perspective. Moreover, in the 2000s, IUCN undertook cautious steps to broaden its understanding of

---

[22] Interview, IUCN staff, 15 May 2013, Gland.
[23] For IUCN see IUCN 2003: 61; 2005a: 6 and 61; 2007: 4; for the members see also Government of India 2011; Conservation International 2011; Botanic Gardens Conservation International quoted in Conservation International 2011; Swedish Ministry of the Environment 2012; interview member of IUCN member NGO, 17 May 2013, Gland.

science even further as evidenced in occasional signs of opening up for 'soft' science and knowledge. Thus, reports acknowledged that IUCN also needed to incorporate findings from social science (IUCN 2003: 54), pay attention to traditional ways of natural resources management (IUCN 2009: 4), or integrate local people's view of the holiness of nature into its guidelines (IUCN 2009: 24). The most visible expression of this new development certainly is IUCN's support for the Intergovernmental Science-Policy Platform for Biodiversity and Ecosystem Services (IPBES) (IUCN 2013: 18). IPBES is not only intended to become an authoritative independent knowledge provider for governments but it also undertakes notable efforts to be open to local and traditional knowledge (Esguerra et al. 2017). Yet, in contrast to other developments, these new ones rarely feature in members' statements. Overall, members show little sensitivity for other than 'traditional academic' knowledge, and they only occasionally call on IUCN to learn from the practical experience of local organizations (IUCN 1997b: 25, NGO from Malaysia), regional teams (IUCN 1990: 57, NGO from Australia), or indigenous peoples (summary of a workshop discussion quoted in IUCN 1994: 74–5).

Finally, a further manifestation of the increasing centrality of 'the people' in the legitimation contest can be seen in the growing recognition of indigenous peoples' rights. Internationally, IUCN has always been at the forefront of pushing protected areas as a conservation method and has been involved in the establishment and management of many of them (Stevens 1997a). Its policies and practices therefore have always had significant repercussions for the livelihoods of indigenous peoples, as many of them have traditionally lived in and around protected areas. And yet, until the late 1980s, indigenous peoples' concerns received only sporadic attention in the IUCN network (an exception being for instance a 1975 resolution on indigenous rights in protected areas, see Stevens 1997a: 35–9). But from then on, awareness evolved among IUCN leadership and parts of membership that indigenous peoples had not been sufficiently integrated into IUCN's work (e.g. IUCN President quoted in IUCN 1988: 36; 1997b: 26, NGO from Australia). In 1991, *Caring for the Earth* endorsed the 'rights of indigenous peoples to their lands and resources' and emphasized the need to cooperate with indigenous peoples in conservation management (IUCN et al. 1991: 61). Throughout the 1990s, IUCN followed up with a couple of policy guidelines in this spirit (Chapin 2004: 20; Stevens 1997b: 40–3), while attention dedicated to the issue in annual reports at the time was moderate and mostly focused on the importance of indigenous traditional knowledge (e.g. IUCN 1990: 51; 1995: 12). Occasionally, more traditionally oriented member NGOs voiced concerns that indigenous resource use might threaten conservation goals (IUCN 1994: 63, WWF; 1997b: 34, Sierra Club), and some state members such as Canada, New Zealand, or India expressed their principled reluctance to govern indigenous peoples matters through global agreements rather than domestically (e.g. IUCN 1997b: 27 and 29). But the overall thrust of discussion with and among members was that IUCN should include indigenous peoples in conservation management and respect their contributions to conservation as well as their (cultural and economic) rights.[24]

The indigenous rights agenda gained further traction after the turn of the millennium. In 2000, the Theme on Indigenous and Local Communities, Equity and Protected Areas (TILCEPA) was initiated to promote good practice in protected areas management (Brosius 2004: 609). This was an essential precursor for the adoption of the Durban Accord[25] at the 2003 IUCN World Parks Congress (Brosius 2004: 609), which formally recognized the rights of people living in protected areas, and which observers have assessed as 'a major step forward' (Adams and Hutton 2007: 163; see similarly Brosius 2004: 611; Colchester 2004: 145). Ever since, the IUCN bureaucracy has regularly emphasized how its work promotes the rights, interests, and participation of indigenous peoples in conservation policy, stating for example that (IUCN 2003: 23): 'IUCN's work with indigenous and local communities responds to the need to address the complex relationships between poverty alleviation, the maintenance of biological and cultural diversity and the fundamental rights of indigenous and traditional peoples.'[26] In parallel, the institutional development continued; notably, IUCN became one of the founding members of the Conservation Initiative on Human Rights[27] in 2009—which quickly came to be considered a flagship initiative by the global conservation community. The preliminary culmination of institutional development was the establishment of a third chamber for indigenous peoples at WCCs, in 2016, 'in recognition of the role they play in conserving the planet' (IUCN 2016c: 40).[28]

Thus, overall, indigenous rights are on the rise; and while the concerns of indigenous peoples were taken up within the IUCN network later than elsewhere in the international community, and the process had a relatively slow start, the support for their rights has accelerated on rhetorical and institutional design levels since the turn of the millennium. The trend towards a more diversified *people-based* legitimation is thus unabated. Translating this and the other developments described above into our bubbles model, we see a significant increase in the size of the human well-being bubble from the moment that sustainable development became a paramount reference frame

---

[24] E.g. workshop discussion summarized in IUCN 1988: 21; several workshop discussions summarized in 1990: 19, 62 and 67–8; 1994: 63, WWF; workshop discussion summarized in 1994: 67; workshop discussions summarized in 1997b: 42.

[25] See http://www.danadeclaration.org/pdf/durbanaccordeng.pdf (last accessed 14 July 2018).

[26] For further examples along these lines see e.g. IUCN 2005a: 26; 2007: 28; 2008: 10 and 34; 2011: 18; 2017: 40; 2018: 40.

[27] See http://www.thecihr.org/ (last accessed 14 July 2018).

[28] On earlier moves to enhance indigenous peoples' visibility at Congresses see also Paulson et al. 2012: 262.

in the discourse. With the broadened understanding of participation and expertise, the related bubbles primarily changed their colour (= meaning) but the participation bubble also grew in size (= relevance). Moreover, from the turn to local stakeholder participation and knowledge a new but closely connected bubble, labelled 'indigenous rights', emerged.

BEYOND ENVIRONMENTAL LAW MAKING
AND PROTECTED AREAS: THE RISE
OF MARKET-BASED NORMS

A second major shift we observe concerns the rise of market-based approaches as a *means* of conservation, and the contestation over the role such approaches should play in IUCN's work. To some extent, this squares with concerns about the *performance* of international organizations, as market-based conservation measures and the economic valuation of nature are increasingly presented by the IUCN Secretariat as the most effective and efficient conservation tools.[29] In particular, some NGO members contest this assumption and highlight the incompatibility of some business partnerships with human rights, and the intrinsic value of nature, but as the following sections will show their opposition is too weak to stop this trend.

For a long time, the Union refrained from addressing economic policies at all, as evidenced already by its initial approach to the notion of sustainable development. This is mirrored in a similarly hesitant approach to businesses. Until the mid-1990s, IUCN engaged only rarely with economic actors and, if so, in a rather ad hoc manner (e.g. IUCN 1971: 25; 1990: 25). An early call for a sustained dialogue between governments, the private sector, and the conservation movement was launched in *Caring for the Earth* which elaborates the need for business to adopt sustainable practices but also names benefits that business can reap from preventing pollution, including lower operational costs and reduced liability for clean-up (IUCN et al. 1991: 96–105). Yet, only in 1996 did the WCC adopt two resolutions that urged IUCN to expand dialogue, 'productive relationships', and interaction with the private sector in order to influence the latter's assessment of environmental risks and damages (resolutions 1.81 and 1.82). At that time, business cooperation was of little interest to the members but having adopted the pertaining motions a majority of them obviously approved of this move. Some members overtly shared the expectation that IUCN could change business practices and support

---

[29] Note, though, that this move to corporate engagement is complementing rather than replacing protected areas as a key conservation method.

conservation effectiveness through cooperation with business (IUCN 1997b: 17, Zoological Society of London).

In the aftermath of the adoption of these motions, activities by the Secretariat provided a boost to business cooperation which then also became much more contested. To develop a more systematic cooperation, the IUCN Secretariat set up a *Business and Biodiversity Programme* (BBP) in 2003.[30] It conducts joint projects with corporations from different sectors, including Shell, Holcim, and Nespresso, to devise environmental management plans with and for them. In terms of justification, IUCN's reports repeatedly emphasize the positive impact on the corporate ecological footprints of its business partners (e.g. IUCN 2008: 3, 7, and 8; IUCN-BBP 2011: 1 and 8). This trend continues well beyond 2010 (e.g. IUCN 2018: 24–5; IUCN-BBP 2012: 1, 7, 13 and 16; 2017: 15). Institutionally, moreover, IUCN adopted a *Business Engagement Strategy* in 2012, with the aim 'to encourage transformational and demonstrable change at the company level to value biodiversity' (IUCN 2013: 15), and new corporate partnerships have recently been announced, for instance with Toyota Motor Corporation (IUCN 2017: 18).

The practical cooperation with business has moreover been embedded by the Secretariat in a broader neoliberal agenda that supports norms of *efficiency* and the *economic value of nature*. IUCN reports vividly illustrate how conservation yields economic efficiency gains (IUCN 2005a: 51):

> For decades, IUCN conserved a bird, wasp, orchid or soft coral species for its beauty and from our moral responsibility. Yet today the Union is harnessing an equally powerful incentive to keep habitats whole: economics ... Wildlife makes us all much richer, aesthetically and financially. Grain-eating crows can be a pest to farmers, but songbirds in agricultural nations produce billions of dollars in free pest control services.

In addition, they praise IUCN for actively participating in the economic valuation of nature, highlighting for instance (IUCN 2007: 22) how IUCN:

> contributes to making the hidden wealth of biodiversity explicit, and changing the exchange rate. We promote rigorous economic valuation of ecosystem goods and services to clarify the role that ecosystems play in the livelihoods of the poor and the economies of nations. In 2006, we put a price on environmental damages, estimated the return on investment of restoration efforts, and calculated the benefits of healthy ecosystems.[31]

This became a major strategic approach followed by the Secretariat, after IUCN participated in the UNEP-led so-called TEEB study on *The Economics of Ecosystems and Biodiversity* (IUCN 2010: 22). Within a few years of its launch by Germany and the European Commission in 2007, TEEB (Kumar

---

[30] Interview, IUCN staff, 17 May 2013, Gland.
[31] See also IUCN 2003: 33–4; 2009: 35; 2011: 22–3; IUCN-BBP 2011: 2.

2012) became the international reference framework for the monetary valuation of nature and the economic costs associated with its loss. The IUCN report for 2010 took pride in IUCN having been a 'key contributor' (IUCN 2011: 22) to TEEB. Moreover, from the 2009 annual report onwards, several reports also contained sections on 'greening the world economy' in which they refer back to TEEB and/or point out how IUCN attempts to work for the establishment of global economic incentives for conservation (IUCN 2010: 22; 2011: 22; 2012b: 23). In the same vein, one observer of the 2012 WCC notes 'the language of "natural capital", "ecosystem services", "economic valuation", "green growth", and the like was pervasive' (Fletcher 2014: 334).

While the original call on IUCN to cooperate with business to change its conduct was very generic, as its manifestations became more visible over time, opposition emerged among parts of the membership.[32] It primarily demanded that IUCN should not cooperate with firms from the extractive industries which are involved in large-scale landscape destruction and frequent human rights violations.[33] According to Kenneth MacDonald's participatory observations, these voices were very pronounced at the 2003 World Parks Congress and the 2004 WCC where audiences openly attacked IUCN's business strategies (MacDonald 2010b: 257–8). The 2008 WCC, then, appears as both a culmination point and a watershed in this regard. Contention arose around a number of motions related to the way the IUCN Secretariat engaged with business, but it was a motion to terminate the cooperation with Shell that marked the pinnacle of these debates (MacDonald 2010b: 270). Though it was supported by more than 70 per cent of the NGO membership, it was nevertheless turned down as only fifteen governments were in support of it (Friends of the Earth International 2009: 2).

At the same time, protest against the mounting presence of businesses during the WCC was already less apparent in 2008 than back in 2004 (MacDonald 2010b: 258). This trend, as observed by Robert Fletcher, continued at the 2012 WCC where dissent with IUCN's business cooperation was voiced mostly in the hallways rather than in public settings (Fletcher 2014: 335). Accounts of public protests at the 2016 WCC against IUCN's economic agenda have not transpired in the media, Congress reports, or academic scholarship. But our interviews from 2013 support the impression that it is a rather small number of NGOs that keep up the criticism that business cooperation is detrimental to conservation,[34] and/or human rights protection.[35] Some even argue that IUCN should focus on the conservation

---

[32] This criticism is rarely found in the proceedings of the General Assemblies and WCCs, so most information in this section relies heavily on interviews and secondary literature.

[33] Skype interview, member of IUCN member NGO, 12 June 2013.

[34] Interviews IUCN staff 13, 14, 15, and 16 May 2013, Gland.

[35] Skype interview, member of IUCN member NGO, 12 June; personal communication with commission working group member, 15 October 2015, Amsterdam. At the same time, even

of nature for its own sake instead of what they perceive as a betrayal of IUCN's original conservationist values through economic valuation.[36] However, especially smaller NGO members rarely have the capacity to follow up on IUCN's activities in this regard and hence are hardly aware of it.[37] Some other members share the view that business cooperation is an appropriate avenue to conservation effectiveness.[38]

Interestingly, in contrast to earlier debates about sustainable development, these criticisms are hardly officially acknowledged at the Secretariat level—and to the extent that they are, this pertains only to a couple of years after the main disruptions over IUCN's business strategy in the mid- and late 2000s. During this time span, IUCN reports treated challenges with regard to private-sector engagement merely as an ongoing debate over how to best realize the mandate for engaging with the private sector (IUCN-BBP 2010: 15). In so far as the reports explicitly acknowledged the criticism of IUCN's business partnerships, they countered this criticism by insisting that market-based approaches are a powerful tool for conservation (e.g. IUCN 2005a: 52; IUCN-BBP 2012: 15). Moreover, in response to concerns, the Secretariat committed to being transparent about IUCN's business partnerships (IUCN-BBP 2010: 21; 2011: 1). However, since about 2012, no more hints at criticism of IUCN's economic agenda can be found in the reports. This mirrors Robert Fletcher's (2014: 335) observations that, at the 2012 WCC, the daily official summaries of members' discussions emphasized broad agreement on the need to bolster market-based conservation approaches, while lively informal debates took place about the desirability of the neoliberal agenda. In light of this downplaying of critical NGO positions, it is hardly surprising that IUCN's move to market-based conservationism continues. Most notably, in 2016, the Union joined the World Business Council for Sustainable Development and other major environmental organizations and corporations in drafting the *Natural Capital Protocol*,[39] which is geared to helping businesses measure their dependency and impacts on nature (IUCN 2017: 20).

In sum, the practical shift to cooperation with business and its embedding in the broader neoliberal agenda jointly reflect IUCN's alignment with 'liberal environmentalism' that was characteristic of the UN system from the 1970s onwards (Bernstein 2001). This is especially the case as IUCN began to engage in a broader debate about the role and potential of sustainable growth in the

---

critics of corporate engagement acknowledge that IUCN works well and on a sustainable basis with small-scale businesses at the local level (personal communication commission working group member, October 2015).

[36] Interview, IUCN staff, 13 May 2013, Gland.

[37] Skype interview, member of IUCN member NGO, 12 June 2013.

[38] Interviews, IUCN staff, 13, 15, and 17 May 2013, Gland.

[39] https://www.wbcsd.org/Programs/Redefining-Value/Business-Decision-Making/Measurement-Valuation/Natural-Capital-Protocol (last access 14 July 2018).

international economic system. Evidently, these developments stand in stark contrast to notions of the sacredness of nature that motivated IUCN's early supporters as well as to some members' concerns over conservation effectiveness and human rights. The Secretariat reacts to criticism of business partnerships by either overlooking it or by defending and expanding this practice. Critical NGOs thus had much less influence in this case than in the first normative shift. In consequence, once market liberal norms had entered the picture, the bubble continued to grow and became ever more important as a normative reference point for IUCN's work.

PATHWAYS OF NORMATIVE CHANGE

Looking at the dynamics that made the two main normative changes possible, we can distinguish between three broad pathways. The first two pathways explain the first norm change. The first path relates to the confluence of different actors pushing for a more development-oriented agenda. The second path combines the push by interest groups with self-reinforcing dynamics in the wake of earlier normative change. Finally, the third path explains the second norm change; it highlights how key figures in the IUCN Secretariat successfully pushed for the uptake of neoliberal norms of market-based conservationism.

Development-Oriented Norm Entrepreneurship

As to the first pathway of change, the growing importance of Southern actors' development concerns, and a higher institutional density in the environmental policy field provided the context within which the Secretariat set IUCN on the path of sustainable development through the adoption of the WCS. The choice of this path was reinforced by pressure from IUCN's Southern members and other organizations in the field.

As briefly described in the section on the historical context, from the early 1970s onwards, it was well noted in international environmental policy circles that Southern actors' cooperation in international environmental policies could not be gained unless development concerns were simultaneously addressed. Moreover, as the field of (international) environmental politics was populated by more and more institutions from the 1970s onwards, IUCN's role as the single most important international environmental organization was increasingly threatened. This new context helped those actors pushing for a more social agenda to steer IUCN away from its traditional wildlife focus.

The key driving force behind the strengthening of human well-being norms was the IUCN Secretariat which was primarily responsible for preparing the various drafts of the WCS (Holdgate 1999: 150; Talbot 1980: 266). In the late 1960s and early 1970s, the IUCN Secretariat had already been sensitive to the need to think of conservation and development together more consistently.[40] The initial institutionalization of human well-being concerns at the 1969 New Delhi General Assembly was a first attempt to strengthen environmental policies 'in a way that would carry support in the developing countries' (Holdgate 1999: 109). In the drafting of the WCS from 1975 onwards, the need to translate the tight relationship between conservation and development into a policy strategy became even clearer (Talbot 1980: 265–6). This boost in conservation-and-development thinking clearly reflects the altered setting in which IUCN operated at the time. While IUCN's annual reports rarely explicitly situated its work in the context of development-oriented policies, and barely took note of the outcomes of the Stockholm Conference (for this observation see also McCormick 1989: 98), the Union's leadership was aware that its activities had to be in line with the policy ideals of the time in order for IUCN to stay relevant (Lausche 2008: 203). Eventually, the personal background of key figures certainly also played a vital role in this. While the top leadership previously exclusively had a Northern background, in the years before the adoption of the WCS, for the first time, IUCN had a Southern Director General, Gerardo Budowski from Venezuela (1970–6), and President, Mohamed Kassas from Egypt (1978–84) (Holdgate 1999: 258).

Besides better representation at the leadership level, the share of Southern members consistently rose from the 1970s onwards (see Figure 6.1), and their voice gained weight in IUCN's bicameral governance system. Just as we have observed in our case study of the WTO (Chapter 3), Southern members enhanced the pressure on IUCN to become more open to notions of sustainable development.[41] In particular, during the discussion of the draft WCS at the 1978 General Assembly, Southern members insisted that conservation was to be firmly aligned with development objectives (Holdgate 1999: 151; McCormick 1989: 165).

In addition to the impact of actors within the IUCN network, the process of developing the WCS gave other organizations in the field the opportunity to push for a firmer commitment to development goals. The members, hundreds of scientific advisors, and the main partner organizations in this endeavour, namely the UN Food and Agricultural Organization, UN Educational, Scientific and Cultural Organization, UNEP, and WWF, could comment on every new draft version (Holdgate 1999: 150; Talbot 1980: 266). Particularly, a handful of socially concerned key UNEP staff members insisted that IUCN

---

[40] Interview, IUCN Environmental Law Centre, 22 July 2013, Bonn.
[41] Interview, IUCN Environmental Law Centre, 22 July 2013, Bonn.

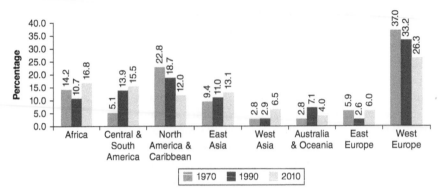

Figure 6.1. Share of national IUCN members from different world regions (total number of national members: 1970: 254; 1990: 663; 2010: 1138)

Source: own compilation from IUCN annual reports

ought to integrate development concerns more firmly in the strategy and made clear that UNEP would otherwise not accept the text (Holdgate 1999: 151).

In sum, a changed understanding in the Secretariat about the objectives of conservation, shifts in the membership structure, and the rising prominence of development concerns in other international institutions active in the environmental field jointly pushed for the acknowledgement of such goals in IUCN as well.

Normative Path Dependence

The second pathway starts from the firm establishment of the sustainable development norm by the WCS. This provided a new normative context that can be seen as the beginning of a normative path dependence—which was, however, supported by Southern and indigenous actors. According to Martin Holdgate, Director General from 1988 to 1994, the adoption of the WCS, in conjunction with the even stronger social orientation that the WCED had introduced in the environmental policy field, encouraged IUCN to put people in Southern countries centre stage in the organization's work (quoted in IUCN 1988: 217). This, in turn, provided opportunities for Southern actors to add further demands. The results were deepened regionalization, strengthened democratic norms, and a broadened understanding of valuable knowledge, all accompanied by a reinforcement of human well-being norms and its expansion to indigenous peoples.

A first development that directly and logically followed from the WCS was IUCN's regionalization. A greater presence in the regions had become a functional necessity if IUCN wanted to support Southern countries in the implementation of sustainable development. In contrast to IUCN's original focus on support for countries' environmental policy and law making

(Lausche 2008; Olivier 2005), the effective implementation of the WCS's emphasis on sustainable development required IUCN to become more active on the ground (Talbot 1983: 8–9). Key to the approach was the development of national conservation strategies. In order to put this strategy to work, support was seen as particularly necessary in regions outside Europe and North America (Holdgate 1999: 149; McCormick 1986: 185). This stronger focus on *activities* in the South, however, could neither be effective nor legitimate unless it was paired with greater sensitivity to the diversity of conservation-related *concerns* in these regions and at the local level.

At the same time, Southern members used the momentum of the adoption of the WCS to actively push the Secretariat to expand IUCN's presence in the field in the Global South.[42] First, they demanded that the Secretariat was more active in the regions to support capacity building for members, so that they could develop and implement national conservation strategies in line with the WCS.[43] Second, they called for more regionalization in order to better align IUCN's activities with members' needs and interests (IUCN 1995: 2). Third, these members believed that IUCN would eventually be more effective in conservation if it worked more through the regions. IUCN's move to the regions in the 1980s and 1990s was thus (also) a response to these powerful demands by Southern country members (Holdgate 1999: 207; IUCN 1993: 15).[44] As put by IUCN President Jay Hair and Director General David McDowell in a letter to the members on this issue, in 1995 (quoted in IUCN 1995: 2): 'We listened to you and as your new leaders, we committed ourselves to respond.'

The turn to regionalization, on its part, also encouraged a further deepening and broadening of *people-based* norms. In this sense, the increasing focus on regional and local conditions accounts for the continuous consolidation of *human well-being* norms which we have described above. The IUCN Secretariat explicitly pointed out that this was necessary because its own activities at the regional and local level could only be successful if they took local people's material needs into account (IUCN 1995: 25). But the deepening of human well-being norms was also aided by further pushes from Southern IUCN leadership figures and Southern members. In the first regard, IUCN Presidents Monkombu Swaminathan from India (1984–90) and Shridath Ramphal from Guyana (1990–4) were widely recognized for being very outspoken on the need for IUCN to integrate conservation and development (Casey-Lefkowitz 1991: 19; Rabbinge 2015: 445; Toro-Pérez 2005: 87 and 89). In the second

---

[42] IUCN 1993: 15; 1990: 57, island nations of the South Pacific; 1994: 9, government members Jordan and Oman; 1994: 22, NGO from Jamaica; 1996: 24), NGO from Malaysia; 2008: 13 NGO from Guatemala; telephone interview former councillor, 5 July 2013.

[43] Interview, IUCN staff, 15 May 2013, Gland.

[44] Telephone interview, former IUCN councillor, 5 July 2013.

regard, Southern members, not only but especially NGO members, remained adamant that IUCN needed to follow a sustainable development agenda.[45]

In addition to the strengthening of *human well-being norms*, the turn to regionalization provided a boost to the *differentiation of people-based legitimation* in three main regards. First, awareness grew in the Secretariat that sustainable development objectives were closely tied to participatory conservation approaches. As the number of field projects multiplied, it acknowledged that their conservation success relied on the participation and ownership of local communities (e.g. IUCN 1993: 16; 1995: 20 and 25; 2009: 48; 2011: 16), and that collaboration with local partners and people could support more socially desirable and equitable solutions (IUCN 2003: 25 and 54). Without local people's participation it would be impossible to know what their needs really were, and it would therefore be impossible to design socially beneficial conservation activities. Second, local knowledge gained recognition in much the same way. The reports thus explained that IUCN attempted to integrate local stakeholders' knowledge precisely because this yielded the promise of more successful local conservation projects (IUCN 1999: 23, 26, and 32).

Third, norms related to well-being, participation, and local knowledge have been extended to indigenous peoples with some time lag. This suggests that, by the early 2000s, these norms were widely accepted within the IUCN network and the core question rather was which constituency they should be applied to. In terms of normative path dependence, according to the IUCN bureaucracy, 'lessons learned from field experience' motivated IUCN to work more for the recognition of indigenous peoples' rights (IUCN 2003: 32). More concretely, for instance, consultations with indigenous communities were acknowledged as important for successful local conservation action (IUCN 2005a: 26), as was indigenous knowledge about the useful properties of local species (IUCN 2005a: 43).

Additional impetus for this development came from the growing strength of the indigenous rights movement. A 'relatively small but dedicated group of civil society and indigenous peoples' organizations' (Jonas 2017: 148) had initially undertaken considerable effort to strengthen awareness for indigenous peoples' contributions to conservation, from the late 1990s to the mid-2000s and thereafter, to push an explicitly rights-based conservation approach. Particularly, the adoption of the indigenous rights-recognizant Durban Accord at the 2003 World Parks Congress was the result of preparatory work by indigenous peoples' organizations (Brosius 2004: 609; Colchester 2004: 150). These initiatives, however, found fertile ground as the IUCN bureaucracy itself had become more open for indigenous concerns— which, in particular, manifested itself in the setting up of TILCEPA in 2000

---

[45] Interview, IUCN staff, 15 May 2013, Gland.

(Brosius 2004: 609). Eventually, IUCN's indigenous rights agenda cannot be understood without noting the significant interdependencies between IUCN and the CBD's work on protected areas. Not only was IUCN actively involved in the drafting of the CBD (McGraw 2002: 10), but its 2003 Durban Accord also provided a major impetus for the adoption of the CBD's Programme of Work on Protected Areas (PoWPA) in 2004 (Kothari et al. 2013: 2). The PoWPA, in turn, includes a strong requirement that the establishment and management of protected areas should be in full respect of the rights of indigenous peoples and local communities, and puts a strong emphasis on the participatory governance of protected areas (United Nations 2004). It has been assessed by observers as a break with the old paradigm of top-down exclusionary protected areas (e.g. Stevens 2014: 60). Moreover, it provided the background for resolutions adopted at the 2004 and 2008 WCCs that took IUCN's indigenous rights agenda further (Kothari et al. 2013: 2).[46]

In summary, normative path dependence in the aftermath of the adoption of the WCS goes a long way in explaining the multifaceted turn to people-based norms, but it was aided by leadership figures in the Secretariat, and the influence of Southern members and indigenous rights groups.

Neoliberal Norm Entrepreneurship

While the shift to market-based legitimation norms followed a different path, like the rise of human well-being norms it was strongly influenced by broader ideas that gained traction in response to the world political context. In the first case, sustainable development norms provided that context; in the second case, the (nearly) global turn to neoliberalism after 1990 became reflected in the environmental policy field and in IUCN. And similarly to the first case, the influence of the world political context materialized for IUCN only after a considerable time lag, and only when influential norm entrepreneurs— notably the IUCN Secretariat and its leading figures—seized the opportunity to jump on the neoliberal bandwagon and push for transforming the ways IUCN would approach conservation.

The beginning of IUCN's systematic and formalized cooperation with business through the two 1996 resolutions was an initial expression of the perceived need to influence the behaviour of corporations, in addition to that of governments. Within the IUCN Secretariat, a market-based conservation

---

[46] In the light of these developments, it may come as a surprise that the 2007 adoption of UNDRIP does not seem to have had further impact on the legitimation discourse and institutional practice. Possibly, the milestones achieved with the 2003 Durban Accord and the CBD's 2004 PoWPA have much more tangible consequences for conservation work on the ground and therefore appear as much more influential.

logic started to gain traction in the early 2000s, mainly out of a frustration with traditional conservation approaches. Previous strategies of providing expertise, working with governments in environmental law making, and implementing conservation projects on the ground were increasingly perceived as unhelpful to solve the environmental crisis.[47] For instance, former Director General Julia Marton-Lefèvre emphasized that all the specialist knowledge gathered about the threats of biodiversity loss had not been able to stop it (Monfreda 2010: 279). Moreover, there was a strong awareness of the expanding influence of the private sector in the world economy, and of its significant impact on the environment as well as on human well-being.[48] Against this background, the neoliberal economic *zeitgeist* seemed to offer promising new solutions to the extinction crisis.

Proponents of the market-based conservation agenda in IUCN expected that conservation goals could be addressed more forcefully by cooperating with businesses and speaking a language that business can relate to, namely the language of economic valuation of nature (IUCN 1997a: 4 and 8; 2005a: 17; for the observation of the frequent invocation of this argument during Congress discussions see also Fletcher 2014: 335).[49] This belief was strongly held in the IUCN Secretariat and its staff capitalized on its influential role in the organization, with other IUCN bodies providing relatively little input on this agenda.[50] Several reasons account for the strength of the Secretariat: first, WCCs only take place every four years, and the members have limited possibilities to influence IUCN's policies in between.[51] Moreover, the motions members adopt at WCCs may be binding for the Secretariat, but they are often rather unspecific and thereby provide considerable leeway for interpreting them in different ways.[52] Finally, the relations between IUCN and other actors are generally managed by the Secretariat, and it maintains frequent and good relations with some business actors.[53] Beyond that, observers of WCCs have noted that the Secretariat also very skilfully designed the set-up of recent Congresses and framed their (interim) results in ways that concealed sustained criticism (Fletcher 2014; MacDonald 2010b). As also observed in our case

[47] Skype interview, member of IUCN member NGO, 12 June 2013; interview IUCN staff, 17 May 2013, Gland.
[48] Interview, IUCN staff, 17 May 2013, Gland; Skype interview member of IUCN member NGO, 12 June 2013.
[49] Interview, IUCN staff, 17 May 2013, Gland; Skype interview member of IUCN member NGO, 12 June 2013.
[50] Interview, IUCN staff, 17 May 2013, Gland; personal communication, commission working group member, October 2015, Amsterdam.
[51] Telephone interview, member of an IUCN national committee, 29 May 2013.
[52] Interview, IUCN staff, 13 May 2013, Gland; Skype interview, former councillor, 26 August 2013.
[53] Skype interview, former councillor, 26 August 2013.

study on the Organisation of African Unity/African Union (Chapter 4), the task of reporting thus gives leading bureaucrats considerable framing powers.

Within the Secretariat, several of the more recent leadership figures supported the organization's business and biodiversity agenda (Holdgate 1999: 222; MacDonald 2010b: 266). An outstanding proponent was Valli Moosa, who remained in the energy industry during his term as IUCN President from 2004 to 2008 (MacDonald 2010a: 540). But Julia Marton-Lefèvre, who was Director General from 2007 to 2014, too, expressed hope that communicating the economic value of nature to policy makers, the business community, and the public would be more effective to raise support for conservation than the traditional regulatory approach. Indeed, she actively used her leadership power to push IUCN's tight alignment with the TEEB study and agenda (Monfreda 2010: 279). As a result of such firm beliefs in the environmental benefits of (the right kind of) economic incentives held by key actors in a powerful Secretariat, the market-based conservation agenda could receive a strong boost within a relatively short time span. In contrast, the critical NGO community was small and weak because by the time these debates became prevalent, many conservation NGOs had already subscribed to the market-based agenda and participated in public–private partnerships (MacDonald 2010b: 258 and 272). However, those NGOs that had remained critical were increasingly marginalized in the debates. This also explains how the neoliberal agenda could become dominant in spite of the fierce opposition that parts of the membership, at times, exhibited.

CONCLUSIONS

IUCN's slogan for the 2012 WCC was 'Nature+'. It was to convey the message that 'there is so much more to nature than what we know about', and that nature relates to a wide variety of aspects of life and policy such as 'nature + climate, nature + economy, nature + people and so on' (Cherny-Scanlon 2012). In its own view and that of its members, IUCN still has an important function to fulfil as Noah's Ark that conserves species. But its journey through more than four decades of changes in the broader field of environmental policy, together with its own decisions, have steered the organization into a position in which it has to take many additional normative considerations into account. As in other cases we study in this book, the list of legitimacy standards IUCN needs to fulfil has become longer over time.

Regarding its own governance, IUCN has always been a very progressive organization due to its bicameral structure that has given NGOs an equal say in the Union's decision making from early on. Yet, it was strikingly conservative for a long time; its approach to conservation and the way it treats local stakeholders, affected by its policies and projects, have changed only slowly. In particular, IUCN was, for a long time, a very traditional conservation organization that aimed to conserve species largely for their own sake. Against this background, the two normative changes we describe in this chapter tell the story of a gradual dissolution of the perceived contradictions between nature and its use by humans. The milestone event for the first change was the adoption of the WCS in 1980, through which IUCN firmly committed itself to the goal of sustainable development. In its aftermath, the legitimation norms associated with this commitment have steadily deepened and broadened. More recently, a second normative change first introduced and then strengthened liberal notions of conservation in IUCN's work. In particular, IUCN has subscribed to market-based instruments and to the idea of putting a price tag on nature. In contrast to the first change, the beginnings of this second shift went largely unnoticed by many members; only as market-based conservation approaches became more institutionalized within IUCN did a small number of outspoken critics start to fiercely contest this development. Even though both of these changes affect the dominant conception of the relation between nature and the economy, they ought to be understood as separate from each other. On the one hand, the deepening and broadening of human well-being concerns could have continued in the same manner, without the parallel commitment to a market logic from the late 1990s. On the other hand, the ideals of market-based conservationism do not depend on the previous adoption of a more social agenda in order to attract political support.

What, then, do these developments tell us about the rise of *people-centred and procedural* legitimation norms? In terms of the latter, IUCN's governance structure that endows governmental and non-governmental organizations with a vote is a constant positive reference point for all participants in the discourse, so that no fundamental rise in *procedural* norms can be observed at this level. Nonetheless, with regard to regionalization and the mounting attention to local participation in concrete conservation measures, adherence to democratic decision making becomes more important. As a result, a legitimation contest over the right procedures comes to complement the legitimation contest over the performance of IUCN. And yet, this development only follows suit from the overarching shift to *people-centred* legitimation norms expressed in the rise of human well-being as a central standard of legitimacy.

In terms of the *pathways* of normative change, IUCN stands out as an example of an organization that is strongly driven by internal developments, namely the normative path dependence initiated by the turn to sustainable development and the leadership of a strong Secretariat. Regarding *normative path dependence*, once the WCS set IUCN firmly on the path to sustainable development, other normative adjustments became more or less 'logical' to fully realize this new perspective. In addition, both the turn to sustainable development and human well-being as well as to market-based conservation mechanisms have found vigorous supporters in the Secretariat; in both cases, the Secretariat also initially came up with concrete plans to modify IUCN's strategic course, thus acting as a *powerful norm entrepreneur*. For the first change, the *rise of the Global South* and later of the indigenous rights movements presented additional driving forces that supported the Secretariat in advocating for the new norms.

At the same time, it is striking how rarely exceptional external events (e.g. the Stockholm Conference or the report of the WCED) were mentioned in the legitimation discourse in the early decades we have analysed, and how big the time lag was with which IUCN took up key developments in the policy field. Certainly, the influence of the external environment can be seen. On the one hand, *political globalization* in the form of rising institutional density in international environmental politics required IUCN to modify some of its objectives in order to stay relevant in the field. Hence, the boost in attention to human (economic) well-being through the WCS also followed from the recognition by the IUCN leadership that a rising number of other organizations in the field had already been committed to the notion of sustainable development, and that this was the route international environmental politics would take in future. On the other hand, *economic globalization*, characterized by the rising impact of multinational corporations and a neoliberal anti-regulatory *zeitgeist*, provided a context that either gave impetus for the Secretariat to modify IUCN's approach to conservation or, at least, facilitated such a modification.

However, the fact that these external forces only made themselves felt long after they had shaped the broader policy field, and once they did this occurred against internal opposition, suggests that IUCN, in many ways, long remained a relatively conservative organization; it avoided too much entanglement with the broader structures of international environmental governance. With IUCN's early involvement in recent flagship initiatives and institutions such as TEEB, the Conservation Initiative for Human Rights, and IPBES, the Union seems to be catching up with current dynamics in the policy field, but only time will tell whether this is a lasting trend, or whether the Union will again fall behind when entirely new normative orientations emerge in the field in the future.

It is only possible to speculate about the reasons for IUCN's long role as a laggard in many ideational developments, but its legacy as a very traditional wildlife-centred conservation organization offers one plausible explanation. Despite all the changes described in this chapter, IUCN still has many wildlife-focused members that are likely to slow down the pace of normative change. Moreover, IUCN flies below the radar of public attention and opinion. In the absence of politicization, it differs from other organizations we study in this book in as much as it does not need to react quickly to the demands of new and very diverse audiences. Thus, the IUCN case does not disconfirm our expectations about the influence of the external context on international organizations' changing terms of legitimation. But it does suggest that international organizations may be receptive to changes in their external environments to different degrees and that this receptiveness may be strongly determined by the historical legacy of the organization. In the IUCN case, this means that a *progressive governance structure* may still lead to conservative policies in an organization with a *traditionally minded membership structure*.

7

Navigating between Refugee Protection and State Sovereignty

Legitimating the United Nations High Commissioner for Refugees

Ellen Reichel

INTRODUCTION

For 2017, the Office of the United Nations High Commissioner for Refugees (UNHCR) recorded 68.5 million forcibly displaced people—a new record high for the sixth year in a row (UNHCR 2018b). The office was founded in 1950 to deal with the remaining caseload of refugees in post-World War II Europe, and was intended to render itself superfluous by finding so-called durable solutions for these refugees. However, the unabatedly high number of refugees, caused by conflicts and crises around the world as well as new groups of persons of concern for the office, make UNHCR 'every bit as relevant as it was when the Office was established in 1950' (UN General Assembly 2011: 1).

This quotation is drawn from a text in which the then High Commissioner António Guterres commemorates the office's sixtieth anniversary. Besides noting the continued relevance of his organization and its mandate, he alludes to two basic challenges for the legitimation of UNHCR. First, he points out that UNHCR's environment is changing and with it the kind and severity of problems UNHCR is set out to resolve. Second, he notes a need to change the balance between concern for national sovereignty and the protection of human rights. However, neither challenge was new to UNHCR in 2010.

According to Alexander Betts, who has written extensively about the organization, UNHCR always needed to adapt its mandate to stay relevant in a rapidly changing world (Betts 2012). Throughout its history, even though the formal mandate remained the same, the actual scope of UNHCR's tasks and persons of concern has constantly been expanded (see also Barnett and Finnemore 2004: 73–4). As a result, the organization frequently needed to act beyond what states had originally agreed to be its proper purpose while giving the impression that it was still acting within the legal boundaries of its mandate. By promoting the image of being *flexible* and *innovative*, UNHCR sought to secure support for expanding its mandate.

Apart from challenges arising from the scope and limits of its legal mandate, UNHCR was also constantly faced with the potential friction between the rights of refugees and the interests of its member states (see Loescher et al. 2008: 2). On the one hand, UNHCR's most basic function is the *protection of refugees' rights*. On the other hand, it is a *service provider for states*, assisting them in the management of refugee flows. As a part of its role, UNHCR is also tasked with monitoring states' compliance with the 1951 Convention relating to the Status of Refugees, sometimes referred to as the Geneva Convention. Yet, by calling out governments for not fulfilling their treaty obligations, UNHCR risks confrontation with its major constituencies.

These two basic challenges—the mismatch between its legal mandate and its actual scope of activities, and the proper balancing between providing services to states and protecting refugee rights—have driven the legitimation contests around UNHCR throughout its history. At the same time, however, we can observe two major changes in the ways in which UNHCR is legitimated.

First, we observe an increasing rhetorical emphasis on individuals as the primary beneficiaries of the activities of UNHCR. This observation supports our general argument that the individual has gained relevance as a reference point for the legitimation of international organizations. However, as UNHCR was never exclusively state-based to begin with, what we witness is not necessarily a linear development *from* state-based *to* society-based legitimation, but rather a *constant navigation and rebalancing* between these two. Seen in this light, the more recent stress on individual rights is not necessarily a one-way street. In fact, it might only be temporary; unilateral state policies such as the closing of European borders in reaction to a rising number of refugees indicate the continued relevance of state sovereignty.

Second, we observe that UNHCR is increasingly assessed in terms of managerial norms like *efficiency, accountability, coherence,* and *coordination*. As we describe more closely in the following sections, these norms gain strength in two particular contexts. On the one hand, the volatile financial resources of UNHCR call for greater efficiency and oversight. On the other hand, the agency's more pronounced role in the coordination of the UN's humanitarian sector generates demands for *coherence and coordination* with other agencies, with which UNHCR increasingly shares its major fields of activity.

To develop these arguments more fully, the following section sketches the historical contours of the policy field in which the legitimation of UNHCR takes place. Subsequently, we lay out the 'traditional' basis of legitimation from which the normative changes we observe depart. The main part of the chapter is then reserved for a detailed reconstruction of the two major changes in the legitimation discourse, and of the pathways that have led to these changes. In a final section, we discuss key findings in light of the broader theoretical framework that informs our study.

THE HISTORICAL CONTEXT: THE INTERNATIONAL REGIME FOR THE PROTECTION OF REFUGEES

To understand the changing contours of the legitimation contests we discuss in this chapter, four contextual aspects in the history of the global refugee regime are particularly relevant: (i) the long history of UNHCR and its predecessor, the High Commissioner for Refugees (HCR), and their often conflicting goals of protecting refugees while assisting states; (ii) the use of the refugee agency as a political instrument despite its formal impartiality; (iii) changing patterns of global refugee flows over time; and (iv) the transformation of UNHCR into a 'humanitarian organization' in the 1990s that altered not only the identity of the organization but also its role and hence the expectations of member states.

When we say that the UNHCR is characterized by a tension between the dual goal of protecting refugees and assisting states, the same holds for its predecessor, the HCR. Established under the auspices of the League of Nations in 1921, the commissioner was to assist European states in coping with the massive inflow of Russian refugees fleeing the revolution as well as the famine of 1921. The challenge, which had partly originated from charitable organizations being overwhelmed by the size of refugee flows, was initially framed in highly political terms. States thus formally limited the HCR mandate to 'people from Russia who claimed to be fleeing political persecution' (Barnett and Finnemore 2004: 77); in fact, however, Western states also accepted other reasons. The formulation of the mandate thus gives an early indication that states saw the refugee agency not only as a functional device to coordinate assistance, but also as a political instrument in times of competing political ideologies. Under the leadership of High Commissioner Fridtjof Nansen, however, the HCR continuously managed to expand the range of its activities, with Nansen '[insinuating] himself into the political and refugee crises in Greece, Turkey, Bulgaria, and elsewhere' as well as securing a number of rights for refugees, among them the right to obtain travel documents, known as 'Nansen passports' (Barnett and Finnemore 2004: 77). Involuntarily, states had thus created an organization whose bureaucratic leaders forcefully campaigned for the rights of refugees, who otherwise had few speaking on their behalf. Yet, because the effectiveness of the HRC depended on the willingness of states to implement its recommendations, the office could not take it too far. In the end, a delicate balance was required between promoting a longer list of refugee 'rights'—a list that would seem at odds not only with state interests but also with the traditional notion of refugee assistance as charity—and serving the interests of states.

This balance remained central when the UN General Assembly established the UNHCR on 14 December 1950. The Statute of the Office, the 1951 Convention Relating to the Status of Refugees and the 1967 Protocol Relating to the Status of Refugees, form the legal basis of the mandate. It tasks UNHCR with providing international protection to refugees and seeking permanent solutions to their plight, as well as with holding states accountable for their obligations that emanate from the 1951 Convention (United Nations 1950; 1951). Monitoring states' compliance was an important role for UNHCR in the beginning (Jacobsen and Sandvik 2016: 3–4). The basic conflict and tension between the protection of refugees and state sovereignty becomes apparent with this task: on the one hand, states created UNHCR to help them cope with protecting and assisting refugees and have an interest in UNHCR fulfilling its tasks. On the other hand, states want to prevent UNHCR from criticizing their own refugee policies.

Like the HCR mandate, the 1951 Convention defines refugees narrowly. It reserves the label for a person who as 'a result of events occurring before 1 January 1951 and owing to well-founded fear of being persecuted for reasons of race, religion, nationality, membership of a particular social group or political opinion' fled to another country. Moreover, the statute determined a mandate for only three years that should only be renewed if a permanent solution had not been found. The General Assembly finally removed this need to constantly renew the mandate in 2003 when it decided 'to continue the Office until the refugee problem is solved' (United Nations 2003).

In 1950, refugees and forced migration were not anticipated to be a long-term and indeed global challenge to which the international community ought to find solutions. This, however, was soon to change. By the end of 1956, the Hungarian crisis became the first new refugee situation and UNHCR was named lead agency for the coordination of the response. The exodus of 200,000 Hungarians into Austria, in the weeks following a student demonstration turned into revolt and halted by Soviet tanks, was met with a timely humanitarian response and a speedy resettlement operation (Colville 2006). The Hungarian crisis was significant for UNHCR because it was designated the lead agency for an emergent refugee situation that occurred after 1951 and was therefore formally outside the temporal scope of the mandate. Moreover, it underscored UNHCR's role and responsibility as a leader for refugee protection. (cf. Loescher 2001: 82ff.).

Other situations, such as the Chinese refugees in Hong Kong and the Algerian refugees in Tunisia in 1957, were legally outside the mandate of UNHCR for geographical reasons. However, either the host states or a parent body requested the office to provide protection and assistance nevertheless (Barnett and Finnemore 2004: 88–9). These activities became known as 'good offices', an approach which allowed UNHCR to expand its activities geographically from Europe to Africa, Latin America, and Asia and has been interpreted by some as a turning point in the history of the organization (Betts 2012: 123–5). By extending its good offices in emerging refugee situations in other world regions, UNHCR was able to overcome the temporal and geographical limitation of its initial mandate. This was legally recognized in the 1967 protocol which broadens the refugee definition accordingly. Furthermore, by successfully extending its good offices and helping to protect refugees in these situations, the UNHCR became 'the centrepiece of the international refugee regime' (Loescher 2001: 81). By becoming the only, or at least the most competent organization to deal with new refugee situations in the eyes of states, UNHCR was able to consolidate its position within the issue area of refugee protection. According to Phil Orchard (2013: 187), UNHCR made itself 'invaluable' to states by responding quickly to new refugee situations in which states could not have acted due to political considerations, especially during the Cold War. It became a 'gatekeeper' to other international governmental organizations by being lead agency and a coordinator to non-governmental organizations (NGOs) by taking over the management of relief operations.

In a way, the continuous broadening of its mandate was legitimated by an incremental process of 'normalizing' new tasks over time. In the early 1970s, many member states criticized the good offices approach for being outside the mandate, distracting from the core mandate, or using up funds for other purposes. As the tasks that UNHCR performed within the good offices approach became framed more often and more explicitly as functionally similar to UNHCR's mandated tasks, and which were increasingly considered as addressing an important humanitarian concern, apprehension subsided among member states that good offices distracted UNHCR from its core tasks. Like in the 1920s, the bureaucratic leaders played a key role in this development. 'At each and every opportunity,' Michael Barnett and Martha Finnemore (2004: 91) recount, 'the high commissioner was on the scene, arguing that his office had the expertise to assist, offering legal interpretations of the mandate that connoted that his office had the delegated authority, and using his moral authority to speak on behalf of the displaced.'

At the same time, patterns of refugee flows began to change from the 1970s. Initially, Western states had sound ideological reasons to welcome refugees fleeing communist regimes to enter the 'free world'. Yet, they increasingly perceived rising numbers of asylum seekers from the Third World as an undue

burden on their societies and economies. The result was that asylum regulations became more politically contested and more restricted in Western
societies. Moreover, developing countries, too, became less hospitable to
refugees and increasingly made their willingness to bear the costs of hosting
them conditional on international assistance (Barnett and Finnemore 2004:
94–5). In sum, the expanded mandate resulting from the good offices
approach, and the politicization of refugee issues resulting from altered patterns of refugee flows came to constitute a key background for the legitimation
contests we discuss in this chapter.

Another relevant background is the transformation of UNHCR from a legal
protection organization into a 'humanitarian agency'. Similarly to the previous
development, this transformation also originates from an expansion of the
UNHCR mandate; this time in connection with the groups of 'persons of
concern', meaning the groups of people under the jurisdiction of the office.
Over the decades, these groups gradually expanded from refugees to include
rejected asylum seekers, returnees, stateless persons, internally displaced persons (IDPs), and victims of human-made and natural disasters. The end of the
Cold War contributed to this transformation in so far as it sparked hopes for a
'decade of repatriation', where many long-standing conflicts could be resolved
and many refugees could return to their home country (UNHCR 1992). This
shifted the focus of UNHCR from countries of asylum to countries of origin,
and added returnees to the list of persons of concern.

The increased international attention to the plight of IDPs in the wake of
the 1991 Gulf War, and the growing awareness about new types of conflict,
changed the perception of the role of UNHCR within the global refugee
regime.[1] By providing assistance to IDPs and returnees in Iraq, UNHCR
consolidated its role in the countries of origin. The question of how to regulate
the protection of IDPs, however, was not yet answered. For that, Francis Deng,
the first Representative of the Secretary General on IDPs, laid the groundwork
by (re)defining 'sovereignty as responsibility' (Deng et al. 1996) of a state to
protect its citizens (including IDPs), and by issuing the 'Guiding Principles on
Internal Displacement'. As the proposal to make UNHCR the designated
agency for IDPs led to a 'turf war among UN agencies', an ad hoc collaborative
system was introduced in 1998, which did not work well and was eventually
replaced by the so-called cluster approach (Orchard 2013: 193–4). The cluster
approach is a result of the reform process of the UN humanitarian sector from
1998 to 2005, driven by the Inter-Agency Standing Committee of the Office
for the Coordination of Humanitarian Affairs (OCHA). It is a coordination

---

[1] One characteristic of many intra-state conflicts that erupted in the early 1990s was the
(deliberate) targeting of civilians, which produced high numbers of IDPs. According to the
Internal Displacement Monitoring Centre, there were 16.5 million IDPs in 1989, 28 million in
1994, and 38 million in 2014 (IDMC 2015).

mechanism intended to avoid duplication of efforts and structures among humanitarian agencies (UN, non-UN, and NGOs) by identifying sectors of problems or clusters. Specific agencies are assigned to lead the coordination of the humanitarian response in each sector according to their expertise. UNHCR was designated the 'lead agency for the protection, emergency shelter and camp management clusters in conflict-generated situations of internal displacement' (UN General Assembly 2007: 1) together with the International Federation of Red Cross and Red Crescent Societies (shelter), and the International Organization for Migration (IOM; camp coordination and management). Hence, UNHCR was officially mandated to lead humanitarian efforts in support of IDPs. When the cluster approach was implemented in pilot countries in 2006, the number of IDPs under UNHCR's care grew 'by 93 per cent from 6.6 million in 2005 to 12.8 million in 2006' (Lanz 2008: 200).

By assuming responsibility for IDPs, the status of sovereignty became redefined. UNHCR was now involved in situations that were previously defined as internal matters (Loescher 2001: 297). The IDP mandate therefore signifies a change in the culture of the global refugee regime or rather the global forced migration regime—as it now included IDPs—with UNHCR still at its core.

Finally, from the mid-1980s onwards, the so-called *root cause debate* gained prominence in debates over international refugee issues. As violent political conflicts across the globe kept the number of refugees high, demands for prevention became a key mantra and spurred debates about the role of UNHCR in finding long-term solutions. This *root cause debate* called into question UNHCR's humanitarian foundation on neutrality and impartiality,[2] and paved the way for a more active involvement of UNHCR in ongoing conflicts and civil wars throughout the 1990s. Notably, UNHCR's role as lead agency for the coordination of humanitarian assistance in Bosnia transformed the office from a legal protection agency into a humanitarian agency (Crisp 2001; Ogata 2005). In addition to traditional functions such as the legal protection of refugees and technical and legal assistance to states, UNHCR became a humanitarian relief organization by incrementally increasing its assistance operations and involving itself in development activities.[3]

---

[2] The term 'humanitarian' has two meanings throughout this chapter. In the sense of humanitarian relief/aid organization, it applies to the sector of emergency assistance in natural and human-made disasters. However, the humanitarian foundation or character of UNHCR's work implies impartiality and is used in contrast to a more political role. It is important to keep in mind that a stronger involvement in humanitarian relief operations can entail the necessity to take on a more political (and therefore less humanitarian in the sense of impartial) role, for instance when it becomes necessary to take sides in a conflict in order to reach civilian populations in need of assistance. For an overview of UNHCR's humanitarian dilemmas, see Weiner 1998.

[3] UNHCR's involvement in development activities is interesting, especially as it relates to questions of mandate overlap and competition over funding with other organizations such as the

With this, over time, UNHCR took on entirely new roles beyond overseeing compliance with the 1950 Geneva Convention and providing protection and assistance to a limited number of refugees in a limited geographical area. UNHCR made itself 'invaluable' as the 'gatekeeper' for a wide range of international governmental organizations and NGOs working in the global forced migration regime with UNHCR 'at the heart' (Orchard 2013). While UNHCR had always collaborated with NGOs for the implementation of assistance programmes, its new role coincided with a steady growth in the number and importance of NGOs the UNHCR worked with as well as the amount of money spent through them.[4] With growing regime complexity, UNHCR became a 'challenged institution' in the sense that its mandate overlapped with those of other international organizations, thereby allowing states to engage in forum shopping (Betts 2013). Especially IOM and the UN Development Programme (UNDP) became competitors when the UNHCR expanded its scope of activities from human rights protection into development, humanitarianism, peacebuilding, security, and migration (Betts 2013: 73–5). Since IOM became a related organization to the UN in July 2016, the option of forum shopping is even more available to states. States also pay more attention to IOM and connect the migration regime with refugee issues (IOM 2016). This is illustrated by the fact that IOM was not mentioned at all in the Executive Committee (ExCom) debates—where states come together to discuss UNHCR policy and approve the budget—in 2013 and only rarely referred to in 2015. After becoming a related organization, IOM was mentioned sixteen times in the ExCom debate of 2017. Although it is still too early to tell how the relationship between UNHCR and IOM will develop, the increasing presence of IOM in ExCom debates shows that the (potential) mandate overlap with IOM is a challenge that UNHCR will have to face in the future.

In sum, if 'the UNHCR of the 1970s bore little resemblance to the UNHCR at its birth' (Barnett and Finnemore 2004: 91), the same could be said for the UNHCR of the 1970s and that of today. The Office of the High Commissioner had used its legal and moral authority to considerably expand the scope of its mandate once more; the ideological dimension of its work had not vanished entirely but receded to the background. New kinds of intra-state conflicts that heavily targeted civilians had replaced interstate wars as the predominant type of violent conflict across the world, producing unprecedented numbers of

---

UNDP. Due to space limitations, this aspect will not be discussed here. For a critical analysis of UNHCR's major development initiatives and policies from the 1960s to 2000 see Crisp 2001.

[4] In 1978, UNHCR had relations with 'over 100 voluntary agencies' (UN General Assembly 1979: 49). By 1990, this number had doubled (UN General Assembly 1991: 39). In 2010, UNHCR had implementing partnership agreements with 687 national and international NGOs, through which it channelled 28 per cent of its total expenditure (544 million USD) (UNHCR 2010: 69).

refugees and other persons of concern. UNHCR had taken on a leading role in the UN's humanitarian sector that further enhanced its authority in some ways but also made it vulnerable in others. It is in light of these developments that we need to make sense of the legitimation challenges the organization experienced in the four decades we examine in this book.

LEGITIMATING THE UNHCR: THE NORMATIVE BASELINE

UNHCR is a humanitarian agency with a rather low level of legal authority over states in areas such as rule making and enforcement. Institutionally, UNHCR is governed by the UN General Assembly and the UN Economic and Social Council (ECOSOC), with a separate UNHCR ExCom consisting of over 100 states that oversee the budget and advise the High Commissioner in the exercise of his or her functions. The institutional set-up is complemented by the High Commissioner and their staff which, in 2015, amounted to 9,700 staff members working in 126 countries and managing a budget of over 7 billion United States dollars (USD) (UNHCR n.d.).

UNHCR was created, *inter alia*, to oversee state compliance with international refugee law but without the power to enforce it. Yet this does not render UNHCR powerless. First, based on its expertise in refugee matters as well as its knowledge through operations in the field, UNHCR does wield crucial expert authority (Barnett and Finnemore 2004: 73). Second, UNHCR has considerable authority vis-à-vis one particular group of persons, namely refugees. This authority manifests itself in the area of refugee status determination, but also in the agency's ability to make and implement the rules that govern the lives in refugee camps (Barnett and Finnemore 2004: 113; Agier 2011). This authority implies that not only states that withhold contributions or refuse to obey international refugee law, but also refugee groups who speak out against specific activities of UNHCR have the potential to challenge the organization's legitimacy.

UNHCR's financial situation is also crucial to its legitimation. Article 20 of the statute determines that only administrative costs shall be covered by a regular budget provided by the UN. For all other expenses, UNHCR is dependent on *voluntary* contributions. During its first years, the office therefore struggled to secure sufficient funding in order to protect and assist the approximately 1 million refugees remaining in Europe. With an annual budget of USD 300,000 and thirty-three staff members at the end of 1951, the first High Commissioner, Gerrit van Heuven Goedhart, was confronted with a lack of resources. Thanks to his leadership skills as a 'good speaker', being 'charming' and 'well-informed', he convinced the UN General Assembly to allow his office to appeal independently to governments and to the private sector for additional funding and to collaborate with NGOs for the implementation of material and legal assistance programmes (Corduwender and Reinalda 2012). Towards the end of our period of investigation, governments were still the largest donor group. In 2010, 89 per cent of voluntary contributions were received from governments (including the EC), 3.6 per cent were received from private donors, and the administrative budget covered by the UN represented 2 per cent of contributions received (United Nations 1950: 12; UNHCR 2010: 83).

Throughout the four decades under investigation, UNHCR needed to respond to three major normative demands that roughly correspond to our questions of what, for whom, and how international organizations ought to govern. In brief, UNHCR thus had to show its *ability to address refugee crises*, to strike *the right balance between the protection of refugees and the provision of services for states*, and to demonstrate its *flexibility* in adapting to a changing world.

First, with regard to *what* to govern, an expanding scope of tasks and persons of concern meant that UNHCR faced a constant need to negotiate the interpretation of its mandate, understood as 'the legitimate scope of the Office's work at any given point in time' (Betts 2012: 118). In order to do so, it needed to prove the worth of its expanding activities to member states, donors, and other stakeholders. The central justification for expanding activities to new groups of persons of concern was that 'the situation of a given group of people is analogous to that of refugees' (UN General Assembly 1971: 2). This way, UNHCR could create the public image of acting within the limits of its mandate while at the same time making the necessary adjustments when tasked to do so by the competent authorities.

Moreover, when UNHCR describes the inclusion of new groups of persons of concern or its engagement beyond the confines of the mandate, it usually refers to its delegated authority to take over this new task. Standard explanations refer to explicit requests by the UN Secretary General, the governmental authorities concerned, decisions by the ExCom or resolutions of the General Assembly, or ECOSOC, thereby further accentuating the image of UNHCR working within the boundaries set by the will of states or its parent bodies. For example, the formulation by UNHCR of programmes for the voluntary repatriation and resettlement of refugees from Guinea-Bissau and Mozambique in 1974 occurred 'pursuant to the decision of the Executive Committee of the High Commissioner's Programme at its twenty-fifth session, and to General Assembly resolution 3271 (XXIX), and upon the specific requests of the Governments of the Territories concerned' (UN General Assembly 1975: 2).[5]

---

[5] The aforementioned example is particular in its enumeration of various sources of authorization. For other examples in the same vein see the following annual reports: UN General Assembly 1975: 10 and 33; 1979: 11, 15, 17, 48, and 49; 1983: 6 and 32; 1991: 21 and 28–9.

Second, in response to the question *for whom* UNHCR was working, the most basic normative foundation of UNHCR's work is the protection of refugees' rights. By amply describing the activities undertaken to protect refugees in the annual reports, UNHCR creates its image as the *protector of refugees*. Yet, UNHCR's role as a *service provider for states* at times indirectly challenges this image. The potential tension in the mandate becomes apparent when states fail to fulfil their obligations towards refugees. The *Toscani Report* of 1983 is a case in point. In a climate of 'asylum fatigue' in the Western world, UNHCR was under pressure to defend refugees' rights against restrictive state policies. After an internal report criticizing West Germany's asylum policies was leaked to the press, the relationship between UNHCR and the West German government worsened considerably, and the High Commissioner had to postpone a trip to Bonn as he was not sure he would be welcomed. Eventually, West Germany did not reduce its funding, but instead increased it from around USD 16 million in 1982 to USD 19.5 million in 1983. Nonetheless, the leaked *Toscani Report* showed UNHCR that 'the margins of error associated with such a strategy [of confrontation, ER] are very narrow' (Milzow 2008: 88; see also Loescher et al. 2008: 237–46; UN General Assembly 1983: 50; 1984: 52; UNHCR ExCom 1983: 9, 354th meeting).

In its own publications, UNHCR does not refer to the balancing of states' and refugees' interests as a potential source of conflict. Instead, the office applies a strategy of parallel legitimation in which it describes its activities for the benefit of states and for the benefit of refugees separately. Throughout the four decades, UNHCR thus describes a wide range of technical and legal assistance services for states such as the issuing of identity cards to refugees (UN General Assembly 1975: 11; 1979: 9), the publication of handbooks (UN General Assembly 1979: 11), the facilitation of voluntary repatriation (UN General Assembly 1983: 21; 1995: 19), the determination of refugee status (UN General Assembly 1971: 6; 1991: 23), the organization of workshops and training seminars (UN General Assembly 1983: 14; 2003: 7), as well as the provision of expertise in drawing up national legislation (UN General Assembly 1979: 44).

Yet, even though the organization extensively presents states as the beneficiaries of UNHCR's policies and assistance activities, the annual reports and Global Reports explicitly assert that its 'primary purpose is to safeguard the rights and well-being of refugees' (UNHCR 1998: Mission Statement). UNHCR's self-image of being a 'voice for the voiceless' (UNHCR 1998: 21) is expressed in the particular attention it pays to the most vulnerable groups (for example UN General Assembly 1971: 29–36). This narrative can be found throughout all four decades, supporting the image of UNHCR as a *protector of refugees*.

Third, questions relating to *how* UNHCR managed refugee crises also fed into the normative baseline according to which the office was legitimated. For instance, UNHCR managed to increase the scope of its activities by arguing that due to changing external circumstances new challenges and tasks arose, which were nevertheless *functionally similar* to the tasks assigned in the organization's initial mandate. Such changing external circumstances include, for instance, large-scale refugee flows created by human-made or natural disasters such as in Cyprus and Indo-China in 1974, the severe drought and famine in several African countries in 1985/6, or mass flight in Rwanda and the former Yugoslavia in 1994 (cf. the introductory sections in UN General Assembly 1975, 1979, 1983, 1986, 1987, and 1995). Other unforeseen circumstances include the outbreak of diseases in refugee camps, deteriorating security situations, the asylum–migration nexus, and more recently climate change refugees. In all these cases, UNHCR presented itself as a flexible agency that was able to react to these challenges in *a timely and innovative manner*. In this context, UNHCR emphasizes its ability to redeploy staff even on a short notice or to adapt its responses 'through a process of experimentation' to find adequate solutions (UN General Assembly 1975: 2).[6]

Against the background of the temporal limitation of the statute and the need to renew the mandate every three to five years, this self-portrayal as a flexible organization helped to prove UNHCR's usefulness and ability to carry out its mandate. Moreover, by showing its ability to recognize or even anticipate new challenges and to react adequately, it justified UNHCR's role as the most appropriate UN body to deal with refugee situations. Accordingly, *flexibility* became a central and stable reference point for UNHCR's legitimation over the years.

BEYOND LEGAL PROTECTION: THE RISE OF THE INDIVIDUAL

Although UNHCR, by its mandate and the nature of its tasks, is drawn in a normative conflict between states and individuals (Betts 2015), one can nevertheless trace that, from the mid-1980s onwards, individuals and their interests become increasingly central in UNHCR's rhetoric. This manifests itself in two ways. On the one hand, the debate about UNHCR's role as an impartial humanitarian agency led to calls for giving the agency a more political role to be able to tackle the root causes of displacement, such as

---

[6] For further examples of UNHCR upholding the norm of flexibility see UN General Assembly 1971: 2 and 29; 1975: 35 and 47; 1983: 16; 1991: 1 and 9; 1995: 1, 4, 10, 16, and 35; 2003: 1 and 11; 2007: 1, 10, 13, 14, 16, and 18; 2011: 1, 4, 6, 9, and 11.

human rights abuses. The *root cause debate* is linked to the rise of the individual because an increasing role for UNHCR in political conflicts means taking side against one conflicting party, which are often states. Less consideration for the political position of certain states and more consideration for human rights, however, represents a shift in the balance between the interests of states and individuals to the benefit of refugees.

The second way in which a concern for individuals becomes evident relates to the changing perception and portrayal of refugees from vulnerable and needy recipients of assistance to proactive agents and stakeholders, who should have a voice in the work of UNHCR. This change in the way UNHCR communicates is carried forward in the empowerment discourse, which demands broader participation of refugees. As we discuss below, both discursive changes run counter to a 'normalization of repatriation' which Barnett and Finnemore (2004: 98–105) observe in the practice of UNHCR. As the emergence of a 'repatriation culture' strengthened state interests at the cost of refugee rights, this suggests a strong decoupling of organizational talk from organizational decisions and action.

Rebalancing the Refugee Rights versus State Interest Equation

The onset of the root cause debate in the early 1980s calls into question the non-political role of UNHCR. It frames the task of finding durable solutions for refugees as interlinked with resolving political conflicts and preventing human rights abuses that cause refugee flows. This, however, conflicts with article 2 of the statute which stipulates that the 'work of the High Commissioner shall be of an entirely non-political character; it shall be humanitarian and social' (United Nations 1950: 6).

The root cause debate was triggered by a study on human rights and mass exoduses prepared by former High Commissioner Prince Sadruddin Aga Khan for the UN Commission on Human Rights in 1981 (E/CN.4/1503), and the Report of Governmental Experts on International Co-operation to Avert New Flows of Refugees (A/41/324) in 1986 (United Nations 1981, 1986). The reports conveyed the idea that armed conflict, the denial of human rights to specific groups or the population in general, and socio-economic factors such as food insecurity triggered mass displacement and therefore needed to be resolved by political means to avert refugee flows.

Before 1982, we do not find statements arguing for a political role of UNHCR in the proceedings of ExCom. Instead, member states emphasize that the political neutrality of the office is a source of efficiency and success. At the 1970 ExCom meeting, a Turkish delegate could thus argue that 'the successful record of UNHCR was largely due to the fact that its aims were wholly humanitarian', and that 'his country warmly commended the political neutrality shown by the Office' (UNHCR ExCom 1970: 22, 204th meeting).[7]

Since 1982, ExCom members increasingly acknowledge that the work of the UNHCR is embedded in a political context. Still, most commentators want the office to preserve its unique, humanitarian character or assign the responsibility to deal with political questions to other actors such as governments or the international community as a whole. The summary records of the 1982 ExCom meeting, for instance, cite a Canadian delegate as arguing that (UNHCR ExCom 1982: 11, 343rd meeting),

> One discouraging feature of the refugee situation was that millions of refugees who desired only to return to their homes were forced to await political settlements to political problems. The strictly humanitarian mandate of UNHCR did not allow it to become involved in political problems, but States Members of the United Nations had a political responsibility to deal with those questions.[8]

In contrast, proponents of a more political role for UNHCR argue that a holistic approach to refugee protection and assistance has to take into account a policy to prevent refugee flows by tackling its root causes. Again at the 1982 ExCom meeting, a Ugandan delegate stated that (UNHCR ExCom 1982: 16, 345th meeting),

> He could not agree that the Committee should refrain entirely from talking about the root causes of the refugee problem. Such causes were part of the environment in which the High Commissioner operated and he should therefore be aware of them. Furthermore, as a United Nations agency, UNHCR would influence other agencies directly engaged in tackling those causes.[9]

Up until 1998, member states do not have a unified position on the question of UNHCR's political neutrality. Some states warn against the risk of UNHCR losing its ability to negotiate with all concerned parties to secure the effective provision of humanitarian aid to refugees. Proponents of a

---

[7] Other states, for example (West) Germany, also voice this opinion: 'In periods of tension, the needy could often be helped, irrespective of the political system, only through UNHCR. His delegation was pleased to note that, for UNHCR, humanitarian questions were more important than short-term political aims, and that the High Commissioner adhered strictly to his mandate, and was thus able to cope with his assignments more efficiently' (UNHCR ExCom 1978: 2, 294th meeting).

[8] Other like-minded statements include the United Kingdom (UNHCR ExCom 1982: 2, 343rd meeting), Finland (UNHCR ExCom 1982: 6, 343rd meeting), Vietnam (UNHCR ExCom 1986: 9, 404th meeting), Austria (UNHCR ExCom 1990b: 4, 456th meeting), and Nigeria (UNHCR ExCom 1994: 14, 491st meeting).

[9] Other statements in a similar vein were made by delegates from Algeria (UNHCR ExCom 1982: 4, 346th meeting), Colombia (UNHCR ExCom 1986: 4, 401st meeting and 1990b: 6, 457th meeting), Nepal (UNHCR ExCom 1994: 8, 493rd meeting), and the Republic of Korea (UNHCR ExCom 1994: 10, 494th meeting).

strictly humanitarian role for UNHCR also stress that the solution of political problems is beyond UNHCR's mandate, responsibility, and competence.

Other states demand a more active engagement of UNHCR in tackling the root causes of refugee flows, by linking it to one of UNHCR's core tasks, namely to find lasting solutions for refugees. Still, most proponents of a more political role for UNHCR are cautious and propose coordinated efforts in that regard with other actors such as governments, the UN Security Council, and the UN system as a whole, while asking UNHCR to act as a 'catalyst' to 'mobilize public opinion' (Tanzania: UNHCR ExCom 1986: 8, 407th meeting and Iran: UNHCR ExCom 1986: 8, 405th meeting). It is important to note that the broad concept of root causes provided states with a catch-all phrase. This allowed them to demand more development aid, call for an end to armed conflict, or deplore authoritarian and racist regimes with reference to the common idea of root causes.

By 1998, the idea of UNHCR engaging politically in order to avert refugee flows seems to have become less controversial. Of the thirteen statements found in the ExCom debates from 1998 to 2011 on that question, only three argue against a more political role for UNHCR. More states argue in favour of UNHCR tackling the root causes as it is part of a concerted, holistic approach, and individual member states demand a political intervention by UNHCR directly without justificatory remarks about why UNHCR should have this role (see for example the statement by Guinea: UNHCR ExCom 1998: 3, 530th meeting or Venezuela: UNHCR ExCom 2002: 15, 563rd meeting). However, with the growing role of UNHCR in conflicts in the former Yugoslavia, Afghanistan, Rwanda, and elsewhere, the debate also gains a new dimension in the 1990s. As the lead agency for UN humanitarian action in the former Yugoslavia, UNHCR *necessarily* becomes involved in the politics of the war, such as 'negotiating away substantial quantities of relief aid as the price for access', or facing the dilemma of either being implicated in ethnic cleansing or abandoning the transiting of people in an effort to facilitate 'organised flight' (Goodwin-Gill 1999: 226–32; see also Loescher 2001; Ogata 2005). Thus, the question no longer is whether UNHCR should be more political, but *how* it can best protect the rights of refugees in a conflict environment.

Sadako Ogata, High Commissioner from 1991 to 2000, was a driving force behind this new self-image of UNHCR as an active advocate of refugees in ongoing, often highly politicized conflicts. In her memoir of that time, *The Turbulent Decade*, she describes for example how she used an invitation to address the UN Security Council 'to speak on behalf of the refugees', and to press for political solutions for the humanitarian crises UNHCR was confronted with (Ogata 2005: 169). Furthermore, Ogata used the suspension of relief efforts to draw attention to the lack of resources and will to find a political solution by the UN and the governments in Yugoslavia and the

Democratic Republic of the Congo. She did so without the knowledge or consent of the UN Secretary General, in order to pressure political actors to assume their responsibility (Ogata 2005: 83 and 247; Schechter 2014). By being outspoken, advocating on behalf of refugees, and not refraining from using controversial tactics, Ogata contributed to a more political role for UNHCR.

This expanded role, however, came at a cost for the legitimation of UNHCR. By expanding the scope of its activities, UNHCR could now be evaluated on its performance in this new field of activity. The humanitarian dilemmas, referred to by UNHCR officials as 'the price of protection' (Richburg 1992), are poignantly summarized by David Rieff (1999):

> Humanitarian workers have found themselves in a cruel dilemma. They thought that bringing aid to suffering people was an unimpeachably good thing to do; but in places like Ethiopia, the Congo and Bosnia, they discovered to their horror that they had become logisticians to the war efforts of belligerents. If a warlord knows that he can depend on a relief agency to feed his civilian population, he may be freer to act solely on the basis of his military imperatives... [W]hether it was in the camps of central Africa or in Sarajevo, they were in a lose-lose situation and they knew it.

Sadako Ogata was well aware of these dilemmas as she often demanded political solutions for refugee situations (Ogata 2005). Even years after Amnesty International had criticized UNHCR for its role in the repatriation of Rwandan refugees from neighbouring countries that Amnesty deemed unsafe (Amnesty International 1997), Ogata felt the need to address the critique. In her justification of UNHCR's action at the time, she admits that UNHCR and herself could have done more to protect refugee rights during the repatriation (Ogata 2005: 255). However, she also contends that she is

> not certain if UNHCR could have prevented... the course from turning so disorderly and violent. We might have stood aside and condemned the rough handling by the military. We might have disassociated ourselves from the operation. Instead, what we did was compromise, to save what little there was to save. (Ogata 2005: 255)

Two conclusions can be drawn from this justificatory statement. First, UNHCR uses the centrality of moral standards and the rights of refugees within its mandate to argue that if UNHCR was not involved in such situations, there would be no protection for refugees at all. That is to say, that an imperfect protection is better than no protection. Second, this statement also shows that UNHCR cannot ignore NGOs and their public criticism.

The role of NGO critique and the media in the legitimation of the UNHCR became evident in the case of Kosovo in 1999. Amnesty International and Human Rights Watch were quite successful in putting pressure on UNHCR during that time. Based on a search for UNHCR, Amnesty International, and Human Rights Watch in the media database Factiva, there is a sharp increase in the number of media articles that mention UNHCR and the two NGOs.[10] In its own right, increased public attention is at least an indicator for a second audience becoming more important for UNHCR: it forced the organization to listen to and manage the demands and critique. Looking more closely at the content of the media articles of 1999, the Kosovo crisis is the topic of the majority of them. Firstly, in March, when the NATO bombing campaign led to mass flight and an overload of UNHCR's response capacity, and secondly, in September, when Serbian refugees had to be protected against retaliatory violence and acts of vengeance by returning Albanians. In some media articles UNHCR is not criticized but presented as the protector of refugees; a witness to accounts by a large number of refugees that flee from atrocities, such as systematic rape (Nordland 1999; Farid 1999). However, when UNHCR is criticized for its role or lack of action on behalf of refugees, the criticism is harsh. Janine di Giovanni (1999) reports that when she approached UNHCR for an article about rape and prostitution in Kosovo, UNHCR was 'concerned but out of touch, and said it would look into the matter'; eventually, UNHCR only responded and brought the matter to the UN Security Council, after the *Times* ran the story. Elsewhere, Human Rights Watch criticized that UNHCR had not moved the refugee camps in Guinea away from the border despite repeated calls to help protect refugees against brutal and atrocious attacks (HRW 1999).

UNHCR reacted to various accusations and critique on three different levels. First, it facilitated the relocation of refugees from Myanmar residing close to the border in Thailand further inland (Agence France-Press 1999). Although this relocation effort in Thailand took place in a different world region than the one the critique of the situation in Guinea had referred to, this operation nevertheless allowed UNHCR to point to its relocation activity in order to protect refugees. Second, it refuted critique by using its right of reply, answering directly to criticisms in the same newspapers. For example, when Human Rights Watch accused UNHCR of supporting the controversial policy of transmigration in East and West Timor (Jones 1999), the director of UNHCR's Bureau for Asia and the Pacific published an article in an effort to right the 'twisted picture' presented by Human Rights Watch only three days later (Fouinat 1999). Third, UNHCR conceded its failure in the Kosovo situation in the annual report of 1999. While it still pointed out that the 'mass exodus from Kosovo was one of the most complex and intensely political

---

[10] In 1999, there were 140 articles mentioning UNHCR and Amnesty International, a rather high number compared to previous years. The Factiva search covered the years from 1970 to 2018 and yielded the first result in 1982 (one article, as in 1983, 1984, and 1988). The number of articles prior to 1999 was never higher than 105 (in 1996) and oscillated between sixteen articles (in 1991) and sixty-four articles (in 1997) for most of the 1990s. For Human Rights Watch, there were seventy-eight articles in 1999 mentioning it in conjunction with UNHCR whereas the number never exceeded forty-two articles in previous years.

refugee emergencies in history', it nevertheless clearly stated that '[t]he humanitarian challenges temporarily exceeded the capacities of UNHCR and its humanitarian partners' (UN General Assembly 2000b: 16).

In sum, by becoming more involved in political crisis situations, UNHCR made itself more vulnerable to criticism. Advocacy NGOs put pressure on UNHCR to position itself even more clearly against states that did not uphold refugee rights through publicity and the media. The increased public attention and the various reactions by UNHCR show that these criticisms and demands were important enough for UNHCR not to ignore.

Empowering Refugees

One answer to the question of *how* UNHCR could better protect the rights of refugees was that those concerned should become more directly involved in policy planning and implementation. The image of refugees thus shifted from voiceless victims to independent agents. The shift from the image of UNHCR as a representative of destitute and vulnerable refugees to a discourse of empowerment and participation supports the assumption about the growing importance of the individual in International Relations. UNHCR's self-image of being a 'voice for the voiceless' (UNHCR 1998: 21) is expressed in the particular attention it pays to the most vulnerable and needy groups, whereas the groups considered to be most in need, and therefore 'voiceless', change over time.

The portrayal of women, in particular, follows a more general trend in the depiction of refugees, from burden to 'assets' for the receiving country or community. Looking at their representation in the annual reports and Global Reports, women used to be mainly mentioned as beneficiaries of programmes to counter sexual and gender-based violence, or in need of special services such as the provision of sanitary materials (UNHCR 2010: 32–5). In these contexts, the role of UNHCR was characterized as being the protector of a group that is especially vulnerable. Beyond women, Christina Clark-Kazak (2009) also identifies a 'vulnerability discourse' in the textual and visual representation in UNHCR's global appeals and Global Reports relating to children as well as disabled and elderly persons (Clark-Kazak 2009). However, the positive impact of the empowerment and participation of women is increasingly acknowledged from 2002 onwards. Already in its 1998 annual report, UNHCR for instance argues that (UN General Assembly 1999b: 8), 'It is generally recognized that the participation of women is central to promoting a culture of peace. UNHCR has thus been a lead participant in inter-agency workshops on women in conflict prevention and peace-building in Africa, the Americas and the Caucuses.' Historically, the idea of participation first comes up in the mid-1980s when 'ways and means to involve refugees themselves were...examined' in the context of tripartite commissions for voluntary repatriation (UN General Assembly 1987: 9). It is taken up again in 1994, but only gains considerable momentum in the late 1990s and early 2000s when its implementation through programmes such as the participatory assessment of needs also becomes a standard practice (UNHCR 2006: 23).[11]

In the 2002 *Global Report*, UNHCR (2002a: 6) thus no longer primarily presents itself in the role of a protector, but instead as promoting participation as a strategy to empower refugees:

> Although not a new approach, working with communities has proved a powerful means of improving refugees' capacity to meet their own needs and solve their own problems. This is in line with the High Commissioner's emphasis on seeing refugees as assets rather than burdens on the host community. It has meant involving them as active partners in all stages of programming and decision-making, thereby empowering them to enhance their own protection.

Attesting to the norm shift, the mission statements contained in the Global Reports, published form 1998 onwards, present the idea of participation quite prominently. UNHCR, they state, 'is committed to the principle of participation, believing that refugees and others who benefit from the organization's activities should be consulted over decisions which affect their lives' (UNHCR 1998: 3).

Beyond communications by UNHCR itself, media articles reporting on the activities of the organization largely support the protector image, by portraying UNHCR as an advocate of refugees. This often-repeated narrative typically involves the description of some kind of mistreatment of refugees by governments such as life-threatening conditions in refugee camps, unlawful detention of asylum seekers, or harassment and intimidation of refugees, followed by a description of UNHCR's advocacy efforts (Reddy 2001; see also Cheesman 2001 and Patiyasevi 1999).

NGOs, however, indirectly challenge UNHCR's claim to representation and protection of refugees by presenting themselves as being in the field, working directly with refugees, and therefore having more expertise on and insights into the needs of refugees (UNHCR ExCom 1978: 11, 294th meeting; 1986: 7, 405th meeting; UNHCR NGO Liaison Unit 2002: 55–6). By insisting on the inclusion of beneficiaries in the planning, implementation, and evaluation of UNHCR programmes (UNHCR NGO Liaison Unit 2002: 18), demanding the creation of accountability mechanisms such as complaint and response mechanisms (UNHCR Inter-Agency Unit 2010: 11), and criticizing the attitude that sees refugees as 'objects of charity' (UNHCR Inter-Agency Unit 2008: 5), NGOs position themselves as the true representative of refugee interests.

---

[11] A critique of UNHCR's participatory mechanisms concerns the question of how much participation they actually allow; see Kaiser (2004).

What is important in the context of legitimation of UNHCR is the latent framing contest about who could be considered the legitimate representative, advocate, and protector of refugees. This framing of the question of representation is challenged, and conflicts 'arise, when the viewpoints held by these groups of allegedly 'weak and voiceless people' contradicts those their advocates hold for them' (Hahn and Holzscheiter 2013: 7). In the case of UNHCR, the discontent of refugees and other persons of concern is rarely reflected in the official communications of the organization, in the deliberations of the member states, or in the reports of the annual consultations with NGOs, where refugee voices are also largely absent. Nonetheless, press articles reporting on refugees protesting against UNHCR by camping out at the agency's compounds, hunger strikes, or even attacks on UNHCR premises and staff show how particular conflicts are silenced in the agency's official discourse (cf. Moulin and Nyers 2007). Yet, there remains a qualitative change in the perception of refugees. That change is relevant for the legitimation of UNHCR because it partially—and at least rhetorically—transforms the purpose of the agency from protecting refugees as 'helpless' recipients of assistance to empowering refugees as independent agents.

This trend continues after 2010. Even in the proceedings of the ExCom, where states come together to discuss UNHCR policy and approve the budget, there are a few statements referring to 'collective accountability towards individual human beings' (UNHCR ExCom 2015: 3, 691st meeting), and the need 'to implement a new model that placed the rights, interests and capabilities of refugees ... at the heart of a comprehensive response' (UNHCR ExCom 2017: 2, 701st meeting). Interestingly, in the 2017 ExCom meeting, the US refers to individuals and their participation in three different interventions throughout the debate, demanding to 'strengthen refugees' ability to provide for themselves and their families' in order to allow for more dignity, placing 'people at the heart of [UNHCR's] activities', and to make sure that 'refugee voices were reflected', as well as pointing out the need 'to empower refugees as decision makers'(UNHCR ExCom 2017: 9, 707th meeting, 6, 708th meeting, and 8, 708th meeting). Looking more closely at one of the statements, it becomes clear that the US supports participation for functional reasons: participation, understood as self-sufficiency, can relieve the UNHCR budget and consequently donor governments. The US delegate explains accordingly that (UNHCR ExCom 2017: 9, 707th meeting), '[a] major focus of the Comprehensive Refugee Response Framework and the conversations on developing the global compact on refugees was the question of how to strengthen refugees' ability to provide for themselves and their families. Ultimately, greater self-reliance led to greater self-protection and dignity.' In the Global Reports after 2010, we can also see the continuing trend of the rise of the individual. A case in point is the Global Report of 2017, in which an increase in individual storytelling can be observed. Throughout the report, there are short testimonials about individual refugees' stories and their inter-action with UNHCR, including quick response codes that lead to accompany-ing videos (UNHCR 2018a). This individual storytelling may help to counteract the perception of global refugee flows as faceless masses, and contribute to making their fate more relatable. In the annual consultations with NGOs after 2010 we can also find calls for a 'people-centred approach' and 'empowerment' of refugees, seeing them as 'assets' instead of a 'burden' (UNHCR Partnership Section 2015: 9, 17, 36).

In sum, the two arguments we have presented boil down to the observation that, in the *communication* of the UNHCR and its member states, the balance between refugee rights and state interests has gradually tilted towards the former. Yet, this observation stands in marked contrast to the attack on refugee rights others have observed in the *practice* of UNHCR in the same period. Barnett and Finnemore argue that from the late 1970s onwards, UNHCR developed a 'repatriation culture'. This culture elevated repatriation from one policy option, alongside asylum and third-country resettlement, to the default option pursued by the office. They argue that the underlying logic and effect of this change, however, was to favour the interests of states hosting large numbers of refugees while putting refugee rights at risk. It did so mainly in two ways. First, the shift in UNHCR's policy signalled to countries of first asylum that the international community no longer demanded them to naturalize refugees as a 'permanent solution'. Instead, it asked for a more limited form of refugee assistance until a 'durable solution', understood as the now 'preferred solution' of repatriation, could be found. Second, UNHCR redefined the notion of 'voluntary repatriation' in a way that effectively allowed the office, rather than individual refugees, to determine 'objectively' whether a home state was to be considered safe for refugees to return to (Barnett and Finnemore 2004: 98–118).

How do we reconcile these conflicting observations? Basically, there are two ways to interpret the contradictory evidence. On the one hand, it might simply point to the limitations of the sources on which our study relies. Whereas Barnett and Finnemore mainly use expert interviews and UNHCR policy documents such as the *Notes on International Protection*, we reconstruct the legitimation discourse by triangulating UNHCR communications, member state statements, and 'external voices' that made it through the media filter. Thus, these sources might lead us to overlook an important discursive shift in the international refugee regime towards the 'repatriation culture' identified by Barnett and Finnemore. Yet, while possible, this interpretation would imply that the shift remained invisible in the communications we examine—in other words, that it was not strongly contested within UNHCR itself. If states were to limit the rights of refugees significantly and if the 'pragmatist' camp—though not the 'fundamentalists' (Barnett and Finnemore 2004: 96–7)—within the UNHCR bureaucracy concurred that this was politically necessary, there simply would not be a prominent voice that spoke out on behalf of refugees.[12] The result would be a silencing of their views and interests at an important political turning point.

Alternatively, a second reading interprets the diverging observations as evidence for a decoupling of talk on the one hand, and decisions and action on the other. On this account, organizations confronted by heterogeneous and often conflicting demands from their organizational environments develop a tendency to secure their survival by talking in one way, deciding in another, and acting in a third way (Brunsson 2002). From this vantage point, the rhetorical strengthening of refugee rights would thus accompany the weakening of refugee rights in practice, hence pointing to a similarity with rise of a development rhetoric—but not of development activities—observed in the International Atomic Energy Agency case (see Chapter 5). Importantly, such a perspective would not see decoupling as cynical but as a necessity—perceived or real—that allows an organization to maintain at least some balance between conflicting demands, rather than rejecting outright, or giving up on a particular ambition.

AFTER THE CRISIS: THE RISE OF MANAGERIAL NORMS

Beyond the rise of the individual described in the previous section, we also observe a rise of managerial norms in the legitimation contests around UNHCR. Two events sparked the rise of these norms after 1990. First, the financial crisis of 1989/90 rendered the accountability relationship between UNHCR and its member states visible and sparked major management reforms over the next decade. Second, the reform of the UN humanitarian sector highlighted the need for coherence in the coordination of the humanitarian sector which, in turn, became an important normative basis for UNHCR activities as well. A common feature of these normative changes is their focus on procedural norms. As a result of their rise, the question *how* UNHCR should carry out its mandate thus receives greater attention.

The Budget Crisis

In 1989, UNHCR faced a budget deficit of approximately 60 million USD (UNHCR ExCom 1989: 4, 437th meeting) and had to downgrade its assistance

---

[12] Barnett and Finnemore (2004: 105) argue that the number of 'fundamentalists' decreased over time when veteran staff departed and more pragmatic personnel were hired, leading to a gradual, yet substantial change in the organizational culture of UNHCR.

programmes for 1990. Gil Loescher even estimates the original deficit (before a first downgrading of programmes) at over 100 million USD. He also describes the temporal overlap of the financial crisis with a financial scandal involving High Commissioner Hocke, which led to his resignation by the end of 1989. The financial scandal concerned a special fund set up by Denmark for the former High Commissioner Hartling, a Danish national, used by Hocke to cover travel expenses for himself and his wife including first-class upgrades and Concorde flights (Loescher 2001: 262–4; see also Lewis 1989). This instance of bad leadership by High Commissioner Hocke exacerbated the financial crisis by lowering staff morale and the confidence of donor governments. The ExCom only approved a semi-annual budget for 1990 which was to be managed by a temporary working group. This group presented its report to an extraordinary session of ExCom in May 1990 that had to approve the budget for the second half of 1990 and reviewed the office's strategy for overcoming the financial crisis (UNHCR ExCom 1990c). This 'most humiliating development' (Loescher 2001: 263) for UNHCR—losing control over its financial management—helps to explain the scale of (management) reforms undertaken in its wake.

Through a general downscaling of programmes and the voluntary contributions received throughout 1990, the budget crisis was eventually overcome. UNHCR blamed the lack of adequate funding for being unable to properly fulfil its mandate. In his attempt to ascribe responsibility for overcoming the financial crisis to member states, the High Commissioner appealed for more predictable funding (UNHCR ExCom 1990a: 3–6, 448th meeting and UNHCR ExCom 1990b: 3, 450th meeting). By contrast, the most important donor government, the US, blamed bureaucratic mismanagement for the budget deficit. The US delegate made a very direct statement to this effect, stating that (UNHCR ExCom 1990a: 4, 450th meeting), 'His delegation felt obliged to point out that some of the impact of the current crisis described in document A/AC.96/744 [UNHCR ExCom 1990c] was attributable to a lack of prioritization and of technical management rather than to a shortage of funds.' The appointment of a working group to oversee the budget, and the 'summoning' of the High Commissioner during the extraordinary session to present his strategy to tackle the financial crisis, make the accountability relationship between the bureaucracy and member states visible. Moreover, the financial scandal and its aftermath show that member states are keen to protect their sovereign prerogatives.

Management Reforms

In the wake of the financial crisis, standards not only of 'accountability', but also of 'efficiency' and 'effectiveness', became increasingly relevant for the legitimation of UNHCR. From 1990 onwards, a series of overlapping reform efforts highlighted these norms. As a reaction to the financial crisis, the High Commissioner appointed an ad hoc Review Group on the Role and Structure of UNHCR in late January 1990 which presented its report, including fifty-eight recommendations, by early March 1990. The main task of the group was 'to conduct a comprehensive review ... in order to identify ways to provide for optimum effectiveness in implementing its mandate and programmes' (UNHCR 1990: 2). Hence, the programme management system that had been used since 1979, 'underwent an in-depth review in 1990' (UN General Assembly 1991: 13).

By April 1993, High Commissioner Ogata set up an Internal Working Group on Programme Management and Operational Capacity which recommended reforms to increase the effectiveness of programme delivery, flexibility, and accountability (UN General Assembly 1994b: 17; 1995: 16). While member states mainly applauded these efforts, they also demanded further rationalization and an 'efficient management of resources' (UNHCR ExCom 1994: 14 and 17, 491st meeting).

By the end of 1994, the High Commissioner directed yet another multiyear reform effort, which brought extensive changes to the way UNHCR was organized and carried out its mandate (UN General Assembly 1997b: 15–17). Over the three phases of this so-called *Project Delphi*, the Change Management Group developed a conceptual framework (December 1994–May 1996), devised an action plan (June–October 1996), and implemented a wide range of management reforms (April 1997–8 and beyond) (UNHCR 1996).

The main outcomes of the latter were summarized in the annual report of 1998: a new operations management system, a protection database, a new supply chain management, the integration of computer systems (IPS), a new human resource and career management system, as well as the decentralization of financial services (UN General Assembly 1999b: 11). The integrated systems project took several years to be implemented and was renamed as Management Systems Renewal Project (MSRP) and rolled out from 2003 onwards (UNHCR 2002a: 87ff. and UNHCR 2002b). Results-based management (RBM), introduced in 2002, was hence complemented by a multiyear extensive management reform that entailed the development of management systems and specialized software for UNHCR purposes (such as the results-based management software FOCUS, introduced in 2008, or proGres, a biometric refugee registration standardized information technology, among others). The description of these diverse reform initiatives takes increasingly more room in the self-legitimation of UNHCR as well as in ExCom debates. What unites the different reform projects and reports is a new public management language based on efficiency and cost-benefit calculations, and focused on rationalization, strategic objectives and outputs, deliverables, impact assessment, evaluation, oversight, and management tools. For example, the 2006 *Global Report* informs that (UNHCR 2006: 20),

The benefits far outweigh the costs in implementing [the MSRP]. The return on investment include the improved control of funds and expenditures, the integration between previous separate systems that will streamline processes and reduce data processing functions, and the reduction of costs in maintaining ancient legacy systems. Being internet-based, MSRP enables UNHCR to have the option to de-centralize, or out-post. MSRP is therefore instrumental in UNHCR present efforts to reform.

Accountability

In the wake of reforms, accountability became a core standard of legitimacy. However, it encompasses different meanings, as there is no systematic or shared understanding over the various contexts in which accountability is mentioned (Türk and Eyster 2010: 160). According to Katja Lindskov Jacobsen and Kristin Bergtora Sandvik, references to accountability in UNHCR policy documents date back to 1980 (Jacobsen and Sandvik 2016: 6–8). Yet, the authors identify several changes in UNHCR's understanding of accountability: a turn towards more accountable management structures after the end of the Cold War, the recognition of the 'potential of political dynamics to undermine UNHCR's protection mandate' after failures in Rwanda and Kosovo, and an 'emerging focus' on downward accountability to beneficiaries, as a direct reaction to scandals involving the abuse of refugees by humanitarian workers.

Although the term accountability is not explicitly used, the reaction of member states to the financial crisis made the accountability relationship between UNHCR and its members visible. During the extraordinary session of ExCom in 1990, the High Commissioner literally had to account for the funds provided by states and for how he planned to overcome the financial crisis. Financial accountability was important for the legitimation of UNHCR in handling the crisis, a finding that fits Jacobsen and Sandvik's observation that UNHCR's early understanding of accountability mainly focused on 'the cost-effective use of public funds' (Jacobson and Sandvik 2016: 6).

In the context of Project Delphi, UNHCR used 'managerial accountability', understood as authority of managers taking ownership of operations, to legitimate a delegation of authority from headquarters to the field (UNHCR 1996: 8–11, 20–1, 27–33, and 52). Finally, the organization introduced the first edition of the Global Report in 1998 to satisfy the reporting demands of a diversified donor base that increasingly included non-traditional donors from the private sector. The introduction of the Global Report, 'the main account to donors' (UNHCR 1998: 8 and foreword), therefore fits the image of financial accountability.

Its different meanings notwithstanding, accountability becomes a more frequent term in ExCom deliberations from 2002 onwards. In 2002, ExCom members primarily refer to it in the context of the West Africa scandal which involved allegations of sexual abuse and exploitation of refugee children by humanitarian workers in Guinea, Liberia, and Sierra Leone, brought to light by a joint UNHCR/Save the Children report in 2002 (UNHCR/Save the Children 2002 and Naik 2003). NGOs welcomed the introduction of the Code of Conduct, including oversight and disciplinary mechanisms, as an important tool to enhance the accountability of UNHCR and implementing partner staff. However, they warned against overstating its impact during a discussion at the annual consultations with NGOs (UNHCR NGO Liaison Unit 2002: 14–15).

By 2010, another layer of meaning is added. When member states refer to accountability, they increasingly demand the development of oversight and audit mechanisms (UNHCR ExCom 2010: 9, 640th meeting; 2010: 4 and 9, 641st meeting). In subsequent years, the focus of accountability talk becomes more heterogeneous, covering issues such as 'results-based management', age, gender and diversity mainstreaming, or internal posting processes. In 2010, many delegations also commend the UNHCR for having reformed and effectively strengthened its internal oversight and audit processes. The reform process of financial accountability to donors culminated in the adoption of the International Public Sector Accounting Standards in 2012, which is reported as a success in the annual report (UN General Assembly 2013: 12). Although many delegations welcome the adoption of the accounting standards during the 2013 ExCom (see for example the statements of the United Kingdom, 669th meeting, the Netherlands and Germany, 672nd meeting, as well as the Republic of Korea and Spain, 673rd meeting), it is again the delegation of the US that is most explicit in its demands for better oversight. Notably, the US delegate criticizes that (UNHCR ExCom 2013: 2, 673rd meeting),

> Although many of the recommendations made by the Board of Auditors in 2011 had been followed up, around 40 of them, particularly regarding risk management, remained outstanding. She continued to be concerned at the ineffective control over implementing partners reported by the Board of Auditors and the Office of Internal Oversight Services, and commended the responsiveness to the proposal made by the Member States to establish an Internal Compliance and Accountability Committee.

Hence, the process of internal management reform continues after 2010 as there are further demands by member states to increase efficiency, transparency, and accountability. Given that the internal logic of efficiency runs against the idea of a state of perfect efficiency that could not be enhanced further, some parallels thus emerge to the self-reinforcing normative dynamics we observe in our case studies of the General Agreement on Tariffs and Trade/ World Trade Organization (Chapter 3), of the African Union (Chapter 4), and of the International Union for Conservation of Nature (Chapter 6).

Reforming the Humanitarian Sector of the UN:
Coherence and Coordination

The reform of the UN humanitarian sector from 1998 to 2005 brought a different set of managerial norms to the fore. In particular, coherence and coordination with other actors in the same sector feature prominently during this period.

In a changing institutional environment, UNHCR had to be flexible to stay relevant. By 2005, the UN General Assembly and ECOSOC had formally authorized UNHCR to take over new tasks related to IDPs. UNHCR reports on its assistance activities for 'persons displaced inside the country' as early as 1974. A growing awareness for the protection needs of IDPs in the beginning of the 1990s, however, leads states to demand a greater involvement by UNHCR. Such demands are based on the similar situation of IDPs and refugees, and on the link to the traditional functions of UNHCR. At a 1994 meeting of the UNHCR's ExCom, for instance, a Chilean delegate commented (UNHCR ExCom 1994: 3, 494th meeting; see also 1994: 16, 489th meeting and 10, 490th meeting):

> Durable solutions had to be found for internally displaced persons who were outside the scope of institutionalized protection. A broader interpretation of UNHCR's humanitarian task and its mandate would enable it to assume responsibility for the protection, on a permanent basis, of internally displaced persons, whose plight was no less serious than that of other refugees.

Other member states challenged this endorsement of UNHCR's new role. As in the following statement by the Indian delegate, their warnings were based on a concern for UNHCR's core mandate as well as a respect for state sovereignty (UNHCR ExCom 1994: 17, 492nd meeting): 'Discussion on the question of internally displaced persons should bear in mind that those persons were within the administrative and territorial jurisdiction of their own States. The consent of the State concerned was therefore a prerequisite before action could be taken to help them.'[13] While UNHCR has always presented itself as a cooperative partner (UN General Assembly 1971: 46 and 1979: 47), system-wide coherence and coordination with other members of the UN system became more central as legitimacy standards after 1990. In addition to presenting coordination efforts as a means to increase efficiency, UNHCR has also promoted the idea of greater system-wide coherence and interagency coordination as a way to mobilize more resources for the office (UN General Assembly 1991: 35–6).[14]

---

[13] See also UNHCR ExCom (1994: 12, 490th meeting) for similar concerns voiced by Australia.

[14] 'In this context, and given the need to augment the resources available to assist refugees and returnees, UNHCR has paid greater attention to inter-agency cooperation as an area of activity with significant potential resource-mobilization for complementary assistance to refugees and returnees.'

Among ExCom members, we observe a similar picture. While states insist on cooperation for the sake of efficiency gains throughout all four decades, demands for a comprehensive and concerted approach for IDPs and programmes that complement each other intensify around 1994 (UNHCR ExCom 1994: 16, 489th meeting and 8, 490th meeting). At the same time, member states seem optimistic about the potential for new forms of coordination. The Swiss government, for instance, is quoted as welcoming 'the new enthusiasm for a relationship between the humanitarian agencies and OCHA, as well as the increase in consultations and inter-agency groups'— a development which it expects can 'only strengthen humanitarian action, its coordination, consistency and resolve' (UNHCR ExCom 1998: 14, 532nd meeting).

Overall, the description of coordination in the context of the cluster approach for IDPs takes up an increasingly significant share of UNHCR reporting. Moreover, it is presented as largely self-evident, with few explicit explanations or justifications given. Unsurprisingly, the focus on the procedures in the context of management reform, from the 1990s onwards, added procedural norms to the legitimation basis of UNHCR. Although efficiency and coordination had been important norms, the new impetus with which they were used in the legitimation of UNHCR justifies speaking of a rise of procedural norms.

PATHWAYS TO NORM CHANGE

Like in the preceding case study chapters, the normative developments we sketch can be traced to multiple sources. Overall, four pathways appear to be particularly relevant in the UNHCR case. The first originates from the rise of 'new wars' after the Cold War. While civilians increasingly became the targets of armed violence in these wars, 'failed states' could only insufficiently protect those who had fled conflict regions, hence giving impetus to international efforts to protect refugees. A second pathway is linked to UN reform in the humanitarian sector, which rendered managerial norms of efficiency more central to the work of UNHCR. Third, as in other cases we reconstruct in this book, normative change originates from the rise of a 'second audience' from which UNHCR seeks legitimacy and whose norms and values it therefore needs to take on board. This time, however, the second audience is neither civil society nor the media system but 'new donors' from which UNHCR seeks support to broaden its financial basis. Finally, we can add organizational learning that follows instances of organizational behaviour constructed as 'scandalized misconduct', as a fourth source of normative change.

New Wars, New Roles

The end of the Cold War is often described as a turning point in international relations. For UNHCR, it has indeed had widespread ramifications (Jacobsen and Sandvik 2016: 6). The office recognized the profound changes early on. In the annual report published in 1990 (UN General Assembly 1990: 1), it writes:

> The period covered by this report witnessed occurrences or developments which were in many ways epochal, and whose impact will in all probability be felt throughout the last decade of the twentieth century... The impact of these developments on current and future refugee problems, and indeed the role of the Office, has yet to become apparent or to be fully grasped.

In hindsight, the end of the Cold War changed the predominant types of conflict and war, presenting new challenges to the office in relation to its assistance operations in the field, its culture of neutrality and humanitarianism, as well as its financial administration and management system. These changes and their corresponding effects on the work of UNHCR provided the conditions upon which both norm changes have to be understood.

Reflecting on her tenure as High Commissioner from 1990 to 2000, Sadako Ogata (2005: 17–18) sums up the challenges of the early 1990s as follows:

> The world was undergoing enormous geopolitical changes without effective and up-to-date means to counteract them... The demise of the cold war... accelerated political changes and brought solutions to long-standing international confrontations. At the same time, the loosening grip of superpower domination resulted in the proliferation of civil and community-based conflicts... No effective formulas to deal with uprisings dominated by nationalism and localism were yet in view.

On the one hand, 'solutions to long-standing international confrontations' provided UNHCR with the opportunity to repatriate large groups of refugees. The lightening of UNHCR's caseload through repatriation was cause for some optimism (UNHCR 1992). On the other hand, 'the proliferation of civil and community-based conflicts' caused new refugee flows and increased the number of IDPs dramatically.

New emergencies, especially IDP situations, challenged UNHCR to become flexible in its response, but the additional operations tied up large parts of its budget. In 1994, for example, humanitarian assistance programmes in the former Yugoslavia, Rwanda, and Burundi accounted for over 60 per cent of the special programmes budget (UN General Assembly 1995: 9). On the one hand, these events directed international attention to the 'humanitarian plight of refugees' (UN General Assembly 1991: 1). This plight was particularly acute since the nature of violent conflict had changed and the civilian population increasingly became the target in the so-called new wars. As they were often fuelled by ethnic conflict, 'forced human displacement became an issue of primary strategic importance' (Ogata 2005: 326). Combined with the partial or complete breakdown of the state in conflict regions, calls for the 'international community' to step in and protect those who had to flee conflict zones became louder. Our observation that individuals became a more central reference point in the rhetoric of UNHCR can, at least for the 1990s, be interpreted as a response to such calls.

On the other hand, new conflicts force UNHCR to become politically involved. Protecting and assisting IDPs thus bears the risk of confrontation. By definition, IDPs have not crossed a border to obtain protection from a government other than their own. Hence, they can find themselves in a similar, yet even more precarious situation than refugees. Based on the similarity of their protection needs, some member states argue for UNHCR's involvement (UNHCR ExCom 1994: 16, 489th meeting, 15, 493rd meeting; 1998: 15, 530th meeting; 2002: 1, 563rd meeting). However, UNHCR risks confronting governments, that are either unable or unwilling to protect their uprooted citizens, and thereby infringing upon their sovereignty. This political dimension of UNHCR's involvement came to the fore when refugee camps were militarized or populations at risk could only be reached by negotiating with conflict parties (cf. Weiner 1998).

In sum, external developments following the end of the Cold War forced UNHCR to balance the traditional norm of neutrality with the newly introduced idea of decisive action for people in need, even in politically charged contexts. At the same time, it is important to note that demands for a more political role of UNHCR had already gained prominence by the 1980s. Thus, by the time states, NGOs, and the UNHCR uttered such demands in the context of the 'new wars' of the 1990s, the *root cause* debate had already prepared the ground on which the stronger domestic involvement of UNHCR to protect refugees and IDPs could find wide acceptance.

New Tasks and UN Reform

Initially, the High Commissioners only reluctantly accepted responsibility for IDPs. In the end, they gave in to the demands made by the Secretary General. They were supported by many states to act as lead agency in humanitarian crises and thereby take on a more political role that seemed to contradict its humanitarian and impartial tradition. While UNHCR acknowledged UNDP's lead role in providing assistance to IDPs in 1990, by 1998, the office had developed a growing awareness for the need to participate in the protection of IDPs. UNHCR was increasingly interested in, and claimed jurisdiction over, IDPs, by describing its engagement in various IDP situations in subsequent reports (UN General Assembly 1999b: 4 and 15; 2003: 1 and 10; 2007: 1–2 and

12; 2011: 4 and UNHCR 2002a: 60; 2006: 40–3; 2010: 49–53). Additionally, in 1998, UNHCR acknowledged the importance of the humanitarian sector reform, and underlined its full involvement and proactive engagement in the process. In 2002, the office continued to point to its active participation and important contributions to interagency coordination within the framework of the Inter-Agency Standing Committee, its 'catalytic role' as the coordinator for internal displacement in Colombia, and signalled its willingness to assume responsibility for other IDP situations in a letter to OCHA's Emergency Relief Coordinator (UN General Assembly 2003: 12, for a similar statement: UNHCR 2002a: 60). After the launch of the cluster approach, UNHCR praised itself for having actively fought for this IDP mandate (UN General Assembly 2007: 12).

Considering the institutional density in the humanitarian sector, with UNDP as a direct competitor for core competencies,[15] a growing number of humanitarian NGOs, as well as plans to establish a special agency for IDPs (UNHCR ExCom 2002: 14, 562nd meeting), it becomes clear that UNHCR had to participate in the cluster approach to stay relevant. UNHCR's fear of marginalization was not new (UN General Assembly 1991: 36 and UNHCR ExCom 1994: 12, 489th meeting). However, when the reorganization of the humanitarian sector was speeding up, UNHCR became increasingly involved in the process. It based its claim on a functional argument: as it became more and more difficult to distinguish between refugees, returnees, IDPs, and other persons of concern in complex emergencies, UNHCR, the expert agency on displacement and camp management, should lead the coordination of efforts in this sector. External developments, namely new conflicts after the end of the Cold War, originally led UNHCR to assume greater responsibility for a more diverse range of persons of concern. Yet, UNHCR also proactively took the opportunities provided by these circumstances to stay relevant. In particular, the determined way in which it secured the IDP mandate points to a strategic use of rhetoric by UNHCR to legitimate itself.

At the same time, the introduction of the cluster approach turned the 'system-wide coherence' into a central demand in the UN system. To achieve coherence, the coordination of the various activities, undertaken by different international organizations, built on a common management logic that had been inspired by New Public Management ideas. The discussion about the accountability of UNHCR in the context of the cluster approach—for

---

[15] The involvement in development activities has a long tradition in UNHCR (see for example Crisp 2001). Development aid provided by UNHCR is presented as a corollary of assistance to persons of concern without which durable solutions could not be achieved. However, UNDP's main activity is development so competition over competencies and funding seem inevitable. On institutional density, see also Betts 2013.

instance, when delegations commend 'the Office's involvement in dialogue to improve the humanitarian coordinator system and the accountability thereof' (UNHCR ExCom 2010: 9, 639th meeting)—suggests that this logic feeds the rise of managerial norms we describe in this chapter. As a result of UNHCR's efforts to stay relevant, it needed to accept the new norms that had come with it, and had to integrate them in its legitimation.

New Audiences

Besides demanding UNHCR to step up international refugee protection and, in so doing, take on a more political role, the violent conflicts of the 1990s also required the office to raise additional funds for the management of its operations. In this context, UNHCR strongly emphasizes participatory as well as managerial norms in its Global Reports, a publication geared towards keeping new donors up to date with the work of the office.

The idea of participation first came up in the context of self-sufficiency projects and UNHCR's development activities, with early references mentioning the risk of a dependency syndrome if aid was handed down to 'voiceless' recipients (UN General Assembly 1983: 18). As UNHCR cooperated with aid agencies like the World Bank on 'refugee aid and development', and as these more traditional development agencies had already implemented community participation projects in the 1970s, we can assume that UNHCR adopted ideas on how to plan and implement development projects from the expert organizations (Paul 1987; UN General Assembly 1983: 30; 1987: 1; 1991: 13; 1995: 2; 1999b: 2; 2003: 11). This points to a learning process that feeds the rise of participation, and the empowerment discourse which is based on the need to fund refugee assistance. Self-sufficiency of refugees promises to relieve the UNHCR budget as refugees find employment and sources of income, and thus become less reliant on long-term UNHCR assistance programmes that blur into development aid. Refugees involved in income-generating self-sufficiency programmes are no longer 'voiceless recipients' of aid but agents engaged in bettering their own lives. In the 1982 annual report, the UNHCR explicitly states this purpose (UN General Assembly 1983: 18):

> Even in its care and maintenance programmes, UNHCR seeks to include income-generating and other activities leading to the partial, and eventually, the total self-sufficiency of the refugees. This policy of encouraging and promoting self-sufficiency is due in part to the desire to reduce the financial burden on the host Government and the international community for the continued care of the refugees. At the same time, this policy also reduces the dependency syndrome often associated with refugee situations by encouraging refugees to assume responsibility over as much of their daily lives as possible.

It becomes clear in this statement that 'self-sufficiency' programmes and the reduction of the 'dependency syndrome' are motivated by the wish to reduce the financial burden on the UNHCR budget and consequently donor governments. Seeing participation as a tool rather than a value in itself is what Ghazalea Mansuri and Vijayendra Rao call the 'instrumental value' of participation, as opposed to an 'intrinsic value' (Mansuri and Rao 2013: 16).

However, we find explicit expressions of a belief in the moral rightness of participation in the mission statements of the Global Reports since 1998. While this might be the result of a learning or socialization process, the observation that participatory ideas are more pronounced in the Global Reports than in the annual reports suggests that UNHCR seeks to resonate with the values of its different audiences by tailoring its messages. According to its first edition in 1998, UNHCR introduced the Global Report to satisfy the needs of a diversified donor base, including the private sector (NGOs, foundations, and business actors). During ExCom sessions, mainly NGOs and consultants mention the positive impact of participation.[16] Moreover, Getachew Dinku Godana argues that international, mainly Western, NGOs 'are among the organizations that pioneered participatory approaches' and 'uphold participation as a noble democratic value', although they do not necessarily achieve genuine citizen participation in their programmes (Godana 2014: 12–13). Overall, this supports the assumption that participatory ideas gained strength in the legitimation contest over UNHCR as the office sought to broaden its legitimation constituency.

However, the questions remain: how and when have participatory norms of the development sector become a normative yardstick for UNHCR? Mansuri and Rao (2013) describe a first wave of participatory development in the 1950s and 1960s. As a reaction to the paternalism of development under colonial power, organizations involved in development aid such as the UN and USAID increasingly advocated for more participation of beneficiaries. As community-driven development projects did not yield the expected results, economists and their theories of structural adjustment became more influential in policy making. Accordingly, the interest in participation waned during the 1970s and early 1980s. However, as the social cost of structural adjustment programmes became increasingly evident in the late 1980s and early 1990s, a second wave of participation was driven by activists and scholars who emphasized bottom-up approaches to empower and include the poor and most vulnerable. This second wave of participation in development coincides with increasing

---

[16] A keyword search for 'participation' in ExCom meeting records yielded seventeen results of which only six were voiced by member states. The limited searchability of some summary records (due to the quality of available electronic copies) limits the interpretation of this figure to some extent. Nevertheless, even if member states refer to participation, they do not demand more participation, nor do they seem to have internalized the idea yet.

financial pressure on the UNHCR budget, due to more extensive assistance programmes and a high number of protracted refugee situations, and the growing awareness of the nexus and overlap between refugee aid and development. In 1986, for example, UNHCR describes the 'advanced stage' (UN General Assembly 1987: 1) of negotiations with the World Bank to co-finance projects for refugees in various countries, and by 1990, the term 'Refugee Aid and Development' has its own paragraph in the important developments section, discussing the delivery of assistance to refugees, in the UNHCR's annual reports (UN General Assembly 1991: 12). In light of the financial pressure on UNHCR, its increasing interest in cooperation with development aid organizations, and their renewed interest in participation and empowerment, we can draw the conclusion that UNHCR had to adapt to 'development speak' and emphasize participation in order to achieve co-financing for long-term refugee aid and development projects. In these early references to participation, its instrumental dimension seems to be a strong incentive to adopt ideas of participation from the development sector. By trying to appeal to new audiences such as the private sector and NGOs in the Global Report from 1998 onwards, the intrinsic value of participation seems to be more accentuated, which points to a process of learning and internalization of normative expectations that were originally adopted from important cooperating partners in the development sector.

The Legacy of Scandal

As indicated in the previous section, the financial crisis in 1989 and 1990 was a window of opportunity to demand a higher level of (financial) accountability and a more efficient use of funds. Member states used the budget deficit to firmly state their demands for efficient administrative structures. Subsequently, UNHCR's new role as lead agency in conflicts after the end of the Cold War added further pressure to reform the office as it overextended the administration.

The temporary loss of control over its budget strongly influenced UNHCR. To repair its legitimacy, UNHCR needed to respond to the demands of the temporary working group and embrace the idea of reform. In this atmosphere of state control, it is not surprising that High Commissioner Stoltenberg addressed the extraordinary session of ExCom in a tone of accountability and only cautiously voiced his discontent over cutbacks and the discontinuation of programmes. This strategy seems to have been successful as many member states expressed their satisfaction with UNHCR's progress in implementing the recommendations by the temporary working group (UNHCR ExCom 1990b: 2 and 10, 455th meeting, 5 and 11, 456th meeting, 3, 5, 9, and 16, 457th meeting).

Appointing an ad hoc group to review UNHCR's structure seemed like a promising strategy to regain some independence from member states. Yet, as the ad hoc review group envisaged a rather comprehensive reform programme and the implementation of far-reaching structural reforms took time, techno-logical advances created a further impetus to modernize the management systems.

Exacerbated by the increased availability and reduced cost of database applications and internet-based software, UNHCR continued to renew its management procedures and systems beyond the demands of the financial crisis. The introduction of various databases by the Change Management Group, and the development of specialized software in the context of the MSRP illustrate this dynamic. UNHCR grew increasingly aware that the new humanitarian tasks had overextended its management systems. This led the High Commissioner to set up another working group and thereby keep the momentum for further reforms going (UN General Assembly 1994b: 17 and Loescher 2001: 286–301).

The kind of normative path dependency we have identified in previous chapters can also be observed in the UNHCR case. The increased use of 'new public management' language makes optimal efficiency the ultimate objective and normative yardstick. Being discursively trapped by the idea of optimiza-tion, it is difficult to even imagine an endpoint to reforms, which puts the organization on track for continued improvement through a dynamic man-date. The increasing rate and comprehensiveness of reform efforts from 1990 onwards attest to this dynamic.

In summary, the financial crisis of 1989/90 constituted an important trigger for normative change. However, further contributing factors, namely overex-tended administrative structures, discursive entrapment, technological change, and an intellectual climate in which 'new public management' norms had gained clout, were equally relevant to determine the pace and course of the rise of managerial norms.

CONCLUSION

When, in 2006, the Canadian delegation to the UNHCR ExCom demanded reforms that would make UNHCR rely on 'modern management practices that [focus] on results and on accountability, not only to States but to the people it served' (UNHCR ExCom 2006: 5, 599th meeting), it gave expression to a general development we sketch in this book. To earn their legitimacy, international organizations face two challenges. First, they need to show how they serve the interests not only of states, but also of the individuals that make up these states. Second, they need to show how their activities help to achieve the desired outcome, but also how the procedures that have led to the selection of ends and means—the way the organization is 'governed'—adhere to commonly shared standards of appropriateness. This chapter shows that UNHCR is no exception.

The legitimation of UNHCR from 1970 to 2010 can be described as the constant negotiation of the legitimate scope of activities between UNHCR, its member states, and NGOs. The informal expansion of its mandate was constant and wide-ranging, to reflect the continuous and profound changes in UNHCR's environment. This chapter has shown how stipulations of the mandate created basic challenges for UNHCR, which in turn determined a basic set of normative demands to which UNHCR had to respond.

The first basic challenge concerns the agency's temporally and geographically limited mandate. UNHCR had to be flexible while acting within the limits set by states, mainly because of its financial dependency on the voluntary contributions by states. The second challenge arose from the question for whom UNHCR works: states or refugees. UNHCR had to balance the interests of refugees, its primary beneficiaries, with the interests of states, its primary contributors, which the statute also mentions as beneficiaries of UNHCR assistance.

These basic normative principles of functionality, flexibility, and legality were expanded by changing meanings and new norms that were added in light of the changes UNHCR faced towards the end of the Cold War. We described the rise of the individual, evidenced by the focus on human rights in the wake of the root cause debate, and the increased attention on civilians and IDPs as victims of new types of conflict. Another element is the empowerment discourse which promoted the norm of participation. This changes the role of refugees from beneficiaries to stakeholders that should be consulted in decisions affecting them, at least in theory.

The second norm change concerns the rise of managerial norms, namely financial accountability and efficiency, after the financial crisis and the overextension of administrative structures by UNHCR's new role as a humanitarian agency. As the humanitarian sector of the UN was reformed, coordination and coherence became important normative foundations for UNHCR as well. These norms pertain to the question of how UNHCR should work.

To some extent, UNHCR reacted to this multitude of norms and coped with the complex set of demands by avoiding a decision, and instead engaged in parallel legitimation: communication geared towards member states was institutionally separated from communication geared towards other donors as well as the wider public. Moreover, the normalization of exceptional tasks was identified as one of the agency's constant strategies to deal with the dilemma of a restricted legal mandate, and expanding challenges and (normative) expectations. This strategy allowed UNHCR to dissolve the paradox of constantly expanding the mandate, and taking over new tasks, without a formal change to its mandate. UNHCR also successfully negotiated the legitimate scope of its activities amid drastically changing external circumstances. In addition, it managed to allay concerns of overburdening, voiced by member states, and to fight for important mandates and competencies to stay relevant when faced with competition originating from an increasing institutional density in the fields in which the organization acted.

Overall, this chapter has shown how external developments such as the end of the Cold War and the financial crisis set in motion norm changes that were accelerated by further contributing factors such as technological change or normative path dependency. Finally, the silence of refugee voices in the official legitimation discourse is striking. The protection of refugees is the most basic function of the UNHCR and it nourishes the agency's image as a moral authority (Barnett and Finnemore 2004: 84). Yet, refugees are also deeply affected by UNHCR decisions and policies. Therefore, refugees and other persons of concern can become a potential source of discontent and contestation. However, rather than being organized at the annual consultations with NGOs or other forums, contestation by refugees is only ad hoc, as reported in press articles or in the academic literature (Moulin and Nyers 2007; Zetter 1991; Scheel and Ratfisch 2013; Powell 2013; Hyndman 2000; Fresia 2014; Crisp 1999).

Ultimately, the concept or definition of refugees itself might help to explain this silence. Michael Barnett and Martha Finnemore have shown that refugees are defined as powerless and therefore do not have to be consulted in decisions affecting them (Barnett and Finnemore 2004). In a similar vein, Ian Clark argues that vulnerability is inextricably linked to the category of refugees (Clark 2013). Although the empowerment discourse has slowly started to change this perspective, the image of refugees as vulnerable victims in need of protection is still powerful. For UNHCR, the tension inherent in these contradictory perspectives on refugees have not become a major legitimation problem thus far. Nevertheless, the participatory assessment of needs the organization has advocated more recently, or the consultation of refugees in designing camps, seem to be promising routes to detach the protection needs of refugees from categories of vulnerability and powerlessness.

8

Legitimating Global Governance in a Post-National World

Conclusions

Klaus Dingwerth

> Dear, dear! How queer everything is to-day!
> And yesterday things went on just as usual.
> I wonder if I've been changed in the night?
>
> Lewis Carroll, *Alice in Wonderland*

We began working on the research reported in this book about eight years ago. At the time, our main interest was to reconstruct how the *quality* of the political discourse in which international organizations gain, maintain, and repair their legitimacy has changed since the end of the Cold War. More precisely, we set out to examine how the norms and values that underpin the justification, appraisal, and critique of international organizations have shifted in the post-1990 world. Compared to the 1970s and 1980s, has *sovereignty* indeed become a weaker reference point in evaluating global governance institutions, as some predicted in the turbulent days of the 1990s when a new world order was about to be crafted? Have *democracy, transparency,* or *accountability* been on the rise as powerful protests against the World Trade Organization (WTO), the International Monetary Fund (IMF), or the World Bank suggested? And if so, what has made the rise of new legitimacy standards possible?

Eight years later, after examining countless primary documents, and the arduous process of interpreting what we found in these documents in view of the existing literature about the organizations we study, we see stability but also a significant amount of normative change. To our surprise, however, one of the major conclusions we draw focuses not on the quality but on the *quantity of legitimacy standards* to which international organizations are subjected. International organizations, we observe, are subjected to a longer and more demanding list of normative expectations than they were at the beginning of our period of investigation. This leads to a paradox: in times when many people feel that international organizations are needed the most to cope with the consequences of economic globalization, their legitimation has become more challenging than ever. In brief, international organizations have come under pressure—among other factors—because they need to match more, and more heterogeneous, normative expectations to convince relevant audiences that they are valuable.

In this concluding chapter, we summarize the main findings of our study and discuss their implications. We do so in three broad steps. In the first section, we describe and systematically organize the changes we see. The key argument in that section is that the legitimation narrative of the national constellation is increasingly complemented by a post-national legitimation narrative that centres on people-based and procedural standards of legitimacy. In the second section, we sort and discuss our observations on the pathways along which normative change has occurred. We argue that the politicization of international authority is one important causal mechanism that feeds the rise of people-based and procedural norms, but that this rise has several other sources in addition to politicization. In the third section, we discuss the major theoretical, practical, and normative implications of our findings as well as some limitations of the approach we have taken in this study.

CHANGING NORMS OF GLOBAL GOVERNANCE: THE RISE OF PEOPLE AND PROCEDURES

Each of our case studies describes the two most relevant normative changes in the legitimation of the selected international organizations. Since we examine five organizations, this provides us with ten stories—or cases—of normative changes (see Table 8.1). Taken together, these ten stories serve as a basis for responding to the questions that motivate our study. So, how have the norms and values that underpin evaluations of international organizations changed since the end of the Cold War? Is there a common theme or thread that unites change in the *terms of legitimation* across the five organizations? Or is each organization—and maybe even each norm shift within the organizations we study—unique, lacking shared features that would allow us to subsume the different observations under a common heading?

Our most general conclusion is simple. The legitimacy standards of the national constellation remain in place. But they are increasingly complemented by the legitimacy standards of the 'post-national constellation' (Habermas 2001). While the former rest on the norms of 'international society' and emphasize state sovereignty, functional cooperation, and non-coerciveness,

Table 8.1. Normative change in the legitimation of international organizations

Organization	Observed normative change	Strengthening of people and procedures
GATT/WTO	Rise of non-trade values	↑ People—↑ Procedures
	Rise of democracy	↑ People—↑ Procedures
OAU/AU	Rise of performance standards	↑ People—↑ Procedures
	Rise of participation and human rights	↑ People—↑ Procedures
IAEA	Rise of nuclear safety	
	Rise of watchdog role and image/rise of development	↑ People
IUCN	Rise of human well-being (including growing interest in indigenous people)	↑ People—↑ Procedures
	Rise of market norms	
UNHCR	Rise of the individual/growing informal role in relation to IDPs	↑ People—↑ Procedures
	Rise of managerial norms	

the latter build on 'world society' norms that conceptualize individuals as rights holders and are guided by a cosmopolitan ideal of inclusive global governance (Clark 2007b).

Moving down one step on the ladder of abstraction, this general claim translates into two specific shifts: a *rise of people-based legitimation norms* and a *rise of procedural legitimacy standards*. These shifts affect all five organizations we study (see Table 8.1), albeit in different forms and to different degrees. Theoretically speaking, the rise of people-based legitimation norms speaks to approaches that theorize the changing interactions between international and world society (Clark 2007b). Notably, it matches the assumption of world polity theorists that 'the underlying entities of the global social world, entitled to its protection and empowered to manage it, are human individuals' (Meyer 2009: 46). In contrast, the rise of procedural norms corresponds to the ideas of a rational-legal culture in which processes of organizing are increasingly standardized (Brunsson and Jacobsson 2000; Steffek 2003; Barnett and Finnemore 2004).

The Rise of People-Based Norms

Seven of the ten normative changes we observe imply a strengthening of people-based legitimacy standards. Moreover, each organization we study in this book experiences at least one rise of people-based norms, while none of the ten normative shifts we observe diminishes the role of 'the people' as a reference point for the legitimation of the international organizations we study. The norms we observe to be rising are 'people-based' in at least one of the following two senses: they either reference 'the people', individuals, or communities other than entire member states as the beneficiaries of international organizations and their work, or they acknowledge the right of 'the people', of individuals, or of communities other than nation states to have their voices heard and considered in the decision-making processes of international organizations. Yet, while standards based on these twin ideas are clearly added to the menu, they neither replace the more traditional legitimation narratives nor remain uncontested.

The rise of people-based norms is strongest and most unequivocal in the International Union for Conservation of Nature (IUCN) case where the conservation of nature for nature's sake gradually makes way for the idea that nature ought to be conserved for the sake of humans. As we show in Chapter 6, this development has ramifications for many areas of IUCN's work. It implies not only a stronger consideration of the interests of communities living in or nearby protected areas—often, these are indigenous communities—but also a greater role for local participation and knowledge in the design and implementation of conservation activities. At the same time, however, IUCN is a special case to begin with. Like other organizations we study, IUCN emphasizes how its activities help states to address global challenges—in this case conservation. Unlike the other organizations we cover, however, it has never conceived of states as its primary constituency. The rise of human well-being norms thus does not pit states and individuals against each other, rather it asks to reconcile the organization's primary 'conservation' rationale with a focus on 'development'. The counternarrative to people-based legitimation is therefore not a state-based or sovereignty-based but a nature-based legitimation narrative that has its roots in the early years of IUCN. Owing to the fear that nature's intrinsic value will be undermined if the organization does not speak up on its behalf, some members continue to subscribe to this narrative. But in general, the organization builds its legitimacy on the principle that conservation and development should go hand in hand, and that the voices of indigenous peoples need to be included just like those of all other local residents and their specific rights respected in conservation efforts.

Beyond IUCN, a growing importance paired with a continued contestation of people-based norms also characterize the discursive shifts we observe in the General Agreement on Tariffs and Trade (GATT) and WTO. In the first of our two stories we reconstruct for the WTO—the rise of 'non-trade values'—individuals become a more prominent reference point when labour standards are discussed. Framed in the language of rights, the discussion primarily focuses not on the prospects of national economies but of individual workers. In the late 1990s and early 2000s, the rise of democratic norms then adds further weight to people-based legitimacy standards. Notably, it ties the legitimacy of the WTO to respecting democratic policy decisions by member states, to the inclusion of civil society voices in the WTO's decision-making process, or to the extent the

WTO makes information about its decision-making process transparent to the public. Furthermore, at the Seattle protests, 'the people' also made themselves heard and seen in front of a global media audience.

Nonetheless, the WTO's own appropriation of the democratic deficit discourse gives the democratic legitimation narrative a different twist when it emphasizes the consensus principle, and understands the FIT formula of 'full inclusiveness and transparency' primarily as the WTO's need to respect and promote the equality of *all member states*, and enhance its transparency *towards those member states*. Thus, we are left with a legitimation contest that accepts 'democracy' as a new terrain for negotiating the legitimacy of the WTO but in relation to which two competing visions of *intergovernmental* and *global democracy* collide.

Next, we see people-based legitimacy standards promoted in the African Union (AU) when the latter reinvents itself as a 'people-centred union', and explicitly turns 'the people' into a primary category of beneficiaries and stakeholders. The development we reconstruct in Chapter 4 takes place in two distinct forms. On the one hand, the policy agenda of the Organisation of African Unity (OAU) and later the AU increasingly turns towards the promotion of 'human security', democracy, human rights, and the rule of law. The continental organization thus asks its member states to recognize—in words but also in deeds—the interests, desires, and rights of 'the people'.

On the other hand, the AU establishes the Pan-African Parliament, formalizes and expands its engagement with civil society, and explicitly aspires to become a 'people-friendly' and 'people-oriented' AU itself. As in the other cases we discuss, the development is not always harmonious. While AU member states support the turn towards 'the people' only reluctantly, civil society observers are critical that the new AU institutions fail to live up to the ideals the organization proclaims. Despite all the participatory talk and participatory mechanisms, the critics hold, the organization remains too exclusive, insufficiently transparent, and inaccessible to the wider public.

In Chapter 7, we observe that references to individuals also become stronger in the justificatory discourse of the Office of the United Nations High Commissioner for Refugees (UNHCR). Like in the GATT and the WTO case, the strengthening of individuals as a reference point is linked to a rights-based frame, this time tied to the UNHCR's mandate to protect the rights of refugees and—subsequently—internally displaced persons (IDPs). Unlike in the other cases we study, however, the inclusion of rights language in the organizational mandate means that individuals have always been a *raison d'être* of the organization. Thus, what we observe is not the emergence of a people-based legitimacy standard per se, rather a shift in the relative importance attached to that standard.

This importance becomes visible in a rhetorical emphasis on how the activities of UNHCR help to protect refugee rights. Moreover, it figures in the strong use of testimonies and images of refugees to raise awareness for their plight—an activity that in itself is a part of the organization's legitimation efforts—and in the increasing recognition of refugees not only as vulnerable groups in need of protection but also as 'assets' or 'stakeholders' whose views and voices need to be included in decision making. As in other cases we study, however, a closer look reveals the ambivalence of this rise of the individual in the language used to legitimate the UNHCR. In this case, it is contested not so much in the discourse itself but rather by a practice that turns 'voluntary' resettlement into the default option. Because this practice of responsibilization primarily serves host states, however, it limits rather than expands the protection of refugees' interests.

Finally, ambivalence also characterizes the rise of people-based norms in the International Atomic Energy Agency (IAEA) case. Here, the organization increasingly stresses how the development component of its work benefits individuals in member states, but that emphasis does not show in the organization's budget for development activities. Overall, the other two pillars of the IAEA's work—nuclear security and nuclear safety—remain the primary terrain on which the legitimacy of the IAEA is negotiated. Normative change is also less contentious than in other organizations we study, in part because the public debate takes little notice of the development work of the IAEA and remains focused on the non-proliferation challenge instead. In addition, while the hopes developing countries had in the 'nuclear promise' may once have been high, their stakes in an organization that provides only limited assistance to them are lower today. In the absence of a better alternative, however, the power of developing countries to call for an expansion of the IAEA's development pillar is equally limited.

In sum, world society norms associated with governing for and with 'the people' have come to complement the international society norms that stand at the core of the legitimation narrative, inherited from the national constellation. Since many of the developments we sketch occur after 1990, our broader picture partly fits with a narrative that sees 1989/90 as a turning point in international political history. However, two caveats need to be noted: first, people-based legitimacy standards were invented long before and merely gained strength more recently; and second, people-based legitimacy standards remain contentious in most organizations. Consequently, they rarely become specific in identifying which 'people' ought to benefit from the activities of international organizations, or whom international organizations need to include in their decision making to deserve legitimacy.

The Rise of Procedural Norms

In addition to the rise of people-based legitimation norms, five of the ten normative changes we observe speak to the rise of procedural legitimacy standards. With the exception of the IAEA, all organizations experience at least one instance when a new procedural norm is added to the legitimation menu. Moreover, as with the rise of people-based norms, we do not identify any normative changes that work against the trend. In brief, the question *how* an international organization is governed therefore gains wider currency for evaluating international organizations. In the documents we examine for this study, relevant audiences no longer hold the organization to account only for what it accomplishes but increasingly also for the ways in which decisions are made. In contrast to the people-based standards described above, the rise of procedural norms is subject to less contestation and it also comprises relatively specific behavioural standards. Much like the rise of people-based standards, however, it expands the list of normative expectations international organizations are meant to fulfil.

In the GATT and the WTO case, procedural standards initially gain traction in relation to the emerging debate over 'non-trade values' and then become central in response to the democratic deficit challenge. In the former case, the main arguments were substantive: the GATT and the WTO should respect environmental concerns and food safety standards and refrain from undermining core labour rights. But the debate over non-trade values also entailed a procedural dimension in that it required the organization to coordinate and align its regulatory work with institutions in neighbouring issue areas—the International Labour Organization (ILO) on labour issues, multilateral environmental agreements on environmental issues, and the Food and Agricultural Organization (FAO) and World Health Organization (WHO)'s Codex Alimentarius Commission on food safety. Together with the 'coherence mandate' in which member states had formally asked for a stronger coordination between the WTO, the IMF, and the World Bank, this new demand meant that the WTO was to be evaluated in terms of how well it managed its relations with key organizations elsewhere (Bernstein and Hannah 2012). However, while this new standard of coherence was added to the menu, it never became as central as the core norms that form the 'GATT gospel' we describe in Chapter 3.

The second normative change is different in this regard. The democratic deficit challenge and the specific ways in which the WTO responded to it significantly strengthen the place of procedural considerations in the legitimation of the organization. Although the details of what these standards mean remained to be negotiated, it was widely acknowledged that, to deserve legitimacy, the WTO had to be 'inclusive', 'transparent', and 'accountable'. Moreover, building on a procedural element of the GATT gospel—the consensus principle—the WTO not only argued that it was, in fact, a firmly democratic organization but also turned this feature into a core element of its projected identity. Similarly to the AU's portrayal as a 'people-friendly' and 'people-oriented' union, the WTO's affirmation and appropriation of democratic legitimacy standards thus represent a case where performance-based and procedure-based standards *as well as the personality* of an international organization are first amended, and then invoked to bolster the latter's claim to legitimacy.

In the OAU and the AU, the strengthening of procedural norms equally comes in the form of democratic principles. Initially referring to democracy promotion as a substantive concern, democratic standards are quickly applied to the international organization as well. As in the WTO case, the introduction of this new legitimacy standard itself is not questioned openly. Instead, contestation in the OAU/AU case focuses on whether the measures the organization takes go far enough to live up to the promise of being a 'democratic' organization. At the same time, procedural norms also rise in response to the OAU/AU's substantive aspirations. As the organization becomes more and more concerned to prove its effectiveness 'on the ground', new standards to measure efficient policy planning, organizational coherence, and sound financial management become important benchmarks to evaluate the OAU/AU.

In relation to IUCN, the human well-being norms we have described above are substantive in nature but they equally give rise to procedural standards. IUCN's bicameral structure has always given governmental and non-governmental actors an equal say in the governance of the organization and in its programmatic decisions. But especially regarding IUCN's local activities, the newly gained focus on conserving nature for the people's sake translates into demands for including 'the people' as well as their knowledge in the decision making about conservation measures. In response to these demands, as we show in Chapter 6, concepts like 'inclusiveness' or 'local knowledge'— often including indigenous knowledge—become more central in IUCN's communications, and the organization also pays attention to corresponding procedures in its practices. Once more, the discursive change has implications for our *personality* dimension. Notably, it deepens and diversifies the way in which IUCN conceives and presents itself as a democratic conservation forum on the one hand, and as an inclusive expert and knowledge hub on conservation issues on the other.

Finally, our UNHCR story differs in as much as procedural standards rise independently of people-based standards and take a different form. Rather than focusing on 'democratic' procedures, they thus tie the legitimacy of UNHCR to the efficiency and accountability of its management procedures. While UNHCR is, in Rittberger and Zangl's (2006) terminology, both a 'programme organization' that develops international rules and policies and an 'implementation agency' that works to put existing rules in practice, the more recent legitimation contest we observe tends to focus on the aspect of implementation. Like in the AU, the procedural and performance dimension of legitimacy are also closely linked in the UNHCR case: while procedural standards may have gained some autonomy in the organization's discourse and practice, they are ultimately justified as a means to achieve performance-based ends.

In sum, like people-based legitimacy standards, the 'principles of rightful conduct' (Clark 2005) to which international organizations are subjected are not entirely novel. But they have expanded from the original assumption, codified in the 1969 and 1986 Vienna Conventions on the Law of Treaties, that state consent and the absence of coercion establish the legitimacy of international institutions, to now include criteria such as the proper coordination with other international organizations, the democratic quality of decision making, or the efficiency and accountability of international bureaucratic processes.[1] What these standards have in common is that they evaluate international organizations based not on what they achieve but on how they work.

DYNAMICS OF NORMATIVE CHANGE:
POLITICIZATION AND BEYOND

What made the rise of people-based and procedural legitimacy standards in global governance possible? The contemporary literature on international organizations suggests that *the politicization of expanding international authority* is a major driver. Because decisions made by international organizations increasingly affect 'the people', the latter increasingly ask international organizations to demonstrate why and how these decisions serve the interests not only of governments but also the individuals the governments represent. Moreover, because the authority of international organizations reaches increasingly further, governments as well as stakeholders beyond governments

---

[1] Article 51 of the 1969 Vienna Convention on the Law of Treaties stipulates that 'the expression of a State's consent to be bound by a treaty which has been procured by the coercion of its representative through acts or threats directed against him shall be without any legal effect'. Article 52 of the same convention further complements that 'A treaty is void if its conclusion has been procured by the threat or use of force in violation of the principles of international law embodied in the Charter of the United Nations'. Finally, article 51 of the Vienna Convention on the Law of Treaties between States and International Organizations or between International Organizations (established in 1986, but not in force) states: 'The expression by a State or an international organization of consent to be bound by a treaty which has been procured by the coercion of the representative of that State or that organization through acts or threats directed against him shall be without any legal effect'.

ask for procedural guarantees that enhance the transparency, predictability, and accountability of international organizations and their activities (Zürn et al. 2012; Zürn 2018).

Our case studies of the GATT/WTO and the OAU/AU confirm the relevance of this causal pathway. Yet, our reconstruction of organizational legitimation discourses also reveals further dynamics that feed to the rise of people-based and procedural norms. Roughly in line with our distinction between change 'from the outside' and change 'from within' in Chapter 2, they fall into two broad categories. In the *organizational environment*, dynamics of change include the rise of new legitimation audiences that are sometimes, but not necessarily, linked to the dynamics of politicization; changes in the broader ideational climate that make specific legitimation frames resonate; and singular crisis events that offer an opportunity to either introduce new or strengthen existing narratives. In terms of *internal dynamics*, the norm entrepreneurship of international bureaucracies, the formation of broad discursive coalitions, and the self-reinforcing dynamics of normative change we describe as normative path-dependence matter in several of our case studies.

The Politicization of International Authority

The politicization argument suggests that a post-national legitimation narrative that builds on people-based and procedural standards should be particularly strong in those international organizations that either wield most authority, or have expanded their authority most strongly over time. Our case studies of the GATT/WTO, the OAU/AU, and the IAEA pose some questions to the first of these arguments but lend support to the second.

While international authority is notoriously difficult to pin down with precision, the measures Liesbet Hooge, Gary Marks, and colleagues have recently developed for their Measuring International Authority dataset provide some guidance (Hooghe et al. 2017). Understanding authority in terms of either pooling or delegation, their study of seventy-two regional and multi-regional organizations since the 1950s also includes three of the organizations we study: the IAEA, the OAU/AU, and the WTO (though only from 1995 onwards). The measures for *pooling*—the capacity of an organization to take important decisions by qualified or simple majority—show the IAEA at first place, with an average score of 0.61 (on a scale from 0 to 1) for different areas of organizational decision making, ranging from budgeting and policy making to the acceptance of new or the suspension of existing members. The WTO follows at second with a score of 0.42, the AU is at third place with a score of 0.35 as opposed to the OAU's score of 0.125. Looking at the *delegation* of authority to organizational bodies that enjoy significant independence from member states, the OAU/AU scores highest (0.25 since 2001, as opposed to 0.06 in its early years) while the IAEA (0.13) and the WTO (0.11) follow at lower levels.[2]

If authority levels, via their politicization, were the key driver of the post-national legitimation frames, we should expect the IAEA to be particularly affected. Among the seventy-two organizations included in the Measuring International Authority dataset, only three have a higher score of pooling: the UN Educational, Scientific and Cultural Organization, the WHO, and the International Civil Aviation Organization. Yet, while our case study shows that the IAEA has indeed been 'politicized', the legitimation contest we observe in relation to the Agency has not significantly shifted towards people-based or procedural norms. In conclusion, unless we argue that international security politics is exceptional and follows a different logic to other policy fields—a possibility we discuss further below—a simple link between authority, politicization, and discursive shifts in legitimation contests does not seem to hold.

A second interpretation that builds on *change in authority levels* seems more plausible. Whereas the IAEA's formal authority, measured in terms of pooling and delegation, may be relatively high, it is noteworthy that Hooghe, Marks, and colleagues see it remain at the same level since the IAEA's establishment in 1957. Those who cared about the work of the Agency, one could argue, were used to the authority the organization wields. This is different for the other two cases where the shift from the GATT and the OAU to the WTO and the AU created windows of opportunity for changing the terms of legitimation. Thus, in both cases, we face quasi-constitutional changes that expand the authority of the international body markedly, visibly, and explicitly. No wonder, then, that those who either opposed the expansion, or sought to advance their own values and interests in the context of a constitutional shift, found ways to 'politicize' the two organizations at this moment in time; no surprise that the memories of such constitutional moments became sticky and reminded audiences of the authority the organizations wielded; and no miracle that the expansion of authority was accompanied not only with high hopes but also with fear, thus leading a broad range of actors to demand 'inclusiveness', 'transparency', or 'accountability'.

In the legitimation of the European Union (EU), for example, discursive change (Biegoń 2016; Sternberg 2013) and institutional change (Rittberger

---

[2] As an alternative measure, Zürn (2018: 107–11) also includes results from his, thus far, unpublished International Authority Database, where values are assigned based on what the statutory documents reveal about the scope and bindingness and autonomy of an organization's decision-making competences. His list of thirty-four international organizations ranks the AU fourth (behind the EU, UN, and IMF), followed by the WTO at eighth place. The IAEA, IUCN, and the UNHCR are not included in his list.

2005) have regularly followed in the wake of constitutional moments in which a visible expansion of regional authority needed to be moderated. As another poster-child case of the politicization of international authority, the legitimation of the WTO shows a comparable pattern and, though less contested, we can interpret the OAU/AU case in similar terms. Nonetheless, a generalization to international organizations *as such* seems difficult because looking at the 'authority-legitimacy nexus' merely through the lens of pooling and delegation may miss out an important element. Notably, it fails to take into account what international organizations actually decide. The International Civil Aviation Organization and the World Meteorological Organization may thus wield significant international authority in their respective fields, but it seems fair to assume that few people care about the decisions they take. Many issues these two organizations address resemble coordination and not collaboration games, and the decisions they take will therefore have fewer distributive or even redistributive consequences than decisions taken in the AU, the WTO, the IMF, or the UN.

Overall, our study thus helps to qualify how authority and its politicization matter for the legitimation of international organizations in four ways. First, it suggests that post-national legitimation narratives thrive in particular where international authority is expanded but not necessarily where it is high. Second, expanded international authority is likely to trigger or further promote a post-national legitimation narrative only where a link between such authority and the stakes of affected groups beyond governments is successfully established. Third, it might well be that dynamics in international security follow their own logic (see also Tallberg et al. 2013), thus suggesting that the legitimation cultures that prevail in specific institutional fields serve as a filter for the broader normative developments in global governance. Fourth, the post-national legitimation narrative also flourishes in organizations like IUCN where formal international authority has not expanded in the same way. This implies that other dynamics beyond politicization contribute to the developments we sketch in this book. It is to these dynamics we turn in the following. Building on the argument developed in Chapter 2, we distinguish between change resulting from transformations in the world that surrounds international organizations, and change resulting from the specific dynamics of legitimation discourses themselves.

World-Order Dynamics: Change from the Outside

Several ingredients of the normative changes we observe originate in the environment of international organizations. Notably, we identify crisis events, changes in the broader ideational climate, and the rise of new legitimation audiences as recurrent conditions that facilitate the rise of post-national legitimacy standards.

Crisis Events

Four of our five case studies demonstrate how a set of events perceived as a 'crisis' can open a window of opportunity for actors to push for discursive change. In the IAEA case, the Chernobyl (and later Fukushima) nuclear accidents demand a response. On the one hand, they raise doubts as to the feasibility of 'nuclear safety', a core idea on which the IAEA and its mandate rest. On the other hand, Chernobyl further reduces the credibility of the IAEA's original promise to provide affordable nuclear energy for the developing world. The result is, first, a heightened role for the IAEA as a coordinator of international cooperation on nuclear safety standards and their implementation; and second, an emphasis on how nuclear science and technology benefit the developing world even when the promise of affordable nuclear energy does not materialize. In response to the latter emphasis, we also see a clear focus on 'human development' in which the organization makes extensive use of testimonies and images to demonstrate how individuals in developing countries benefit from its activities.

In the WTO case, the Seattle protests are widely perceived as a crisis in need of a response. As Chapter 3 has shown, the organization gives a twofold response. It acknowledges the major legitimation frames stressed by the critics but deals with them in different ways. The WTO reinterprets environmental concerns as 'sustainable development' and incorporates them in its preamble. It outsources labour rights issues to the ILO, and food safety as well as other regulatory concerns to standard-setting bodies acting in conformity with the International Organization for Standardization. Finally, the WTO confronts the democratic challenge by exploiting the linguistic openness of 'democracy' and redefines the term in ways that suit the organization best.

In the OAU/AU case, the violent conflicts and declining economies of the early 1990s constitute a set of almost chronic crises to which the organization seeks to respond, increasingly in vain. This crystallizes *inter alia* in the failure of the OAU to prevent and effectively address the genocide in Rwanda in 1994, which became an international symbol of the crisis of international conflict management. As we reconstruct in Chapter 4, the experience of this failure and the OAU's own efforts to learn from this through the work of the International Panel of Eminent Personalities provide an important anchor for justifying that institutional as well as normative transformations were necessary. Against this background, the organization turns to 'outcomes', especially in the realm of peace and security, and seeks to demonstrate its willingness to work with and for 'the people' rather than merely for states or incumbent governments.

Finally, the UNHCR story differs because the 'financial crisis' of 1989/90 has little to do with events taking place outside the organization. Yet, it equally shows how the successful framing of an event or a series of events as a crisis renders calls for fundamental change plausible. Counterfactually, it is difficult to imagine the accountability language to become as central to the legitimation of UNHCR in the absence of events that could have been characterized as a 'scandal' or a 'crisis of accountability'. Crises, in other words, open windows of opportunity because, as 'extraordinary' events, they demand an 'extraordinary' response. In sum, our emphasis on crisis introduces some contingency but it does not mean that change happens randomly. Whether or not a crisis exists, and 'of what' it might be a crisis, is thus necessarily subject to—and hence the result of—political contestation. In this contestation, existing norms and values and their interpretations will serve as a baseline. What precise response must follow, however, will rarely be clear in advance but subject to negotiation, and actors may also seize the opportunity to introduce new normative frames in such moments.

Ideational Climate

Talking of contingency, our case studies also illustrate that ideational fads and fashions matter. Windows of opportunity may allow new ideas to be introduced and existing ones to be either strengthened or weakened. But which ideas relevant audiences will find plausible depends, at least in part, on the broader ideational climate of the day.

In the WTO case, the failure of labour rights standards provides the clearest example. Carrying a 'socialist' flavour, these demands faced high hurdles to appear compatible with the post-1990 neoliberal ideology. In contrast, environmental demands could partially be aligned with neoliberal economic thinking—for instance in the form of externalities or as drivers for technological innovation—or be reframed in the language of 'sustainable development'. In addition, the neoliberal turn of the 1980s and 1990s meant that liberalization was increasingly constructed as a necessary—and often also sufficient—condition for development and not as an impediment to it (Geck and Weinhardt 2019; see also Eagleton-Peirce 2016). Similarly, in the more recent normative changes we observe in the IUCN case, neoliberal ideas render two novel ideas plausible: first, that ecosystem services ought to be economically valorized; and second, that IUCN should work with, rather than against, multinational corporations. Finally, the rise of managerial norms in the UNHCR case builds on new public management ideas that were spreading fast and widely, and were closely linked to a neoliberal understanding of 'lean' politics.

Beyond neoliberal ideas, the 'end of history' (Fukuyama 1989) climate of the early 1990s also shines through in our case studies of the OAU and the AU, of the GATT and the WTO, and of IUCN. In all three cases, we see a significant strengthening of democratic frames. Finally, the 'human' adjective in newly popular concepts such as 'human security' and 'human development' provided a powerful hook for norm entrepreneurs in the AU and IUCN; it also allowed the IAEA to claim its own development contribution. At the same time, the WTO case also illustrates that 'human development' does not rise everywhere. Instead, the more traditional understanding that construes development as a feature of national economies remains sticky in this specific discursive context, where it has played a central role since the early days of the GATT.

The Second Audience and the Rise of Non-State Actors

Third, we observe that the audiences from which international organizations seek legitimacy have expanded over time (see also Zaum 2013a; Symons 2011). In addition to states as the primary constituencies of international organizations, we thus observe the rise of various 'second audiences' from which international organizations seek recognition as rightful authorities, and whose expectations therefore come to matter in the legitimation contests we observe.

In the GATT and the WTO case, civil society literally stands at the door of the WTO and disrupts meetings, demanding its voice to be heard. The protests increase public awareness and attention, and they also turn the media into another relevant legitimation constituency as reporting on the WTO increases in line with the organization's growing importance as regulatory authority. Moreover, protests and media visibility mean that 'the public' begins to care about the WTO. Taken together, these expansions imply that the organization no longer legitimates itself to a trade community alone and consequently, a technocratic language no longer suffices to gain, maintain, or repair its legitimacy. Faced with a constituency in which key concepts from trade theory do not resonate much, the WTO needs to defend itself in a language that its new constituencies can make sense of: a language in which the GATT can quickly become 'GATTzilla' and the WTO a 'monster'; in which turtles count as much as trade statistics; and in which 'democracy' provides a normative anchor no less powerful than 'growth'.

The IAEA case presents a further case in which media attention grows significantly once the unipolar moment of the post-1990 world allows the United States (US) and its allies to use the organization in pursuit of their political goals. The role of the IAEA in international conflicts with Iraq, North Korea, and Iran puts the Agency on the front pages of the global news media. For an organization with an identity as a technical organization, based on science and expertise on the one hand and impartiality on the other, this implies a need to move out of its comfort zone and, like the WTO, learn to communicate to a broader range of stakeholders. As a symbolic event, award-ing the 2005 Nobel Peace Prize to the organization and its Director General, Mohamed ElBaradei, signals to this broader audience that the IAEA stands 'on the right side of history'. At the same time, however, it also puts the spotlight on an agency that is used to flying below the radar of public attention, and which fears that growing scrutiny will hinder rather than help it to accomplish the functions member states have assigned to it.

Finally, our case studies of the OAU and the AU, and of the UNHCR, illustrate that the rise of new audiences is not limited to civil society organ-izations (CSOs), the media, and 'the public', but also includes donors. The AU faces incentives to meet the normative expectations of some of its major international partners which, like the EU or the UN, also support a move towards democratic legitimation norms. In the UNHCR case, the search for a more diverse funding basis and the accountability the organization wishes to signal to non-traditional funders motivate the publication of the 'Global Report' that 'provides information for governments, private donors, partners and others interested in our activities and achievements' (UNHCR 2017).

Taken together, our observations boil down to three points. First, non-state actors have gained centrality in legitimation contests. Often, these 'external actors', as we define them in Chapter 2, are CSOs which others have rightly identified as a 'third force' (Florini 2000), and as an essential component of the contemporary world of international organizations (Karns and Mingst 2015). Our chapters on the WTO, on the AU, and on IUCN are clearest in this regard. Second, the range of non-state actors which contribute to legitimation contests has expanded over time. In the WTO case, it includes social movement organizations, the business community, and international trade lawyers. In the AU, it includes non-governmental organizations (NGOs) but also other states and the EU. In the IAEA, we note the strength of a nuclear epistemic community for which the Agency serves as a focal point. In the IUCN case, indigenous peoples seek and gain recognition, and in the UNHCR, new donors play key roles in bringing about normative change. In sum, our results stress not only the mind-boggling heterogeneity of James Rosenau's (1990) 'multi-centric world of world politics' but also a diversification of legitimacy-granting audiences (Koppell 2010; Symons 2011) that makes the task of legitimation more challenging for international organizations. Finally, the mediatization of the legitimation game makes a difference. As international organizations gain attention in the media, we see the potential for greater scrutiny rising even in cases where civil society remains relatively silent. In brief, the WTO attracts civil society activism, but the IAEA does not. Nevertheless, as our discussions in Chapters 3 and 5 reveal, both get greater scrutiny.[3]

---

[3] We are grateful to Margaret Karns for pointing out this specific implication of our observations.

Beyond the major influences discussed above, we also find some evidence—in descending order—for the discursive effects of *growing institutional density, global power shifts*, and *democratization* discussed in Chapter 2. With regard to the first, the *growing density of international organizations* plays a role in four of our five case studies. While the absence of competitors added to the legitimacy of the GATT/WTO in the post-1990 world, the proliferation of regional and bilateral trade agreements after 2005 is the major background for the most recent legitimacy crisis in which observers have come to question whether 'we still need the WTO'. Moreover, the 'coherence' norm becomes relevant as a result of growing overlaps between trade and other areas of global governance. In the OAU and the AU, in contrast, competition with other regional organizations on the African continent, particularly over external financial resources, provided an impetus to live up to international norms of 'good governance'. Similarly, IUCN's adoption of economic legitimation frames follows a more general development in the field of global environmental governance. It occurs at a time when other organizations threaten to compete on IUCN's turf, when IUCN sees a need to cooperate with these organizations in specific areas of its work, or when IUCN simply decides to follow the example set by its peers. Finally, the UNHCR is subject to competitive pressures in the UN's densely populated humanitarian cluster. This results in an uptake of 'coordination' and 'coherence' norms, and feeds, in addition, the need to take 'efficiency' and 'accountability' seriously. In contrast, the pressures of 'contested multilateralism' are weaker in the IAEA case where the organization remains largely unchallenged as a focal point on nuclear security as well as nuclear safety.

Next, all five case studies confirm the fundamental *global power shifts* international organizations experienced when decolonization turned developing countries into a majority in global organizations, and gave regional organizations like the OAU their initial purpose to assist in the struggle for liberation. The strength of development frames across all organizations we study has its origin in this tectonic shift. Subsequently, the global power shifts of 1989/90 added to the legitimacy of the GATT as the major international trade club, a legitimacy which the growth in the organization's membership only seemed to underline. For the OAU, in contrast, the end of the Cold War implied that Western powers became preoccupied with other world regions, resulting in the need to organize an African response to African problems. The new wars added urgency to this need and they also enhanced pressures on the UNHCR to find 'durable solutions' for the ensuing refugee crises. Finally, the IAEA case shows how the end of the Cold War allowed the US, as the remaining superpower, to use the neutral clout of international organizations as a hegemonic tool in its efforts to shape the regional orders of the post-1990 world. Yet, this 'laundering' effect (Abbott and Snidal 1998), as we show in Chapter 5, contributed to a politicization of the IAEA, as did the ambitions of

Iraq, Iran, Libya, and North Korea to use an assumed power vacuum to develop nuclear weapons programmes.

In brief, the end of the Cold War thus had a disruptive effect on many international organizations, including on their legitimation contests—but the precise consequences vary greatly across our cases. At the same time, we observe only few discursive effects that can be linked directly to the more recent global power shifts associated with the rise of Brazil, China, and India. With regard to these power shifts, the most visible effect is the WTO's legitimation crisis linked to the deadlock of multilateral trade negotiations in the Doha Round in which the rise of emerging markets plays an important role (Hale et al. 2013; Zangl et al. 2016). Moreover, as indicated above, the politicization of the IAEA also results from the more assertive behaviour of a number of regional powers. Overall, however, the effects of the most recent global power shifts remain marginal in the cases we study.

In part, of course, this observation is an artefact of our decision to focus primarily on normative change in the 1990s and 2000s and of our exclusion of organizations like the IMF or the World Bank. In these organizations, Chinese pressures to alter the weighted voting scheme had already gained strength by 2010; moreover, rising powers had begun to set up their own competitors to Northern-dominated development banks. A look at recent developments helps to illustrate this point. Zangl and colleagues, for example, have worked out how rising powers use the standstill in the Doha Round to demand a greater say in the WTO's decision making. In the absence of concessions, rising powers question the legitimacy of the organization: in their view, it does not reflect the realities of contemporary global power structures (Zangl et al. 2016). Moreover, as we have seen in Chapter 3, the ability to stall negotiations undermines the rationale of the organization for other members, as well, thereby creating a new legitimacy challenge.

At the same time, our analysis in Chapters 4 to 7 shows that, even if we take the more recent years into account, most trends we observe for the period until the 2000s continue and the effects of normative demands rising powers make do not become particularly visible in many organizations. One plausible conclusion could thus be that, had we focused not on developments until but *after* 2010, the picture would have looked different *for those organizations in which the political stakes are particularly high*. In terms of implications, that difference would most likely have reduced the role of people-based arguments at the cost of sovereignty-based arguments, as witnessed, for instance, in debates about the responsibility to protect (Jaganathan and Kurtz 2014; Liu and Zhang 2014; Stuenkel and Tourinho 2014). At the same time, it would probably have added further strength to one of our central messages: namely, that international organizations face an increasingly heterogeneous set of normative expectations which renders their legitimation more challenging.

Finally, while *democratization* would be a plausible driving force in the three cases in which democratic legitimation frames are on the rise—the GATT and the WTO, the OAU and the AU, and IUCN—its effects seem weak across the board. In the GATT/WTO case, the question whether some of the new members should subject themselves to a strong and highly intrusive international governance scheme, only a few years after their societies finally gained the right to govern themselves democratically, helped to spur the 'democratic deficit' critique as did the general triumph of democracy in the 1990s. Overall, however, this frame resonated mostly among the WTO's 'second audience' but found less support in debates among member states. The latter, moreover, moderated the challenge by reframing the demand as a need for 'policy space'. In contrast, in the AU case, the democratization agenda the organization had embarked upon was not only a response to the ideals of newly democratized African states but also to the normative demands of Western donors. Moreover, in the IUCN case, democratic norms were enshrined in the very governance structure of the organization; in addition, the relatively early strengthening of the role of members in the regions and of local stakeholders was primarily linked to the rising number of members from the developing world. Finally, the IAEA and the UNHCR experienced a democratization of member states but no turn towards democratic legitimacy standards. The particular legitimation culture of the humanitarian field and the observation that the UNHCR had, by the 1990s, mostly become an organization that implemented rather than developed policy programmes might help to account for this variation. But overall, the mixed results imply that our evidence for a democratization effect on the legitimation discourses of international organizations remains weak. The weakness of this link is further supported by the fact that, in the intergovernmental debates we examine, 'democratic' legitimacy claims originate from democratic and non-democratic countries alike (see also Eisentraut 2013).

In sum, we find several of the propositions we formulated in Chapter 2 confirmed. At the same time, the effects of individual external factors are very heterogeneous, thus working against the assumption that external pressures simply translate into altered normative expectations. Moreover, while our discussion in Chapter 2 presented the various 'external' influences on legitimation contests largely in isolation, our discussion hints at important connections between them. Crisis events like the Seattle protests, for instance, are inherently linked to new audiences, and the success of new groups to make their voices heard in a legitimation contest will depend on how well they can link their demands to traditional norms in a field. Yet, how the various ingredients combine into a full-fledged recipe for normative change is best seen in conjunction with the 'internal' ingredients we discuss in the following section.

Discursive Dynamics: Change from Within

Developments in the environment in which international organizations are embedded facilitate normative change. Ultimately, however, change is triggered by actors who succeed at pushing for it. In addition, dynamics that are best characterized as internal to the legitimation discourse itself make some efforts more likely to succeed than others. In our case studies, we identify three forces as particularly relevant in this regard: the presence of norm entrepreneurs, the presence of broad discursive coalitions, and the self-reinforcing dynamics that unfold once legitimation contests are set on a new track.

Norm Entrepreneurship

While the structural factors we have described in the previous section may facilitate normative change, such change is unlikely to occur unless someone asks and mobilizes support for it. Not all actors will be equally powerful when it comes to mobilizing for normative change, but our theoretical model leads us to expect the range of powerful actors to become more varied after 1990. Our case studies partly confirm this expectation. At the same time, they reveal that international bureaucracies and their leaders are particularly powerful in shaping the legitimation contests we observe.

In our study of the GATT and the WTO, non-traditional actors like environmental NGOs, international trade union federations, and transnational social movements were amongst those pushing the most strongly for 'non-trade values'. Yet, their discursive power had proven to be limited to redefining the terrain on which the legitimacy of the new WTO was to be negotiated; it did not include the power to define the new terms of legitimation themselves. Instead, the executive heads—notably Mike Moore and Pascal Lamy, aided by long-serving WTO spokesperson Keith Rockwell, and supported by key member states—managed to carefully select from the menu offered by protesters, and to thereby lead the way in reinterpreting environmental concerns as sustainability demands, and calls for global democracy as requests for equal participation and transparency among governments. Moreover, our study illustrates how power structures within civil society mattered; for instance, a Northern NGO like Oxfam became a 'spokesperson' for development in the international media discourse, while major Southern counterparts like the Third World Network received less attention in comparison. Because Southern voices tended to utter a more radical critique of the world trade system than Oxfam, this implied that such a critique, while voiced among some activists, was effectively silenced in the legitimation contests we observe.

The strong role of the secretariat and its leaders also shows in our case studies on the OAU/AU and IUCN. In the IUCN case, protest is largely absent. In the first normative change we reconstruct, changed perceptions in the secretariat, pressure from Southern members, and the leadership of other international organizations in the field coalesced to strengthen human well-being norms. Leadership mattered in this context: the years that preceded the adoption of the World Conservation Strategy—the document in which sustainable development was first enshrined in the organization—saw the first Southern IUCN Director General and IUCN President taking office. Moreover, as Ina Lehmann writes in Chapter 6, IUCN Presidents Monkombu Swaminathan from India (1984–90) and Shridath Ramphal from Guyana (1990–4) further pushed IUCN towards integrating the conservation and development agendas.

In the second normative change that leads to a strengthening of economic legitimation frames, the secretariat and its leaders become more central as norm entrepreneurs, with IUCN President Valli Moosa and Director General Julia Marton-Lefèvre actively using their leadership roles to advance cooperation projects between IUCN and the business sector. Here, the strong role of the bureaucracy is facilitated by organizational structures: notably the formal rule that IUCN members only meet every three to four years, and the informal practice that IUCN primarily serves as an international hub for many NGO members, offering excellent networking opportunities in the global conservation community. As a result, the members' stakes in IUCN tend to be moderate, and even if some members might disagree with the organization's position, they may not invest a great deal of energy in opposition work but campaign for their own positions domestically instead. In this sense, organizational purpose and design make the IUCN bureaucracy relatively powerful in comparison to most other international organizations.

In the AU case, the secretariat is a key force behind the rise of democratic norms, which it uses not only to please donors and avoid hypocrisy but also to build itself a basis of support among African CSOs. Again, the chapter identifies the leadership of a small set of norm entrepreneurs within the OAU/AU bureaucracy—notably OAU Secretary General Salim Ahmed Salim but also Jean Ping—as a decisive factor in instigating normative change.

The IAEA case, in turn, illustrates the importance of support by a relevant epistemic community in times of crisis. A particularly interesting feature of the case is that, since Chernobyl, the organization remains largely shielded from the direct critique of environmental groups even though its explicit goal is to promote nuclear energy. Purpose and design also matter here because the main responsibility for nuclear energy programmes and their safety remains with governments; the IAEA mainly provides assistance in information sharing and standard setting. Yet since its creation in 1957, the IAEA has also developed into the focal institution of an epistemic community, united by shared beliefs in the potential and feasibility of nuclear energy. These shared beliefs keep critics at a distance and allow the Agency to play a role in rebuilding confidence in the technology after the catastrophe. The Secretariat, whose members form part of the epistemic community, is therefore best described not as a norm entrepreneur but as a shield that protects the organization against fundamental normative change in times of crisis. More recently, however, our second story of normative change also points to the leadership of individuals, as illustrated by Mohamed ElBaradei's emphasis on development norms in the Nobel Peace Prize lecture.

Finally, the UNHCR case also attests to the different roles leaders can play in bringing about normative change. On the one hand, we thus saw how the failure of leaders to abide by the rules triggered the introduction of a stricter accountability regime. On the other hand, we also noted the impact individual executive heads had on what it meant for UNHCR to be 'a guardian of international refugee norms and as the holder of specialized knowledge and expertise on refugee issues' (Loescher 2001: 140). This way, individual leaders played their part in defining the normative yardsticks in view of which the organizations was to be evaluated.

Discursive Coalitions

Furthermore, our case studies underline that norm entrepreneurs will more likely succeed if they become part of broad discursive coalitions that support, though maybe for different reasons, the envisaged normative change. In the GATT and the WTO case, for example, the transformation of environmental concerns into a sustainable development frame allowed the norm to be supported by both Northern and Southern members. Similarly, Northern and Southern members could rally behind democracy-based slogans: the former because the political ideology to which they publicly subscribed did not allow them to contradict such slogans; the latter because democratic demands for 'a seat at the table' served their political interests. In contrast, labour rights did not have the backing of Southern members, leading calls for the inclusion of such rights in the GATT and the WTO to meet with little success.

In our reconstruction of legitimation contests at the OAU and AU, it is difficult to say whether the power of major donors like the EU or the UN, the interest of the AU bureaucracy in building a 'citizen-based' constituency for its work, or the growing strength and norm entrepreneurship of African civil society alone would have been sufficient to strengthen democratic norms. Yet, it seems clear that all three influences had pointed in the same direction and that they reinforced each other. Similarly, the fact that donor states demanded accountability from the UNHCR in the wake of the 'financial crisis' fitted well with UNHCR's desire to respond to the expectations of new donors. Meanwhile, IUCN could not have embarked on its path towards a more 'economic' conservation ideology without complementary moves from the corporate sector that signalled the intent to develop more 'ecological' business approaches (see also Pattberg 2007). Overall, the observations from our case studies of the AU and the UNHCR thus illustrate how different degrees of dependence, and hence different configurations of accountability relations, shape the legitimation contest.

Normative Path Dependence

Finally, one of the most striking findings from our case studies is that normative change is often self-reinforcing. In other words, once they set in, changes in the justificatory patterns of international organizations can themselves become a source of further normative change. Hinting at the analogue mode of endogenous change in institutional theory, we term this phenomenon normative path dependence. The label suggests that, first, when an organization is set on a new justificatory path, it not only faces incentives to 'walk the walk' but also to deepen its commitments by adhering to the broader set of values associated with that path. Second, normative path dependence suggests that this deepening will make it costlier for the organization to switch to a different path in the future.

The cases that exhibit this dynamic most clearly are the IUCN and the GATT/WTO, but we also observe similar dynamics in the OAU/AU and the UNHCR. In the IUCN case, it is the shift from conservation for nature's sake to conservation for humans' sake that triggers a range of additional changes in the way the organization justifies itself as well as its activities. While the old image allows IUCN to speak on behalf of a voiceless nature, the communities for whom it purports to act under the new image do have a voice. In particular, the turn to sustainable development deepens and broadens the norms of human well-being and participation. Evidently, if IUCN wanted to promote sustainable development, it needed to be more present in the regions and at the local levels, thereby giving Southern actors more clout to demand their effective inclusion. This step further entrenched social well-being norms and spurred additional demands for inclusion, for example from indigenous peoples who had largely been neglected as a relevant stakeholder group. At a more abstract level, the shift in a central *performance norm* thus triggers a shift in *procedural norms* that not only deepens the initial change but ultimately alters the *personality*—the very identity—of the organization. This may not make the change we observe irreversible. But it makes future norm shifts that negate this new foundation costlier, indeed.

In the WTO case, acceptance of the 'democracy' frame after 1999 sets the organization on a new justificatory path. Building its defence on the claim that its consensus-based decision-making procedures make the WTO the 'most democratic' among contemporary international economic organizations, the WTO is able to score a quick victory in the legitimation contest against its adversaries. But that victory comes with a price tag attached. Notably, it further solidifies the consensus norm and makes reforms that tinker with this norm more costly. In a context where the legalization of dispute settlement under the WTO has significantly reduced the flexibility to interpret new agreements, and where the organization has grown from originally twenty-three to 163 members, this price is hardly negligible. To be sure, the deadlock of the Doha Round has numerous sources. However, in contrast to common interpretations, our study suggests that the legacy of Seattle is one of them.

In sum, our evidence on norm entrepreneurs and on discourse coalitions will sound familiar to scholars of normative change (cf. Keck and Sikkink 1998). Similarly, our findings resonate with the ideas of 'rhetorical entrapment' (Schimmelfennig 2001), 'coercive arguing' (Krebs and Jackson 2007), or 'normative pressures' (Grigorescu 2015) we have alluded to in Chapter 2. At the same time, they go beyond these ideas in that they point to a specific dynamic that leads an organization to deepen its commitment to a norm, by either adding further norms that belong to the same 'family of values' or redefining existing legitimacy standards in light of the new commitment. So, while Grigorescu's perspective might lead us to conclude that the WTO has 'deflected' normative pressures since Seattle, the notion of normative path dependence suggests that this 'deflection' has, in fact, entangled the organization more deeply in the web of democratic legitimation, with major constraints for how to repair its legitimacy in future crises. The result of normative path dependence is, in other words, a fundamental shift in the legitimacy game.

BROADER IMPLICATIONS

What do our findings imply? In the following, we discuss the major implications our results have for our efforts to make sense of global governance, as well as for the efforts of international organizations to address the policy problems they confront.

Theoretical Implications

In Chapter 2, we have argued that legitimation contests can be conceptualized at different levels of analysis. At the level of *actors*, they are constituted by the discursive interactions among the members of an organization, the international bureaucracy, and a broad range of external actors who comment on the organization and its activities. At the level of *structures*, we have conceived of legitimation contests as constituted by the relations among the discursive frames actors use to advance their legitimacy claims. These discursive frames can be diagnostic as well as normative, with the former delineating 'what is' and the latter 'what has value' (Boltanski 2011). Finally, we have argued that legitimation contests not only shape world politics but that they are themselves affected by material and ideational developments in the broader context of world politics. We use the following paragraphs to review and qualify key assumptions of our heuristic model, in light of the empirical evidence.

The Inner Circle: Who Speaks?

In relation to the actors in the 'inner circle' of our bubbles model, our empirical evidence speaks to the key role international bureaucracies and their leaders play in legitimation contests. In addition, however, it also challenges the idea of coherent legitimation discourses itself. Notably, we observe that *in 'normal times'* member states and the international bureaucracy tend to describe and evaluate international organizations and their activities in a different language than the various 'second audiences' we study. While international bureaucracies and member states use one set of normative frames, NGOs, the media, and other 'external actors' voice their concerns in others. Since the underlying frames in the types of sources we study overlap only to a limited extent, the idea of parallel-running *partial discourses* seems to be the most supported by our evidence for these periods of organizational legitimation contests. Yet, this is different when we look at *periods of normative change*. In the latter, demands from external actors or newly relevant audiences are recognized and taken up in the annual reports of international organizations, as well as in the contributions member states make to intergovernmental debates. As a result, we observe a stronger interaction among bureaucratic, governmental, and civil society frames and therefore a more coherent legitimation discourse in these periods.

Theoretically, this leads to two important arguments: first, organizational legitimation is constituted by a core (the members and the administration) and a periphery (our 'external actors'); and second, organizational legitimation works differently in 'normal times' and in 'times of crisis'. In contrast to what we assumed in Chapter 2, only the latter periods are characterized by a close interaction of the discursive dynamics in the core and in the periphery. In this context, however, the observation that various external actors have recently become important legitimation constituencies is significant. It might signal that, for international organizations, a practice that was previously reserved for the 'crisis mode of legitimation' has actually become the new normal.

The Outer Circle: About What?

In terms of the normative structures of legitimation contests, our first observation is that legitimacy standards are rarely dropped from the menu once they become part of the organizational repertoires. The decline of 'peace' as a normative reference point in the justification of the GATT and later the WTO remains an exception in this regard.

Second, new legitimacy standards emerge and gain strength. As we have argued above, the standards that have been on the rise share two commonalities at a relatively abstract level. Falling broadly in line with Ian Clark's distinction between rules of rightful membership and rules of rightful conduct (Clark 2005), they strengthen people-based and procedural norms as the twin components of a post-national legitimation narrative. While people-based legitimacy standards define who is to take part in and benefit from 'governing the globe' (Avant et al. 2010), procedural norms define the rules to which decision making must adhere to count as legitimate. At a high level of generality, this suggests homogenization undergirded by legitimacy standards that broadly resonate with the theoretical insights of the 'world polity' school. According to these insights, modern organizations in the Western cultural account are guided by an institutional script of rationalization for which the individual is the ultimate reference point (Meyer et al. 1987; 1997; Meyer 2009; Drori et al. 2006).

However, we can also see that people-based and procedural norms allow for different 'localizations' (Acharya 2004). 'People-based' legitimacy claims in the IAEA thus differ from 'people-based' claims in the WTO; and challenges based on procedural norms are not the same in IUCN and the UNHCR. In important ways, these localizations follow the logic and legitimation cultures that characterize the diverse policy fields we investigate, thus limiting homogenization and promoting differentiation instead. Following the logic of our case selection outlined in Chapter 1, our case studies thus lend support to the idea of the *issue area as a variable*.

For the GATT and the WTO, Chapter 3 has thus elaborated on the 'GATT gospel' that was formed early in the organization's history and continues to provide the essential background for any legitimation contests we observe. Substantially, these background norms are tied to a broader set of norms, centred around notions of 'growth' that are characteristic of global economic governance more generally. The centrality of the 'GATT gospel' does not render normative change impossible. But it structures the changes that can be imagined as well as the strategies that actors must pursue to make their desired changes resonate with inherited discursive practices.

Beyond global economic governance, the IUCN and the IAEA cases further illustrate how issue-specific legitimation cultures channel normative change. Contrary to what might be expected, the IUCN case is thus characterized by little politicization but a significant strengthening of democratic legitimation frames; in contrast, the IAEA case displays significant politicization but no rise of democratic legitimation. Both developments are plausible if we take the participatory tradition of conservation governance and the sovereignty-based, more technical, and more secretive culture of nuclear safety and non-proliferation governance, as part of the wider field of global security governance, into account.

Moreover, while the AU does not have the 'issue culture' in the same way as the IAEA or IUCN, its comprehensive agenda—much like that of the EU to which the AU or its ambitions are occasionally likened—lends itself to the introduction of democratic legitimation frames. Finally, the UNHCR is traditionally characterized by a fine-tuned balance between the normative logics that inform the practice of sovereign states and the global rights practice—or international and global society—as the constitutive macro-practices of the global political realm (Lechner and Frost 2018). As a result, it mainly provides space for normative frames that do not tilt the balance too strongly in one or the other direction.

Finally, our third observation in relation to the normative structures of legitimation contests is that international organizations work in increasingly dense institutional fields. Consequently, a common language as well as common normative foundations limit the extent to which justifications may become differentiated. In sum, our close look at five international organizations shows a complex picture in which homogenizing and differentiating forces are largely in balance. The primary mode of change in which the two forces are reconciled is layering—a process in which 'the new does not replace the old, but is added to it' (Van der Heijden 2011: 9). While layering has some resemblance to sociological institutionalism's idea that organizations can integrate competing demands from their constituencies in different ways (Brunsson 2002), the heuristic framework we develop in Chapter 2 pays little attention to this specific mechanism. Discovering that it is a default option in practice thus also makes us aware that the conceptual toolkit of historical institutionalism might comprise instruments that can help us describe and make sense of the normative changes we observe (see further below).

Beyond the Circles: Which Macro-Structures Make a Difference?

In the model we outlined in Chapter 2, we had identified a number of macro-developments which we expected to have an impact on legitimation contests, traced over four decades. In addition to the power shifts discussed above, they include decolonization, economic globalization, technological change, the rise of transnational civil society, and institutional density.

As discussed in the previous section, we can conclude that decolonization changed the legitimacy game by giving developing countries—and hence, also the justificatory logic pushed by developing countries—a numerical advantage in virtually all intergovernmental organizations with a global reach. The impact of this change is felt across the four global organizations we study: the GATT, the IAEA, IUCN, and the UNHCR. On some occasions, decolonization lends support for development-related norms and values; in others, it appears in the form of the 'North–South' cleavage, a fierce contestation over the right course of action to be pursued by the organization. Moreover, decolonization is a foundational value for the OAU and the AU; once all African states became formally independent from their colonial powers, the rationale—and also its contestation—largely shifted to the conceptual terrains of liberation and the full realization of independence.

Beyond decolonization, the big picture becomes a bit more blurry. In the particular way *globalization* has unfolded, it renders the neoliberal norms and values we find in the GATT/WTO, in the UNHCR, and in IUCN plausible. But globalization also becomes a bone of contention when protesters single out and successfully oppose the WTO as the beast of neoliberalism, or when IUCN members oppose the economic valuation of nature. *Technological change*, the *rise of transnational civil society*, and the *globalization of media* combine to make the most powerful international organizations visible and widely known, and to generate 'second audiences' for some of the less well-known organizations, too. But that development appears to make a difference only in some cases—for instance, when media coverage of the IAEA increased significantly in the 1990s and 2000s—while others like IUCN continue to fly below the radar of public attention.

Finally, reflecting upon what our results mean and why they matter in more general terms, Rainer Forst's thinking on 'social orders of justification' (*soziale Rechtfertigungsordnungen*) provides a useful starting point. Forst argues that power is rooted in accepted justifications—that it takes a primarily 'noumenal' form (Forst 2015: 65). On this account, to have power means to be able 'to influence, make use of, define, occupy or even seclude' the realm of accepted justifications for others (2015: 66).[4]

This interpretation of 'noumenal power' also specifies why and how the object of our study matters from a normative point of view. When the terrain for negotiating the legitimacy of global governance structures shifts towards people-based and procedural norms, actors with a high credibility on these conceptual terrains will gain power, while those with a lower standing in relation to the task of defining 'people-based' or 'procedural' legitimacy stand to lose. In sum, the ability to define the conceptual terrain on which legitimacy is negotiated is a *general* source of power. In addition, our case studies further reveal that the ability to define for others what it means to work for the benefit of 'the people' and to follow the 'right procedures' in doing so have become *specific* forms of power in global governance.

In terms of positive theorizing, moreover, the theoretical construct we arrive at may lack the coherence of Michael Zürn's *A Theory of Global*

---

[4] Translations of Forst (2015) are our own.

Governance. In Zürn's account, the transfer of rule-making competence—and, to a lesser extent, of epistemic authority—triggers a politicization of international organizations which is then followed by a broadening of legitimation narratives (Zürn 2018). To be sure, the stories we recollect in our case study of the GATT and the WTO roughly match this pattern. Yet, the GATT and the WTO are not necessarily representative, and focusing on the 'big five' may therefore lead us to draw inadequate conclusions for international organizations in general. Do we then face a situation in which the most visible international organizations have come under pressure while others may continue as business as usual? Our case studies suggest that this is not the case. In contrast, all organizations we examine are subject to broader and more heterogeneous normative expectations. Some sources of this broadening are more general; others are specific to some (kinds of) organizations. Consequently, the resulting patterns of normative change are therefore similar to some extent, but differ significantly in other regards.

In general terms, the *liberal script of individualism and proceduralism* that John Meyer and others have always emphasized in their writings affects all organizations we study. In addition, however, two dynamics that shape the ways in which normative change unfolds apply only to some organizations. On the one hand, authority transfer may well be a necessary condition for societal actors to engage in *strong politicization* and hence trigger rapid and deep changes in the content of legitimation contests. On the other hand, where such strong pressures are absent, *issue area cultures* seem to channel the more mundane discursive changes that characterize the long-term trajectories of any legitimation contests. Seen from this angle, we are thus once more confronted with a differentiation between legitimation 'in times of crisis' versus legitimation 'in normal times'. By and large, the global governance literature, with its predominant focus on the strongest and most visible international organizations, may thus have taught us a great deal about the crisis mode, but neglected legitimation 'in normal times'. To understand the dynamics to which the legitimation of international organizations has become subject, we need to know both. In that sense, our study complements existing theories of global governance, notably where such theories claim to speak for international organizations as a general category.

Practical Implications

Our results also have practical implications. Three of them are particularly noteworthy. First, our observation that the list of normative expectations to which international organizations are subject to has grown ever longer adds yet another source of *gridlock* to the list that Thomas Hale, David Held, and Kevin Young (2013) have compiled in their eponymous book. Hale et al. argue that multipolarity, institutional inertia, harder problems, and institutional fragmentation have jointly contributed to the failure of contemporary international institutions to deliver the global cooperation the world is in need of. Our study suggests that an ever longer list of normative expectations, that contemporary international organizations are expected to fulfil, adds to the pressures these organizations face in similar ways. The rise of post-national legitimation norms provides yet another piece in the larger puzzle called gridlock.

Like the other sources Hale et al. discuss, however, the growing list of legitimacy standards does not occur in isolation. In contrast, as we show throughout our study, the rise of new legitimacy standards is itself connected to the rising number of organizational members (*multipolarity*), to the legacies of the founding moment to which organizations respond with layering rather than fundamental reform (*institutional inertia*), to the increasingly intrusive nature of regulations devised by international organizations (*harder problems*), and to competition with other international and transnational organizations (*institutional fragmentation*). At the same time, the changes in the major legitimation contests international organizations confront cannot be reduced to these four factors; they constitute a distinct development of their own. Like in Hale et al.'s account, some of the standards that have been added to the menu are difficult to imagine in the absence of the previous successes of international cooperation after 1945: it is, for instance, much more plausible to expect international organizations to advance the well-being of individuals where these organizations have demonstrated their ability to govern 'behind the borders' in the past. Moreover, like for many contributing factors the authors of *Gridlock* identify, we can imagine the consequences of the expanding list of legitimacy standards to go both ways. In theory, a longer list of expectations could thus allow international organizations to cherry-pick the standards they can meet most easily and hence facilitate legitimation; or it could enhance the risk of failure in relation to one important standard, thereby making legitimation more difficult. For the time being, the empirical analysis we undertake in this book renders the latter assumption more plausible. The addition of new legitimacy standards, we conclude, adds to the pressures international organizations confront.

A second implication is complexity. If international organizations are expected to do well in relation to more—and more heterogeneous—normative yardsticks, the societies they are mandated to serve will need to learn to cope with complexity. Satisfying all or most standards in a coherent way will be more difficult; organizational hypocrisy becomes a more likely feature, and justifications of organizational structures and activities will inevitably need to be a bit more complicated. This implication seems particularly problematic in view of the rise of populist movements that Western democracies—the founders and, for a long time, ardent supporters of international cooperation—have experienced in recent years. With voters either asking for or tempted by simple solutions, the proliferation of populist movements has shaken the foundations of party systems in many democracies. The spread of populism also suggests that many contemporary societies have little tolerance for complexity. Unsurprisingly, international organizations have received their fair share of criticism from nationalist movements that view anything international with great scepticism. The leaders and supporters of international organizations have yet to find a powerful response. While our study describes how international organizations have responded to a more 'individualist' world after 1989/90, their most recent challenge thus is to find answers to a more nationalist, a more populist, and, last but not least, a more complex world.

Third, in developing their legitimation strategies, the leaders and supporters of international organizations will need to be aware that short-term fixes may have long-term consequences. In several of our cases studies, we observe that responses to legitimacy challenges work in the short term but generate their own challenges at a later stage. When the WTO responds to Seattle, its acknowledgement of a democratic legitimacy standard 'works'; yet the commitment to democratic norms severely constrains the organization in its responses to the deadlock of the Doha Round. Similarly, when IUCN responds to developing country demands and adopts a focus on human well-being, the response 'works', but it also triggers further demands for participation and for the inclusion of local knowledge. Finally, when the AU expands its legitimacy claims based on the notion of a performance-oriented and people-centred organization, the boldness of its claims may 'work' initially. Yet, it also renders the organization vulnerable when measured in view of its aspirations.

Overall, this observation hints at the risks of a 'legitimation trap' whereby a specific response to a legitimacy challenge generates new and unforeseen challenges in the future—a possibility for which several of our case studies provide evidence. Taken together, this leads us to another simple, yet important conclusion: while institutional design matters for legitimacy (see also Grigorescu 2015; Tallberg et al. 2013), legitimacy itself cannot be designed. Due to its fundamentally political nature, legitimacy remains 'organic'. Its substance is not only contested by definition, but also contingent in ways that defy single actors (who may surely influence or 'shape' the definition of legitimacy at a given time) to exercise control. In brief, the legitimacy of international organizations is what states—and increasingly also a variety of non-state actors—make of it.

POSTSCRIPT

Quite naturally, while our study answers some questions, it also raises new ones. These new questions open up avenues for further research. Theoretically, for instance, our emphasis on 'layering' and 'normative path dependence' hints at the possibility of developing a more genuinely *historical institutionalist account of normative change* in global governance. Given the conceptual toolkit that historical institutionalist approaches offer and given the progress research has recently made in applying this toolkit to international institutions (Fioretos 2011; 2017; Hanrieder 2015), such an approach could be very fruitful indeed. At the same time, our evidence suggests that historical institutionalists themselves could benefit from directing their gaze not only at material but also at ideational structures—a focus the initial historical institutionalists still had, but has been lost along their own development path (Hall and Taylor 1996; Farrell and Finnemore 2016).

Second, our study traces normative change mostly in language, but not in *practices*. A further leftover therefore lies in the application of a more practice-oriented lens to the legitimation of international organizations. Informed by social anthropology, the practice perspective does not so much search for norms in official linguistic expressions but is primarily interested in the order that emerges from the everyday routines, habits, or 'practices' in which actors engage. Here, too, recent advances in applying different variants of practice theory to the global realm—some more focused on the micro-level, others on the macro-level—could facilitate such an effort (Adler and Pouliot 2011; Bueger and Gadinger 2014; Lechner and Frost 2018). Moreover, while some practice theorists have been reluctant to engage with norms, the recent works of Antje Wiener (2018) and of Silvia Lechner and Mervyn Frost (2018) can help to bring both literatures into a more fruitful debate.

Third, the approach we have taken in this study remains relatively 'global': we examine documents from international organizations, from the governments of their member states, and from external actors whose interventions make it through the filter of the international media. In consequence, our study says little about the many local variations of legitimation contests. In brief, local opposition to the WTO may vary between Ireland and Italy; IAEA safeguard inspections may be challenged on different grounds in different countries; and the AU may well be contested in different ways in the urban versus rural parts of many of its member states. To arrive at a more complete and more nuanced understanding of global normative change, further research that examines how the norms we sketch are 'localized' in different contexts, and which additional norms that we do not observe to be strong at the global level matter locally, would seem particularly useful (Wiener 2018; Zimmermann 2017).

Fourth, the normative implications of the observations we make deserve further scrutiny. Is the rise of post-national legitimacy standards good news? Does it represent 'moral progress' or provide grounds for more 'humane governance' (Falk 1995)? Should we therefore welcome people-based and procedural norms where we observe their growing relevance? Or are the developments we sketch problematic from a normative point of view, so that we should seek to obstruct rather than support their rise? Any answer to these questions would need to come in two parts: it would need to examine the normative quality of the post-national legitimacy standards *as such*, but also reflect upon whether the *addition* of post-national legitimacy standards to the existing menu is desirable. As we have suggested above, Rainer Forst's work on social orders of justification might provide a starting point for such an analysis. Yet, it will not be trivial to work out how the changes we map in our analysis would relate to Forst's (2015: 109) twin demands, that morally progressive orders can be 'justified in reciprocal and general ways', and that they include 'institutions for generating such justifications'. As an alternative to Forst's roots in political philosophy, the sociologically rooted but ethically sensitive approach we find in the English School's engagement with the emerging field of international political theory could provide a basis for studies that seek to clarify what the changes we observe imply in normative terms (Brown 2014; Linklater 1998; Lechner and Frost 2018).

Finally, there is the present. Because our study is interested in change that occurred 'after the end of the Cold War', our primary period of analysis includes two decades before as well as after 1989/90. This desire to learn something about the emergence of a genuine normative order in the post-1990 world of 'global governance' evidently raises the question how much of what we find still holds today. This question becomes particularly pressing if we assume that the international order has changed dramatically not only after 1989/90—an assumption that provided the basic rationale for our project—but also during the very years in which we conducted our analysis. Since then, China has grown stronger, and more rapidly so, leading some observers to declare the end of the American (Acharya 2014) or Western (Stuenkel 2016) world order. The global financial crisis has hit the world economy. A refugee crisis has generated much political turmoil in many parts of the world. The global environmental crisis has gained further momentum. Authoritarianism has celebrated an unlikely revival. Democracy—the gold standard few people in 1989/90 would have imagined to become challenged soon—is tumbling in Western as well as non-Western societies (Levitsky and Ziblatt 2018). The electorate in Europe's third largest economy have voted to leave the EU. The US, as the 'liberal Leviathan' (Ikenberry 2011) of the post-war international order, has become a deeply divided country; under the Trump administration, it has also turned its back on its long-standing allies as well as on the multilateralism which held the post-war international order together.

In brief, does the post-1989/90 normative order we sketch in this book still exist? Or have we depicted the normative contours of an 'era of global governance' that has already been replaced, lasting no longer than the interwar period of the previous century? In the end, we do not know. Finalizing our manuscript, we have cast our net more broadly to normative changes in the most recent annual reports as well as in other documents from the organizations we study. Yet, as we document in Chapters 3 to 7, we found much continuity in the trends we describe in this book. The pressures on the WTO have continued to mount, but the legitimation narratives have not changed a great deal. The extinction of species and ecosystems is accelerating, but IUCN continues to build and defend its legitimacy on a mix of participatory, knowledge-based, and market-based claims. The AU may get even less attention from Western states these days, but its legitimation rhetoric still centres around the idea of a people-centred union that delivers on the ground. The IAEA had to deal with the consequences of the Fukushima nuclear accident, but much like Chernobyl, it used the event to cultivate its image as a technical rather than a political organization. Finally, the UNHCR was much in demand to help states cope with a steep surge in the number of refugees worldwide. While the question 'why we need' the UNHCR was not on the agenda at all, the justificatory rhetoric continues to strike a delicate balance between state interests and the protection of the rights of refugees. In the end, if there has been a further transformation in the norms in view of which international organizations are evaluated, it either does not exist in our cases or in the kinds of sources on which our study is based, or the international discourses we examine are simply slow to respond. Once more, further research that systematically engages with the differences between the post-1989/90 and the post-2008 normative orders and/or examines such changes based on a variety of sources will be most useful.

Practically speaking, however, our findings have implications for today's world even if we cannot tell how lasting they will turn out to be. Notably, we observe a relative strengthening of 'world society norms' versus 'international society norms', of people-based 'cosmopolitan' norms versus 'Westphalian' norms, and of a 'global rights practice' versus a 'practice of sovereign states'. Such oppositions suggest an important rift in the liberal script that informs the post-war order. In the context of the post-war global order, international society norms as well as world society norms form part of a liberal vision in which the sovereign state practice shields states from interference by other states, while the global rights practice protects individuals from the power of states. In theory, both are complementary to the extent that they share a common foundation in liberal values, broadly understood. Nevertheless, they stand in tension where, as in the debate over a responsibility to protect, the rights of states in international society and the rights of individuals in world society collide.

At a time when the liberal vision has come under attack domestically as well as internationally, this rift in the liberal script could be detrimental to the extent that it divides or casts doubt on the liberal project. Yet, the tension between the norms of 'international society' and 'world society' can also become productive. It can force the communities rallying behind the liberal vision to seek common ground and restate their normative project in light of contemporary challenges like global warming, state failures, or the deprivation of human rights; and it can induce 'the West' to reformulate its political vision in ways that allow various traditions to subscribe to it. As social scientists, we can highlight, describe, and seek to understand the tensions that exist. Much like the legitimation contests we reconstruct in this book, however, resolving the tensions between the norms of international and world society remains a profoundly political task.

Overview of Organizational Meetings Attended and Interviews Conducted for This Study

Meetings Observed

World Trade Organization

WTO Public Forum	19–21 September 2011	WTO, Geneva

Organisation of African Unity/African Union

Open Session of the Peace and Security Council on Operationalizing African Peace and Security Architecture	24 April 2013	AU HQ, Addis Ababa
ISS Seminar OAU/AU 50 years	15 May 2013	AU HQ, Addis Ababa
Workshop of the State of the Union Project	16 May 2013	AU HQ, Addis Ababa
Being a Pan-African	17 May 2013	AU HQ, Addis Ababa
Journalist Training on the AU (in collaboration with Friedrich-Ebert-Foundation)	18 May 2013	AU HQ, Addis Ababa
Open Sessions of the 50th Anniversary Celebrations	25 May 2013	AU HQ, Addis Ababa

Case Study on the International Atomic Energy Agency: Participation in Meetings of the Organization

IAEA General Conference	17–21 September 2012	IAEA HQ, Vienna

Office of the UN High Commissioner on Refugees

Annual Consultations with NGOs	11–13 June 2013	UNHCR, Geneva

Interviews Conducted

Organisation of African Unity/African Union

Member African NGO	3 April 2012	Addis Ababa
Long-term serving OAU/AU staff (peace and security)	24 April 2013	AU HQ, Addis Ababa
Long-term serving OAU/AU staff (interpreter)	25 April 2013	AU HQ, Addis Ababa
AU staff (communications)	26 April 2013	AU HQ, Addis Ababa
Long-term serving OAU/AU staff (peace and security)	28 April 2013	AU HQ, Addis Ababa
Long-term serving OAU/AU staff (interpreter)	7 May 2013	AU HQ, Addis Ababa
Member African NGO	14 May 2013	Addis Ababa
AU staff (communications)	16 May 2013	AU HQ, Addis Ababa
AU staff (Office of the Chairperson)	19 May 2013	AU HQ, Addis Ababa
Long-term serving OAU/AU staff (political affairs)	21 May 2013	AU HQ, Addis Ababa
Member African NGO	22 May 2013	Addis Ababa
AU staff (political affairs)	24 May 2013	AU HQ, Addis Ababa

International Union for Conservation of Nature

IUCN staff member	13 May 2013	IUCN HQ, Gland
IUCN staff member	13 May 2013	IUCN HQ, Gland
IUCN staff member	14 May 2013	IUCN HQ, Gland
IUCN staff member	15 May 2013	IUCN HQ, Gland
IUCN staff member	16 May 2013	IUCN HQ, Gland
IUCN staff member	17 May 2013	IUCN HQ, Gland
IUCN national committee	29 May 2013	Telephone
Member of IUCN member NGO	17 May 2013	Gland
Member of IUCN member NGO	12 June 2013	Skype
Former Councillor	5 July 2013	Telephone
IUCN Environmental Law Centre	22 July 2013	Bonn
Former Councillor	26 August 2015	Skype
Commission Working Group Member	October 2015	Amsterdam

Office of the United Nations High Commissioner for Refugees

Member of national NGO	14 June 2013	Geneva
Member of international NGO	20 June 2013	Geneva
UNHCR staff member, Inter-Agency Unit	21 June 2013	Geneva
UNHCR staff member, communication	21 June 2013	Geneva

References

Abbott, Kenneth W. and Duncan Snidal (1998) 'Why States Act through Formal International Organizations' *Journal of Conflict Resolution* 42 (1), 3–32.

Abbott, Kenneth W., Jessica Green, and Robert O. Keohane (2016) 'Organizational Ecology and Institutional Change in Global Governance' *International Organization* 70 (2), 247–77.

Abdelal, Rawi and John G. Ruggie (2009) 'The Principles of Embedded Liberalism: Social Legitimacy and Global Capitalism' In *New Perspectives on Regulation*, edited by David Moss and John Cisternino, pp. 151–62. Cambridge, MA: Tobin Project.

Acharya, Amitav (2004) 'How Ideas Spread: Whose Norms Matter? Norm Localization and Institutional Change in Asian Regionalism' *International Organization* 58 (2), 239–75.

Acharya, Amitav (2014) *The End of American World Order*. Cambridge: Polity Press.

Acharya, Amitav (2016) 'Studying the Bandung Conference from a Global IR Perspective' *Australian Journal of International Affairs* 70 (4), 342–57.

Adams, William M. (1990) *Green Development. Environment and Sustainability in the Third World*. London: Routledge.

Adams, William M. and Jon Hutton (2007) 'People, Parks and Poverty: Political Ecology and Biodiversity Conservation' *Conservation and Society* 5 (2), 147–83.

Adedeji, Adebayo et al. (2007) *Audit of the African Union*. Addis Ababa: African Union.

Adler, Emmanuel and Vincent Pouliot, eds. (2011) *International Practices*. Cambridge: Cambridge University Press.

Adotey, Bing (1991) 'Salim A. Salim on the OAU and the African Agenda' *Review of African Political Economy* 18 (50), 60–9.

AFRODAD, AfriMAP, and Oxfam (2007) *Towards a People-Driven African Union: Current Obstacles and New Opportunities*. Nairobi: AFRODAD.

Agence France-Press (1999) 'Thousands of Myanmar Refugees to Be Relocated in Thailand', *AFP*, 19 August.

Agier, Michel (2011) *Managing the Undesirables: Refugee Camps and Humanitarian Government*. Cambridge: Polity Press.

Albert, Mathias, Barry Buzan, and Michael Zürn (2013) 'Introduction: Differentiation Theory and International Relations' In *Bringing Sociology to International Relations: World Politics as Differentiation Theory*, edited by Mathias Albert, Barry Buzan, and Michael Zürn, pp. 1–24. Cambridge: Cambridge University Press.

AllAfrica (2002) 'Welcome to the African Union', 23 July. Available at: https://allafrica.com/stories/200207230315.html (accessed 23 November 2018).

Alter, Karen J. and Sophie Meunier (2009) 'The Politics of International Regime Complexity' *Perspectives on Politics* 7 (1), 13–24.

Amate, C. O. C. (1986) *Inside the OAU: Pan-Africanism in Practice*. London: Macmillan.

Amnesty International (1997) 'Rwanda: Human Rights Overlooked in Mass Repatriation'. Available at: https://www.amnesty.org/en/documents/AFR47/002/1997/en/ (accessed 8 July 2018).

Anaya, S. James (2004) *Indigenous Peoples in International Law*. Oxford: Oxford University Press.

Anderson, Brilé, Thomas Bernauer, and Aya Kachi (2017) 'Does International Pooling of Authority Undermine the Legitimacy of Global Governance?' Unpublished manuscript.

Anderson, John Ward (2006) 'Iran to Face Security Council: Tehran Defiant on IAEA Vote', *Washington Post*, 5 February.

Andresen, Steinar (2002) 'The International Whaling Commission (IWC): More Failure than Success?' In *Environmental Regime Effectiveness: Confronting Theory with Evidence*, edited by Edward L. Miles, Arild Underdal, Steinar Andresen, Jorgen Wettestad, Jon Birger Skjaerseth, and Elaine M. Carlin, pp. 379–404. Cambridge, MA: MIT Press.

Annan, Kofi (2001) 'Address by UN Secretary-General to the Summit of the Organization of African Unity', Lusaka, 9 July.

Araya, Selome (2007) 'The African Diaspora and the United States of Africa', Pambazuka News Issue 309, http://pambazuka.org/en/category/comment/42081 (accessed 22 March 2017).

Arden-Clarke, Charles (1991) 'Reform urged on environmental impact of GATT', *Guardian*, 13 September.

Associated Press (1991) 'Trade Experts Criticize US Dolphin Protection', 24 August.

AU (2002a) Protocol Relating to the Establishment of the Peace and Security Council of the African Union. Durban: African Union.

AU (2002b) Statutes of the Commission of the African Union. ASS/AU/2(I)-d. Durban: African Union.

AU (2013) Indian Prime Minister Sends Congratulatory Message to the AUC Chairperson for Celebrations of OAU-AU Golden Jubilee. Addis Ababa: African Union. Available at: https://www.au.int/en/newsevents/26657/indian-prime-ministers-sends-congratulatory-message-auc-chairperson-celebrations (accessed 22 March 2017).

AU Assembly (2008) Decision on the Single Legal Instrument on the Merger of the African Court on Human and Peoples' Rights and the African Court of Justice. Assembly/AU/Dec.196 (XI). Sharm el-Sheik: African Union.

AU Assembly (2013) 50th Anniversary Solemn Declaration. Addis Ababa: African Union.

AU Assembly (2016a) Decision on the Institutional Reform of the African Union. Assembly/AU/Dec.606(XXVII). Kigali: African Union.

AU Assembly (2016b) Decision on the Outcome of the Retreat of the Assembly of the African Union. Assembly/AU/Dec.605(XXVII). Kigali: African Union.

AU Commission (2004a) Assembly of the African Union, Third Ordinary Session. Fifth Ordinary Session of the Executive Council. Report of the Commission, EX.CL/104 (V). Addis Ababa: African Union.

AU Commission (2004b) Strategic Plan of the African Union Commission. Volume 1: Vision and Mission of the African Union. Addis Ababa: African Union.

AU Commission (2004c) Strategic Plan of the African Union Commission. Volume 2: 2004–2007 Strategic Framework of the Commission of the African Union. Addis Ababa: African Union.

AU Commission (2005) Report of the AU Commission for the Period from January to June 2005. Sirte: African Union.

AU Commission (2006) Report of the Commission for the Period January–June 2006. Banjul: African Union.

AU Commission (2007) African Union Commission Annual Report 2007. Addis Ababa: African Union.

AU Commission (2008a) Activity Report of the Commission for the Period January to June 2008. Addis Ababa: African Union.

AU Commission (2008b) Comments by the Commission on the Report of the High-Level Panel on the Audit of the African Union. Addis Ababa: African Union.

AU Commission (2009) Strategic Plan 2009–2012. Addis Ababa: African Union.

AU Commission (2010) Report of the Chairperson on the Activities of the Commission Covering the Period January to June 2010. Addis Ababa: African Union.

AU Commission (2011) Letter from the Chairperson: Transforming the Commission into the Engine of Africa's Renaissance. Issue 2. Addis Ababa: African Union.

AU Commission (2013) Annual Report of the Chairperson on the Activities of the Commission Covering the Period January to December 2012. Addis Ababa: African Union.

AU Commission (2014) Draft Strategic Plan 2014–2017 for the African Union Commission. Addis Ababa: African Union.

AU Commission (2015) Annual Report of the Chairperson on the Activities of the African Union Commission Covering the Period January to December 2014. Addis Ababa: African Union.

AU Commission (2016) Annual Report of the Chairperson of the African Union Commission for the Period January to December 2015. Addis Ababa: African Union.

AU Commission (2017) *African Union Handbook 2017*. Addis Ababa: African Union.

AU Commission (2018) *African Union Handbook 2018*. Addis Ababa: African Union.

AU Executive Council (2013) Project Document for the Commemoration of the 50th Anniversary of the OAU/AU. Ext/EX.CL/4(XIV). Addis Ababa: African Union.

AU Monitor (2010) Voices of the Civil Society on Peace and Security: Recommendations of Civil Society Organisations on Peace and Security ahead of the 15th Ordinary Session of the African Union Summit. *AU Monitor*. Available at: http://www.pambazuka.org/aumonitor/comments/2708/ (accessed 1 August 2013).

Avant, Deborah D., Martha Finnemore, and Susan K. Sell, eds (2010) *Who Governs the Globe?* Cambridge: Cambridge University Press.

Ba, Alice D. (2013) 'The Association of Southeast Asian Nations: Between Internal and External Legitimacy' In *Legitimating International Organizations*, edited by Dominik Zaum, pp. 132–61. Oxford: Oxford University Press.

Barkenbus, Jack (1987) 'Nuclear Power Safety and the Role of International Organization' *International Organization* 41, 475–90.

Barker, Rodney (2001) *Legitimating Identities: The Self-Presentations of Rulers and Subjects*. Cambridge: Cambridge University Press.

Barnett, Michael (2002) *Eyewitness to a Genocide: The United Nations and Rwanda*. Ithaca, NY: Cornell University Press.

Barnett, Michael and Martha Finnemore (2004) *Rules for the World: International Organizations in Global Politics*. Ithaca, NY: Cornell University Press.

Bechhoefer, Bernhard G. (1959) 'Negotiating the Statute of the International Atomic Energy Agency' *International Organization* 13 (1), 38–59.

Beetham, David (2013) *The Legitimation of Power*, 2nd edition. Basingstoke: Palgrave Macmillan.

Bernstein, Steven (2001) *The Compromise of Liberal Environmentalism*. New York: Columbia University Press.

Bernstein, Steven (2011) 'Legitimacy in Intergovernmental and Non-State Global Governance' *Review of International Political Economy* 18 (1), 17–51.

Bernstein, Steven and Erin A. Hannah (2012) 'The WTO and Institutional (In) Coherence in Global Economic Governance' In *The Oxford Handbook on the World Trade Organization*, edited by Amrita Narlikar, Martin Daunton, and Robert M. Stern, pp. 776–808. Oxford: Oxford University Press.

Betts, Alexander (2012) 'UNHCR, Autonomy, and Mandate Change' In *International Organizations as Self-Directed Actors: A Framework for Analysis*, edited by Joel E. Oestreich, pp. 118–40. New York: Routledge.

Betts, Alexander (2013) 'Regime Complexity and International Organizations: UNHCR as a Challenged Institution' *Global Governance* 19 (1), 69–81.

Betts, Alexander (2015) 'The Normative Terrain of the Global Refugee Regime' *Ethics and International Affairs* 29 (4), 363–75.

Betts, Alexander and Louise Bloom (2014) Humanitarian Innovation: The State of the Art. Occasional Policy Paper 009. New York: UN OCHA.

Bexell, Magdalena, ed. (2015) *Global Governance, Legitimacy and Legitimation*. London: Routledge.

Bhagwati, Jagdish (1993) 'Environmentalists against GATT' *Wall Street Journal*, 19 March.

Biegoń, Dominika (2016) *Hegemonies of Legitimation: Discourse Dynamics in the European Commission*. Basingstoke: Palgrave Macmillan.

Biermann, Frank (1998) *Weltumweltpolitik zwischen Nord und Süd. Die neue Verhandlungsmacht der Entwicklungsländer*. Baden-Baden: Nomos.

Biermann, Frank and Bernd Siebenhüner, eds (2009) *Managers of Global Change: The Influence of International Environmental Bureaucracies*. Cambridge, MA: MIT Press.

Biermann, Frank, Philipp Pattberg, Harro van Asselt, and Fariborz Zelli (2009) 'The Fragmentation of Global Governance Architectures: A Framework for Analysis' *Global Environmental Politics* 9 (4), 14–40.

Binder, Martin and Monika Heupel (2015) 'The Legitimacy of the UN Security Council: Evidence from Recent General Assembly Debates' *International Studies Quarterly* 59, 238–50.

Black, Julia (2008) 'Constructing and Contesting Legitimacy and Accountability in Polycentric Regulatory Regimes' *Regulation and Governance* 2 (2), 137–64.

Boltanski, Luc (2011) *On Critique: A Sociology of Emancipation*. Cambridge: Polity Press.

Braithwaite, John and Peter Drahos (2000) *Global Business Regulation*. Cambridge: Cambridge University Press.

Brassett, James and Eleni Tsingou (2011) 'The Politics of Legitimate Global Governance' *Review of International Political Economy* 18 (1), 1–16.

Brosius, J. Peter (2004) 'Indigenous Peoples and Protected Areas at the World Parks Congress' *Conservation Biology* 18 (3), 609–12.

Brown, Chris (2014) *International Society, Global Polity: An Introduction to International Political Theory*. London: Sage.

Brunsson, Nils (2002) *The Organization of Hypocrisy: Talk, Decision and Actions in Organizations*. Copenhagen: Copenhagen Business School Press.

Brunsson, Nils and Bengt Jacobsson (2000) *A World of Standards*. Oxford: Oxford University Press.

BuaNews (2007) 'Africa: AU to Focus on Traditional Leaders'. Available at: http://allafrica.com/stories/200710290976.html (accessed 22 March 2017).

Buchanan, Allan and Robert O. Keohane (2006) 'The Legitimacy of Global Governance Institutions' *Ethics and International Affairs* 20 (4), 405–37.

Bueger, Christian and Frank Gadinger, eds (2014) *International Practice Theory: New Perspectives*. Basingstoke: Palgrave Macmillan.

Bukovansky, Mlada (1999) 'The Altered State and the State of Nature: The French Revolution and International Politics' *Review of International Studies* 25 (2), 197–216.

Bukovansky, Mlada (2002) *Legitimacy and Power Politics: The American and French Revolution in International Political Culture*. Princeton, NJ: Princeton University Press.

Bukovansky, Mlada (2010) 'Institutional Hypocrisy and the Politics of Agricultural Trade' In *Constructing the International Economy*, edited by Rawi Abdelal, Marc Blyth, and Craig Parsons, pp. 68–89. Ithaca, NY: Cornell University Press.

Business Day (2002) Business Needs to Drive NEPAD and AU, 2 July.

Buzdugan, Stephen and Anthony Payne (2016) *The Long Battle for Global Governance*. London: Routledge.

Carroll, Lewis (1998 [1865/1871]) *Alice's Adventures in Wonderland and Through the Looking Glass and What Alice Found There*, edited and with an introduction and notes by Hugh Haughton. London: Penguin Books.

Carson, Rachel (1962) *Silent Spring*. Boston, MA: Houghton Mifflin.

Casey-Lefkowitz, Susan (1991) 'IUCN: 18th General Assembly Report' *Environmental Policy and Law* 21(1), 16–19.

Castells, Manuel (2008) 'The New Public Sphere: Global Civil Society, Communication Networks, and Global Governance' *Annals of the American Academy of Political and Social Science* 616, 78–93.

CCP-AU (2008a) Report of the Citizens' Continental Conference on the African Union Summit. Addis Ababa: Centre for Citizens' Participation in the African Union.

CCP-AU (2008b) A People-Centred African Union: CSO Engagement in a Peaceful and Prosperous Industrialising Africa. Addis Ababa: Centre for Citizens' Participation in the African Union.

CCP-AU (2009) Fifth Citizens' Continental Conference on the AU Summit: African Citizen's Communique. Addis Ababa: Centre for Citizens' Participation in the African Union.

CCP-AU (2010) Civil Society Briefing Notes: Regional Integration. Adddis Ababa: Centre for Citizens' Participation in the African Union.

Červenka, Zdenek and Colin Legum (1980) 'The Organization of African Unity in 1978: The Challenge of Foreign Intervention' In *Africa Contemporary Record: Annual Survey and Documents 1978–1979*, edited by Colin Legum, pp. A25–A39. New York: Africana.

Červenka, Zdenek and Colin Legum (1981a) 'The Organization of African Unity in 1979' In *Africa Contemporary Record. Annual Survey and Documents 1979–1980*, edited by Colin Legum, pp. A58–A71. New York: Africana.

Červenka, Zdenek and Colin Legum (1981b) 'The OAU in 1980. Focus on Economic Problems and Human Rights' In *Africa Contemporary Record: Annual Survey and Documents 1980–1981*, edited by Colin Legum, pp. A64–A71. New York: Africana.

Chapin, Mac (2004) 'A Challenge to Conservationists', *World Watch* Magazine, November/December, 17–31.

Cheeseman, Nic (2015) *Democracy in Africa: Successes, Failures, and the Struggle for Political Reform*. Cambridge: Cambridge University Press.

Cheesman, Bruce (2001) 'Pakistani border at flashpoint', *Australian Financial Review*, 29 October.

Cherny-Scanlon, Xenya (2012) 'How Nature+ Was Born'. Available at: https://web.archive.org/web/20140811165729/https://portals.iucn.org/blog/2012/09/11/how-nature-was-born/ (accessed 8 November 2015).

Chesterman, Simon (2004) *You, the People: The United Nations, Transitional Administration, and State-Building*. Oxford: Oxford University Press.

Chesterman, Simon, ed. (2007) *Secretary or General? The UN Secretary-General in World Politics*. Cambridge: Cambridge University Press.

Christoffersen, Leif E. (1997) 'IUCN: A Bridge-Builder for Nature Conservation' In *Green Globe Yearbook 1997: Yearbook of International Cooperation on Environment and Development*, edited by Helge O. Bergesen and Georg Parmann, pp. 59–69. Oxford: Oxford University Press.

Cilliers, Jakkie and Julia Schünemann (2013) Future of Intrastate Conflict in Africa: More Violence or Greater Peace? *ISS Paper 246*. Pretoria: Institute for Security Studies.

Clark, Ian (2005) *Legitimacy in International Society*. Cambridge: Cambridge University Press.

Clark, Ian (2007a) *International Legitimacy in World Society*. Cambridge: Cambridge University Press.

Clark, Ian (2007b) 'Legitimacy in International and World Society' In *Legitimacy in an Age of Global Politics*, edited by Achim Hurrelmann, Steffen Schneider, and Jens Steffek, pp. 193–210. Basingstoke: Palgrave Macmillan.

Clark, Ian (2007c) 'Setting the Revisionist Agenda for International Legitimacy' *International Politics* 44, 325–35.

Clark, Ian (2013) *The Vulnerable in International Society*. Oxford: Oxford University Press.

Clark-Kazak, Christina (2009) 'Representing Refugees in the Life Cycle: A Social Age Analysis of United Nations High Commissioner for Refugees Annual Reports and Appeals 1999–2008' *Journal of Refugee Studies* 22 (3), 302–22.

Coicaud, Jean-Marc (2010) 'Deconstructing International Legitimacy' In *Fault Lines of International Legitimacy*, edited by Hilary Charlesworth and Jean-Marc Coicaud, pp. 29–86. Cambridge: Cambridge University Press.

Colchester, Marcus (2004) 'Conservation Policy and Indigenous Peoples' *Environmental Science and Policy* 7, 145–53.

Colville, Rupert (2006) 'Fiftieth Anniversary of the Hungarian uprising and refugee crisis: UNHCR'. Available at: http://www.unhcr.org/news/latest/(2006)/10/453c7adb2/fifti eth-anniversary-hungarian-uprising-refugee-crisis.html (accessed 22 March 2017).

Commission on Global Governance (1995) *Our Global Neighbourhood: The Report of the Commission on Global Governance.* Oxford: Oxford University Press.

Conservation International (2011) 'Another Leap towards the Barometer of Life'. Available at: http://www.conservation.org/newsroom/pressreleases/Pages/IUCN-Red-List-Leap-Towards-Barometer-Life.aspx (accessed 22 March 2017).

Corduwender, Jeroen and Bob Reinalda (2012) 'Van Heuven Goedhart, Gerrit Jan: United Nations High Commissioner for Refugees, 1951–1956', *IO BIO: The Biographical Dictionary of Secretaries-General of International Organizations.* Available at: http://www.ru.nl/politicologie/io-bio-bob-reinalda/io-bio-biographical-dictionary-sgs-ios/#h52a17323-d702-0f6a-24fb-2acef47316d7 (accessed 22 March 2017).

Cottrell, Patrick (2016) *The Evolution and Legitimacy of International Security Institutions.* Cambridge: Cambridge University Press.

Cox, Robert (1983) 'Gramsci, Hegemony and International Relations: An Essay in Method' *Millennium: Journal of International Studies* 12 (2), 162–75.

Crisp, Jeff (1999) '"Who Has Counted the Refugees?" UNHCR and the Politics of Numbers' *New Issues in Refugee Research*, Working Paper no. 12. Geneva: UNHCR Policy Research Unit.

Crisp, Jeff (2001) 'Mind the Gap! UNHCR, Humanitarian Assistance and the Development Process' *International Migration Review* 35 (1), 168–91.

Curzon, Gerard and Victoria Curzon (1973) 'GATT: Traders' Club' In *The Anatomy of Influence: Decision-Making in International Organization*, edited by Robert W. Cox and Harold K. Jacobson, pp. 298–333. New Haven, CT: Yale University Press.

Cuvellier, Thierry (2016) 'ICC, Out of Africa', *New York Times*, 7 November. Available at: http://www.nytimes.com/2016/11/07/opinion/the-icc-out-of-africa.html (accessed 24 November 2016).

Dahl, Robert A. (1999) 'Can International Organizations Be Democratic? A Skeptic's View' In *Democracy's Edges*, edited by Ian Shapiro and Casiano Hacker-Cordón, pp. 19–34. Cambridge: Cambridge University Press.

Daily News (2002) 'Exit Bungling OAU, It Comes Toothless AU', *Daily News*, 15 July.

Daily Yomiuri (2009) 'Incoming IAEA Chief Amano Ready for Challenges Ahead', *Daily Yomiuri*, 3 October.

Deephouse, David and Mark C. Suchman (2008) 'Legitimacy in Organizational Institutionalism' In *The SAGE Handbook of Organizational Institutionalism*, edited by R. Greenwood, C. Oliver, R. Suddaby, and K. Sahlin-Andersson, pp. 49–77. Thousand Oaks, CA: Sage.

Deguignet, Marine, Diego Juffe-Bignoli, Jerry Harrison, Brian MacSharry, Neil Burgess, and Naomi Kingston (2014) *2014 United Nations List of Protected Areas.* Cambridge: UNEP-WCMC.

Deitelhoff, Nicole and Lisbeth Zimmermann (2013) 'Things We Lost in the Fire: How Different Types of Contestation Affect the Validity of International Norms' HSFK Working Paper 18/2013. Frankfurt: HSFK.

Dellmuth, Lisa M. and Jonas Tallberg (2016) 'Elite Communication and Popular Legitimacy in International Organizations'. Available at https://papers.ssrn.com/sol3/papers.cfm?abstract_id=2757650 (accessed 4 July 2018).

Demaret, Paul (1995) 'The Metamorphoses of the GATT: From the Havana Charter to the World Trade Organization' *Columbia Journal of Transnational Law* 34 (5), 123–71.

Deng, Francis M., Sadikiel Kimaro, Terrence Lyons, Donald Rothchild, and I. William Zartman (1996) *Sovereignty as Responsibility: Conflict Management in Africa.* Washington, DC: Brookings Institution Press.

Di Giovanni, Janine (1999) The Rape of Kosovo: Investigation, *Times*, 19 June.

Dingwerth, Klaus (2019) 'Democracy' In *The Language of World Trade Politics: Unpacking the Terms of Trade*, edited by Klaus Dingwerth and Clara Weinhardt, pp. 80–96. London: Routledge.

Dingwerth, Klaus, Henning Schmidtke, and Tobias Weise (2018) 'Speaking Democracy: Why International Organizations Adopt a Democratic Rhetoric'. Unpublished manuscript.

Dlamini-Zuma, Nkosazana (2003) Statement of the Outgoing Chairperson of the Executive Council of Ministers of the African Union HE Dr Nkosazana Dlamini-Zuma, Maputo, 6 July.

Doub, William O. and Joseph M. Dukert (1975) 'Making Nuclear Energy Safe and Secure' *Foreign Affairs* 53 (4), 756–72.

Dowie, Mark (2011) *Conservation Refugees. The Hundred-Year Conflict between Global Conservation and Native Peoples.* Cambridge, MA: MIT Press.

Drori, Gili S., John W. Meyer, and Hokyu Hwang, eds (2006) *Globalization and Organization: World Society and Organizational Change.* Oxford: Oxford University Press.

Dunne, Nancy (1992) 'Fears over "Gattzilla the Trade Monster": US Greens Lead a Growing Lobby Worried about a Loss of Sovereignty' *Financial Times*, 30 January, 3.

Eagleton-Pierce, Matthew (2016) *Neoliberalism: The Key Concepts.* London: Routledge.

East African (2002) 'Will the AU Be Any Different?' *East African*, 15 July.

Ecker-Ehrhardt, Matthias (2016) 'Why Do Citizens Want the UN to Decide? Cosmopolitan Ideas, Particularism and Global Authority' *International Political Science Review* 37 (1), 99–114.

Edwards, Martin S. (2009) 'Public Support for the International Economic Organizations: Evidence from Developing Countries' *Review of International Organizations* 4 (2), 185–209.

Eisentraut, Sophie (2013) 'Autokratien, Demokratien und die Legitimität internationaler Organisationen: Eine vergleichende Inhaltsanalyse staatlicher Legitimationsanforderungen an die UN-Generalversammlung' *Zeitschrift für Internationale Beziehungen* 20 (2), 3–33.

Eiser, Richard J., Bettina Hannover, Leon Mann, Michel Morin, Joop van der Pligt, and Paul Webley (1990) 'Nuclear Attitudes after Chernobyl: A Cross-National Study' *Journal of Environmental Psychology* 10, 101–10.

ElBaradei, Mohammed and International Atomic Energy Agency (2007) *Atoms for Peace: A Pictorial History of the International Atomic Energy Agency, 1957–2007.* Vienna: International Atomic Energy Agency.

Elsig, Manfred and Cédric Dupont (2012) 'Persistent Deadlock in Multilateral Trade Negotiations: The Case of Doha' In *Oxford Handbook of the World Trade Organization*, edited by Amrita Narlikaer, Martin Daunton, and Robert M. Stern. Oxford: Oxford University Press.

Engel, Ulf (2013) 'The Changing Role of the AU Commission in Inter-African Relations: The Case of APSA and AGA' In *Africa in World Politics: Engaging a Changing Global Order*, edited by John W. Harbeson and Donald Rotchild, pp. 186–206. Boulder, CO: Westview Press.

Engel, Ulf and João Gomes Porto, eds (2010) *Africa's New Peace and Security Architecture: Promoting Norms, Institutionalizing Solutions*. Farnham: Ashgate.

Engel, Ulf and João Gomes Porto, eds (2013) *Towards an African Peace and Security Regime: Continental Embeddedness, Transnational Linkages, Strategic Relevance*. Farnham: Ashgate.

Esguerra, Alejandro, Silke Beck, and Rolf Lidskog (2017) 'Stakeholder Engagement in the Making: IPBES Legitimization Politics' *Global Environmental Politics* 17 (1), 59–76.

Essy, Amara (2002a) Statement by Mr Amara Essy, Secretary-General of the OAU, Special Session of the AU Council of Ministers, Durban, 1 July.

Essy, Amara (2002b) Message of the OAU Secretary-General, Mr Amara Essy, on the Occasion of the 39th Anniversary of the OAU, Addis Ababa, 25 May.

Eurobarometer (2011) Standard Eurobarometer 74 (Autumn 2010): Public Opinion in the European Union. Brussels: European Commission.

Fahamu (2008) *Towards a Continental Government: Collected Contributions*. Nairobi: Pambazuka.

Falk, Richard (1995) *On Humane Governance: Toward a New Global Politics*. Cambridge: Polity Press.

Farid, Ahmed (1999) Kosovo Tragedy: An Overview, *Independent*, 14 May.

Farrell, Henry and Martha Finnemore (2016) 'Global Institutions without a Global State' In *The Oxford Handbook of Historical Institutionalism*, edited by Orfeo Fioretos, Tulia G. Falleti, and Adam Sheingate, pp. 572–89. Oxford: Oxford University Press.

Fassbender, Bardo (1998) *UN Security Council Reform and the Right to Veto: A Constitutional Perspective*. Leiden: Martinus Nijhoff.

Fawcett, Louise (2005) 'Regionalism from an Historical Perspective' In *Global Politics of Regionalism: Theory and Practice*, edited by Mary Farrell, Björn Hettne, and Luk van Langenhove, pp. 21–37. London: Pluto Press.

Fickling, Meera and Gary Hufbauer (2012) 'Trade and the Environment' In *The Oxford Handbook on the World Trade Organization*, edited by Martin Daunton, Amrita Narlikar, and Robert M. Stern, pp. 719–39. Oxford: Oxford University Press.

Fierke, Karin (2004) 'World or Worlds? The Analysis of Content and Discourse' *Qualitative Methods: Newsletter of the American Political Science Association* 2 (1), 36–9.

Findlay, Trevor (2012) *Unleashing the Nuclear Watchdog: Strengthening and Reform of the IAEA*. Waterloo, Ontario: Cenre for International Governance Innovation.

Fioretos, Orfeo (2011) 'Historical Institutionalism in International Relations' *International Organizations* 65 (2), 367–99.

Fioretos, Orfeo, ed. (2017) *International Politics and Institutions in Time*. Oxford: Oxford University Press.

Fischer, David (2000) 'Nuclear Safeguards: Evolution and Future' In *Verification Yearbook 2000*. London: VERTIC.

Fischer, David and IAEA (1997) *History of the International Atomic Energy Agency: The First Forty Years*. Vienna: International Atomic Energy Agency.

Fletcher, Robert (2014) 'Orchestrating Consent: Post-Politics and Intensification of Nature TM Inc. at the 2012 World Conservation Congress' *Conservation and Society* 12 (3), 329–42.

Florini, Ann (2000) *The Third Force: The Rise of Transnational Civil Society*. Washington, DC: Carnegie Endowment.

Foroyaa (2007) 'Heads of State on the Next Step Forward', 6 July.

Forst, Rainer (2012) *The Right to Justification: Elements of a Constructivist Theory of Justice*. New York: Columbia University Press.

Forst, Rainer (2015) *Normativität und Macht: Zur Analyse Sozialer Rechtfertigungsordnungen*. Berlin: Suhrkamp.

Fouinat, Francois (1999) 'Letters to the Editor: Refugee Protection', *International Herald Tribune*, 30 September.

Franck, Thomas (1990) *The Power of Legitimacy among Nations*. Oxford: Oxford University Press.

Franke, Benedikt and Romain Esmenjaud (2008) 'Who Owns African Ownership? The Africanisation of Security and Its Limits' *South African Journal of International Affairs* 15 (2), 137–58.

Fresia, Marion (2014) 'Building Consensus within UNHCR's Executive Committee: Global Refugee Norms in the Making' *Journal of Refugee Studies* 27 (4), 514–33.

Frey, Marc, Sönke Kunkel, and Corinna R. Unger (2014) 'Introduction: International Organizations, Global Development, and the Making of the Contemporary World' In *International Organizations and Development, 1945–1990*, edited by Marc Frey, Sönke Kunkel, and Corinna R. Unger, pp. 1–22. Basingstoke: Palgrave Macmillan.

Friends of the Earth International (2009) 'Letter to IUCN'. Available at: http://www.foei.org/wp-content/uploads/2014/04/IUCN_FoEI-letter-09-jan-09.pdf (accessed 22 March 2017).

Frost, Mervyn (2013) 'Legitimacy and International Organizations: The Changing Ethical Context' In *Legitimating International Organizations*, edited by Dominik Zaum, pp. 26–40. Oxford: Oxford University Press.

Fukuyama, Francis (1989) 'The End of History' *National Interest* 16 (Summer), 3–18.

Gamson, William A. and André Modigliani (1989) 'Media Discourse and Public Opinion on Nuclear Power: A Constructionist Approach' *American Journal of Sociology* 95, 1–37.

GATT (General Agreement on Tariffs and Trade) (1970) *GATT Activities in 1969/70*. Geneva: GATT.

GATT (1972) GATT Activities in 1971. Geneva: GATT.

GATT (1973) GATT Activities in 1972. Geneva: GATT.

GATT (1974a) Contracting Parties, Thirtieth Session: Summary Record of the Third Meeting, Held at the Palais des Nations, Geneva, on Wednesday, 20 November 1974, at 10 a.m. (GATT Document SR.30/3). Geneva: GATT.

GATT (1974b) Contracting Parties, Thirtieth Session: Summary Record of the Fourth Meeting, Held at the Palais des Nations, Geneva, on Thursday, 21 November 1974, at 10 a.m. (GATT Document SR.30/4). Geneva: GATT.

GATT (1975a) GATT Activities in 1974. Geneva: GATT.

GATT (1975b) Contracting Parties, Thirty-First Session: Summary Record of the First Meeting, Held in the Palais des Nations, Geneva, on Wednesday, 26 November 1975, at 10.30 a.m. (GATT Document SR.31/1). Geneva: GATT.

GATT (1975c) Contracting Parties, Thirty-First Session: Summary Record of the Fourth Meeting, Held in the Palais des Nations, Geneva, on Thursday, 27 November 1975, at 3 p.m. (GATT Document SR.31/4). Geneva: GATT.

GATT (1976) Contracting Parties, Thirty-Second Session: Summary Record of the Second Meeting, Held in the Palais des Nations, Geneva, on Tuesday, 23 November 1976, at 10.30 a.m. (GATT Document SR.32/2). Geneva: GATT.

GATT (1978a) GATT Activities in 1977. Geneva: GATT.

GATT (1978b) Contracting Parties, Thirty-Fourth Session: Summary Record of the Third Meeting, Held in the Palais des Nations, Geneva, on Tuesday, 28 November 1978, at 3 p.m. (GATT Document SR.34/3). Geneva: GATT.

GATT (1979a) Contracting Parties, Thirty-Fifth Session: Summary Record of the Third Meeting, Held in the Palais des Nations, Geneva, on Wednesday, 28 November 1979, at 10.20 a.m. (GATT Document SR.35/3). Geneva: GATT.

GATT (1979b) Contracting Parties, Thirty-Fifth Session: Summary Record of the Fourth Meeting, Held in the Palais des Nations, Geneva, on Wednesday, 28 November 1979, at 3.20 p.m. (GATT Document SR.35/4). Geneva: GATT.

GATT (1979c) Contracting Parties, Thirty-Fifth Session: Summary Record of the Fifth Meeting, Held in the Palais des Nations, Geneva, on Thursday, 29 November 1979, at 10.25 a.m. (GATT Document SR.35/5). Geneva: GATT.

GATT (1980) GATT Activities in 1979. Geneva: GATT.

GATT (1986a) Contracting Party, Forty-Second Session: Peru, Statement by H. E. Mr José Carlos Mariátegui Arellano, Ambassador, Permanent Representative (GATT Document No. GATT SR.42/ST/2, 16 December). Geneva: GATT.

GATT (1986b) Contracting Party, Forty-Second Session: Poland, Statement by Mr Janusz Kaczurba, Deputy Minister of Foreign Trade (GATT Document No. GATT SR.42/ST/12, 16 December). Geneva: GATT.

GATT (1986c) Contracting Party, Forty-Second Session: Korea, Statement by H. E. Mr Sang Ock Lee, Ambassador, Permanent Representative (GATT Document No. GATT SR.42/ST/9, 16 December). Geneva: GATT.

GATT (1986d) Contracting Party, Forty-Second Session: Chile, Statement by H. E. Mr Mario Barros van Buren, Ambassador, Permanent Representative (GATT Document No. GATT SR.42/ST/33, 22 December). Geneva: GATT.

GATT (1986e) Forty-Second Session of the GATT Contracting Parties: Opening Statement by the Chairman Ambassador Kazuo Chiba (Japan) (GATT Document No. GATT/1401, 24 November). Geneva: GATT.

GATT (1986f) Contracting Party, Forty-Second Session: Switzerland, Statement by H. E. Mr Pierre-Louis Girard, Ambassador, Permanent Representative (GATT Document No. SR.42/ST/10, 16 December). Geneva: GATT.

GATT (1986g) Contracting Party, Forty-Second Session: Austria, Statement by H. E. Mr Georg Reisch, Ambassador, Permanent Representative (GATT Document No. SR.42/ST/14, 17 December). Geneva: GATT.

GATT (1986h) Contracting Party, Forty-Second Session: Sri Lanka, Statement by Mr P. Nagaratnam, Permanent Representative (GATT Document No. SR.42/ST/22, 18 December). Geneva: GATT.

GATT (1986i) Contracting Party, Forty-Second Session: Chile, Statement by H. E. Mr Mario Barros van Buren, Ambassador, Permanent Representative (GATT Document No. SR.42/ST/33, 22 December). Geneva: GATT.

GATT (1986j) Contracting Party, Forty-Second Session: Federal Republic of Germany, Statement by Mr Gerhard Abel, Director, Federal Ministry of the Economy (GATT Document No. SR.42/ST/37, 22 December). Geneva: GATT.

GATT (1987) Contracting Parties, Forty-Third Session: India, Statement by H. E. Mr S. P. Shukla, Ambassador, Permanent Representative (GATT Document SR.43/ST/16, 22 December).

GATT (1988) Contracting Parties, Forty-Fourth Session: India, Statement by H. E. Mr S. P. Shukla, Ambassador, Permanent Representative (GATT Document SR.44/ST/17, 23 November). Geneva: GATT.

GATT (1991a) GATT Activities in 1990: An Annual Review of the Work of the GATT. Geneva: GATT.

GATT (1991b) United States: Restrictions on Imports of Tuna: Report of the Panel, GATT Document No. DS21/R, 3 September. Geneva: GATT.

GATT (1993) GATT Activities in 1992: An Annual Review of the Work of the GATT. Geneva: GATT.

GATT (1994a) GATT Activities in 1993: An Annual Review of the Work of the GATT. Geneva: GATT.

GATT (1994b) Contracting Parties, Fiftieth Session: Canada, Statement by H. E. Mr Gerald E. Shannon, Ambassador, Permanent Representative (GATT Document SR.50/ST/2, 22 December). Geneva: GATT.

GATT (1994c) Contracting Parties, Forty-Ninth Session: Colombia, Statement by H. E. Mr Gillermo Alberto Gonzalez, Ambassador, Head of Delegation (GATT Document SR.49/ST/12, 18 February). Geneva: GATT.

Geck, Angela and Clara Weinhardt (2019) 'Development' In *The Language of World Trade Politics: Unpacking the Terms of Trade*, edited by Klaus Dingwerth and Clara Weinhardt, pp. 132–51. London: Routledge.

Gill, Stephen (1998) 'New Constitutionalism, Democratisation and Global Political Economy' *Pacifica Review: Peace, Security and Global Change* 10 (1), 23–38.

GiMAC (2007) 10th Pre-Summit Consultative Meeting on Gender Mainstreaming in the African Union. Accra: Gender Is My Agenda Campaign.

GIMPA (2007) Report of the Continental Civil Society Conference on the Proposed African Union Government. Accra: Ghana Institute for Management and Public Administration.

Githongo, John and William Gumede (2008) 'Let the African Union Set Democratic Standards', *Financial Times*. Available at: https://www.ft.com/content/22a2637e-469d-11dd-876a-0000779fd2ac (accessed 22 March 2017).

Godana, Getachew Dinku (2014) 'The Rhetoric of Community Participation: NGOs' Discourses and Deliberative Practices with Communities in Ethiopia' *Communication Studies: Theses, Dissertations, and Student Research* 30, 1–304. Available at http://digitalcommons.unl.edu/commstuddiss/30 (accessed 30 January 2018).

Goldstein, Judith and Lisa Martin (2000) 'Legalization, Trade Liberalization, and Domestic Politics: A Cautionary Note' *International Organization* 54 (3), 603–32.

Gómez-Baggethun, Erik, Rudolf de Groot, Pedro L. Lomas, and Carlos Montes (2010) 'The History of Ecosystem Services in Economic Theory and Practice: From Early Notions to Markets and Payment Schemes' *Ecological Economics* 69, 1209–18.

Goodwin-Gill, Guy S. (1999) 'Refugee Identity and Protection's Fading Prospect' In *Refugee Rights and Realities: Evolving International Concepts and Regimes*, edited by Frances Nicholson and Patrick M. Twomey, pp. 220–49. Cambridge: Cambridge University Press.

Göthel, V., G. Voigt, and W. Burkart (2007) 'Atomenergie zum Nutzen von Umwelt und Gesundheit' In *50 Jahre Internationale Atomenergie-Organisation IAEO. Ein Wirken für Frieden und Sicherheit im Nuklearen Zeitalter*, edited by Dirk Schriefer, Walter Sandtner, and Wolfgang Rudischhauser, pp. 121–35. Baden-Baden: Nomos.

Government of India (2011) 'Press Brief: India to Host IUCN Council Meeting 14–17 November, Ministry of Environment and Forests. Available at: http://moef.nic.in/downloads/public-information/Press%20brief_India%20to%20host%20IUCN%20Council%20meet_17th%20June.pdf (accessed 22 March 2017).

Graham, Thomas R. (1979) 'Revolution in Trade Politics' *Foreign Policy* 36, 49–63.

Gregoratti, Catia and Bart Slob, eds (2015) *Rethinking the UN Global Compact*. London: Pluto Press.

Grigorescu, Alexandru (2007) 'Transparency of Intergovernmental Organizations: The Roles of Member States, International Bureaucracies and Nongovernmental Organizations' *International Studies Quarterly* 51, 625–48.

Grigorescu, Alexandru (2010) 'The Spread of Bureaucratic Oversight Mechanisms in Intergovernmental Organizations' *International Studies Quarterly* 54 (3), 871–86.

Grigorescu, Alexandru (2015) *Democratic Intergovernmental Organizations? Normative Pressure and Decision-Making Rules*. Cambridge: Cambridge University Press.

Guastaferro, Barbara and Manuela Moschella (2012) 'The EU, the IMF, and the Representative Turn: Addressing the Challenge of Legitimacy' *Swiss Political Science Review* 18 (2), 199–219.

Haas, Peter M. (1992) 'Introduction: Epistemic Communities and International Policy Coordination' *International Organization* 46 (1), 1–35.

Habermas, Jürgen (2001) *The Postnational Constellation: Political Essays*. Cambridge, MA: MIT Press.

Hahn, Kristina and Anna Holzscheiter (2013) 'The Ambivalence of Advocacy: Representation and Contestation in Global NGO Advocacy for Child Workers and Sex Workers' *Global Society* 27 (4), 497–520.

Hale, Thomas N., David Held, and Kevin Young (2013) *Gridlock: Why International Cooperation Is Failing When We Need It Most*. Cambridge: Polity Press.

Hall, Peter A. and Rosemary C. R. Taylor (1996) 'Political Science and the Three New Institutionalisms' *Political Studies* 44 (5), 936–57.

Hanrieder, Tine (2009) 'Die Weltgesundheitsorganisation unter Wettbewerbsdruck: Auswirkungen der Vermarktlichung globaler Gesundheitspolitik' In *Die Organisierte Welt: Internationale Beziehungen und Organisationsforschung*, edited by Klaus Dingwerth, Dieter Kerwer, and Andreas Nölke, pp. 165–88. Baden-Baden: Nomos.

Hanrieder, Tine (2015) *International Organizations in Time: Fragmentation and Reform*. Oxford: Oxford University Press.

Harman, Sophie (2011) 'Searching for an Executive Head? Leadership and UNAIDS' *Global Governance* 17 (4), 429–46.

Harrer, Gudrun (2014) *Dismantling the Iraqi Nuclear Programme: The Inspections of the International Atomic Energy Agency, 1991–1998*. London: Routledge.

Hartmann, Christof (2016) 'Subsaharan-Africa' In *The Oxford Handbook of Comparative Regionalism*, edited by Tanja A. Börzel and Thomas Risse, pp. 271–94. Oxford: Oxford University Press.

He, Hongwei and Andrew D. Brown (2013) 'Organizational Identity and Organizational Identification: A Review of the Literature and Suggestions for Future Research' *Group and Organization Management* 38 (1), pp. 3–35.

Held, David, Anthony McGrew, David Goldblatt, and Jonathan Perraton (1999) *Global Transformations*. Redwood City, CA: Stanford University Press.

Helleiner, Eric (2014a) *The Forgotten Foundations of Bretton Woods: International Development and the Making of the Postwar Order*. Ithaca, NY: Cornell University Press.

Helleiner, Eric (2014b) 'Southern Pioneers of International Development' *Global Governance* 20 (3), 375–88.

Herald (1993) 'Test Case for the IAEA', *Herald*, 14 March, 10.

Herald (2007) 'African Union Failed the Crucial Test', *Herald*, 11 July.

Holdgate, Martin (1999) *The Green Web: A Union for World Conservation*. London: Earthscan.

Hollande, François (2013) 'Intervention de M. le président de la République lors du 50e anniversaire de l'Union Africaine à Addis-Abeba'. Available at: https://web.archive.org/web/20170427135215/http://www.elysee.fr/declarations/article/intervention-de-m-le-president-de-la-republique-lors-du-50e-anniversaire-de-l-union-africaine-a-addis-abeba/ (accessed 22 March 2017).

Holzscheiter, Anna (2010) *Children's Rights in International Politics: The Transformative Power of Discourse*. London: Palgrave Macmillan.

Hooghe, Liesbet, Gary Marks, Tobias Lenz, Jeanine Bezuijen, Besir Ceka, and Svet Derderyan (2017) *Measuring International Authority: A Postfunctionalist Theory of Governance*, Vol. III. Oxford: Oxford University Press.

Hopgood, Stephen (2006) *Keepers of the Flame: Understanding Amnesty International*. Ithaca, NY: Cornell University Press.

HRW (Human Rights Watch) (1999) Refugees in Guinea must be protected, *All Africa* (via *COMTEX News*), 1 June.

HRW (2010) AU Summit: Focus on Human Rights Consequences of Conflicts, press release. London: Human Rights Watch.

Hurd, Ian (2007) *After Anarchy. Legitimacy and Power in the United Nations Security Council*. Princeton, NJ: Princeton University Press.

Hurrell, Andrew (2002) 'Norms and Ethics in International Relations' In *Handbook of International Relations*, edited by Walter Carlsnaes, Thomas Risse, and Beth Simmons, pp. 137–54. London: Sage.

Hurrelmann, Achim, Steffen Schneider, and Jens Steffek, eds (2007) *Legitimacy in an Age of Global Politics*. Basingstoke: Palgrave Macmillan.

Hutton, Jon, William M. Adams, and James C. Murombedzi (2005) 'Back to the Barriers? Changing Narratives in Biodiversity Conservation' *Forum for Development Studies* 32 (2), 341–70.

Hyde, Susan D., Judith Kelley, and Daniel L. Nielson (2017) 'The Power of Heuristics: Testing the Sources of Legitimacy Beliefs about International Election Observers'. Unpublished manuscript.

Hyndman, Jennifer (2000) *Managing Displacement: Refugees and the Politics of Humanitarianism*. Minneapolis, MN: University of Minnesota Press.

IAEA (International Atomic Energy Agency) (1956) The Statute of the IAEA. Available at: http://www.iaea.org/About/statute.html (accessed 22 March 2017).

IAEA (1970) One Hundred and Thirty-Sixth Plenary Meeting (IAEA Document No. GC(14)/OR.136). Vienna: IAEA.

IAEA (1971) Annual Report, 1 July 1970–30 June 1971 (IAEA Document No. GC(15)/455). Vienna: IAEA.

IAEA (1974a) Record of the One Hundred and Seventieth Plenary Meeting (IAEA Document No. GC(XVIII)/OR. 170). Vienna: IAEA.

IAEA (1974b) Record of the One Hundred and Seventy-Fifth Plenary Meeting (IAEA Document No. GC(XVIII)/OR. 175). Vienna: IAEA.

IAEA (1974c) Record of the One Hundred and Sixty-Ninth Plenary Meeting (IAEA Document No. GC(XVIII)/OR. 169). Vienna: IAEA.

IAEA (1975) Annual Report, 1 July 1974–30 June 1975 (IAEA Document No. GC(19)/544). Vienna: IAEA.

IAEA (1977) Twenty Years International Atomic Energy Agency (1957–1977). Vienna: IAEA.

IAEA (1978a) Record of the Two Hundred and Second Plenary Meeting (IAEA Document No. GC(22)/OR.202). Vienna: IAEA.

IAEA (1978b) Record of the Two Hundred and Third Plenary Meeting (IAEA Document No. GC(22)/OR.203). Vienna: IAEA.

IAEA (1979) The Annual Report for 1978 (IAEA Document No. GC(23)/610). Vienna: IAEA.

IAEA (1982a) Consideration of the Suspension of Israel from the Exercise of the Privileges and Rights of Membership if, by the Time of the General Conference's Twenty-Sixth Regular Session, It Has Not Complied with the Provisions of United Nations Security Council Resolution 487 of 19 June 1981 (IAEA Document No. GC (26)/675). Vienna: IAEA.

IAEA (1982b) Record of the Two Hundred and Forty-First Plenary Meeting (IAEA Document No. GC(26)/OR.241). Vienna: IAEA.

IAEA (1982c) Record of the Two Hundred and Forty-Second Plenary Meeting (IAEA Document No. GC(26)/OR.242). Vienna: IAEA.

IAEA (1982d) Record of the Two Hundred and Forty-Third Plenary Meeting (IAEA Document No. GC(26)/OR.243). Vienna: IAEA.

IAEA (1982e) Record of the Two Hundred and Thirty-Ninth Plenary Meeting (IAEA Document No. GC(26)/OR.239). Vienna: IAEA.

IAEA (1983) The Annual Report for 1982 (IAEA Document No. GC(27)/684). Vienna: IAEA.

IAEA (1986a) Record of the Two Hundred and Eighty-Eighth Plenary Meeting (IAEA Document No. GC(30)/OR.288). Vienna: IAEA.

IAEA (1986b) Record of the Two Hundred and Eighty-Fifth Plenary Meeting (IAEA Document No. GC(30)/OR.285). Vienna: IAEA.

IAEA (1986c) Record of the Two Hundred and Eighty-Fourth Plenary Meeting (IAEA Document No. GC(30)/OR.284). Vienna: IAEA.

IAEA (1986d) Record of the Two Hundred and Eighty-Ninth Plenary Meeting (IAEA Document No. GC(30)/OR.289). Vienna: IAEA.

IAEA (1986e) Record of the Two Hundred and Eighty-Second Plenary Meeting (IAEA Document No. GC(30)/OR.282). Vienna: IAEA.

IAEA (1986f) Record of the Two Hundred and Eighty-Seventh Plenary Meeting (IAEA Document No. GC(30)/OR.287). Vienna: IAEA.

IAEA (1986g) The Annual Report for 1985 (IAEA Document No. GC(30)/775). Vienna: IAEA.

IAEA (1987a) Record of the Two Hundred and Ninety-Fourth Plenary Meeting (IAEA Document No. GC(XXXI)/0R.294). Vienna: IAEA.

IAEA (1987b) The Annual Report for 1986 (IAEA Document No. GC(31)/800). Vienna: IAEA.

IAEA (1988) Record of the Three Hundred and Third Plenary Meeting (IAEA Document No. GC(XXXII)/0R.303). Vienna: IAEA.

IAEA (1990a) Thirty-Fourth (1990) Regular Session: Record of the Three Hundred and Twenty-Eighth Plenary Meeting (IAEA Document No. GC(34)/OR.328). Vienna: IAEA.

IAEA (1990b) Thirty-Fourth (1990) Regular Session: Record of the Three Hundred and Twenty-Fifth Plenary Meeting (IAEA Document No. GC(34)/OR.325). Vienna: IAEA.

IAEA (1990c) Thirty-Fourth (1990) Regular Session: Record of the Three Hundred and Twenty-Ninth Plenary Meeting (IAEA Document No. GC(34)/OR.329). Vienna: IAEA.

IAEA (1990d) Thirty-Fourth (1990) Regular Session: Record of the Three Hundred and Twenty-Seventh Plenary Meeting (IAEA Document No. GC(34)/OR.327). Vienna: IAEA.

IAEA (1990e) Thirty-Fourth (1990) Regular Session: Record of the Three Hundred and Twenty-Sixth Plenary Meeting (IAEA Document No. GC(34)/OR.326). Vienna: IAEA.

IAEA (1990f) Thirty-Fourth (1990) Regular Session: Record of the Three Hundred and Twenty-Third Plenary Meeting (IAEA Document No. GC(34)/OR.323). Vienna: IAEA.

IAEA (1994a) Plenary Meetings. Record of the Eighth Plenary Meeting (IAEA Document No. GC(38)/OR.8). Vienna: IAEA.

IAEA (1994b) Plenary Meetings. Record of the Fifth Plenary Meeting (IAEA Document No. GC(38)/OR.5). Vienna: IAEA.

IAEA (1994c) Plenary Meetings. Record of the Sixth Plenary Meeting (IAEA Document No. GC(38)/OR.6). Vienna: IAEA.

IAEA (1994d) Plenary Meetings. Record of the Third Plenary Meeting (IAEA Document No. GC(38)/OR.3). Vienna: IAEA.

IAEA (1995) Annual Report 1994. Vienna: IAEA.

IAEA (1998a) Plenary Meetings: Fifth Meeting (IAEA Document No. GC(42)/OR.5). Vienna: IAEA.

IAEA (1998b) Plenary Meetings. Ninth Meeting (IAEA Document No. GC(42)/OR.9). Vienna: IAEA.

IAEA (1998c) Plenary Meetings. Second Meeting (IAEA Document No. GC(42)/OR.2). Vienna: IAEA.

IAEA (1998d) Plenary Meetings. Seventh Meeting (IAEA Document No. GC(42)/OR.7). Vienna: IAEA.

IAEA (1998e) Plenary Meetings. Third Meeting (IAEA Document No. GC(42)/OR.3). Vienna: IAEA.

IAEA (1999) The Annual Report for 1998 (IAEA Document No. GOV/1999/28). Vienna: IAEA.

IAEA (2002) Forty-Sixth Regular Session Record of the Sixth Plenary Meeting, IAEA Document No. GC(46)/OR.6. Vienna: IAEA.

IAEA (2003) IAEA Annual Report for 2002 (IAEA Document No. GC (47)/2). Vienna: IAEA.

IAEA (2006a) Plenary: Record of the Fifth Meeting (IAEA Document No. GC(50)/OR.5). Vienna: IAEA.

IAEA (2006b) Plenary: Record of the Second Meeting (IAEA Document No. GC(50)/OR.2). Vienna: IAEA.

IAEA (2006c) Plenary: Record of the Seventh Meeting (IAEA Document No. GC(50)/OR.7). Vienna: IAEA.

IAEA (2006d) Plenary: Record of the Sixth Meeting (IAEA Document No. GC(50)/OR.6). Vienna: IAEA.

IAEA (2006e) In the Service of Peace: 2005 Nobel Peace Prize. Vienna: IAEA. Available at: https://www.iaea.org/sites/default/files/nobel2005.pdf (accessed 22 March 2017).

IAEA (2007) IAEA Annual Report for (2006) (IAEA Document No. GC(51)/5). Vienna: IAEA.

IAEA (2008) Annual Report (2007) (IAEA Document No. GC(52)/9). Vienna: IAEA.

IAEA (2010a) Plenary: Record of the Fifth Meeting (IAEA Document No. GC(54)/OR.5). Vienna: IAEA.

IAEA (2010b) Plenary: Record of the First Meeting (IAEA Document No. GC(54)/OR.1). Vienna: IAEA.

IAEA (2010c) Plenary: Record of the Fourth Meeting (IAEA Document No. GC(54)/OR.4). Vienna: IAEA.

IAEA (2010d) Plenary: Record of the Seventh Meeting (IAEA Document No. GC(54)/OR.7). Vienna: IAEA.

IAEA (2010e) Plenary: Record of the Sixth Meeting (IAEA Document No. GC(54)/OR.6). Vienna: IAEA.

IAEA (2010f) Plenary: Record of the Third Meeting (IAEA Document No. GC(54)/OR.3). Vienna: IAEA.

IAEA (2011a) Annual Report (2010) (IAEA Document No. GC(55)/2). Vienna: IAEA.

IAEA (2011b) IAEA Chief Yukiya Amano visits Fukushima Daichi. Available at: https://www.youtube.com/watch?v=bA1jojWGt4k (accessed 22 March 2017).

IAEA (2011c) Introductory Statement to Board of Governors by IAEA Director General Yukiya Amano, 21 March. Available at: https://www.iaea.org/newscenter/statements/introductory-statement-board-governors-22 (accessed 16 July 2018).

IAEA (2011d) Draft IAEA Action Plan on Nuclear Safety, IAEA Document No. GC (55)/14. Vienna: IAEA.

IAEA (2015) The Agency's Programme and Budget 2016–2017, IAEA Document No. GC(59)/2. Vienna: IAEA.

IBRD (International Bank for Reconstruction and Development) (1944) Articles of Agreement (as amended). Available at: http://siteresources.worldbank.org/EXTABOUTUS/Resources/ibrd-articlesofagreement.pdf (accessed 4 July 2018).

ICG (2018) Seven Priorities for the African Union in 2018. Africa Briefing No. 135. Brussels: International Crisis Group.

IDMC (Internal Displacement Monitoring Centre) (2015) Global Overview 2015. Available at: http://www.internal-displacement.org/publications/2015/global-overview-2015-people-internally-displaced-by-conflict-and-violence (accessed 27 March 2017).

Ikenberry, John (2011) *Liberal Leviathan: The Origins, Crisis, and Transformation of the American World Order*. Princeton, NJ: Princeton University Press.

Ingram, Paul, Jeffrey Robinson, and Marc L. Busch (2005) 'The Intergovernmental Network of World Trade: IGO Connectedness, Governance and Embeddedness' *American Journal of Sociology* 111 (3), 824–58.

IOM (International Organization for Migration) (2016) IOM Becomes a Related Organization to the UN, press release. Geneva: IOM.

IPSS (2017) APSA Impact Report 2016: Assessment of the Impacts of Intervention by the African Union and Regional Economic Communities in 2016 in the Frame of the African Peace and Security Architecture (APSA). Addis Ababa: Institute for Peace and Security Studies.

Iriye, Akira (2002) *Global Community: The Role of International Organizations in the Making of the Contemporary World*. Berkeley, CA: University of California Press.

IUCN (1971) *IUCN Yearbook 1970*. Morges: International Union for Conservation of Nature and Natural Resources.

IUCN (1972) Eleventh General Assembly: Proceedings (Banff, Alberta, Canada, 11–16 September). Morges: International Union for Conservation of Nature and Natural Resources.

IUCN (1973) *IUCN Yearbook 1972*. Morges: International Union for Conservation of Nature and Natural Resources.

IUCN (1975) *IUCN Yearbook 1974*. Morges: International Union for Conservation of Nature and Natural Resources.

IUCN (1975/6) *IUCN Yearbook 1975–1976*. Morges: International Union for Conservation of Nature and Natural Resources.

IUCN (1977) Thirteenth (Extraordinary) General Assembly: Proceedings (Geneva, Switzerland, 19–21 April 1977). Morges: International Union for Conservation of Nature and Natural Resources.

IUCN (1980) World Conservation Strategy: Living Resource Conservation for Sustainable Development. Gland: International Union for Conservation of Nature and Natural Resources.

IUCN (1981) Achievements 1978–1981. Gland: International Union for Conservation of Nature and Natural Resources.

IUCN (1984) Triennial Report 1982–1984. Gland: International Union for Conservation of Nature and Natural Resources.

IUCN (1987) Triennial Report 1985–1987. Gland: International Union for Conservation of Nature and Natural Resources.

IUCN (1988) 17th Session of the General Assembly of IUCN and 17th IUCN Technical Meeting: Proceedings (San José, Costa Rica, 1–10 February 1988). Gland: International Union for Conservation of Nature and Natural Resources.

IUCN (1990) Triennial Report 1988–1990. Gland: International Union for Conservation of Nature and Natural Resources.

IUCN (1993) Annual Report 1992. Gland: International Union for Conservation of Nature and Natural Resources.

IUCN (1994) 19th General Assembly: Proceedings, 19th Session of the General Assembly of IUCN, the World Conservation Union (Buenos Aires, Argentina, 17–26 January 1994). Gland: International Union for Conservation of Nature and Natural Resources.

IUCN (1995) Annual Report 1994. Gland: International Union for Conservation of Nature and Natural Resources.

IUCN (1997a) Annual Report 1996. Gland: International Union for Conservation of Nature and Natural Resources.

IUCN (1997b) Proceedings: World Conservation Congress (Montreal, Canada, 13–23 October 1996). Gland: International Union for Conservation of Nature and Natural Resources.

IUCN (1999) Annual Report 1998. Gland: International Union for Conservation of Nature and Natural Resources.

IUCN (2001) Proceedings: World Conservation Congress (Amman, Jordan, 4–11 October 2000). Gland: International Union for Conservation of Nature and Natural Resources.

IUCN (2003) An Assessment of Progress: The IUCN Programme 2002. Gland: International Union for Conservation of Nature and Natural Resources.

IUCN (2005a) Forging Linkages: An Assessment of Progress 2004. Gland: International Union for Conservation of Nature and Natural Resources.

IUCN (2005b) Proceedings of the Members' Business Assembly: World Conservation Congress (Bangkok, Thailand, 17–25 November 2004). Gland: International Union for Conservation of Nature and Natural Resources.

IUCN (2007) Working for Conservation: Programme Report 2006. Gland: International Union for Conservation of Nature and Natural Resources.

IUCN (2008) Building the Future: A Report on the IUCN Programme 2005–2008. Gland: International Union for Conservation of Nature and Natural Resources.

IUCN (2009) Proceedings of the Members' Assembly: World Conservation Congress, Barcelona, 5–14 October 2008. Gland: International Union for Conservation of Nature and Natural Resources.

IUCN (2010) Natural Assets: Annual Report 2009. Gland: International Union for Conservation of Nature and Natural Resources.

IUCN (2011) The Nature of Progress: Annual Report 2010. Gland: International Union for Conservation of Nature and Natural Resources.

IUCN (2012a) Statues (of 5 October 1948, revised on 22 October 1996 and 13 October 2008 and last amended on 14 September 2012) and Regulations (revised on 22 October 1996 and last amended on 14 September 2012). Gland: International Union for Conservation of Nature and Natural Resources.

IUCN (2012b) 2011 IUCN Annual Report: Solutions, Naturally. Gland: International Union for Conservation of Nature and Natural Resources.

IUCN (2013) 2012 IUCN Annual Report: Nature+. Towards Nature-Based Solutions. Gland: International Union for Conservation of Nature and Natural Resources.

IUCN (2016a) Statutes (of 5 October 1948, revised on 22 October 1996 and last amended on 10 September 2016) and Regulations (revised on 22 October 1996 and last amended on 9 February 2017). Gland: International Union for Conservation of Nature and Natural Resources.

IUCN (2016b) Annual Report. IUCN 2015. Gland: International Union for Conservation of Nature and Natural Resources.

IUCN (2016c) Proceedings of the Members' Assembly: World Conservation Congress, Honolulu, Hawai'i, 6–10 September 2016. Gland: International Union for Conservation of Nature and Natural Resources.

IUCN (2017) IUCN 2016. International Union for Conservation of Nature. Annual Report 2016. Gland: International Union for Conservation of Nature and Natural Resources.

IUCN (2018) IUCN 2017. International Union for Conservation of Nature. Annual Report 2017. Gland: International Union for Conservation of Nature and Natural Resources.

IUCN (International Union for Conservation of Nature and Natural Resources)-BBP (Business and Biodiversity Programme) (2010) On the Move: Business and Biodiversity Programme Annual Report 2009. Gland: International Union for Conservation of Nature and Natural Resources: Business and Biodiversity Programme.

IUCN-BBP (2011) Scaling Up: Global Business and Biodiversity Programme Annual Report 2010. Gland: International Union for Conservation of Nature and Natural Resources: Business and Biodiversity Programme.

IUCN-BBP (2012) Shaping the Future with Business: Global Business and Biodiversity Programme Report 2011–2012. Gland: International Union for Conservation of Nature and Natural Resources: Business and Biodiversity Programme.

IUCN-BBP (2017) Highlights 2016: Business and Biodiversity Programme. Gland: International Union for Conservation of Nature and Natural Resources: Business and Biodiversity Programme.

IUCN, UNEP, and WWF (1991) *Caring for the Earth: A Strategy for Sustainable Living.* Gland: IUCN, UNEP, and WWF.

Jacobsen, Katja Lindskov and Kristin Bergtora Sandvik (2016) 'Introduction: Quest for an Accountability Cure' In *UNHCR and the Struggle for Accountability: Technology, Law and Results-Based Management*, edited by Kristin Bergtora Sandvik and Katja Lindskov Jacobsen, pp. 1–25. New York: Routledge.

Jaganathan, Madhan Mohan and Gerrit Kurtz (2014) 'Singing the Tune of Sovereignty? India and the Responsibility to Protect' *Conflict, Security and Development* 14 (4), 461–87.

Japan Times (2009) 'Mr Amano Heads IAEA', *Japan Times*, 7 July.

Johnson, Stanley (2012) *UNEP: The First 40 Years: A Narrative*. Nairobi: United Nations Environment Programme.

Johnson, Tana (2014) *Organizational Progeny: Why Governments Are Losing Control over the Proliferating Structures of Global Governance*. Oxford: Oxford University Press.

Johnstone, Ian (2007) 'The Secretary-General as Norm Entrepreneur' In *Secretary or General? The UN Secretary-General in World Politics*, edited by Simon Chesterman, pp. 123–38. Cambridge: Cambridge University Press.

Jolly, Richard, Louis Emmerij, and Thomas G. Weiss (2009) *UN Ideas that Changed the World*. Bloomington, IN: Indiana University Press.

Jonas, Holly C. (2017) 'Indigenous Peoples' and Community Conserved Territories and Areas (ICCAs): Evolution in International Biodiversity Law' In *Biodiversity and Nature Protection Law*, edited by Elisa Morgera and Joana Razzaque, pp. 145–60. Cheltenham: Edward Elgar.

Jones, Sidney (1999) 'Don't Betray the Refugees Trapped in West Timor', *International Herald Tribune*, 27 September.

Junne, Gerd C. A. (2001) 'International Organizations in a Period of Globalization: New (Problems of) Legitimacy' In *The Legitimacy of International Organizations*, edited by Jean-Marc Coicaud and Veijo Heiskanen, pp. 189–220. Tokyo: United Nations University Press.

Kagame, Paul (2017) The Imperative to Strengthen Our Union. Report on the Proposed Recommendations for the Institutional Reform of the African Union. Addis Ababa: African Union.

Kaiser, Tania (2004) 'Participation or Consultation? Reflections on a "Beneficiary Based" Evaluation of UNHCR's Programme for Sierra Leonean and Liberian Refugees in Guinea, June–July 2000' *Journal of Refugee Studies* 17 (2), 185–204.

Kaluzynska, Eva (1990) 'GATT Finale Opens to Pessimism and Protest', *Reuters News*, 3 December.

Karns, Margaret and Karen Mingst (2015) *International Organizations: The Politics and Processes of Global Governance*. Boulder, CO: Lynne Rienner.

Kasperson, Roger E., Gerald Berk, David Pijawka, Alan B. Sharaf, and James Wood (1980) 'Public Opposition to Nuclear Energy: Retrospect and Prospect' *Science, Technology, and Human Values* 5, 11–23.

Keck, Margaret E. and Kathryn Sikkink (1998) *Activists beyond Borders*. Ithaca, NY: Cornell University Press.

Keohane, Robert O. (1984) *After Hegemony: Cooperation and Discord in the World Political Economy*. Princeton, NJ: Princeton University Press.

Kerry, John (2013) 'Remarks at the African Union 50th Anniversary Summit Leaders Dinner'. Available at: https://2009-2017.state.gov/secretary/remarks/2013/05/209965.htm (accessed 22 March 2017).

Kikwete, Jakaya Mrisho (2009) Statement by His Excellency Jakaya Mrisho Kikwete, the Outgoing African Union Chairman and President of the United Republic of Tanzania at the 12th Summit of Heads of State and Government of the African Union, Addis Ababa, 1–3 February.

Kim, Younghwan, Minki Kim, and Wonjoon Kim (2013) 'Effect of the Fukushima Nuclear Disaster on Global Public Acceptance of Nuclear Energy' *Energy Policy* 61, 822–8.

Kioko, Ben (2003) 'The Right of Intervention under the African Union's Constitutive Act: From Non-Interference to Non-Intervention' *International Review of the Red Cross* 85 (852), 807–25.

Köhler, Horst (2003) The IMF: A Reliable Partner for Africa, Maputo, 10 July. Available at: http://www.imf.org/external/np/speeches/2003/071003.htm (accessed 22 March 2017).

Koppell, Jonathan G. S. (2005) 'Pathologies of Accountability: ICANN and the Challenge of "Multiple Accountability Disorder"' *Public Administration Review* 65 (1), 94–108.

Koppell, Jonathan G. S. (2010) *World Rule: Accountability, Legitimacy and the Design of Global Governance*. Chicago, IL: University of Chicago Press.

Korea Times (2001a) 'NK Accuses IAEA of Siding with US', *Korea Times*, 18 July.

Korea Times (2001b) 'P'yang Refuses IAEA Inspection', *Korea Times*, 19 July.

Korea Times (2004) 'IAEA Inspection to Focus on Unreported Uranium', *Korea Times*, 16 September.

Kothari, Ashish, Philip Camill, and Jessica Brown (2013) 'Conservation as if People also Mattered: Policy and Practice of Community-Based Conservation' *Conservation and Society* 11(1), 1–15.

Kratochwil, Friedrich (2006) 'On Legitimacy' *International Relations* 20 (3), 302–8.

Krebs, Ronald K. and Patrick Thaddeus Jackson (2007) 'Twisting Tongues and Twisting Arms: The Power of Political Rhetoric' *European Journal of International Relations* 13 (1), 35–66.

Kubálková, Vendulka, Nicholas Onuf, and Paul Kowert, eds (1998) *International Relations in a Constructed World*. London: M. E. Sharpe.

Kumar, Pushpam, ed. (2012) *The Economics of Ecosystems and Biodiversity: Ecological and Economic Foundations*. New York: Routledge.

Lanz, David (2008) 'Subversion or Reinvention? Dilemmas and Debates in the Context of UNHCR's Increasing Involvement with IDPs' *Journal of Refugee Studies* 21 (2), 192–209.

Laporte, Geert and James Mackie, eds (2010) *Building the African Union: An Assessment of Past Progress and Future Prospects for the African Union's Institutional Architecture*. Maastricht: ECDPM.

Lausche, Barbara (2008) *Weaving a Web of Environmental Law*. Berlin: Erich Schmidt Verlag.

Lechner, Silvia and Mervyn Frost (2018) *Practice Theory and International Relations*. Cambridge: Cambridge University Press.

Legum, Colin (2000) 'The Organization of African Unity: Facing Up to the Failure of Its Mediation Efforts' In *Africa Contemporary Record: Annual Survey and Documents 1992-1994*, Vol. 24, edited by Colin Legum, pp. A33–A38. New York: Africana.

Levitsky, Steven and Daniel Ziblatt (2018) *How Democracies Die*. New York: Penguin Press.

Lewis, Paul (1989) 'UN Refugee Chief Quits over His Use of Funds', *New York Times*, 27 October.

Linklater, Andrew (1998) *The Transformation of Political Community*. Cambridge: Polity Press.

Linzer, Dafner (2004) 'IAEA Leader's Phone Tapped. US Pores over Transcripts to Try to Oust Nuclear Chief', *Washington Post*, 12 December.

Liu, Tiewa and Haibin Zhang (2014) 'Debates in China about the Responsibility to Protect as a Developing Norm: A General Assessment' *Conflict, Security and Development* 14 (4), 403–27.

Loescher, Gil (2001) *The UNHCR and World Politics: A Perilous Path*. Oxford: Oxford University Press.

Loescher, Gil, Alexander Betts, and James Milner (2008) *The United Nations High Commissioner for Refugees (UNHCR): The Politics and Practice of Refugee Protection into the Twenty-First Century*. New York: Routledge.

Lotze, Walter (2013) 'Building the Legitimacy of the African Union: An Evolving Continent, and Evolving Organization' In *Legitimating International Organizations*, edited by Dominik Zaum, pp. 111–31. Oxford: Oxford University Press.

Lulie, Hallelujah and Jakkie Cilliers (2016) 'Salim at the Organization of African Unity' In *Salim Ahmed Salim: Son of Africa*, edited by Jakkie Cilliers, pp. 67–85. Addis Ababa: Institute for Security Studies.

MacDonald, Kenneth I. (2010a) 'The Devil Is in the (Bio)diversity: Private Sector "Engagement" and the Restructuring of Biodiversity Conservation' *Antipode* 42 (3), 513–50.

MacDonald, Kenneth I. (2010b) 'Business, Biodiversity and New "Fields" of Conservation. The World Conservation Congress and the Renegotiation of Organisational Order' *Conservation and Society* 8 (4), 256–75.

MacKenzie, David (2010) *A World beyond Borders: An Introduction to the History of International Organizations*. Toronto: University of Toronto Press.

Mansuri, Ghazala and Vijayendra Rao (2013) Localizing Development: Does Participation Work? Washington, DC: World Bank.

Marceau, Gabrielle (1994) *Anti-Dumping and Anti-Trust Issues in Free-Trade Areas*. Oxford: Clarendon Press.

Martin, Adrian (2017) *Just Conservation: Biodiversity, Wellbeing and Sustainability*. London: Earthscan.

Masire, Quett Ketumile Joni et al. (2000) *Rwanda: The Preventable Genocide*. Addis Ababa: Organization of African Unity.

Mazower, Mark (2012) *Governing the World: The History of an Idea, 1815 to the Present*. New York: Penguin Press.

McCormick, John (1986) 'The Origins of the World Conservation Strategy' *Environmental Review* 10 (3), 177–87.

McCormick, John (1989) *Reclaiming Paradise: The Global Environmental Movement*. Bloomington: Indiana University Press.

McGraw, Désirée (2002) 'The Story of the Biodiversity Convention: From Negotiation to Implementation' In *Governing Global Biodiversity: The Evolution and*

Implementation of the Convention on Biological Diversity, edited by Philippe G. LePrestre, pp. 7–38. Aldershot: Ashgate.

Meadows, Donella, Dennis Meadows, Jorgen Randers, and William W. Behrens III (1972) *The Limits to Growth: A Report for the Club of Rome's Project on the Predicament of Mankind*. New York: Universe Books.

Mert, Ayşem (2015) *Environmental Governance through Partnerships: A Discourse Theoretical Study*. Cheltenham: Edward Elgar.

Meyer, John W. (2009) 'Reflections: Institutional Theory and World Society' In *World Society: The Writings of John W. Meyer*, edited by Georg Krücken and Gili S. Drori, pp. 33–63. Oxford: Oxford University Press.

Meyer, John W. and W. R. Scott (1983) 'Centralization and the Legitimacy Problems of Local Government' In *Organizational Environments: Ritual and Rationality*, edited by John W. Meyer and W. Richard Scott, pp. 199–215. Beverly Hills, CA: Sage.

Meyer, John W., John Boli, and George M. Thomas (1987) 'Ontology and Rationalization in the Western Cultural Account' In *Institutional Structure: Constituting State, Society, and the Individual*, edited by George M. Thomas, John W. Meyer, Francisco O. Ramirez, and John Boli, pp. 12–27. London: Sage.

Meyer, John W., John Boli, George M. Thomas, and Francisco O. Ramirez (1997) 'World Society and the Nation State' *American Journal of Sociology* 103 (1), 144–81.

Milliken, Jennifer (1999) 'The Study of Discourse in International Relations: A Critique of Research Methods' *European Journal of International Relations* 5 (2), 225–54.

Milzow, Katrin (2008) 'Anatomy of a Crisis: Relations between the United Nations High Commissioner for Refugees and the Federal Republic of Germany from the 1970s to the 1980s' *Refugee Survey Quarterly* 27 (1), 74–88.

Monfreda, Chad (2010) 'Setting the Stage for New Global Knowledge: Science, Economics, and Indigenous Knowledge in "The Economics of Ecosystems and Biodiversity" at the Fourth World Conservation Congress' *Conservation and Society* 8 (4), 276–85.

Moore, Mike (2002) 'Democracy, Development and the WTO'. Speech delivered at the Qatar Conference on Democracy and Free Trade, 26–27 March, Doha, Qatar.

Moretti, Franco and Dominique Pestre (2015) 'Bankspeak: The Language of World Bank Reports' *New Left Review* 92, 75–99.

Morris, Justin and Nicholas J. Wheeler (2007) 'The Security Council's Crisis of Legitimacy and the Use of Force' *International Politics* 44 (2), 214–31.

Morse, Julia and Robert O. Keohane (2014) 'Contested Multilateralism' *Review of International Organizations* 9 (4), 385–412.

Moulin, Carolina and Peter Nyers (2007) '"We Live in a Country of UNHCR": Refugee Protests and Global Political Society' *International Political Sociology* 1 (4), 356–72.

Müller, Harald, David Fischer, and Wolfgang Kotter (1994) *Nuclear Non-Proliferation and Global Order*. Stockholm: SIPRI.

Mulligan, Shane (2004) 'Questioning (the Question of) Legitimacy in IR: A Reply to Jens Steffek' *European Journal of International Relations* 10 (3), 475–84.

Murithi, Timothy (2005) *The African Union: Pan-Africanism, Peacebuilding and Development*. Aldershot: Ashgate.

Murithi, Timothy (2012) 'The African Union at Ten: An Appraisal' *African Affairs* 111 (445), 662–9.

Murphy, Craig N. (1994) *International Organizations and Industrial Change: Global Governance since 1815*. Cambridge: Polity Press.

Mustapha, Mukhtarr (1980) *Big Game in Africa*. Birmingham: Third World Publications.

Naik, Asmita (2003) 'West Africa Scandal Points to Need for Humanitarian Watchdog' *Humanitarian Exchange* 24 (July). Available at: http://reliefweb.int/report/guinea/west-africa-scandal-points-need-humanitarian-watchdog-0 (accessed 22 March 2017).

Najam, Adil (2005) 'Developing Countries and Global Environmental Governance: From Contestation to Participation to Engagement' *International Environmental Agreements* 5, 303–21.

Naldi, Gino (1989) *The Organization of African Unity: An Analysis of Its Role*. London: Mansell.

Nation (2007) 'Atomic Watchdog Agency Turns 50', *Nation*, 20 August.

New Straits Times (2006) 'Ahmadinejad: IAEA Influenced by West', *New Straits Times*, 4 March.

New Vision (2010) 'Uganda: Country Rejects AU Gay Group', *New Vision*, 23 July.

Niehaus, Friedrich (2007) 'Internationale Zusammenarbeit bei der nuklearen Sicherheit' In *50 Jahre Internationale Atomenergie-Organisation IAEO. Ein Wirken für Frieden und Sicherheit im nuklearen Zeitalter*, edited by Dirk Schriefer, Walter Sandtner, and Wolfgang Rudischhauser, pp. 96–107. Baden-Baden: Nomos.

Nordland, Rob (1999) 'In Kosovo, Fear and Hunger. Starvation Stalks the Thousand Still Stuck Inside', *Newsweek*, 2 May.

Novicki, Margaret (1983) 'Interview Peter Onu Secretary-General Ad Interim, Organization of African Unity' *Africa Report* 28 (5), 57.

Novicki, Margaret (1992) 'Interview: A New Agenda for the OAU: Salim Ahmed Salim' *Africa Report* 37 (3), 36.

Nujoma, Sam (2002) Statement by His Excellency Dr Sam Nujoma President of the Republic of Namibia at the OAU/AU Heads of State and Government Summit, Durban, 9–12 July.

Nullmeier, Frank, Dominika Biegoń, Jennifer Gronau, Martin Nonhoff, Henning Schmitke, and Steffen Schneider (2010) *Prekäre Legitimitäten: Rechtfertigung von Herrschaft in der postnationalen Konstellation*. Frankfurt: Campus.

O'Brien, Robert, Anne Marie Goetz, Jan Aart Scholte, and Marc Williams (2000) *Contesting Global Governance: Multilateral Economic Institutions and Global Social Movements*. Cambridge: Cambridge University Press.

O'Neill, Kate (2017) *The Environment and International Relations*. Cambridge: Cambridge University Press.

OAU (Organisation of African Unity) (1963) OAU Charter. Addis Ababa: Organisation of African Unity.

OAU (1980) Lagos Plan of Action for the Economic Development of Africa 1980–2000. Lagos: Organisation of African Unity.

OAU (1990) African Charter for Popular Participation in Development and Transformation. Arusha: Organisation of African Unity.

OAU (2000) Constitutive Act of the African Union. Lomé: Organisation of African Unity.

OAU Assembly (1990) Declaration on the Political and Economic Situation in Africa and the Fundamental Changes Taking Place in the World. AHG/Decl.1 (XXVI). Addis Ababa: Organisation of African Unity.

OAU Secretariat (1970a) Introduction to the Report of the Administrative Secretary General Covering the Period from February 1970 to September 1970. CM/330. Part I. Addis Ababa: Organisation of African Unity.

OAU Secretariat (1970b) Report of the Administrative Secretary General Covering the Period February 1970 to September 1970. CM/330. Part II. Addis Ababa: Organisation of African Unity.

OAU Secretariat (1974a) Presentation of the Annual Report of the Administrative Secretary-General on the Activities of the Organization. CM/571/(XXII). Mogadishu: Organisation of African Unity.

OAU Secretariat (1974b) Report of the Administrative Secretary-General Covering the Period from June 1973 to June 1974. CM/571. Part 2. Addis Ababa: Organisation of African Unity.

OAU Secretariat (1978) Report of the Administrative Secretary General Covering the Period from February to July 1978. CM/875(XXXI). Part II. Khartoum: Organisation of African Unity.

OAU Secretariat (1982) Report of the Secretary General on the Activities of the General Secretariat Covering the Periods between March and July 1982. CM1188 (XXXIX). Part II. Tripoli: Organisation of African Unity.

OAU Secretariat (1990a) Introductory Note of His Excellency Salim Ahmed Salim. CM/1570(LI). Part 1. Addis Ababa: Organisation of African Unity.

OAU Secretariat (1990b) Report of the Secretary-General on the Fundamental Changes Taking Place and in the World and Their Implications for Africa: Proposals for an African Response. CM/1592. Addis Ababa: Organisation of African Unity.

OAU Secretariat (1994a) Introductory Note by the Secretary-General. Tunis: Organisation of African Unity.

OAU Secretariat (1994b) Report of the Secretary-General on the Activities of the General Secretariat Covering the Period February to June 1994. CM/1825(LX). Part II. Tunis: Organisation of African Unity.

OAU Secretariat (1998) Introductory Note to the Report of the Secretary-General. Ouagadougou: Organisation of African Unity.

OAU Secretariat (2000) Introductory Note to the Report of the Secretary-General. Lomé: Organisation of African Unity.

OAU Secretariat (2002a) Introductory Note to the Report of the Secretary General. Durban: Organisation of African Unity.

OAU Secretariat (2002b) Report of the Secretary General on the Activities of the General Secretariat Covering the Period February–June 2002. Durban: Organisation of African Unity.

Ogata, Sadako (2005) *The Turbulent Decade: Confronting the Refugee Crisis of the 1990s.* New York: W. W. Norton.

Okoth, Godfrey (1987) 'The OAU and the Uganda-Tanzania War, 1978–1979' *Journal of African Studies* 14 (3), 152–62.

Olivier, Juliette (2005) *L'Union Mondiale pour la Nature (UICN): Une Organisation Singulière au Service du Droit de l'Environnement*. Brussels: Bruylant.

Olwell, Russell B. (2008) *The International Atomic Energy Agency*, 1st ed. New York: Chelsea House.

Onuf, Nicolas (1989) *World of Our Making: Rules and Rule in Social Theory and International Relations*. Columbia, SC: University of South Carolina Press.

OPEC (Organization of the Petroleum-Exporting Countries) (1983) *Annual Report 1982*. Vienna: OPEC.

OPEC (2012 [1961]) Statute. Vienna: OPEC.

Orchard, Phil (2013) 'Governing Forced Migration' In *Governing the World? Cases in Global Governance*, edited by Sophie Harman and David Williams, pp. 180–96. New York: Routledge.

OSIEA (2008) African Union Must Act on Zimbabwe Now, African States Told, press release. Nairobi: Open Society Initiative for Eastern Africa.

Park, Susan (2010) *World Bank Group Interactions with Environmentalists: Changing International Organisation Identities*. Manchester: Manchester University Press.

Patiyasevi, Rita (1999) 'UNHCR Calls for Refugee Relocation'. *Nation* (Thailand), 31 March.

Pattberg, Philipp (2007) *Private Institutions and Global Governance: The New Politics of Environmental Sustainability*. Cheltenham: Edward Elgar.

Paul, Samuel (1987) 'Community Participation in Development Projects: The World Bank Experience'. *World Bank Discussion Papers* 6. Available at: http://www.ircwash. org/sites/default/files/Paul-1987-Community.pdf (accessed 22 March 2017).

Paulson, Niels, Ann Laudati, Amity Doolittle, Meredith Welsh-Devine, and Pablo Pena (2012) 'Indigenous Peoples' Participation in Global Conservation: Looking beyond Headdresses and Face Paints' *Environmental Values* 21, 255–76.

PAYLF (2007) *1st Pan African Youth Leadership Forum: Democracy in Africa— Renewing the Vision*. Accra: Friends of Africa International.

Peters, Ingo (2013) 'Legitimacy and International Organizations: The Case of the OSCE' In *Legitimating International Organizations*, edited by Dominik Zaum, pp. 196–220. Oxford: Oxford University Press.

Pevehouse, Jon (2005) *Democracy from Above: Regional Organizations and Democratization*. Cambridge: Cambridge University Press.

Pilat, Joseph F., Robert F. Pendley, and Charles K. Ebinger, eds (1985) *Atoms for Peace: An Analysis after Thirty Years*. Boulder, CO: Westview Press.

Powell, Nathaniel K. (2013) 'The UNHCR and Zimbabwean Refugees in Mozambique, 1975–1980' *Refugee Survey Quarterly* 32 (4), 41–65.

PR Newswire (1991) 'Trade Ruling Blows Dolphin Protection out of the Water', 23 August.

Prantl, Jochen (2013) 'The Shanghai Cooperation Organization: Legitimacy through (Self-)Legitimation?' In *Legitimating International Organizations*, edited by Dominik Zaum, pp. 162–78. Oxford: Oxford University Press.

Price, Richard (1998) 'Reversing the Gun Sights: Transnational Civil Society Targets Land Mines' *International Organization* 52 (3), 613–44.

Rabbinge, Rudy (2015) 'M. S. Swaminathan: His Contributions to Science and Public Policy' *Current Science* 109 (3): 439–46.

Radkau, Joachim (2011) *Die Ära der Ökologie: Eine Weltgeschichte.* Munich: Beck.

Rai, Shirin M. and Georgina Waylen, eds (2008) *Global Governance: Feminist Perspectives.* Basingstoke: Palgrave Macmillan.

Ramirez, Francisco O., Yasemin Soysal, and Suzanne Shanahan (1997) 'The Changing Logic of Political Citizenship: Cross-National Acquisition of Women's Suffrage Rights, 1890 to 1990' *American Journal of Sociology* 62 (5), 735–45.

Rauh, Christian and Michael Zürn (2018) 'Endogenous Legitimation Dynamics in Global Economic Governance: Authority, Politicization, and Alternative Narratives'. Unpublished manuscript.

Reddy, B. Muralidhar (2001) 'Poor Support for Tackling Refugee Influx—UNHCR', *Hindu,* 14 October.

Reimerson, Elsa (2013) 'Between Nature and Culture: Exploring Space for Indigenous Agency in the Convention on Biological Diversity' *Environmental Politics* 22 (6), 992–1009.

Reinalda, Bob (2009) *Routledge History of International Organizations: From 1815 to the Present Day.* London: Routledge.

Reis, Ronald A. (2009) *The World Trade Organization.* New York: Infobase.

Renn, Ortwin (1990) 'Public Responses to the Chernobyl Accident' *Journal of Environmental Psychology* 10, 151–67.

Reporter (2007) 'Practicing at Home What One Preaches Abroad', *Reporter,* 9 July.

Reus-Smit, Christian (2007) 'International Crises of Legitimacy' *International Politics* 44 (2), 157–74.

Reuters News (1992) Charity Chief Says Third World Loses in GATT. News report, 8 January.

Richburg, Keith B. (1992) 'In Africa, Lost Lives, Lost Dollars: Incompetence, Negligence, Maladministration among UN Woes', *Washington Post Foreign Service,* 21 September.

Richmond, Oliver and Ioannis Tellidis (2014) Emerging Actors in International Peacebuilding and Statebuilding: Status Quo or Critical States? *Global Governance* 20 (4), 563–84.

Rieff, David (1999) 'The Death of a Good Idea—Kosovo Is Teaching Relief Workers a Bitter Lesson: There Are No Humanitarian Solutions to Humanitarian Problems', *Newsweek,* 2 May.

Rittberger, Berthold (2005) *Building Europe's Parliament: Democratic Representation Beyond the Nation State.* Oxford: Oxford University Press.

Rittberger, Volker and Bernhard Zangl (2006) *International Organization: Polity, Politics and Policies.* Basingstoke: Palgrave.

Rosa, Eugene A. and Riley E. Dunlap (1994) 'Poll Trends: Nuclear Power: Three Decades of Public Opinion'. *Public Opinion Quarterly* 58, 295–324.

Rosa, Hartmut (2013) *Social Acceleration: A New Theory of Modernity.* New York: Columbia University Press.

Rosenau James N. (1990) *Turbulence in World Politics.* Princeton, NJ: Princeton University Press.

Rosenau James N. (1997) *Along the Domestic-International Frontier.* Cambridge: Cambridge University Press.

Roth, Brad R. (1999) *Governmental Illegitimacy in International Law*. Oxford: Clarendon Press.

Ruggie, John G. (1982) 'International Regimes, Transactions, and Change: Embedded Liberalism in the Postwar Economic Order' *International Organization* 36 (2), 379–415.

SABC (South African Broadcasting Corporation) (2013) 'European Leaders Snubbed at AU Event'.

Salim, Salim Ahmed (1998) 'The OAU Role in Conflict Management' In *Peacemaking and Peacekeeping for the New Century*, edited by Olara A. Otunnu and Michael W. Doyle, pp. 245–53. Lanham, MD: Rowman and Littlefield.

Sandbrook, Chris G., Janet A. Fisher, and Bhaskar Vira (2013) 'What Do Conservationists Think about Markets?' *Geoforum* (50), 232–40.

Sandholtz, Wayne and Kendall Stiles (2008) *International Norms and Cycles of Change*. Oxford: Oxford University Press.

Schechter, Michael G. (2014) 'Ogata, Sadako', *IO BIO: The Biographical Dictionary of Secretaries-General of International Organizations*. Available at: https://www.ru.nl/politicologie/io-bio-bob-reinalda/io-bio-biographical-dictionary-sgs-ios/ (accessed 22 June 2018).

Scheel, Stephan and Philipp Ratfisch (2013) 'Refugee Protection Meets Migration Management: UNHCR as a Global Police of Populations' *Journal of Ethnic and Migration Studies* 40 (6), 924–41.

Scheinman, Lawrence (1987) *The International Atomic Energy Agency and World Nuclear Order*. Washington, DC: Resources for the Future.

Schimmelfennig, Frank (2001) 'The Community Trap: Liberal Norms, Rhetorical Action, and the Eastern Enlargement of the European Union' *International Organization* 55 (1), 47–80.

Schmidtke, Henning (2010) 'Die Vereinten Nationen: Gespaltene Legitimität' In *Prekäre Legitimitäten: Rechtfertigng von Herrschaft in der postnationalen Konstellation*, edited by Frank Nullmeier, Dominika Biegoń, Jennifer Gronau, Martin Nonhoff, Henning Schmitke, and Steffen Schneider, pp. 107–46. Frankfurt: Campus.

Scholte, Jan Aart (2005) *Globalization: A Critical Introduction*, 2nd ed. Basingstoke: Palgrave.

Scholte, Jan Aart (2011) 'Towards Greater Legitimacy in Global Governance' *Review of International Political Economy* 18 (1), 110–20.

Schriefer, Dirk, Walter Sandtner, and Wolfgang Rudischhauser, eds (2007) *50 Jahre Internationale Atomenergie-Organisation IAEO: Ein Wirken für Frieden und Sicherheit im Nuklearen Zeitalter*. Baden-Baden: Nomos.

Schwartz-Shea, Peregrine and Dvora Yanow (2012) *Interpretative Research Design: Concepts and Processes*. New York: Routledge.

Seabrooke, Leonard (2007) 'Legitimacy Gaps in the World Economy: Explaining the Sources of the IMF's Legitimacy Crisis' *International Politics* 44 (2), 250–68.

Sending, Ole Jacob (2014) 'The International Civil Servant' *International Political Sociology* 8 (3), 338–40.

Sending, Ole Jacob (2017) *The Politics of Expertise: Competing for Authority in Global Governance*. Ann Arbor, MI: University of Michigan Press.

Shivji, Issa G. (2007) 'The Essential Building Blocks of the Pan-African Vision, *Pambazuka News* 299, 12 April. Available at: https://www.pambazuka.org/pan-africanism/essential-building-blocks-pan-african-vision (accessed 22 March 2017).

Speth, James G. and Peter M. Haas (2006) *Global Environmental Governance*. Washington, DC: Island Press.

State of the Union Project (2010) *Continental Report*. Nairobi: State of the Union Project.

Steffek, Jens (2003) 'The Legitimation of International Governance: A Discourse Approach' *European Journal of International Relations* 9 (2), 249–75.

Steffek, Jens (2006) *Embedded Liberalism and Its Critics: Justifying Global Governance in the American Century*. Basingstoke: Palgrave Macmillan.

Steffek, Jens (2007) 'Legitimacy in International Relations: From State Compliance to Citizens Consensus' In *Legitimacy in an Age of Global Politics*, edited by Achim Hurrelmann, Steffen Schneider, and Jens Steffek, pp. 175–92. Basingstoke: Palgrave Macmillan.

Steffek, Jens (2013) 'Mandatskonflikte, Liberalismuskritik und die Politisierung von GATT und WTO' In *Die Politisierung der Weltpolitik*, edited by Michael Zürn and Mathias Ecker-Ehrhardt, pp. 213–39. Berlin: Suhrkamp.

Steinberg, Gerald M. (2007) 'Why Are the IAEA and ElBaradei Protecting Iran?' *Jerusalem Post*, 6 November.

Stephen, Matthew (2014a) 'Rising Powers, Global Capitalism and Liberal Global Governance: A Historical Materialist Account of the BRICs Challenge' *European Journal of International Relations* 20 (4), 912–38.

Stephen, Matthew (2014b) 'Rising Regional Powers and International Institutions: The Foreign Policy Orientations of India, Brazil and South Africa' *Global Society* 26 (3), 289–309.

Sternberg, Claudia (2013) *The Struggle for EU Legitimacy: Public Contestation, 1950–2005*. Basingstoke: Palgrave.

Stevens, Stan (1997a) 'The Legacy of Yellowstone' In *Conservation through Cultural Survival: Indigenous Peoples and Protected Areas*, edited by Stan Stevens, pp. 13–32. Washington, DC: Island Press.

Stevens, Stan (1997b) 'New Alliances for Conservation' In *Conservation through Cultural Survival: Indigenous Peoples and Protected Areas*, ed. Stan Stevens, pp. 33–62. Washington, DC: Island Press.

Stevens, Stan (2014) 'A New Protected Areas Paradigm' In *Indigenous Peoples, National Parks and Protected Areas: A New Paradigm Linking Conservation, Culture and Rights*, edited by Stan Stevens, pp. 47–83. Tucson, AZ: University of Arizona Press.

Strange, Michael (2011) 'Discursivity of Global Governance: Vestiges of "Democracy" in the World Trade Organization' *Alternatives: Global, Local, Political* 36 (3), 240–56.

Strange, Michael (2013) *Writing Trade Governance: Discourse and the WTO*. London: Routledge.

Strange, Susan (1996) *The Retreat of the State: The Diffusion of Power in the World Economy*. Cambridge: Cambridge University Press.

Streeck, Wolfgang and Kathleen Thelen (2005) 'Introduction: Institutional Change in Advanced Political Economies' In *Beyond Continuity: Institutional Change in*

Advanced Political Economies, edited by Wolfgang Streeck and Kathleen Thelen, pp. 1–39. Oxford: Oxford University Press.

Stuenkel, Oliver (2016) *Post-Western World.* Cambridge: Polity Press.

Stuenkel, Oliver and Marcos Tourinho (2014) 'Regulating Intervention: Brazil and the Responsibility to Protect' *Conflict, Security and Development* 14 (4), 379–402.

Suchman, Mark C. (1995) 'Managing Legitimacy: Strategic and Institutional Approaches' *Academy of Management Review* 20 (3), 571–610.

Swedish Ministry of the Environment (2012) 'Sweden and the IUCN: Information Sheet from the Swedish Ministry of the Environment, Stockholm'. Available at: http://www.government.se/49b75e/contentassets/72cc978dca7f4d30b905d79d218e0b93/sweden-and-the-iucn-m2012.09 (accessed 22 March 2017).

Symons, Jonathan (2011) 'The Legitimation of International Organisations: Examining the Identity of the Communities that Grant Legitimacy' *Review of International Studies* 37 (5), 2557–83.

Szasz, Paul (1970) *The Law and Practices of the International Atomic Energy Agency.* Vienna: IAEA.

Talbot, Lee (1980) 'The World's Conservation Strategy' *Environmental Conservation* 7 (4), 259–68.

Talbot, Lee (1983) 'IUCN in Retrospect and Prospect' *Environmental Conservation* 10 (1), 5–11.

Tallberg, Jonas, Thomas Sommerer, Theresa Squatrito, and Christer Jönsson (2013) *The Opening Up of International Organizations: Transnational Access in Global Governance.* Cambridge: Cambridge University Press.

Tamiotti, Ludivine, Robert Teh, Vesile Kulaçoğlu, Anne Olhoff, Benjamin Simmons, and Hussein Abaza (2009) *Trade and Climate Change: A Report by the United Nations Environment Programme and the World Trade Organization.* Geneva: World Trade Organization.

Terborgh, John (2004) 'Reflections of a Scientist on the World Parks Congress' *Conservation Biology* 18 (3), 619–20.

Third World Network (2017) 'Don't Hold MC11 in Argentina unless Ban on NGOs Is Rescinded', SUNS #8588, 4 December. Available at: https://www.twn.my/title2/wto.info/2017/ti171203.htm (accessed 13 June 2018).

This Day (2007) 'Africans in the Diaspora Seek Strong Unity Government'. Available at: http://www.pambazuka.org/pan-africanism/africans-diaspora-seek-strong-unity-government (accessed 22 March 2017).

Tieku, Thomas (2009) 'The Multilateralization of Democracy Promotion and Defense in Africa' *Africa Today* 56 (2), 75–91.

Torgler, Benno (2008) 'Trust in International Organizations: An Empirical Investigation Focusing on the United Nations' *Review of International Organizations* 3 (1), 65–93.

Toro-Pérez, Catalina (2005) 'Acteurs, scénarios et discours: la mobilisation en réseaux de la Biodiversité' *Cuadernos de Administración* 33: 61–103.

Toups, Catherine (1995) 'Iraqis Fooled Weapons Monitors. Lack of Skepticism at IAEA Faulted', *Washington Times*, 23 August.

Türk, Volker and Elizabeth Eyster (2010) 'Strengthening Accountability in UNHCR' *International Journal of Refugee Law* 22 (2), 159–72.

UN General Assembly (1971) Report of the UNHCR, 1970, UN Document No. A/8412. New York: United Nations.

UN General Assembly (1974) Declaration on the Establishment of a New International Economic Order. UN Document No. A/RES/S-6/3201 (1 May). New York: United Nations.

UN General Assembly (1975) Report of the UNHCR, 1974, UN Document No. A/10012. New York: United Nations.

UN General Assembly (1979) Report of the UNHCR, 1978, UN Document No. A/34/12. New York: United Nations.

UN General Assembly (1983) Report of the UNHCR, 1982, UN Document No. A/38/12. New York: United Nations.

UN General Assembly (1984) Report of the UNHCR, 1983, UN Document No. A/39/12. New York: United Nations.

UN General Assembly (1986) Report of the UNHCR, 1985, UN Document No. A/41/12. New York: United Nations.

UN General Assembly (1987) Report of the UNHCR, 1986, UN Document No. A/42/12. New York: United Nations.

UN General Assembly (1990) Report of the UNHCR, 1989, UN Document No. A/45/12. New York: United Nations.

UN General Assembly (1991) Report of the UNHCR, 1990, UN Document No. A/46/12. New York: United Nations.

UN General Assembly (1992) 47th Plenary Session of the General Assembly, UN Document No. A/47/PV.60. New York: United Nations.

UN General Assembly (1993a) 48th Session of the General Assembly, UN Document No. A/48/PV.60. New York: United Nations.

UN General Assembly (1993b) 60th Plenary Meeting of the General Assembly, UN Document No. A/48/PV.60. New York: United Nations.

UN General Assembly (1994a) 89th Plenary Meeting of the General Assembly, UN Document No. A/49/PV.89. New York: United Nations.

UN General Assembly (1994b) Report of the UNHCR, 1993, UN Document No. A/49/12. New York: United Nations.

UN General Assembly (1995) Report of the UNHCR, 1994, UN Document No. A/50/12. New York: United Nations.

UN General Assembly (1996) 67th Plenary Meeting of the General Assembly, UN Document No. A/51/PV.67. New York: United Nations.

UN General Assembly (1997a) 52nd Plenary Meeting of the General Assembly, UN Document No. A/52/PV.52. New York: United Nations.

UN General Assembly (1997b) Report of the UNHCR, 1996, UN Document No. A/52/12. New York: United Nations.

UN General Assembly (1998) 49th Plenary Meeting of the General Assembly, UN Document No. A/53/PV.49. New York: United Nations.

UN General Assembly (1999a) 73rd Plenary Meeting of the General Assembly, UN Document No. A/54/PV.73. New York: United Nations.

UN General Assembly (1999b) Report of the UNHCR, 1998, UN Document No. A/54/12. New York: United Nations.

UN General Assembly (2000a) 53rd Plenary Meeting of the General Assembly, UN Document No. A/55/PV.53. New York: United Nations.

UN General Assembly (2000b) Report of the UNHCR, 1999, UN Document No. A/55/12. New York: United Nations.

UN General Assembly (2002) 53rd Plenary Meeting of the General Assembly, UN Document No. A/57/PV.53. New York: United Nations.

UN General Assembly (2003) Report of the UNHCR, 2002, UN Document No. A/58/12. New York: United Nations.

UN General Assembly (2004a) 38th Plenary Meeting of the General Assembly, UN Document No. A/59/PV.38. New York: United Nations.

UN General Assembly (2004b) 39th Plenary Meeting of the General Assembly, UN Document No. A/59/PV.39. New York: United Nations.

UN General Assembly (2004c) 40th Plenary Meeting of the General Assembly, UN Document No. A/59/PV.40. New York: United Nations.

UN General Assembly (2006) 39th Plenary Meeting of the General Assembly, UN Document No. A/61/PV.39. New York: United Nations.

UN General Assembly (2007) Report of the UNHCR, 2006, UN Document No. A/62/12. New York: United Nations.

UN General Assembly (2011) Report of the UNHCR, 2010, UN Document No. A/66/12. New York: United Nations.

UN General Assembly (2013) Report of the UNHCR 2012/2013, UN Document No. A/68/12. New York: United Nations.

UN Secretary General (1992) An Agenda for Peace: Preventive Diplomacy, Peacemaking, and Peace-Keeping, UN Document No. A/47/277. New York: United Nations.

UNECA (2014) United Nations Ten-Year Capacity Building Programme for the African Union: Second Triennial Review (2010–2012). New York: United Nations.

UNHCR (Office of the United Nations High Commissioner for Refugees) (1990) Report of the Ad Hoc Review Group on the Role and Structure of UNHCR. UNHCR Archive, Publications, Box 25, Geneva: UNHCR.

UNHCR (1992) Statement by Mrs Sadako Ogata, United Nations High Commissioner for Refugees, at the International Management Symposium, St Gallen, Switzerland, 25 May. Available at: http://www.unhcr.org/admin/hcspeeches/3ae68faec/statement-mrs-sadako-ogata-united-nations-high-commissioner-refugees-international.html (accessed 22 March 2017).

UNHCR (1996) Delphi: The Final Report of the Change Management Group, 1 May 1996, UNHCR Archive, Publications, Box 65. Geneva: UNHCR.

UNHCR (1998) 1998 Global Report. Geneva: UNHCR.

UNHCR (2002a) The Global Report 2002. Geneva: UNHCR.

UNHCR (2002b) 'Impact of Budgetary Reductions', preliminary note. Available at: http://www.unhcr.org/partners/donors/3db5774c9/impact-budgetary-reductions-june-2002.html (accessed 27 March 2017).

UNHCR (2006) The Global Report 2006. Geneva: UNHCR.

UNHCR (2010) The Global Report 2010. Geneva: UNHCR.

UNHCR (2017) 'The Global Report'. Available at: http://www.unhcr.org/the-global-report.html (accessed 22 March 2017).

UNHCR (2018a) Global Report 2017. Geneva: UNHCR. Available at: http://www.unhcr.org/the-global-report.html (accessed 28 August 2018).

UNHCR (2018b) Global Trends: Forced Displacement in 2017. Available at: http://www.unhcr.org/5b27be547.pdf (accessed 27 June 2018).

UNHCR (n.d.) UNHCR website. Available at: http://web.archive.org/web/20161018015524/http://www.unhcr.org/figures-at-a-glance.html (accessed 27 March 2017).

UNHCR ExCom (1970) Summary Records of ExCom meetings, UN Document No. A/AC.96/SR.202–213. Geneva: UNHCR.

UNHCR ExCom (1978) Summary Records of ExCom meetings, UN Document No. A/AC.96/SR.293–303. Geneva: UNHCR.

UNHCR ExCom (1982) Summary Records of ExCom meetings, UN Document No. A/AC.96/SR.342–350. Geneva: UNHCR.

UNHCR ExCom (1983) Summary Records of ExCom meetings, UN Document No. A/AC.96/SR.351–367. Geneva: UNHCR.

UNHCR ExCom (1986) Summary Records of ExCom meetings, UN Document No. A/AC.96/SR.401–412. Geneva: UNHCR.

UNHCR ExCom (1989) Summary Records of ExCom meetings, UN Document No. A/AC.96/SR.437–447. Geneva: UNHCR.

UNHCR ExCom (1990a) Summary Records of ExCom meetings, UN Document No. A/AC.96/SR.448–452 (extraordinary session). Geneva: UNHCR.

UNHCR ExCom (1990b) Summary Records of ExCom meetings, UN Document No. A/AC.96/SR.453–460. Geneva: UNHCR.

UNHCR ExCom (1990c) Report of the Executive Committee Temporary Working Group to the Extraordinary Session of the Executive Committee of the High Commissioner's Programme. A/AC.96/742. UNHCR Archive, Executive Committee Folder, 41st Session. Geneva: UNHCR.

UNHCR ExCom (1994) Summary Records of ExCom Meetings, UN Document No. A/AC.96/SR.489–496. Geneva: UNHCR.

UNHCR ExCom (1998) Summary Records of ExCom Meetings, UN Document No. A/AC.96/SR.525–533. Geneva: UNHCR.

UNHCR ExCom (2002) Summary Records of ExCom Meetings, UN Document No. A/AC.96/SR.561–569. Geneva: UNHCR.

UNHCR ExCom (2006) Summary Records of ExCom Meetings, UN Document No. A/AC.96/SR.549–607. Geneva: UNHCR.

UNHCR ExCom (2010) Summary Records of ExCom Meetings, UN Document No. A/AC.96/SR.639–647. Geneva: UNHCR.

UNHCR ExCom (2013) Summary Records of ExCom Meetings, UN Document No. A/AC.96/SR.666–674. Geneva: UNHCR.

UNHCR ExCom (2015) Summary Records of ExCom Meetings, UN Document No. A/AC.96/SR.684–692. Geneva: UNHCR.

UNHCR ExCom (2017) Summary Records of ExCom Meetings, UN Document No. A/AC.96/SR.701–709. Geneva: UNHCR.

UNHCR Inter-Agency Unit (2008) Report on UNHCR's Annual Consultations with Non-Governmental Organizations. Geneva: UNHCR.

UNHCR Inter-Agency Unit (2010) Report on the Annual Consultations with Non-Governmental Organizations. Geneva: UNHCR.

UNHCR NGO Liaison Unit (2002) Report on Pre-ExCom Consultations with Non-Governmental Organisations. Geneva: UNHCR.

UNHCR Partnership Section (2015) Annual Consultations with NGOS. Geneva: UNHCR.

UNHCR and Save the Children (2002) Note for Implementing and Operational Partners by UNHCR and Save the Children-UK on Sexual Violence and Exploitation. Available at: http://reliefweb.int/report/guinea/note-implementing-and-operational-partners-unhcr-and-save-children-uk-sexual-violence (accessed 22 March 2017).

United Nations (1945) Charter of the United Nations (as amended). Available at: http://www.un.org/en/charter-united-nations/ (accessed 4 July 2018).

United Nations (1950) Statute of the Office of the United Nations High Commissioner. Available at: http://www.unhcr.org/3b66c39e1.html (accessed 22 March 2017).

United Nations (1951) Convention Relating to the Status of Refugees. Available at: http://www.unhcr.org/3b66c2aa10.html (accessed 22 March 2017).

United Nations (1967) Protocol Relating to the Status of Refugees. Available at: http://www.unhcr.org/3b66c2aa10.html (accessed 22 March 2017).

United Nations (1981) 'Question of the Violation of Human Rights and Fundamental Freedoms in Any Part of the World, with Particular Reference to Colonial and Other Dependent Countries and Territories', Study on Human Rights and Massive Exoduses, E/CN.4/1503. Available at: https://documents-dds-ny.un.org/doc/UNDOC/GEN/G82/102/52/PDF/G8210252.pdf?OpenElement (accessed 27 March 2017).

United Nations (1986) 'Report of Governmental Experts on International Co-operation to Avert New Flows of Refugees', UN Document No. A/41/324. New York: United Nations.

United Nations (1992) Convention on Biological Diversity. Available at: https://www.cbd.int/convention/text/ (accessed 2 November 2015).

United Nations (2003) Resolution of the General Assembly, UN Document No. A/RES/58/153. New York: United Nations.

United Nations (2004) Convention on Biological Diversity Decision VII/28: Protected Areas. Available at: https://www.cbd.int/decision/cop/default.shtml?id=7765 (accessed 12 June 2018).

United Nations (2007) United Nations Declaration on the Right of Indigenous Peoples. Available at: http://www.un.org/esa/socdev/unpfii/documents/DRIPS_en.pdf (accessed 22 March 2017).

United Nations (2018) Sustainable Development Goals: 17 Goals to Transform Our World. Available at: https://www.un.org/sustainabledevelopment/sustainable-development-goals/ (accessed 26 June 2018).

Van der Heijden, Jeroen (2011) 'Institutional Layering: A Review of the Use of the Concept' *Politics* 31 (1), 9–18.

Van der Pligt, J. and Cees J. H. Midden (1990) 'Chernobyl: Four Years Later: Attitudes, Risk Management and Communication' *Journal of Environmental Psychology* 10 (2), 91–9.

Van Rooy, Alison (2004) *The Global Legitimacy Game: Civil Society, Globalization and Protest*. Basingstoke: Palgrave Macmillan.

van Walraven, Klaas (1996) *Dreams of Power: The Role of the Organization of African Unity in the Politics of Africa 1963–1993*. Ridderkerk: mimeo.

van Walraven, Klaas (2010) 'Heritage and Transformation: From the Organization of African Unity to the African Union' In *Africa's New Peace and Security Architecture: Promoting Norms, Institutionalizing Solutions*, edited by Ulf Engel and João Gomes Porto, pp. 31–56. Farnham: Ashgate.

Various (2007) An Open Letter to Africa's Present and Future Leaders, Desmond Tutu Fellows, AU-Monitor. Available at: http://www.pambazuka.org/pan-africanism/open-letter-present-and-future-leaders-africa (accessed 22 March 2017).

Various (2010) Recommendations of Civil Society Organisations on Peace and Security ahead of the 15th African Union Summit. Available at: http://www.wanep.org/wanep/attachments/article/186/AU-CSO%20Pre-Summit%20Recommendations%20-%20Kampala%20July%202010%20(2).pdf (accessed 22 March 2017).

Vetterlein, Antje (2012) 'Seeing Like the World Bank on Poverty' *New Political Economy* 17 (1), 35–58.

Vilmer, Jean-Baptiste Jeangène (2016) 'The African Union and the International Criminal Court: Counteracting the Crisis' *International Affairs* 92 (6), 1319–42.

Viola, Lora Anne, Duncan Snidal, and Michael Zürn (2015) 'Sovereign (In)Equality in the Evolution of the International System' In *The Oxford Handbook of Transformations of the State*, edited by Stephan Leibfried, Evelyne Huber, Matthew Lange, Jonah D. Levy, Frank Nullmeier, and John D. Stephens, pp. 221–36. Oxford: Oxford University Press.

von Bogdandy, Armin (2001) 'Verfassungsrechtliche Dimensionen der Welthandelsorganisation, 1. Teil: Entkoppelung von Recht und Politik' *Kritische Justiz* 34 (3), 264–81.

Ward, Michael (2004) *Quantifying the World: UN Ideas and Statistics*. Bloomington, IN: Indiana University Press.

Warrick, Joby (2011) 'Iran Close to Nuclear Capability, IAEA Says', *Washington Post*, 7 November.

Washington, Monica J. (1997) 'The Practice of Peer Review in the International Nuclear Safety Regime' *NYU Law Review* 72, 430–69.

WCED (World Commission on Environment and Development) (1987) *Our Common Future*. Oxford: Oxford University Press.

Weaver, Catherine (2008) *Hypocrisy Trap: The World Bank and the Poverty of Reform*. Princeton, NJ: Princeton University Press.

Weber, Max (1978 [1921]) *Economy and Society*. Berkeley, CA: University of California Press.

Weiner, Myron (1998) 'The Clash of Norms. Dilemmas in Refugee Policies' *Journal of Refugee Studies* 11 (4), 433–53.

Weise, Tobias (2015) 'Between Functionality and Legitimacy: German Diplomatic Talk about the Opening of Intergovernmental Organizations' *Global Governance* 21 (1), 99–117.

Welz, Martin (2013) *Integrating Africa: Decolonization's Legacies, Sovereignty and the African Union*. London: Routledge.

Wiener, Antje (2018) *Constitution and Contestation of Norms in Global International Relations*. Cambridge University Press.

Wilkinson, Rorden (2006) *The WTO, Crisis and the Governance of Global Trade*. New York: Routledge.

Williams, Paul D. (2007) 'From Non-Intervention to Non-Indifference: The Origins and Developments of the African Union's Security Culture' *African Affairs* 106 (423), 263–79.

Wing, Christine and Fiona Simpson (2013) *Detect, Dismantle, and Disarm: IAEA Verification, 1992–2005*. Washington, DC: United States Institute of Peace Press.

Winslett, Gary (2019) 'Protectionism' In *The Language of World Trade Politics: Unpacking the Terms of Trade*, edited by Klaus Dingwerth and Clara Weinhardt, pp. 32–50. London: Routledge.

WIPO (World Intellectual Property Organization) (2001) Annual Report 2000. Geneva: WIPO.

Witt, Antonia (2013) 'The African Union and Contested Political Order(s)' In *Towards an African Peace and Security Regime: Continental Embeddedness, Transnational Linkages, Strategic Relevance*, edited by Ulf Engel and João Gomes Porto, pp. 11–30. Farnham: Ashgate.

Wolfers, Michael (1984) 'The Institutional Evolution of the OAU' In *The OAU after Twenty Years*, edited by Yassin El-Ayouty and William I. Zartman, pp. 85–100. New York: Praeger.

World Bank (2000) Can Africa Claim the 21st Century? Washington, DC: World Bank.

WTO (World Trade Organization) (1994) 'General Agreement on Tariffs and Trade: Multilateral Trade Negotiations Final Act Embodying the Results of the Uruguay Round of Trade Negotiations' *International Legal Materials* 33 (5), 1144–272.

WTO (1996) Annual Report 1996. Geneva: World Trade Organization.

WTO (1997) Annual Report 1997. Geneva: World Trade Organization.

WTO (1999) Annual Report 1999. Geneva: World Trade Organization.

WTO (2000) Annual Report 2000. Geneva: World Trade Organization.

WTO (2001a) Annual Report 2001. Geneva: World Trade Organization.

WTO (2001b) Ministerial Conference, Fourth Session: India, Statement by the Honourable Murasoli Maran, Minister of Commerce and Industry (WTO Document WT/MIN(01)/ST/10, 10 November). Geneva: World Trade Organization.

WTO (2001c) Ministerial Conference, Fourth Session: Norway, Statement by H. E. Mr Jan Petersen, Minister of Foreign Affairs (WTO Document WT/MIN(01)/ST/32, 10 November). Geneva: World Trade Organization.

WTO (2001d) Ministerial Declaration, adopted on 14 November 2001 (WTO Document WT/MIN(01)/DEC/1, 20 November). Geneva: World Trade Organization.

WTO (2001e) Ministerial Conference, Fourth Session: France, Statement by H. E. Mr Laurent Fabius, Minister for Economy, Finance and Industry (WTO Document WT/MIN(01)/ST/15, 10 November). Geneva: World Trade Organization.

WTO (2001f) Ministerial Conference, Fourth Session: Pakistan, Statement by H. E. Mr Abdul Razak Dawood, Minister for Commerce, Industries and Production (WTO Document WT/MIN(01)/ST/6, 10 November). Geneva: World Trade Organization.

WTO (2001g) Ministerial Conference, Fourth Session: Pacific Islands Forum, Statement Circulated by Mr W. Noel Levi, CBE, Secretary General (as an Observer) (WTO Document WT/MIN(01)/ST/29, 10 November). Geneva: World Trade Organization.

WTO (2002) Annual Report 2002. Geneva: World Trade Organization.

WTO (2005) Ministerial Conference, Sixth Session: Norway (WTO Document WT/MIN(05)/ST/30, 14 December). Geneva: World Trade Organization.

WTO (2007) Annual Report 2007. Geneva: World Trade Organization.

WTO (2009a) Annual Report 2009. Geneva: World Trade Organization.

WTO (2009b) Ministerial Conference, Seventh Session: China, Statement by H. E. Mr Chen Deming, Minister of Commerce (WTO Document WT/MIN(09)/ST/113, 2 December). Geneva: World Trade Organization.

WTO (2009c) Ministerial Conference, Seventh Session: Switzerland, Statement by H. E. Councillor Doris Leuthard, Minister of Economic Affairs (WTO Document WT/MIN(09)/ST/2, 2 December). Geneva: World Trade Organization.

WTO (2009d) Ministerial Conference, Seventh Session: Hongkong, China, Statement by Mrs Rita Lau Ng Wai-Lan, Secretary for Commerce and Economic Development (WTO Document WT/MIN(09)/ST/6, 2 December). Geneva: World Trade Organization.

WTO (2009e) Ministerial Conference, Seventh Session: Tanzania, Statement by the Honourable Dr Mary M. Nagu, Ministry for Industry, Trade and Marketing (WTO Document WT/MIN(09)/ST/7, 2 December). Geneva: World Trade Organization.

WTO (2011) Annual Report 2011. Geneva: World Trade Organization.

WTO (2012) Annual Report 2012. Geneva: World Trade Organization.

WTO (2013a) Annual Report 2013. Geneva: World Trade Organization.

WTO (2013b) Ministerial Conference, Ninth Session: France, Statement by H. E. Mrs Nicole Bricq, Minister of Foreign Trade (WTO Document WT/MIN(13)/ST/53, 5 December). Geneva: World Trade Organization.

WTO (2013c) Ministerial Conference, Ninth Session: Republic of Korea, Statement by H. E. Mr Sang Jick Yoon, Minister of Trade, Industry and Energy (WTO Document WT/MIN(13)/ST/14/Rev.1, 6 December). Geneva: World Trade Organization.

WTO (2013d) Ministerial Conference, Ninth Session: United States, Statement by H. E. Mr Michael Froman, Trade Representative (WTO Document WT/MIN(13)/ST/18, 4 December). Geneva: World Trade Organization.

WTO (2015) Understanding the WTO. Geneva: World Trade Organization.

WTO (2016) Annual Report 2016. Geneva: World Trade Organization.

WTO (2017) Annual Report 2017. Geneva: World Trade Organization.

WTO (2018) Address by Mr Roberto Azevêdo, WTO Director-General, MC11 Closing Session, 13 December 2017 (WTO Document WT/MIN(17)/74, 22 January). Geneva: World Trade Organization.

Wunder, Sven (2007) 'The Efficiency of Payments for Environmental Services in Tropical Conservation' *Conservation Biology* 21(1), 48–58.

Young, Oran R. (1989) *International Cooperation: Building Regimes for Natural Resources and the Environment*. Ithaca, NY: Cornell University Press.

Zangl, Bernhard (2008) 'Judicialization Matters! A Comparison of Dispute Settlement under GATT and the WTO' *International Studies Quarterly* 52, 825–54.

Zangl, Bernhard, Frederick Heußner, Andreas Kruck, and Xenia Lanzendürfer (2016) 'Imperfect Adaptation: How the WTO and the IMF Adjust to Shifting Power Distributions among Their Members' *Review of International Organizations* 11 (2), 171–96.

Zaum, Dominik, ed. (2013a) *Legitimating International Organizations*. Oxford: Oxford University Press.

Zaum, Dominik (2013b) 'International Organizations, Legitimacy, and Legitimation' In *Legitimating International Organizations*, edited by Dominik Zaum, pp. 3–25. Oxford: Oxford University Press.

Zaum, Dominik (2013c) 'Conclusion' In *Legitimating International Organizations*, edited by Dominik Zaum, pp. 221–30. Oxford: Oxford University Press.

Zelditch, Morris, Jr. (2001) 'Theories of Legitimacy' In *The Psychology of Legitimacy: Emerging Perspectives on Ideology, Justice, and Intergroup Relations*, edited by John T. Jost and Brenda Major, pp. 33–53. Cambridge: Cambridge University Press.

Zetter, Roger (1991) 'Labelling Refugees: Forming and Transforming a Bureaucratic Identity' *Journal of Refugee Studies* 4 (1), 39–62.

Zimmermann, Lisbeth (2017) *Global Norms with a Local Face: Rule-of-Law Promotion and Norm Translation*. Cambridge: Cambridge University Press.

Zoellick, Robert B. (2012) 'Why We Still Need the World Bank' *Foreign Affairs* 91 (2), 66–78.

Zürn, Michael (2004) 'Global Governance and Legitimacy Problems' *Government and Opposition* 39 (2), 260–87.

Zürn, Michael (2014) 'The Politicization of World Politics and Its Effects: Eight Propositions' *European Political Science Review* 6 (1), 47–71.

Zürn, Michael (2018) *A Theory of Global Governance: Authority, Legitimacy, and Contestation*. Oxford: Oxford University Press.

Zürn, Michael and Matthew Stephen (2010) 'The View of Old and New Powers on the Legitimacy of International Institutions' *Politics* 30 (S1), 91–101.

Zürn, Michael, Martin Binder, and Matthias Ecker–Ehrhardt (2012) 'International Authority and Its Politicization' *International Theory* 4 (1), 69–106.

Index

Index